CROZ
LARRIKIN BIKER

CROZ
LARRIKIN BIKER

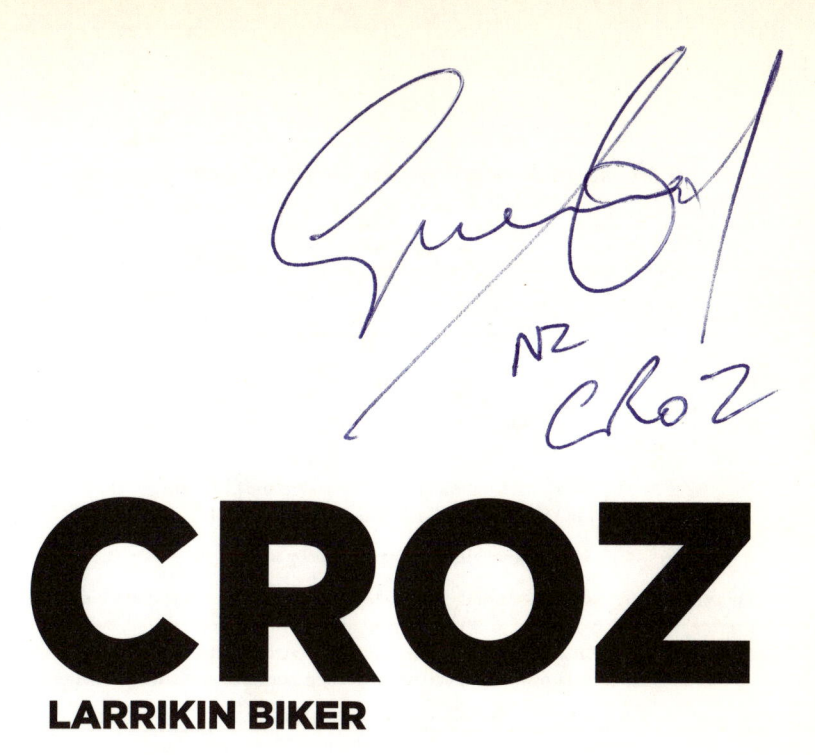

GRAEME CROSBY

HarperSports
An imprint of HarperCollins*Publishers*

To those riders who paid the ultimate price

HarperCollins*Publishers*

Harper*Sports*
An imprint of HarperCollins*Publishers*

First published in 2010
by HarperCollins*Publishers* (New Zealand) Limited
PO Box 1, Shortland Street, Auckland 1140

Copyright © Graeme Crosby 2010

Graeme Crosby asserts the moral right to be identified as the author of this work.
All rights reserved. No part of this publication may be reproduced, stored in a retrieval system or transmitted in any form or by any means, electronic, mechanical, photocopying, recording or otherwise, without the prior written permission of the publishers.

HarperCollins*Publishers*
31 View Road, Glenfield, Auckland 0627, New Zealand
25 Ryde Road, Pymble, Sydney, NSW 2073, Australia
A 53, Sector 57, Noida, UP, India
77–85 Fulham Palace Road, London W6 8JB, United Kingdom
2 Bloor Street East, 20th floor, Toronto, Ontario M4W 1A8, Canada
10 East 53rd Street, New York, NY 10022, USA

National Library of New Zealand Cataloguing-in-Publication Data

Crosby, Graeme.
Croz : larrikin biker / Graeme Crosby.
ISBN 978-1-86950-857-9
1. Motorcyclists—New Zealand—Biography.
2. Grand Prix motorcycle racing. I. Title.
796.75092—dc 22

Cover design by Carolyn Lewis
Cover image courtesy Chris Pearson and Mortons Archive
Typesetting by Springfield West

Printed by Griffin Press, Australia

70gsm Classic used by HarperCollins*Publishers* is a natural, recyclable product made from wood grown in sustainable forests. The manufacturing processes conform to the environmental regulations in the country of origin, Finland.

Wherever possible, the author and publishers have made every attempt to determine the ownership of photographic material used in this book. However, it has not been possible to establish the origin and ownership of some photographs given to Graeme Crosby. If anyone has information about the source of these photographs, please contact the publishers in the first instance.

Contents

Lap 1	STARTING OUT WITH A PASSION	11
	The first few years: 1973–75	11
Lap 2	MARLBORO SERIES AND A TEETH-CUTTING EXERCISE, 1973–74	21
Lap 3	AROUND THE TRAPS GAINING EXPERIENCE	36
	Practice Day, Pukekohe, 1974	36
	Castrol 6 Hour, October 1974	37
	Marlboro Series, 1974/75	40
	Aussie 6 Hour, 1975	44
	1975 Castrol 6 Hour and Marlboro Series	49
Lap 4	SPREADING MY WINGS, 1976	52
	The move across the Ditch	52
	Finding a ride	55
	Marlboro Series, 1976/77	64
Lap 5	BONJOUR, MONSIEUR AND COBBER! 1977	68
	Bathurst and 6 Hour	68
	Bolt the Door (Bol d'Or 24-hour, Le Mans)	71
Lap 6	LIFTING MY GAME, 1978	88
	NZ 6 Hour and Marlboro Series, 1977/78	88
	Bathurst	89
	Aussie titles: Oran Park	91
	Adelaide 3 Hour	95

Lap 7	WHICH WAY DOES THE TRACK GO AND WHAT'S THE LAP RECORD? 1978	97
	Suzuka 8 Hour	97
Lap 8	I CALL AUSTRALIA HOME, 1978–79	117
	Aussie Honda Castrol 6 Hour and NZ 6 Hour	117
	Bol d'Or, Paul Ricard	118
	Swann Series	121
	Team Kawasaki Australia contract	122
	Adelaide 3 Hour and Bathurst	125
Lap 9	GOING GLOBAL, 1979	131
	Isle of Man — my first look	131
	Brands Hatch	134
	Isle of Man Tourist Trophy Millennium	138
	Mallory Park	143
	Donington	144
	Snetterton	146
Lap 10	MORIWAKI KAWASAKI AND THE 'SIT UP AND BEG', 1979	148
	Suzuka 8 Hour	148
	Oran Park	149
	Silverstone	150
	Ulster Grand Prix	151
	Oulton Park	154
	Scarborough	156
	Cadwell	159
	Donington and Imola AGV Cup	160

Lap 11	UNEXPECTED FACTORY RIDE, 1979	165
	Castrol 6 Hour, Amaroo Park	165
	Brands Hatch	166
	Contract with Suzuki for 1980	169
	Going back to New Zealand, November	174
Lap 12	MOVE OVER, HERE I COME, 1980	180
	Testing new bikes in Japan	180
	Suzuki, my new home	187
	Daytona	190
Lap 13	CRISIS OF CONFIDENCE, 1980	199
	Trans-Atlantic	199
	Austrian Grand Prix, Salzburg	205
	Testing at Misano and Brands	211
	Isle of Man preview	213
	Italian Grand Prix, Misano	214
	Spanish Grand Prix, Jarama	217
	French Grand Prix, Paul Ricard	219
Lap 14	RUNNING ON EMPTY? 1980	222
	Isle of Man	222
Lap 15	KNOCKING OFF THE SHARP EDGES, 1980	237
	Post-TT, Mallory Park	237
	Dutch TT, Assen	238
	Belgian Grand Prix, Zolder	238
	Snetterton and Suzuka 8 Hour	241
	Silverstone	247
	Ulster Grand Prix	251

Lap 16	TIDYING UP THE LOOSE ENDS, 1980	254
	Nürburgring	254
	Japan and back	257
	Donington	259
	Cadwell Park	260
	Mallory Park	262
Lap 17	SEE YOU NEXT YEAR — SAME TIME, SAME PLACE, 1980	266
	Using my head	266
	Testing in Japan, home and Swann Series	269
Lap 18	DÉJÀ VU, 1981	281
	Daytona International Speedway	281
	A new season: Cadwell Park	283
	Donington Park	285
	Trans-Atlantic Match Races	287
	Salzburgring, Austria	288
	German Grand Prix, Hockenheim	290
	Italian Grand Prix, Monza	292
Lap 19	CONTROVERSY AND CROZ NEVER FAR APART, 1981	299
	Circuit Paul Ricard	299
	Brands Hatch Short Circuit	301
	Yugoslavia	302
	Isle of Man TT races	304
Lap 20	ANY CHANCE OF A HOLIDAY? 1981	317
	Donington	317
	Dutch Grand Prix, Assen	317
	Spa-Francorchamps	319

	San Marino Grand Prix, Misano	321
	Snetterton	325
	Suzuka 8 Hour	325
	Silverstone	327
Lap 21	CROZ — THE WORLD AND BRITISH CHAMPION, 1981	331
	Imatra, Finland	331
	Anderstorp, Sweden	333
	Ulster Grand Prix	335
	Donington	337
	Oulton Park	338
	Race of the Year, Mallory Park	339
	Brands Hatch	342
Lap 22	FUCK! WHERE DID THAT COME FROM? 1981	344
	Free-fall	344
	Where to now?	348
Lap 23	PICKING UP THE PIECES, 1982	357
	The new team	357
	Our new home in Italy	361
	Daytona	365
	Argentina Grand Prix	368
Lap 24	MUDDLING THROUGH ALONE, 1982	371
	Imola, Italy	371
	Hengelo, The Netherlands	373
	Austrian GP, Salzburg	375
	French Grand Prix, Nogaro	377
	Spanish Grand Prix, Jarama	382

Lap 25	UNABLE TO CONVERT, 1982	384
	Gran Premio delle Nazioni, Misano	384
	Donington ITV and John Player Cup	386
	Dutch Grand Prix, Assen	387
	Spa-Francorchamps, Belgium	391
Lap 26	SKIN, BLOOD AND SCABS, 1982	395
	Yugoslavia	395
	Silverstone	398
Lap 27	OK, BEEN THERE, DONE THAT — WHAT'S NEXT? 1982	408
	Swedish Grand Prix, Anderstorp	408
	Mugello	413
	Hockenheimring	419
POSTSCRIPT, 2010		425
RESULTS		427

1

STARTING OUT WITH A PASSION

THE FIRST FEW YEARS: 1973–75

From where I was sitting under a low hedge I knew I was in deep trouble. My white overalls were soaked with water and grass stains, blood dripped from an open wound on my elbow, and the new visor I'd purchased less than an hour ago was hanging from one dome and scratched with gravel rash. The customer's bike lay beside me, grass and mud smeared down one side and a shiny new scrape mark running along the left-hand muffler. The bike's handlebars were bent and there was a small but conspicuous dent in one side of the tank.

At 17 years of age I had suddenly developed a face like a sucked lemon as I dragged the little Kawasaki from where it had come to rest alongside me under the hedge. 'Shit! I've done it now,' I thought. This was my first day at work, my first assignment, and already I'd made my first major fuck-up.

Playing racer on a client's bike, seeing how fast I could ride in the rain, was not a good start to my employment. I was going over and over it in my mind, asking myself why I'd lost the front end going into that corner. The tyre appeared to be in good condition with lots of tread and the road, although wet, seemed to have grip — though clearly not enough. I decided it must have been sap on the road from the overhanging trees that had brought me down. I put that one in the memory bank for future retrieval — 'watch for sap on corners'.

I had started my motorcycle working career in Auckland in 1972 with Laurie Summers Ltd, the Kawasaki importers for New Zealand at that time. I began in the sales department as a general 'gofer', 'dogsbody' or 'hairy arse', depending on who was addressing me. I had just been to head office in the city to pick up the small daily parts order that included a Vespa exhaust valve. I soon worked this out as being an apprentice initiation test, knowing that Vespas don't have valves, and retaliated by taking a 10-minute break on the way back for a hot chocolate and a fag. I began thinking I was some hotshot racer and decided to take a short-cut through the One Tree Hill Domain which had a series of nice flowing bends. Scuttling around these was fun and, yes, it was raining lightly and the rest is personal history.

'How the hell am I going to explain this to my boss?' I wondered. I managed to kick the handlebars back into a workable position, jumped aboard and kick-started the 350 cc twin rotary disc 2-stroke. It barked back into life as if nothing had happened. I would have to deal with it, just 'fess up as soon as I got back, admit my shortcomings and apologize profusely.

Arriving back at the dealership, I quickly located the boss and explained in depth how 'that' bus had just come out of nowhere and how I'd tried to avoid it but I hit the brakes and skidded off. I told him the big yellow bus didn't even stop, but it must have been one of about 250 belonging to the Auckland fleet. The boss leaned forward in his chair, listened to me intently, paused, then advised me to watch out for buses in the future and told me that bikes are just mechanical things. Anything can be fixed but bodies are a little different so be careful in the future. 'Yes, sir,' I said.

Bob Buchanan was the manager, a fair-faced man with a mop of hair that at first glance resembled Worzel Gummidge's. He wore large black-rimmed spectacles and his roughly trimmed moustache sat proudly above a huge jawbone. Bob was always puffing away on cigarettes. I first met him when I was straight out of school working part-time in a used-car yard. This somewhat seedy looking place specialized in classic English sports cars. There were some wonderful cars on display, including the XK120 and 140 Jaguars plus MGA's, a TF1500 and Triumph TR6 and TR4's. As a cleaner I was encouraged to use whatever it took to make the cars look great. Using my initiative, once I even tried black tyre paint to enhance the sun-ravaged and tired-looking leather on a Sunbeam Rapier. That brilliant idea had to be abandoned after a client returned from a test drive in the car and walked out of the yard with black stains on the seat of his white linen pants.

I worked there for about five weeks before persuading a local copper to issue me a car driver's licence. I'd had a motorcycle licence since the age of 15 so considered myself overdue to have a car endorsement, and as the little book was signed off by the traffic officer I took the opportunity of stealing his pen and adding a heavy trade truck licence endorsement. I was licensed to kill.

Bob visited the car yard one day looking at an XK120 and after a test drive and some talking he offered me a job on the spot at the Kawasaki shop. How could I refuse? Motorcycles were my passion and I started the next day. I can't remember telling the yard boss I wouldn't be turning up for work again but I guess they figured it out.

At such a tender age and a sponge for knowledge, I found Bob was able to teach me a lot about life. He was a hard-drinking man with a penchant for living life to the max. Bob was the most accident-prone person I've ever known. Although he couldn't ride a bike well, he insisted each night on taking home the most expensive and powerful bike in the showroom. He was usually intoxicated and crashed frequently.

I had been at work for less than a month when we received a call to pick up a smashed bike at Mangere Bridge, about 8 km away. I arrived at the scene to find a Kawasaki on the grass verge with its front wheel tucked up neatly between the exhausts under the engine. This 1969 Kawasaki 500 cc H1 triple cylinder 2-stroke was blessed with a powerful engine and a power band as narrow as a knife edge. It was mounted in a thin-wall lightweight tubular chassis that twisted and bent like spaghetti at any suggestion of a corner. The chassis provided virtually no ground clearance and had a set of handlebars so narrow your thumbs almost touched each other. This red-tank model was known to be the most vicious bike ever produced and led to the coining of its nickname, the 'widow-maker'.

Bob was on a hiding to nowhere riding this lethal machine. It took me and two big Samoan boys, who happened to be watching, to manhandle this battered bike onto the company's Morris Oxford utility.

On his return to work from a short stay in hospital, Bob elected to use the Morris Oxford utility as his mode of transport — a safer bet, he thought. He set off for home after work one Friday night full of beer and bravado with his leg still in a plaster cast. The top edge of his plaster got jammed under the dashboard, and with his foot firmly planted on the throttle Bob careered out of control. He shot out through a car park at the back of the shop, across the road and smashed head-on into a brick state house, demolishing its front wall. I can still hear that old engine screaming its lungs out with the rear wheels spinning furiously. Someone eventually had the presence of mind to switch it off.

I was then given the opportunity of selling bikes, and part of the sales process was providing demonstrations to the clients, which usually meant coercing them to climb on the back. They were treated to a 10-minute pillion ride while I clinically demonstrated the bike's various selling points. The features I usually liked to demonstrate included the bike's power and acceleration, its maximum banking angle and the ease with which it could be flicked from side to side at speed while dodging cars and trucks. During all the time I spent doing these demonstration rides, I only once threw a bike away with a customer on the back. I touched an exhaust pipe on the ground while blasting off and turning out from an intersection. The bike spun up the road, leaving me and the prospect on the ground. Although highly embarrassed, I quickly got over it, as did the client, who went on to buy the bike.

It was in July 1973 when news broke from Tahiti that young New Zealander Geoff Perry had been one of the passengers on a Pan Am flight that had crashed as it was taking off from Papeete. The probable cause was put down to instrument failure in the climb-out phase. At about 300 feet from take-off the aircraft entered a turn but the bank angle increased unchecked and the crew evidently failed to take corrective measures. The aircraft crashed and sank in about 700 metres of water, killing all but one of the 79 people aboard.

This was devastating news to the motorcycling fraternity in New Zealand because Geoff was such a promising and talented young rider. A few years earlier he had raced at the Singapore GP on his home-built Suzuki 500 twin and, through Rod Coleman's connections with the factory, secured a TR750 to use the following year. Geoff again used a TR500 at Daytona in 1973 and came close to winning the big one, only to have a chain break on the last lap. His performance at Daytona earned him a ride with Suzuki USA at selected events, which he had to balance against work commitments with Air New Zealand.

Geoff was supported by his fellow apprentice John Allnutt and Allan Franklin, both talented technicians who were charged with looking after the spanners. This team was earmarked by Suzuki Japan to take the RG500 onto the European stage in 1974. Geoff was en route to his first race at Ontario for the 1973 season when the accident happened. He was due to be back on the Tuesday for an apprenticeship exam, so in effect it was truly a flying visit and he had elected to go by himself. Tragedy and luck so often go hand in hand. I thought about Daytona and wondered if one day I would ever get to race on that famous high-banked tri-oval course. Time would tell.

in 1973 plans were being made to stage an international cycle racing series in New Zealand to attract top internationals in Europe and the USA. It appealed to many of these riders, mainly because it was off-season and the five New Zealand circuits offered a cross-section of conditions to test the competitors. It was also a time for fun, relaxation and an opportunity to visit New Zealand. By the time Christmas arrived the organizers had found a series sponsor. Philip Morris would put up $10,000 and brand the events 'The Marlboro Series'.

Riders came from all over the world. The USA was represented by Ron Grant, who had just signed a contract with Suzuki for the season. He brought with him a very young Pat Hennen, who had also been drafted into the Suzuki team.

The opening round drew a big crowd on Boxing Day in Wanganui where the circuit winds itself around a network of tight roads that surround a centrally located cemetery. It also features a railway line crossing that has to be taken at an acute angle, making it quite tricky in the wet. That first race at the 'Cemetery Circuit', as it was named, was dominated by a few very competitive local riders. Dale Wylie eventually took the win on a TR500 twin Suzuki, followed home by Trevor Discombe, Ginger Molloy, Keith Turner and Pat Hennen.

Pukekohe was the second round of the Marlboro Series on 29 December 1973. Initially, I went as a spectator but ended up helping Eric Bone on his production H2. It was like heaven to me. The Castrol 'R' castor-based 2-stroke oil produces a distinctive thick sweet scent that can only be described as being the essence of speed and competition.

I didn't know a lot about these guys but I'd heard of Cal Rayborn. He had starred in *On Any Sunday*, a movie that dramatized the various motorcycle sports in America. Though basic, its feral nature contributed to its popularity amongst motorcycle fans all over the world. Cal was here to do some car racing and hadn't planned on doing any 2-wheel events, but was offered an opportunity to race a TR500 at the Pukekohe round. The bike he was loaned belonged to Colemans, the New Zealand Suzuki importers. With him was his father-in-law who had worked on Cal's bikes over the years, and everyone chipped in to help get him out on the track.

Eric had one of those days you'd want to forget. He crashed during practice when a rider in front of him slowed unexpectedly. He took evasive action but ran off the track and ended upside down in a pile of mud and grass on the edge of a drain. Although he came away relatively unscathed, Eric was bundled off to hospital for observation.

Eric tells the story of arriving at the hospital and having to wait until a doctor came to see him.

> 'I had been sitting patiently in the waiting room when an older nurse came into the room. I got her attention and asked her how long it would be before I was seen. She was obviously at the end of her shift and stressed out, because she snarled back at me, saying that she was pissed off seeing crashed motorcyclists, rugby players, battered wives and drunks taking up the doctors' valuable time when they could be better deployed saving, in her opinion, worthwhile people. Boy, did she cop a mouthful from me. I told her what I thought of her all right!
>
> 'A few minutes later this bossy matron returned, this time snidely remarking that they are still bringing in crashed motorcyclists, even dead ones. As if to prove her point, she said one of your American racing friends is lying dead out there. I stood up and could see a small group of people gathered and I instantly recognized Geoff Perry's older sister Dale. She was in a distressed state with tears running down her face. That's when I discovered that it was Cal Rayborn who had been killed.'

What transpired in this tragic turn of events was that Cal had run the bike successfully in practice but thought he was in need of more power. Talking with mechanic Joe Lett, Cal discovered Joe had already modified the jetting previously so it could be run on alcohol and had all the jets in a box if he wanted to change it over. Joe insisted it didn't improve the power much and it was really a waste of time. Cal and his father-in-law decided that the change to alcohol was necessary, so Joe left them to it to change the carburettor jets and mix up some alcohol fuel for the race.

The facts are a bit sketchy but from all indications some additional modifications were carried out to the slide cut-aways and this may have contributed to the engine running leaner and seizing as Cal was going through Champion Curve at high speed. He was unable to catch the seizure and was thrown off the bike and into a wooden fence, suffering extensive and fatal chest injuries.

The third round was staged around an industrial estate at Gracefield in the Hutt Valley near Wellington. I heard the news that John Boote appeared with the very first TZ700. This 4-cylinder 2-stroke racer was blindingly fast, winning decisively on its first outing. He went on to win again at the last round in Christchurch but missed out on the series win by starting too late.

Joining the Auckland Motorcycle Club was the only way to get issued with a racing licence. This club had been founded back in the 1930s and it ran like clockwork. It was a well-oiled machine, classic in its constitution and committee make-up.

At just 17 I was too young to get a competition licence, so I forged my mum's signature and changed my date of birth. The application was then put to the committee for consideration.

I had been at the dealership for only two months when I decided I could just about afford a small bike. There was nothing in my price bracket that I could consider in our shop but I had had my eye on a nice new green Suzuki AC50 at a dealership only 300 metres up the road. I had often roared past this place, usually on one wheel and invariably with a passenger clinging on for dear life with eyes the size of dinner plates.

From time to time I would drop into this Suzuki shop and chat with its owner, Ken Fletcher. I loved watching Ken prepare his Suzuki TR500 race bike. It was a pristine little workshop and his race bikes were always beautiful to the eye — clean, sparkling and oh that smell of Castrol 'R' and racing fuel. I was becoming hooked on the racing scene and this became the catalyst for me to think of taking to the track.

I dutifully paid $40 deposit and signed up for a three-year hire-purchase term to pay off the balance at some exorbitant finance rate. I jumped aboard my new bike and rode it straight down the hill and back to work. That afternoon I began the work of converting it into a race bike. I didn't know much but a little knowledge is dangerous and my expectations of morphing this little 50 cc bike into a fire-breathing monster were perhaps a little ambitious. Ken Fletcher must have thought I was a wanker. Who in their right mind would want to race a 50 cc Suzuki anyway?

I had a developing interest in the workshop and asked to be transferred under a government apprenticeship scheme. My life as a mechanic began a week later. That's when I got to really know and admire Eric Bone, who was largely responsible for introducing me to road racing. Eric was head mechanic in the workshop but we had already begun travelling to the racetracks together, along with his girlfriend Margaret. She was a big blonde with a ferocious appetite for gin, lime and lemonade plus the capacity to go head to head with anyone until the small hours of the morning. I was certainly in good hands but constantly scared shitless of Marg who would threaten to wipe grease and oil from my face with her spit-dampened handkerchief.

Eric rode a red Kawasaki H1 that the company had given him

as a write-off to rebuild and race under their sponsorship. It really looked just like the bike Bob had crashed earlier with a flattened front end. A very tidy production race bike emerged after some careful disassembly, straightening and rebuilding. It was fun doing the work on it. The front forks had bent almost at right angles under the frame. They must have been under maximum compression at the time of impact because when we took the top nuts off the forks, the inner springs launched themselves skywards, nearly cleaning up Eric and me in the process. This bike never missed a beat on the track but over time eventually became uncompetitive and obsolete. In any case Eric had moved into the Open Production class, racing aboard a H2 750 triple.

My Suzuki AC50 lasted about three months before I sold it and purchased the 1970 A7 Avenger that Eric had raced regularly before his interests became firmly focused on the 500 cc. I still had no racing experience but had done plenty of road riding. A group of friends would gather on Friday nights or at weekends to race each other from Auckland to Wellington via Wanganui or Hamilton and back. These were long rides of over 1200 km. I think it was critical in the learning phase for budding racers but not too popular with the police. I was able to push the bike to its limits, all the time honing my riding skills, and at speed on empty country roads I developed an ability to read the road.

2

MARLBORO SERIES AND A TEETH-CUTTING EXERCISE, 1973–74

I was soon informed that my application had been accepted by the Auckland Motorcycle Club and I paid my fees to become an official member. I was not into the politics of the club but more interested in the social side, sitting down with all these wonderful characters and listening to their entertaining stories. Everyone had a story to tell, but it was those classic European yarns of road racing that were the best to listen to. I would hang on every word, particularly when it was being told from first-hand experience. Like all storytelling, when you get a bunch of guys together, I'm sure there were plenty of cases of 'the older I got the faster I went'.

In the early 1970s the subject at the club that really fired my imagination was racing in the UK and the Isle of Man. Just listening to these guys talking about the Isle of Man and the experiences they had had there was fascinating. The depth of knowledge they had of the circuit 12,000 miles away was incredible and how they were able to describe every corner and section of the Island circuit blew me away. The members would talk about the successes and failures of New Zealand riders as they had attempted to conquer the greatest road circuit in the world. I wondered what it would be like to compete on the tortuous 37¾ mile course.

I studied the TT circuit more out of interest initially than from a desire to race. I read books and pored over the *Motorcycle News* and its rival *Motorcycle Weekly*, which always seemed to arrive about three months after their UK publication.

Now that I had my licence to race, I entered my first club event at Pukekohe and finished a creditable fourth. My Kawasaki A7 was the only one in the field amongst a herd of newly arrived RD350's. My first outing was marred by a spectacular crash during the first practice session. I was hot on the heels of a group of RD350's approaching the chicane on the back straight. Unexpectedly, the rider directly in front of me sat up and braked earlier than I had anticipated. To avoid running up his backside I dived to the left, which put me all out of line to be able to get around the island forming the chicane. Over the top I went, leaping about three feet in the air, but landed all crossed up and was immediately spat off. Down I went at about 130 kph and slid to a stop. The bike slid a little further down the track but remarkably was not damaged beyond bent handlebars and scuffed mufflers. It didn't make much difference cosmetically because the mufflers were already poked, and now it was looking decidedly second-hand.

Often these club races had over 60 entries but what was really bizarre was the method used to get the riders onto the grid. It was a free-for-all with no allocated grid positions for the race and no qualifying. Whoever got to the start line first got the best position. The riders were all lined up in rows about six deep behind a pit gate. Every bike was revving and jostling around; 2-stroke smoke hung in the air as we all waited for the gate to open. But the gate opened inwards, making it virtually impossible to predict who would end up on the front row following the melee as the riders fought for a good spot.

My second race was scheduled to be at Porirua, a circuit close to

Wellington. Eric and Marg drove down in his Austin 1100 land crab towing a trailer with Eric's Kawasaki 500 perched up high but tied down firmly. I attached the rear aluminium race number plates and rode my A7 to the circuit. Its front plate was tied to the seat with a bungee cord.

The race was held around a downtown shopping centre where the course made use of its car parks and a stretch of the surrounding roadways to form a track of about 2.5 km in length. There were lampposts on every corner and hay bales were used to protect the high kerbs. There was nothing unusual about this set-up. After all, it was road racing Kiwi-style and with only a few purpose-built tracks available to use, this would have to do.

My entry into the 350 cc production race almost turned into a nightmare for me. After a solid start and running in third place for most of the race, I was really happy with the way things were going. Then, on the last lap, I made a mistake and ran wide on a corner. I mounted the kerb at speed and up onto the footpath, whistling right through a rope attached to empty 44-gallon drums positioned there to keep the crowd back. Re-entering the track some 50 metres further on, I was still dragging the rope and two drums. I managed to finish third, closely followed by the 44-gallon drums in fourth and fifth place.

Later that day reality set in with the first big crash I ever witnessed. I was watching Eric's race, not believing my eyes that a Triumph T140v of all things was way out in front. A bike that was slow in comparison to Eric's H1 — how could that be possible? As I looked back to watch some of the other riders coming through a fast left-hander, I saw this unfortunate rider on a 500 cc Kawasaki get it completely wrong, run wide and slam straight into a lamppost. It was only lightly protected by a straw bale and on impact it exploded upwards, sending straw and debris from the smashed motorcycle high into the air.

I was stunned by the realization I might have witnessed my first fatality. I immediately thought of those close to him, his mechanics and his girlfriend or wife in the pit area. Perhaps he had children at home; his parents and the list of his loved ones grew in my mind. There is no instruction book on how we are supposed to deal with such a tragedy, so I put the accident out of my mind as soon as I could. The tactic of switching off the emotional aspect of racing's accidents and incidents would assist me in the future.

After the race meeting was over the competitors and supporters met at the local pub where they would gather for a night of beer drinking. Winners and losers alike, each had a race to recall, corner by corner, gear change by gear change. The stories were generally about the 'ifs' in racing. 'If' I had done this or 'if' the flag had came out a lap later. The 'ifs' could continue all night but we all knew this was not confined to motorsport.

Learning the fine art of motorcycle engineering was proving to be enjoyable, with Eric imparting his knowledge to me. Being in a branch workshop, we had to do many repairs in-house. These included painting, wheel rebuilding, cylinder re-boring, welding, tuning, accident repairs and crankshaft rebuilds. I was always the one who ran the errands and picked up parts from head office. So long as the parts could be tied down over a seat or were able to be stuffed into my white overalls, I was the man.

On arrival at head office I would be challenged to better the record to the top of Mt Eden and back. Glen Williams reckoned he had set the record at about four minutes. After three months and 20 attempts I realized I couldn't trust the timekeepers. I was always two to three seconds slower than their own man, according to their stopwatches.

One Friday night I became involved in a heated discussion with Bob at the office about a girl he had been dating. He accused me of getting too close to her and in a fit of jealous rage a fight broke out. I am not normally violent but something broke inside and I decked him with one big left hook. I was surprised at my own strength and Bob fell backwards through a plate-glass window. He suffered lacerations to his arm and forehead, though not severe enough to earn him a trip to the accident and emergency department.

With my chest swollen like a victorious prize fighter I went downstairs to the workshop and collected my tools. With the party still in full swing I scarpered out the back door and began thinking what the next week would bring as an unemployed mechanic. Decking the boss might not have been the smartest thing to do, and I wasn't going to include that in my résumé.

It's often said that as one door closes, another one opens and that's how it was for me. During the next week I got on my bike and started looking for a new job. What I had in mind was working as a mechanic in a place that understood racing. Translated, that meant I wanted a job that allowed me to prepare my race bike during my work hours and take Friday off to travel to the racetracks without feeling like I'd been dodging work.

I took a job at a Yamaha shop that had a contract to service Triumph police bikes. At a time when the Japanese were producing such innovative and relatively fast mid-sized bikes, the old T140P police bike had become something of a dinosaur. Throw a huge cowling on it and a heavy radio and saddlebags and it handled like a roller skate in a gravel patch. I loved tuning and servicing these bikes and, as expected, they all required a meticulous road test that entailed getting on the motorway and winding them out until they vibrated like an out-of-balance concrete mixer.

Late one Friday night I dropped in to check out a recently opened bike shop near my house. It was owned by an eclectic bunch of guys — Jim Halliday, an older ex-Royal Navy man, and his two sons-in-law Ian Beckhaus and Alan Johnson. Ian and Alan were mates and had recently arrived back from a stretch of duty as magistrates in Papua New Guinea. Their job was to maintain some sort of semblance of order in the remote outposts. They were loud, funny and rude with that classic dry Aussie humour. I enjoyed their company and after a few weeks I was asked to join the new venture, working in the workshop.

I packed up my tool-box (again) from the Yamaha shop and started the next day at 'SHAFT Motorcycles'. The new shop had an extraordinary company logo. A rather large erect penis lying horizontally with the byline *'Shaft — a stroke ahead of the rest'* neatly and graphically positioned beneath. Ian fostered a great relationship with the gangs, earning him the nicknames 'Honest Ian' from the bikers and 'the Beak' from others closer to him, presumably either because of his magistrate's status or his nose.

As a new shop, Shaft wanted some public exposure and they readily agreed to sponsor me on my old Kawasaki A7. I would have been happy with a box of beer and a few used tyres, but Ian insisted on promoting his brand to get his mileage. I adopted the corporate orange and yellow paint scheme and repainted the A7. A new set of leathers was ordered in matching orange and yellow. My Bell helmet was painted with a flame design to create an impact and the whole package matched quite nicely. However, once I got my suit on and sat aboard the newly painted A7 it looked a bit like a patchwork quilt.

Following a couple of average performances on my A7, Ian and Jim decided that it needed to be put out to pasture. The company bought another 350 cc Kawasaki but this time the more modern three-cylinder version. One race on the S2 and it was parked up as well; what Shaft wanted was a winner where the limelight was — the Open Production class.

I struggled with being told that I had to move up and ride a 750 cc machine because I thought it was a bit too big and fast for me, and at only 18 I felt not quite ready. Jim told me in no uncertain terms, 'No one's interested in the smaller classes; it's the Open Production class that really matters. Trust me, young fella!'

Finally I agreed, and they bought a used 750 cc Kawasaki. It was prepared by Arthur Randall, our head mechanic. He was a clever and competent Englishman who wouldn't take shit from anyone, but he had a great sense of humour as long as you agreed with everything he said.

I thought it might be a good idea, because he was so humorous, to nail his tool-box to the bench one night after he had gone home. Not a 'dicky bird' was said when he arrived for work the next morning to find his tool-box securely attached to the bench. He removed the nails without a word or fuss and went off to his first job for the day. The following morning when I arrived at work, the bastard had welded up all the hinges on my new tool-box and not only wrecked them but ruined the paintwork. I had to smash it to get my tools out. I was tempted to do something else, like electrifying his workbench, but for the first time in history I used my common sense. It was the best thing because he had already planned a few more nasty surprises in anticipation of my response, as I found out later.

Arthur did a great job of getting the new 750 ready, rebuilding it with all the care and attention afforded an F1 car. We had to overhaul the crankshaft so Arthur took all the new parts home and spent hours fitting new rod kits to it, assembling and balancing the crankshaft. He was so proud when he brought it back, telling us all it was true to less than a thousandth of an inch. But he was also paranoid about anyone touching it, for fear of upsetting his perfect balancing job. He placed it carefully on his bench.

Jim Halliday was lurking around in the workshop as the engine was being reassembled and I pointed to the crankshaft on Arthur's bench.

'Arthur's done the crank, Jim,' I said. 'Here, look at this!' I carefully picked up the three-cylinder crankshaft and proudly turned around to show him. However, as I turned, a sleeve on my overalls got caught on the edge of the bench and pulled my hand off the crank and it dropped to the concrete floor with a solid thud.

While Jim ripped strips off me for being careless and stupid, I was already focusing on how the hell I was going to tell Arthur that all his careful work had been ruined. I didn't have to wait long, though, as he'd heard the commotion and came around the corner to find me with the crank in my hand and a look of terror on my face. He knew straight away what had happened and took the crank from me and went over to the press. He slipped it between some vee blocks, set up the dial gauge indicator and gave it a spin. The needles spun around and back and forth again like a tachometer, suggesting that another two long nights of balancing was needed. Arthur was naturally pissed off and it took a long time before I was able to dig my way out of that one. I needed to show him that all the work he had done would be rewarded by winning at Hamilton the following week.

The annual road race at Hamilton was my first outing on the H2. For this event, the organizers roped off large sections of the road around a city park. What scared me most was that I was up against Eric Bone on his 750 cc Kawasaki. He was my mentor and I had a lot of respect for him but on the other hand I was being given an opportunity to prove my riding capability on the bigger bike. I was constantly being hounded and reminded by Jim and Ian, 'You can do this you young bugger — you can beat Boney!' That made me even more nervous.

The race started and I found myself behind Eric and in front of some other hard-charging challengers who were quite content to chip away at me on the inside of just about every corner. I managed to slip by Eric between two corners and then all of a sudden, as if by default or accident, I found myself leading the pack with just two laps to go. Half-expecting Eric to fly by at any time, I held on to win my first Open Production race.

I was ecstatic but not as much as Ian and Jim, who had literally forced me to make the jump to the big time. I had beaten the master and what a feeling that was. After the race, I talked to Eric and when I did so, I got the feeling he was more thrilled for me than disappointed with his own result.

I could just about see the word 'Grasshopper' appearing on Eric's lips ... as if he was Master Po and I was Caine receiving the ultimate endorsement from my kung fu mentor and teacher.

That night the organizing club held a function in rented rooms above the local Honda shop. It turned out to be a real humdinger with lots of food and wine. My girlfriend Mary was not shy and we decided that a streak might be in order. Streaking was all the rage in the mid-1970s, so off came my clothes, Mary stripped to her knickers and we ran out into the unsuspecting crowd for a quick circuit of the dance floor. With tits and testicles flying about all over the place we barely made a few metres before I was taken down in a flying rugby tackle. I was trapped in a wrestler's hold with all and sundry encouraged to view my private parts. From that day on, I thought streaking was best left to someone else. Eventually, I was released to go and find my clothes and finish the bottle of wine I had started. The room, however, by this time had taken a distinctive lean and it began spinning like a helicopter in slow motion. It was time to head back to the motel. I made a mental note never to drink wine again and to keep my clothes on at all times in public places.

We awoke at about 10 a.m. with the motel owner noisily trying to coax a billy goat off the roof. How it got there we don't know but I had my suspicions. I also denied any knowledge of how his new lawnmower had ended up at the bottom of the swimming pool.

Back in Auckland the three musketeers — Jim Halliday, Ian Beckhaus and Allen Johnson — decided to help out even more with my racing. Jim fancied himself as a talent-spotter and saw potential in my riding style. One afternoon he waltzed into the shop. Ian was busy counting out cash from a brown paper bag with a big brown heavily tattooed biker in attendance. Jim came through to the workshop.

'What's happening, you young buck?' he asked. I was working on my race bike.

'Getting this ready for Manfeild next weekend,' I replied.

Jim looked me straight in the eye. 'Good. You know you have to knock that Collison fellow off, don't you? You've got the best bike now and no excuses, so don't worry about any of those other riders, you can knock them off, just like you did to Eric. You young bugger, all we need to do is try and control you somehow.'

I drove down-country to the recently completed Manfeild racetrack. Its new surface was smooth and fast. Chris Amon had something to do with its layout. Some corners were banked and for once it was a track with some width to it, and no poles or hay bales to worry about. I was nervous as hell and my stomach churned away like a stone-crusher. Being mid-winter it was freezing cold, and the track facilities were quite basic with only cattle yards for shelter. The wind blew from the south and it was raining off and on. I had entered three races on the H2, two production events and the Grand Prix which was open to all comers on any capacity machines. My qualifying time in the wet was surprising in that it was only three seconds slower than the fastest time set in a dry session. That made me nervous, but after winning the first race by a country mile I felt my nerves had settled down and I was beginning to enjoy myself.

The Amco Open Grand Prix race was scheduled to be run midway through the day and had just about every top rider in New Zealand entered. Avant, Boote, Collison, Discombe and runner-up in the 500 cc world championship in 1969, Ginger Molloy. The start was furious, ducking and diving amongst the water spray trying to get into the right position for the first corner. It was wild, with bikes in all directions, but I came out of the corner right up Molloy's exhaust pipe. We traded places for a number of laps, with me getting the better of Ginger on the corners but being blown off down the straights. Ginger had a little 'oops' and slid off his TZ350 Yamaha without injury late in the race, leaving me alone out front. I cruised the remaining laps to the finish flag to win my biggest race to date.

Topping the day off with another easy win in the second production race by a big margin made it three from three. With those victories came the spoils of war — three bottles of locally made plonk and a prize money cheque for $178. Of course I was rapt.

A reporter took a few photos and asked me if it was my biggest win. Naturally I said yes, pointing out it was the biggest race meeting in New Zealand that year. He noticed me holding the bottles of wine and asked if I was going to drink them now. 'Hell no!' I replied. 'These will never be opened; they'll remain as a reminder of my first big win, so they will stay on my mantelpiece back home.'

I was lying through my back teeth and if the bottles had had any life they would have been feeling very nervous right then as I hightailed it back to the truck in search of a glass. Three minutes later we had drained them all.

Back in Auckland, I sat listening to Keith Williams, the best storyteller of all time. He had me in fits of laughter as he talked me through his life experiences and racing career. He was there every Thursday night at the club. Keith had strong opinions on just about everything that mattered and didn't suffer fools or bureaucrats lightly.

But he had one feature that bewildered me. He had lost his vision in one eye following a dog attack when he was young. He had a glass eye installed. He had adapted well to his disability while growing up and although riding a motorcycle is one thing, the thought of him at speed in a racing environment was extraordinary. When you raced against him, any braking or overtaking action had to be done with a fair amount of caution and on the correct side so that Keith could see what was happening. I am sure many a brave rider has attempted to pass him on the wrong side and ended up having the gap closed unintentionally, before being run off the track.

Keith kept on at me to have a go at racing a 'real' bike and although

I knew he was talking about the Yamaha 250 cc and 350 cc racers, I thought they were a little more complicated than my old production bikes with so many changes available to make. They had little triangle-shaped tyres and expansion chambers that pushed out about 110 decibels. They were fast with little weight and the engine had a power band to contend with. It had carburettors that needed constant fettling and fuel that required mixing by hand with racing oil. These 'pukka racers' also had cowlings and big brakes and it seemed to me that I would be more comfortable with a production bike. I could ride it to the racetrack, park it up against a fence, attach the front racing number then change into my racing suit and go racing. Afterwards reverse it all and ride it to the pub. Quite simple, so I thought.

The guys who rode these smaller-capacity racers were invariably arriving with their steeds perched up on a trailer, tool-boxes and spare parts aplenty. Two mechanics and a tart (wife) who sat in the car all day quite happily doing her needlework. All this while her beloved rider, who was covered from head to toe in oil-infused fuel vapour and oil-stained leathers, worked feverishly at changing jets, sprockets and tyres and repairing broken clutch plates.

Keith asked me if I wanted to test his Yamaha 350 cc and even offered his company utility to transport it out to the track and back. I unloaded the bike, mixed the fuel and oil as instructed, checked it out as best I could, and adjusted the seating and handlebar position, not really knowing much about these racers. I set off on a few laps and after two I returned to the pits, convinced that 2-stroke racers were a breed of their own and as long as my arse pointed to the ground I would not get to grips with them at all.

I returned the transporter and bike, cleaned, polished and sparkling as new. I was slightly uneasy as to how I was going to explain that this bike was a dud and handled so badly compared with my production bike that I would not want to use it again. I began by saying, 'Keith, mate, ah thanks but … you know I didn't like the handling and on corners it was kind of, ah, how can I put this ...' Keith interjected by asking what tyre pressures I used. 'Ah, don't know, whatever they had in them I suppose,' I replied sheepishly. Without saying a word, he reached out and grabbed a tyre pressure gauge and checked the front tyre. The gauge registered 13 pounds. Keith looked at me through his one eye and said, 'Pick the bike up next Friday night and take it to Baypark Raceway. But, you idiot, this time at least put some bloody air in the tyres please — 30 pounds should do it.'

Baypark Raceway in Tauranga is about three hours from Auckland. At Tauranga we splashed out and booked a hotel. It had a house bar that was dangerous when we all got together. I was awoken in the small hours of the morning by banging on the outside window and within seconds my room was full of people scampering around looking for a place to hide. Management and police had begun a systematic search of rooms, looking for the culprits responsible for climbing the flag pole and stealing the New Zealand flag. I answered the door looking bleary-eyed and indignantly complained about being woken up. I tried muttering something about trying not to wake my girlfriend who was fast asleep playing possum in the bed. Although we passed inspection, it took another hour for the drunken crowd to filter out the door and off to their respective bedrooms.

Out at the track I dragged Keith's Yamaha and my 750 Kawasaki off the back of the ute. The Kawasaki was thrown against the fence and my attention was focused on the 350. I began by pumping up the tyres to 30 pounds, carried out the check-over, this time with a little more knowledge of its workings, and went out for practice.

Hell, this bike is a missile, I thought on the first lap. It was quick, light to steer, really good suspension and by crikey it went around corners as if on rails. My lap times were really fast but it was an uncomplicated track. It had only four corners, one big sweeping 180-degree curve and three 180-degree hairpins. It was a bit like doing laps around your kitchen.

I rode my Kawasaki 750 to a win in the production race after a hard-fought battle with a local rider. The 350 cc class race was a big thing for me because Ginger Molloy also lined up on the grid. The race started in a flurry of moving machinery and screaming 2-strokes, all jostling for the best position to enter the first turn. As the smoke cleared and the back straight came into view I found myself in about fifth spot but quickly worked my way up to second, a few seconds behind Ginger. It was on about lap 10 of 15 laps that I figured I had his measure and closed to be almost side by side down the straights. My disc brake worked well and I felt very confident under brakes to be able to make a move into the lead.

I out-braked Ginger, only to go a little wide coming out and lose the drive on to the next short straight. Ginger out-accelerated me to take back the lead but it was too late: I could smell the kill. I was riding like a demon possessed, head down, arse up in the traditional style. I began thinking this type of racing was quite exciting. I tucked under the screen and revved the engine out hard. I sat up, braked and pitched the bike into the corner following Ginger. I was nearly up his exhaust pipe, cranking the bike over to what I thought was the maximum bank angle, aiming to get a run on Ginger exiting out of the corner ...

Keith lifted his eyebrow, took one look at the bike and said, 'Croz, it's only superficial damage, but from what I hear from others, you rode its wheels off — well done. To keep up with Ginger was no mean feat, in fact everyone was really impressed.' I was a bit taken aback. I stopped picking at the itchy scab on my forearm that had mysteriously appeared shortly after I dived into the corner following Ginger on his Yamaha. I had expected a less-than-flattering response when I handed back the battle-scarred Yamaha. Keith was no doubt proud of the fact that this bike he had built was able to perform and I had a hand in showcasing it on his behalf. It was not a real TZ350 like Ginger's bike but more of a modified production R5 Yamaha with TZ350 bits on it. Keith had given me my first-hand look at true Grand Prix-style racing and it made me think about what might happen if I was ever to trade in my old production bike and get one of those fancy things.

I still preferred production racing. To me it was about winning the race to the local pub after competition for the day had drawn to a close. In a shower of gravel and flying stones I would fishtail my production bike out of the track, complete with racing plates bungeed to the rear seat. I would have managed to get two rounds of drinks in before the traditional rider, car, trailer with bike and spares combination ground to a halt in the pub car park.

I decided to stick to production bikes because with the regulations as they stood, no modifications could be made. The maintenance was less, therefore I didn't have to be a slave to it.

3

AROUND THE TRAPS GAINING EXPERIENCE

PRACTICE DAY, PUKEHOHE, 1974

Although I'd been working at Shaft, I found myself floating between bike shops as I chased rides in my emerging role as a semi-professional racer. I visited the Mt Eden workshop where Tony Phillips had shown interest in my racing. He was recalling his time in Canada, where he had been helping out with a team in a 24-hour race with Yvon Duhamel riding a screaming H1R 500 cc racer. 'Just like this one, but an earlier model.' He pointed to the lime green H1R-A parked on display in the workshop.

Thinking it might be fun to ride, I interrupted him to ask, 'When are we going to get this thing going?' Before long Tony had a workshop job card made up and the bike was dragged into the workshop with instructions to get it race-ready. The ignition was faulty and, despite spending many hours on it, we had to send it away for a specialist to sort out.

It was made ready for the annual test day at Pukekohe. We had no tyres available but I managed to convince Ken Fletcher to sell me a new wet-weather Dunlop tyre. It was designed to go on a 3½-inch-wide rim to take advantage of the shape. Our Kawasaki rims were a lot smaller and when the tyre was fitted it looked like a big rubber

O-ring. We threw a road tyre on the front, loaded it up and took it out to Pukekohe for a test day.

Ken would have kicked my arse if he'd been able to catch me. In one of the first outings we arrived at the same corner at the same time. Probably more through my inexperience than from a deliberate act of defiance, I wouldn't let him in up the inside going into Railway Corner and chopped him off. I felt the bump and looked around to see Ken tumbling towards the dirt edge, following his brand new and freshly painted TZ700. It was sliding along the track spraying coolant water and brake fluid from the damaged hoses and broken master cylinder.

As I approached the same corner on the next lap I saw him standing beside his damaged bike. I checked if he was OK by giving him the thumbs up and asking beneath my closed visor, 'You OK, mate?' The look on his face told me I should be looking for a place to hide when he got back. Fortunately, when we talked later about the incident he didn't blame me. He said he came in a bit hot and ran up the inside of me. His new, now poked, bike looked a mess and I felt for him as he had worked hard preparing it for this day.

CASTROL 6 HOUR, OCTOBER 1974

The Castrol 6 Hour race in New Zealand was planned as a direct result of the highly successful Australian event of the same name. The major manufacturers were all interested in fielding teams to showcase their various models. Even Honda announced that some poor sod was going to compete in this new race aboard the newly released GL1000 Gold Wing, a big flat-four touring model. This was going to be a sight to see.

It was held at the Manfeild racetrack where I had already tasted victory on my H2 in the rain, so when Eric asked me to partner him in this race on his H2 Kawasaki 750 cc triple, I was in. We stood a good chance of winning with a well-prepared bike. Laurie Summers Ltd offered Ginger Molloy a new Z1 900 to race. He agreed but surprisingly decided to ride it solo, without a break for the whole six hours. It was a good choice of rider and he would push it hard but we doubted if he could go the distance at the pace required. We didn't know too much about the new Z1 900 but felt our older and lighter 2-stroke would be faster and less likely to need replacement tyres or brakes.

The manufacturers showed up with an eclectic mix of oddball makes and models. From the first day of practice everyone had a race plan. The smaller-capacity bikes gambled entirely on their fuel efficiency and reliability to be there at the end.

For the bigger bikes it was a different story. No one knew if the six hours of racing could be completed on just one set of rubber. Getting these heavy bikes to go in a straight line required lots of fuel, so calculations were being made with index fingers on the dusty back windows of cars. If you could get 60 minutes out of a tank of fuel, then it was five stops — but only four if you could wring 72 minutes from a tank.

Eric and I were under no illusions and would need at least six stops. Every stop needed to be lightning fast and at halfway a front brake change would be required. It was easier to re-route the brake lines and change the whole system than to cock around attempting to change just the pads. According to Eric, the rear was a different matter. A few days before the event he had arranged for the local brake shop to bond on the hardest and most durable shoes for the rear brakes. A phone call had assured him they had stock of this hard asbestos material. But when it came time to get the shoes bonded, he discovered the local Suzuki shop had taken the lot, leaving us with no option but to use the standard original shoes. He came steaming into the workshop a day before we had planned to go to the track.

'Those dirty rotten thieving bastards,' he muttered. 'Suzuki have taken all the special shoe material I'd planned to use and left us with bloody nothing.'

The race for us was lost then and there because without the special brake lining, the shoes wear quickly and soon become useless as the adjustment runs out. I had no option but to run the race as hard as I could and hope that with careful use of the rear brake we might have something left in the latter part of the race.

The start was hectic but I soon settled into the groove, pulling a big margin on the rest, including Ginger who was riding smoothly on the big 900. By lap 20 my rear brake was useless, but by using the front brake plus a little engine brake, I was still posting good lap times. Eric was sent out at the 53-minute mark and with a newly adjusted rear brake he kept up the fast times. He came in and handed the riding over again to me for my next stint and I pressed on into the fourth hour.

Although it had been adjusted at the stop, the rear brake was again useless, while the front brake gradually began getting softer, requiring the lever to be pumped a couple of times before going into a corner. Not an ideal situation, especially as the transmission was showing signs of self-destructing. Jumping in and out of fourth gear, I knew we were in deep trouble and it was getting worse. With another fuel stop due soon and still well positioned, I whistled into one of the banked corners only to find I had virtually no brake, causing me to run wide and almost off the track. I recovered and headed for the pit area, hoping like hell my team was ready. They were, but I found I couldn't stop as my front brake was now all but gone.

The whole pit area became a moving target for me as I sped down pit lane not knowing where I would end up. I threw myself off the side of the bike and used my boots as brakes to pull up about 20 metres past my allocated pit area. Eric took one look and made a gesture with his thumb across his throat, indicating he was out and didn't want to risk his life with dodgy brakes. Being younger and more foolhardy, I was reluctant to give away our lead and with another change of brakes I was out there again going for it. With my head down between the tachometer and speedometer and my arse poking up I continued, making up lost ground. Fourth gear was now a lottery and I found myself short-changing into fifth, half-expecting the gearbox to explode between my legs.

The last 40 minutes was like skating on thin ice, wondering if I'd end up off the course after a total brake failure or just get spat onto the road as the gearbox locked up in fourth gear. The old H2 was not handling the best by now but I finally rode it over the line to finish in third place behind Allen Collison and that wily old racer Ginger Molloy, who had circulated smoothly for the whole six hours and didn't even stop for a tyre change. I needed one of those Z1 900's for sure.

Back in the pit area I kicked the back wheel of the H2 and was surprised to see seven broken spokes poking out and the rest about to break off. There was an engraved pewter mug and Castrol ribbon for our efforts plus I got half the third place prize money. Not a bad effort, I thought — and I had survived.

MARLBORO SERIES, 1974/75

'Croz, you can take the J4 van down to Wellington, as long as you bring it back in one piece and look after the H1R,' Tony offered. I was stoked — at least we had a van to take to the first round of the Marlboro Series at Gracefield. It wasn't the most salubrious form of transport but it would get Woody and me and both the bikes from Auckland to Wellington and back via Wanganui for the second round on Boxing Day.

The line-up of riders at Gracefield was remarkable, given that New Zealand is a small country and a long way from anywhere. Pat Hennen turned up again but with two bikes, a TR500 and TR750 Suzuki. John Boote had also returned, this time with his brother and their two TZ750's. Wylie, Fletcher, Discombe, Avant, Molloy and Woodley headed up the local team and a bunch of high-profile

Aussies including brothers Murray and Jeff Sayle crossed the Ditch from Sydney.

I backed up the J4 van and unloaded my H2 and the H1R-A. I was hopeful that the latter's ignition system was finally sorted so I could get in a few more laps than the typical three before grinding to a halt. It sounded raw and nasty when I fired it up for practice the first time. It had a triple-cylinder air-cooled engine that sat rather high in the chassis and had a narrow power band if jetted correctly, even narrower if it wasn't. It was a four-year-old bike that had done virtually no racing mileage, so it looked clean and pretty. It was destined to stay that way because halfway through practice it cried enough. I was wondering if it would ever finish a race. Back into the J4 it went, never again to be ridden in anger.

By contrast, my old production bike was looking a bit sad but it performed flawlessly, like a trained seal, so long as I kept it upright.

'Gidday, son, fancy seeing you here!' I knew the voice, and through the crowd that had just reformed after I sent them diving for cover was my dad. I had been leading the practice on the second lap when approaching a corner off the back straight I pulled on the brake a little too hard. The handlebars went soft, the steering screwed around and down I went, flat on my face at about 120 kph. I rotated my body around and was sliding up the road towards the gutter. The bike was sliding alongside me, making a much greater racket as every exposed edge was being ground off by the tarmac. The mufflers were making that expensive noise but hopefully they would stay attached to the chassis mounts and remain intact. It came to rest up against a hay bale on the edge of the track and I tried to stand up but I was still moving and was shot up on the kerb. All I saw were the backs of people running away, alarmed that the bike or me would end up amongst them. There were deck chairs and chilly bins full of food and drink being scattered everywhere as people dived for cover. When I stopped, I heard Dad call out.

'You silly bugger, what did you do that for?' he said, knowing I was not injured.

'Bloody hell, I didn't expect to see you here. I was going to try and find out where you're living, as Woody and I might need a place to stay tonight. Come on over later to the pits.'

It was a disastrous day but I won the production race and with it about $60 in prize money.

Dad had been transferred to Wellington following a slight indiscretion with a Russian aircraft at Auckland Airport. He was a senior crash fire officer and his duties included inspecting any new aircraft type that landed, going through the interior and documenting its layout in case it was involved in an accident. The data would then be stored 'in the event of an emergency'.

The Russian management didn't believe in sending their crews to a hotel for the night, preferring them to stay aboard on the apron. When Dad arrived late at night for the inspection, he was met by the crew who were already half-cut on vodka. Out of politeness, of course, he had a few with them and for his punishment got demoted and exiled to head office at Wellington Airport. At least Woody and I now had beds if we wanted.

Woody had noticed that the van had been blowing a little smoke out the back. It got worse by the hour as we drove back up the island. Wanganui had its round of the Marlboro Series on Boxing Day. Despite the perceived dangerous state of the circuit, it had a good safety record. Many riders have crashed there but because the speeds are relatively slow, no one gets that far out of control. The railway lines have to be treated with respect but it's a great track and can be fun to ride.

We had booked a hotel in the main street, an old wooden colonial one that has boiler rooms and steam pipes, and a smoking room with a private house bar. It also had the traditional smelly burgundy patterned carpet that was threadbare in places. For the three days it cost us $40 a night plus an extra $20 each for Christmas dinner. Woody and I had a nice dinner in the hotel, then went to a motel where there was a party. We were invited to join a bunch of riders for another Christmas dinner. We couldn't afford it but we figured as it was Christmas, bugger it. 'Chicken today, bones tomorrow, Woody — we'll be OK, trust me.'

Race day brought a new problem as soon as I went out on the track to practise. My rear tyre was poked and I couldn't get traction. Gracefield must have been harder on the rubber than I thought. I had to buy another tyre, which set me back another $80. The new tyre was fitted and balanced and with one last practice I got to run it in nicely before my three races.

'Croz, how much money do you have left?' Woody asked.

'Wouldn't have a clue. Hang on a minute mate, I'll check.' I went to my wallet and pulled out a pile of receipts, invoices and three $5 notes. Then it hit me. 'Fuck-all. How much have you got?' Woody walked to the front of the van and checked his wallet; counting the small change we had exactly $23 between us.

'Is that all? Where's the programme, Croz?' He looked at it for a while, then Woody told me it was my problem.

'What do mean, "my problem"?' I asked.

'Hey! It's not me who's doing the riding, Croz. We need $160 for the hotel. We have $23 and the prize money for winning all three races is $140. We'll have only three fucking dollars to our name before the drive back to Auckland. It's your problem — get out there and win, otherwise we'll be stuck here washing dishes for a month!'

The pressure was now on to win the three races. Riding like a man possessed, I won all three. We paid for the hotel and with some small change we found in the J4, we set off for Auckland billowing out a cloud of white smoke. Not being able to pay for any more accommodation meant it would be an overnight trip.

Rodger Freeth understood our dilemma and offered to drive slowly behind us at least some of the way back to Auckland. If we broke down he would be able to help. Rodger had a beautiful old Porsche that had just been repainted and he tucked in behind us as we drove off. A little way into the journey we struck a long uphill. The J4 struggled and we needed first gear to complete the climb. At the top I stopped and checked the oil — nothing showing on the dipstick, so we poured in the remaining spare engine oil and set off again. The second time we stopped to check the oil level, Rodger pulled up alongside. His Porsche had changed colour and was covered in a sticky oily film. He had thought the window was a little dirty and turned on the wipers, only to discover just how much oil had landed on his car.

He left us at that point and on his arrival in Auckland his car needed a considerable amount of work by painters to restore it to its original splendour.

With no spare engine oil left we had to use Castrol 'R' 2-stroke racing oil to get us to the next service station. We had planned to buy all the petrol we could afford, about $9 worth, but we knew we had reserves in the race bikes' fuel tanks. Our oil consumption had become catastrophic. The next service station we stopped at had an oil disposal and recovery area out the back, which we raided by siphoning out enough discarded oil to get us back to Auckland.

I pulled into the workshop at Kawasaki and handed the keys to Tony. As promised, his bike and the J4 van were both still in one piece.

AUSSIE 6 HOUR, 1975

'Holy shit, I'm off to Sydney for the 6 Hour!' I couldn't believe my luck when Tony Phillips announced the plan. He intended to talk to Kawasaki Australia about trying to get me a ride on a Z1. He probably thought that as I had run third in the New Zealand 6 Hour last year they would be interested in supplying a bike for me to ride. He even mentioned a possibility of co-riding with Gregg Hansford. A few phone calls later it was plain it wasn't going to happen but enough interest was generated for Tony, Brenda and me to go over a few weeks before the race and try to find a ride.

I would have to get an appropriate racing licence but that was a formality through the NSW Auto Cycle Union. We organized a KZ400 bike from a Sydney dealer to use and somehow convinced someone to provide lodgings for us in a house at Kogarah, close to the airport. I must have had rocks in my head: here I was with not two pennies to rub together and grand ideas about taking on the Aussies at Amaroo Park for the Castrol 6 Hour production race — the motorcycle equivalent of Bathurst, the 'great race'. We flew over on one of Air New Zealand's new DC-10's. They had begun taking delivery of these hi-tech airliners in early 1973. This was my first overseas flight, and it made a huge impact on me. I was trying to figure out how these heavy chunks of aluminium could get airborne. From then on I was a very curious boy about aviation.

On the Monday morning Tony and I drove into the city to meet with Neville Doyle. He was in charge of Team Kawasaki Australia — the race team. Gregg Hansford and Murray Sayle rode for them and were planning to team up on a Z1 900 in the 6 Hour. I was determined to find a ride, preferably with Kawasaki, but it was clear Neville couldn't do a lot for us. He referred us to the local area sales manager, Myles Stivano, who might be able to point us in the right direction. I didn't expect he would just give me a new Z1 to race but we had a shot at convincing him we needed to be seriously considered.

Tony began by explaining that I had won the New Zealand Castrol 6 Hour race, riding alone, and was looking for a Kawasaki to ride in the Aussie event. Myles listened for minute or two, with his eyes beginning to glaze over, and he indeed did point us in a certain direction — out over the horizon and back to Auckland. He referred to New Zealanders as bludgers, no-hopers, useless, incompetent and untrustworthy. In my opinion, he was just a mean old bastard who hated Kiwis. Finally, he backed off a little and suggested I call the Australian Triumph importer in Melbourne. Apparently, they were looking for riders for their 750 cc Trident for the 6 Hour. A classic diversionary tactic, I thought.

'Arrogant prick,' I thought as I drove off from Kawasaki NSW in a state of disbelief. 'Go ride a Triumph — fuck off!' This guy didn't deserve to occupy space in my brain but he did make me look for a telephone box to call the Triumph agent in Melbourne. The phone call provided some level of comfort when they offered me a ride, but I felt somewhere out there Lady Luck would appear and I respectfully declined in the hope of finding a better opportunity in Sydney. It was now only days before Australia's greatest ever production race was scheduled to start. I was getting anxious. An article in *Revs* magazine carried a small piece noting I was in Sydney looking for a ride. As a consequence, I finally got a sniff of a possible ride.

That chance of a ride on a 900 Kawasaki eventuated after news that *Revs* reporter Burnie Summers, who was teamed to ride with Sydney rider Chris Wise, had broken his leg in a road accident. This left a slot potentially available for me. I was in boots and all and made the call to Chris. A talented rider, he was slowly moving away from racing due in part to his young family and the fact that he was building his own cartage business, running a twin steer International dump truck. He was an experienced rider with lots of local knowledge on his home track. He would certainly be a good partner.

We were to meet at Amaroo Park for a few laps of practice a week before the race. Amaroo was a really small and tight hilly circuit taking only about 60 seconds to run a lap, really dizzy stuff with mainly right-hand corners. The track was out west towards the Blue Mountains and was built in a natural rocky amphitheatre. This was my first visit to Amaroo Park and I was astounded at the flies and the heat. Constantly swatting at the little bastards hovering around my face, I finally learnt the meaning of the 'great Aussie wave'.

The Castrol 6 Hour event began in 1970 and was seen as an ideal showcase for new road bike models being released on the Aussie market. In 1975 bike sales nationally were booming, and with sales figures set to rise it was an important race. The 6 Hour was a real test of men, machine and tactics and the organizers had carefully orchestrated a system to deny anyone the chance of cheating. A set of strict rules meant that the bikes were eligible with no modifications allowed; they had to be totally stripped and carefully reassembled under the watchful eye of an officious team of scrutineers. The theory was that if the bike passed the pre-race technical check intact it would be classified as being 'standard' and a safe bet to enable the organizers to declare a winner on that last lap. Television had brought its own influence and understandably was demanding a final result that would not be subject to protests after the chequered flag had been waved.

Our old Z1 was in a sad state when I first laid eyes on it. Looking like it had been to the moon and back, it required lots of parts to be replaced just to make the official check-in. When it came time for scrutineering it was another story. We were forced to replace the mufflers because the underside was damaged from cornering and as a consequence it could have been seen as having an advantage at the start of the race. The bikes were supposed to be in showroom condition, to ensure this would be a true production race. The footpegs and any other minor parts showing signs of wear or damage had to be replaced.

The scrutineering took place in a tent with each bike allocated a tiny work area, with sand and flies everywhere late into the night. The odd cheat was found during those checks but for any of those who wanted to try, the official chief technical inspector Chris Peckham was up for the challenge.

Our old bike was finally put together with help from sidecar rider Peter Campbell, who had a workshop close to Liverpool where he worked on his own Z1-powered sidecar. He knew the Z1 engine backwards but had a huge struggle trying to get the correct valve clearances. We were forced to start the race with a distinctive rattle on number three cylinder, the result of not having the correct shims available. Our race started with the hope that it didn't spit a shim out through the camshaft cover and embed itself in my groin.

Practice continued during the week while the technical inspections were under way. Things went well for Chris during practice and I found myself more than able to match it with these Aussie riders.

We started the race in seventh position and pounded our way around until we made a cock-up with our fuel calculation. It was critical to get an hour out of a tank prior to handing over to the co-rider for his stint. This ultimately meant one less stop. We miscalculated our fuel burn rate and ran out of gas and out of contention. However, I did enough to impress onlookers.

The race was won by Gregg Hansford and Murray Sayle on a Z1 900 after a brilliant battle with John Warrian riding a 900 Ducati. Sadly, John was let down mechanically within sight of the finish line and I had to watch Myles Stivano gloat publicly about his boys. I wished he would choke on a beer can.

I thought Sydney was a cool place to live and wanted to be there to race. It was also the novelty of a different country and lifestyle plus the way the Aussies embraced their poor cousins from over the Ditch that made my decision to leave New Zealand in pursuit of a racing career in Australia a reality.

Although they were a hardy bunch, I had to keep reminding them we New Zealanders came from a colonizing, missionary, pioneering and settler stock, unlike Australia which was a big empty place that had plenty of room for Britain's convicts. The banter and piss-taking made life a constant laugh.

That trip to Australia and the race experience proved I could foot it with their best and I decided I wanted more.

1975 CASTROL 6 HOUR AND MARLBORO SERIES

A few weeks after the Aussie 6 Hour, the New Zealand 6 Hour followed. This time I was given a new Z1 900 from Laurie Summers. It was uncrated at the Mt Eden workshops where it was meticulously assembled and checked. The workshop foreman was given the task of putting about 500 km on it before the Z1 900 had its first service and pre-race preparation. I was tossed the keys and told to be at the racetrack on Thursday for technical inspection. It needed the extra kilometres and by the time the bike arrived at Manfeild it had travelled about 1200 km. By far the hardest stretch was the trip from Auckland to the track. For some strange reason, the act of getting it there had become a race in itself. I had to better the time set the previous year and was on target to break the unofficial record.

About 50 km short of my destination I passed a small pub and parked outside was my support vehicle that had left earlier that day. I jumped on the brakes and joined in with the crew for a late afternoon jug of beer. When the publican sent us packing we wobbled off to our motel near the track, leaving the record safe for another year.

This year we had spoken of using a co-rider for the event but I felt I could do the job without one, just like Ginger had last year. It was my decision and a good one because I didn't have to rely on anyone else having to get up to speed with me. Besides, if I treated it as a long high-speed ride, it should be OK. I knew the circuit, I knew the bike was capable and I knew I could concentrate for the duration. The thought of not having to share the prize money was also tantalizing.

We were properly prepared for this race with a game-plan for nearly every eventuality. When the flag dropped it was straight to the front for me and I set about getting into a smooth rhythm on the big 4-cylinder Kawasaki, a rhythm I kept throughout the race.

Sometimes things go so well if you are prepared; it's hard to believe we could have been worried about anything before the race. It would be the first time I understood and experienced the six 'P's' of racing.

These are not necessarily the reserve of motorcycle racing, as the principles apply in all sorts of areas: 'Piss-Poor Preparation equals Piss-Poor Performance'.

We were prepared for almost everything except when, just after my fourth fuel stop, I felt a sensation in my bladder that could mean only one thing. Luckily, I made it to the scheduled fuel stop. As soon as the bike rolled to a stop and was being refuelled, I casually left the pit area and walked to a nearby fence to relieve myself. All males know this, I'm sure, but if it's slightly cold and you have racing gloves on and a racing suit with a small YKK zipper that doesn't go all the way to the bottom, it can prove a tad embarrassing. I was bent over trying to get my 'old fella' out and into a position that would enable me to do what comes naturally. Time ticked by as I fidgeted around, wondering if it would have been easier just to let go on the bike. With a sea of faces in front of me in the grandstand and with my dignity finally destroyed I managed to get the job done, finishing to a chorus of cheers and laughter, though losing a lap in the process.

Back on the bike I cruised to an easy win, comfortable with my decision to ride the whole distance alone. I collected a huge winner's cheque, a trophy and the sash. I drank the plonk, shouted the team whitebait fritters for dinner, then partied all night. It was a long, slow trip back to Auckland, nursing a hangover.

I used the Z1 and followed the Marlboro Series as it travelled down the country. I was winning the production races and generally having a fun time. Timaru was different, though, as Tony had finally fixed the 500 cc H1R racer. I recall going out on it and blasting off down the back straight in hot pursuit of the leaders. That was all I could remember.

I picked myself up off the ground, mindful of the sharp pain in my left shoulder. The first-aid guy had his little black leather bag. Whatever medical marvels he had in there I wouldn't know but I guessed it was probably full of aspirin and sticking plasters. He helped me off the track and I walked back to see Dr Jim Cashman. He had an interest in racing and had been playing around with a little water-cooled Suzuki triple in his spare time. Jim was travelling with the troops, dealing with the gravel rash, bruises and broken bones that invariably happen over a month of racing. He took one look and told me I had broken my collarbone.

I didn't even remember the crash that had left me on the side of the track with a broken collarbone and a mangled bike. I was expecting to be rushed off to hospital and have to undergo surgery, but Jim put me straight. 'Croz, you've broken your clavicle. I can't do anything about it. I'll put it in a sling, though, and see you at the bar tonight at the function.'

That night I was bringing up blood, so I grabbed Dr Jim. 'Doc, I'm bleeding internally and there's blood in my mouth.' He reassured me I was not about to die and reminded me also that it was my shout. I felt a bit better, but at the same time a little poorer as I bought him a beer.

4

SPREADING MY WINGS, 1976

THE MOVE ACROSS THE DITCH, 1976

Back at work in Auckland in January 1976, I began planning for a longer stay in Australia. During a drinking session one night a group of us decided to fly to Melbourne to watch Agostini racing at Laverton Airbase. In Melbourne we all piled into taxis and headed for Laverton to watch the Australian TT. We thought the taxi driver was Greek but when we asked if he could speak English he nodded and spoke in some foreign language he reckoned was Australian. We booked into a cheap hotel that turned out to be infested with fleas.

At Laverton we were standing at the end of the straight in hot sunshine, scratching at fleabites while fending off zillions of flies and with sweat and sunblock dribbling down our faces. We squinted into the distance, desperately awaiting the arrival of Ago's MV.

The scream of the 3-cylinder MV heralded the emergence of shimmering figures appearing from the 42-degree heatwave. Over the PA system we could hear how the race was progressing. The excitement was unbelievable, with Kenny Blake finally crossing the line ahead of a bunch of international stars. Although it was a great event, things turned to custard when the organizers failed to make enough money to pay for all the overheads. Some of the international competitors' bikes were impounded by Customs, who were awaiting payment that had been guaranteed from the organizers.

We had more contacts in Sydney, so with my friends Martyn Aiken and Paul Knight I headed there, leaving our girlfriends to find a flat and jobs in Melbourne. We had allocated $200 towards buying a car and soon located a shady second-hand dealer who wore the regulation gold chains and white shoes. 'Mate, have I got a deal for you!' he said, before stitching us up with an old red '63 Ford Galaxy. It used more water than petrol in the 5 km it took to decide we'd been tucked and with the car running on only six of its eight cylinders we headed back to the dealer's yard. To give him his due, he agreed to exchange it for an HQ Holden, knowing we were off to Sydney and that it would be the last he'd see of us.

Meanwhile, Alan Johnson and his wife Jennifer had moved back to live in Australia, leaving Ian Beckhaus to run Shaft Motorcycles. When he left, he unwisely suggested that if we were ever in Sydney we should look them up and they'd be happy to accommodate us. I think they meant Brenda and me, not three males who turned up on their doorstep at Campbelltown full of testosterone and bravado. Apart from taking Jennifer's hospitality for granted, drinking all of Johno's cold beers and cleaning the fridge out of food on a daily basis, we were the perfect guests. Regardless, they remained the consummate hosts.

Eventually, we settled for a dubious-looking brick apartment block in Cabramatta. Luckily, it had a large garage in the basement that would do as a workshop for all the bikes that were arriving. We had Kiwis coming and going, sleeping on the floor and getting home at all hours of the night. John Woodley was one who had taken up residence and I was intrigued by his commitment to the sport. He was a dedicated sportsman who thrived on looking at the healthy side of life. One of our heated discussions was as a result of my taking the piss out of him, as he wanted to drink the water after cooking vegetables in it. It sounded plausible as he explained the benefits but ultimately it fell on deaf ears as I went looking for another beer. It was the first time I'd experienced true sports professionalism but I was not ready to heed his advice as I was having too much fun partying. John had worked in the New Zealand Air Force and was a capable mechanic with a wealth of knowledge. He was a brilliant rider and not afraid to make radical changes. John was the first rider to replace his twin shock units with a mono-shock on his RG500.

I found work immediately with Adams and Sons as a mechanic and parts person in nearby Liverpool but this lasted only a month. Doing tune-ups, selling spark plugs and answering the phone were the full extent of my day's work. The sales manager led a double life as a local-body alderman and used the bike shop as an office with locals coming and going. There was not a bike being sold and I decided I was out of there.

Joining the Bankstown Wiley Park Motorcycle Club gave me an insight into what grass-roots racing was all about. It was a great place to meet and talk racing with guys in similar situations. A normal job and a passion for racing were the only requirements, plus a healthy thirst with a preference for Tooheys New, the local beer.

Easter was looming and, with it, Bathurst, where everyone went for the annual bike races. I made contact with Peter Carson and he still had the old Z1 I'd used at the 6 Hour. He agreed to bring it to Bathurst for us, ready to go.

I had also been offered an H2 racer that was apparently a very quick bike in its day but had not been ridden for a while. I brought it up on the trailer and did one run down Conrod Straight before it locked up. It was fast and steered OK but I was disappointed to get only one lap at a time before it kept breaking. It was running far too lean but it wasn't the main jets as I expected but the needle jets that were causing the problem. I had no spares, so we loaded it on the trailer, declaring it dead.

As we didn't have much money, sleeping in my recently purchased Valiant was the best option. Brenda bought some cheap cuts of meat and sausages for the barbecue that Bob Levy traditionally set up for all comers.

The production Z1 arrived on a small truck with Peter Carson, who proudly assisted in lifting it off for me. The poor bloke put his hands around the bottom of the fork leg and lifted it OK but as the front wheel touched the ground and rolled backwards it caught his index finger in the disc brake and took the top off it. He squealed as the top of his finger hung on by just the smallest piece of skin. Blood shot out everywhere; he was not happy and required hospital treatment, but even worse, the old Z1 spat out a valve shim after a few laps. It was subsequently also declared terminally ill.

FINDING A RIDE, 1976

By now I was in desperate need of a good job and drove in to Sydney to meet with Ross Hannan. His brother Ralph had been working with Ginger Molloy back in New Zealand at his Hamilton shop and suggested I try Ross for a job if I ever made it to Sydney.

Ross was an exciting and energetic bloke — a human dynamo, full-on dealing with Yoshimura racing product enquiries in Australia. He just loved his racing. Up in his office there were bits of paper and product samples all over his desk and phones were ringing flat out. He was working on a project, trying to assist Yoshimura R&D in America with a problem they had.

Setting up in America had proved troublesome for Yoshimura and Ross was determined to help in any way he could. The American business was experiencing the financial speed-wobbles and was in desperate trouble. Ross decided to throw together a large parts order to get them going again. He didn't know if he could even sell the parts but it was the kick-start the business desperately needed.

Ross had a chubby face with a ruddy complexion and possessed a visibly bent and mangled body that caused him to limp quite badly. The damage to his legs was the result of a horrific accident back when he was racing. He told some cracker yarns and related some incredible stories. He reflected on some sad ones as well, including his own experience with the Isle of Man TT races in 1970. He was involved in a massive pile-up a few miles out from the start. The organizers had decided to experiment with a mass start instead of letting the riders off two at a time at ten-second intervals. Ross arrived at Snugborough, along with several other riders, just before the Union Mills section of the course. They were all bashing fairings and jostling for their own racing lines when a rider ahead crashed. Ross and a few others were caught up in the ensuing carnage. It almost killed him that day and he spent the next 12 months recovering at Nobles Hospital.

It would have been lonely during his stay, with only his bedpan to talk to. And it would have been a lot tougher had it not been for Ross meeting his future wife Carmen, who nursed him back into shape during his recuperation. He was fortunate to have come away alive and semi-intact, a lot luckier than many who have paid the ultimate penalty on the dangerous mountain course.

We had a great discussion and by the time I left Ross to get back to his phone calls I had a paying job. I went downstairs to acquaint myself with the idiosyncrasies of his home-built brake shoe grinding machine and to get a run-down on what was expected of me with the cylinder head performance work. This job was going to suit me right down to the ground.

During those discussions he also hinted at offering me a ride on a Kawasaki Z1 superbike that he was preparing using Yoshimura parts. His idea was to race the bike a few times to promote his business but he'd not decided who was going to ride it. Ralph told Ross that I would be able to do it justice. So it was decided I would be the new 'factory rider' — yee haa!

Ross explained that Myles Stivano from Kawasaki NSW had called him one day, saying that he had the latest Z900 to view. As soon as I heard Myles' name, my eyes began to glaze over with the thought that our paths might cross again. Ross continued, 'Complete with twin front discs and a flash paint job, this is the best Kawasaki yet, Myles reckons.' So Ross wandered down to the Kawasaki shop to check it out, all the time conscious that he hadn't been on a road bike for some time — ever since his big crash, in fact. The idea was beginning to appeal to him. He treated himself by purchasing this new Kawasaki Z900 and was genuinely looking forward to riding again — not racing, but out on the road.

Ross got a call within a few days from Tony Hatton and Ian Cork. 'Ross, it's Tony; look, I wonder if you can help us out?' The two of them had been preparing to drive down to Adelaide for the Advertiser 3-hour production race. 'Maaate,' he said, 'we've just lost our ride in the Adelaide Advertiser 3-hour.'

'So how does that affect me?' Ross asked, beginning to realize what they were wanting. 'Look guys, it's only got 7 k's on the clock and I've hardly even ridden it myself yet.'

Tony must have thought for a split second ... so it's not about whether we can race it or not, he's just making a point that it's still brand new. 'Great,' said Tony, 'we only want it for the weekend and you can have it back after that and it'll be nicely run in for you.'

Ross stammered while trying to find the words to politely say no, but Corky twisted his arm and he reluctantly agreed. Corky picked up the bike the next day and it was last seen driving off into the distance on the back of his trailer, Adelaide-bound. It was prepared meticulously at the track and Tony started in the 3-hour race. Unfortunately, he crashed the bike during the early part of the race coming off the back straight and totalled the new bike. The broken bike and bits were scraped off the track and thrown onto the trailer for the long drive back to Sydney. This would provide plenty of time to work out a strategy to let Ross know what had happened to his pride and joy.

Corky dropped this mangled mess, now with 230 km on the clock, back at Ross's shop. Eventually, when the parts from Yoshimura began to arrive, Ross figured it would be a great idea to make a race bike out of it. Superbikes were just becoming fashionable and it was the way racing appeared to be going.

Ian Cork got the call this time from Ross. 'Corky, you know that new Z900 that you and Hatton fucked at Adelaide, well I've got the parts now and you can fix it! I want to build an American-style superbike to race here in Australia.' Ross reckoned that Corky could be conned into doing this job for him. Ross also mentioned that his brother Ralph had this bloke Crosby who could be a winner on it. Corky was less than impressed. 'Yeah, yeah, yeah, whatever ... another bloody Kiwi ...'

Corky picked up the remains of the bike and loaded it on the back of his ute and went home to deal with it, probably wondering what the hell he'd let himself in for. While he started working on the superbike, I needed to find a bike for the 6 Hour race. Brenda had taken a barmaid's job at a pub in Chullora on the Hume Highway. One of her regulars, Jack Davies, managed Norm Fraser's Ducati dealership in Parramatta Road. Jack was a regular at the pub and we got talking while I was waiting for Brenda to finish work one night.

We discussed the 6 Hour race and he introduced me to his chief mechanic who was Ducati-mad. I had watched the 900SS of Johnny Warrian almost win the previous year and when Jack asked if I wanted to ride the 900SS I agreed in a flash. We tested it at Amaroo Park and found it to be a slow-steering beast that dragged its exhaust pipe on the ground. My co-rider Phil Leslie had ridden these things for some time and seemed to know all the technical details about the bike. It had no real appeal to me because it felt long in the wheel base. It wouldn't change direction fast enough for me. We had a rear tyre fitted on the front to solve our ground clearance problems, which was fine, but it under-steered severely. I found I was stuck in the Ducati groove on the track, unable to be aggressive and attack so it was always going to be a steady-as-she-goes race. I did my part on the bike and we were running up front in a good position and keeping in contact with the leaders. When Phil crashed and ended our run on the big Duke I was disappointed, although riding those air compressors perhaps wasn't really me.

A few weeks later in New Zealand, Laurie Summers provided me with another bike — this time it was the updated Z1000, which had only two mufflers instead of the more classic four separate pipes. Again I elected to run it solo which I guess was a bit selfish, but having control of my own destiny gave me the comfort level I wanted.

I thought about how having control works, theorizing that the worry about crashing out didn't figure in my thinking because I had confidence in myself. The added problems of using a second rider opened up questions of comparison of lap times, riding style — as far as how hard on the bike he will be — and the question of keeping it upright on the track. They all played on my mind but by removing the distraction I felt I could be more focused.

There was a start-line crash that my friend Woody Kitney would rather forget about. He had just picked up his new Z1000 only a few days before the event and got rammed at the start from behind, literally ripping the exhaust system off his new bike. I rode around keeping out of trouble and had what proved to be an easy win, completing 250 laps. This was my second win riding solo.

I was keen to get back to Australia and set eyes on this mysterious bike Ross had talked about. Not many people knew he was rebuilding it. Corky's wife Shirley was not too pleased when it turned up because they didn't really have enough garage space at home, so it ended up on the lounge floor, balanced precariously on a beer crate during the assembly process. The whole job was to take only a few weeks but it had dragged on for months, by which time Shirley's patience was wearing thin. I'm sure she was initially really pleased when I started visiting Corky's house, because it put extra pressure on him to finish it.

When I first sighted the bike I got quite excited. I began imagining what it would be like to ride. While I slouched on the settee watching *Coronation Street* on the TV perfectly framed through the chassis, I sensed that Ian was a little less enthusiastic than me about getting on with the job. But in true 'persistence-removes-resistance' fashion, I encouraged Corky to think about getting it ready for Lakeside in a few weeks' time.

Over the next week I would drop into Corky's place on the pretence of checking on the bike or dropping off the odd bits he needed. Secretly I just loved the company and the stories that he told me of when he was a younger man. He confided to me that he'd been prone to brawling and fighting once he had a skinful of beer. I thought that must have been another man because Corky seemed a very strong-willed person who refused to drink alcohol and knew he could not trust himself any more if he had a few. 'Hey no worries, you have the fizzy drinks, Corky, and do the interstate driving and leave the beer drinking to me,' I told him.

The date with Lakeside drew nearer and progress was slow. I began to think we would miss the race by a few days but Corky must have had a brainwave or finally got the message that he could be out and away from all this pressure if he just put his head down and got on with finishing the bike. All his troubles would be gone, including having to put up with me drinking all his family's beer and eating half the food.

I arrived one night to find it all ready to go, the newly painted red and white tank along with matching side covers gleaming like wet leather in the sunlight. A pair of new tyres mounted on Morris racing wheels topped it off. But the telltale smell of racing fuel meant we were ready to race. I wanted to fire up the beast there and then.

Corky told me to piss off, commenting that she'd be right on the day and we didn't need to wake up the neighbours. I was not about to argue with this ex-pub fighter now showing the signs of tiredness from the long hours he had been putting in. It was a massive last-minute effort just to finish the beast so I could go and play racer with it.

In true Ross Hannan fashion, he had conned Corky into taking the bike to Lakeside and I would share driving with some other friends independently in my Valiant. Ross had promised Corky he could drive the new XJ6 Jaguar that Ross had just taken delivery of. Corky and Ross set off with Corky at the wheel and the new bike perched untested up on the trailer. It had developed attitude and seemed to be saying, 'Hey, look at me!' It was almost as if it was champing at the bit to be released from its tie-downs. 'Let me at 'em! Bring it on,' I could almost hear it say.

While the bike was bouncing around on the trailer, in the car Ross was trying to instil some energy into Corky, who didn't really want to be there. He was looking tired from all the late nights but he wouldn't let on, nor would he let Ross behind the wheel of his own car. Although Ross was a little disappointed at Corky's lack of enthusiasm, he was also anxious about how the bike and I would perform.

We had no radio or heater and with the windows continually fogging up it made for an unpleasant drive. Wrapped in a blanket in the front bench seat, I could feel the old Valiant churning away, tracing the inland route up through Tamworth. It was midwinter and bloody cold, I was tired and desperately in need of sleep but if we'd stopped we wouldn't have made the track in time. We arrived at Lakeside sore and weary but recovered quickly with morning stretches and some scrotum scratching. I gave Corky a hand to release the shackles from the beast and unload it, and went about the business of checking it for safety and making sure it was good for scrutineering. I pushed the brightly painted bike down into the scrutineering bay where it was meticulously checked for any sign that could mean danger for the rider and others on the track. I was given a sticker and we were now ready to race.

There were some admiring looks from people in the paddock area and complimentary remarks about the paint job. However, for all intents and purposes, it was a fairly standard-looking bike. What many people didn't know, and I was about to find out, was just how quick this fire-breathing monster was. Corky flooded the new 31 mm smooth-bore Mikuni carburettors in preparation for the start and I went around the back to give it an almighty push. I fired it up and the raspy four-into-one Yoshimura pipe cracked out its war cry. It was crisp and responsive to the throttle and the exhaust note suggested a finely tuned and very powerful engine. My chest swelled and I felt a stirring in the loins. This was going to be some bike. It warmed up quickly and with no sign of oil leaks we shut it down to await my turn for practice.

Corky and I walked over to the Armco guardrail to check out the other riders practising. We hung over the fence beside the approach to a quick left-hand uphill bend, watching as they emerged before us under heavy braking from the tunnel of steel barrier fencing. Swooping up and around the bend, they disappeared over the crest of the hill.

I was nervous about this track and worried about the closeness of the steel barriers designed to protect both cars and spectators. We had no option, though — if we wanted to race, it had to be under terms negotiated by the strongest users. We could not compete against the influence of the car-racing fraternity. We were being treated as second-class citizens or poor cousins, and the thought of head-butting an Armco wall was always on my mind. 'Be safe and avoid the steel barriers at all costs,' I told myself, but I knew I wouldn't be thinking about this when I dropped the clutch for the first lap.

SPREADING MY WINGS, 1976

Corky and I had walked over to see Gregg 'Harry' Hansford. He was due to ride a few practice laps on the Team Kawasaki KR250. When Harry turned up, it was on his arse sliding down the road towards us. He had slipped off coming down the hill under brakes and literally slid by us at speed, so close that I could hear the scuffing and scraping of his green leathers doing their job of protecting his skin. He slid almost to a complete halt, stood up and casually jogged off the track and back to the pits as if nothing had happened. Corky and I were blown away by this cool dude.

Corky was cynical about this 'Kiwi import rider' and I could tell he had little confidence in my ability. However, it was not his decision to give me the ride.

Practice was all about learning the track and setting up the new 'beast'. I had a few adjustments to do after the practice but I wasn't sure what effect they would have. Ross had told me that just getting tyres and shocks had been a problem. But now everything seemed spot on — all I had to do was to change the gearing. Best thing I'd ever ridden.

What surprised me, though, was just how much horsepower I had available. Having power was one thing, but tyres would be the limiting factor. Ross had managed to get me two that would kind of do the job. These were not slick tyres but more like wet-weather-treaded Dunlops. On the cost front, Ross, Corky and I were now stepping up to the big league. We had no experience with actual racing tyres because until now we had only used basic production tyres. In the back of my mind it registered that I could get a few quick laps in before they started to heat up and loose traction. It then became a case of hanging on for dear life as I slipped and skidded my way around the circuit.

I jostled for a start position. It was a clutch start and the beast leapt off the line as if it had a rocket up its bum. It had me flapping grimly off the high bars trying to hold on. I led into the first turn and stayed ahead for the first lap until one by one the hotshots closed in and passed me. I was expecting to continue working my way backwards but finished in the top four. On my first ride, this was an unexpected and welcome result.

By the time I got back to the pit area, Corky had had a change of heart and was showing some interest at last. He was genuinely surprised that I could ride so well. The bike performed flawlessly and it proved a powerful weapon; his new rider was, well, 'OK'. In a single day he had turned from a sceptic into my greatest fan. He stopped complaining about me drinking his beer and eating his family's food.

Already Ross had plans to compete in other upcoming races. Monday back at work it was a very different Corky who said I could join him as a mechanic at his new shop at Bankstown. Ross did not object to my changing jobs as he could never rely on me turning up for work anyway.

Alas, good things don't last, though I didn't expect to blot my copybook so soon after we got back. Shirley had a birthday party at home and I was invited. I bought some small plastic sealed fluorescent nightsticks. I drilled a small hole in the end of one and swung it around a darkened room. The contents spilled out and created a fabulous speckled fluorescent effect on the lounge wallpaper. I also ruined her friend's $800 leather jacket, which I had to replace. Bugger!

For some obscure reason I'd now earned the nickname 'Greenbottle', presumably after the Peter Sellers character Bluebottle in *The Goon Show*. So I became Greenbottle or 'Greenie', or just plain 'Bottle'.

MARLBORO SERIES, 1976/77

Rosko agreed to send the superbike over to New Zealand to contest the Marlboro Series. Superbikes had been gaining in popularity with races attracting some top international riders. I went out on a limb, taking what was the only 4-stroke machine to compete in the series.

The overall results were not brilliant but I made an impact visually on the racing. The crowd could see this standard-looking bike hightailing down the straight, leading for a few laps before getting worn down and passed through a genuine lack of speed. It had the grunt out of corners but with the frontal profile I was always going to be struggling.

I worked on the basis that if I could get a good start I might be able to hang on long enough to get a placing by the time the chequered flag was waved. On the streets of Wanganui where the straights were short and the corners bumpy, I had the best chance of holding off the competition. On ultra-fast tracks like Pukekohe I was relegated to scrapping with the minor placegetters.

I called in a favour from Ian Beckhaus of Shaft Motorcycles. As part of the Australian contingent I had teamed up with Peter Campbell and Doug Chivas, who had brought over their Kawasaki-powered outfit and needed an extra car. Our borrowed Austin A40 Farina valve-bounced its way around both the North and South Islands. Into a strong headwind carrying five people, it was so slow it needed to be pushed along from behind by our CF Bedford van — also on loan.

The depth of talent was incredible, with more than 20 foreign riders from seven countries. Randy Mamola was on his second visit Down Under and though he'd matured a little over the past year, he still showed signs of being a spoilt brat. We gave him some leeway because of his age, and we all recognized that he was a brilliantly talented rider.

The first round at Auckland was a waste of time for me. I was simply too slow down the long back straight. Gregg Hansford had been talking with me and during the conversation I offered to let him do a few laps on the bike and he accepted, probably out of curiosity.

'How did she go, Harry?' I asked, expecting him to be impressed with the power and handling qualities of my beautiful superbike.

'Better you than me,' he said, walking away and shaking his head.

The streets of Wanganui were more my style. I was able to get the jump on the field and lead for a few laps. Then the inevitable happened — first one then another would slip by until I was left languishing in sixth or seventh spot. But I was building on my reputation as a never-give-up, carefree kind of rider with an ability to entertain the crowd.

At Gracefield it was much the same. I drifted back as the race progressed but still put on a show for the crowd. Amongst the high-pitched 2-stroke chorus it was easy to distinguish the sound of my unmuffled 4-stroke in full flight.

One day Gregg and I were playing pool for a few dollars and the contest had reached a critical stage when Randy suddenly leapt out of nowhere and swept the balls across the table with his outstretched arms, scattering them in all directions. Then he made a run for the door.

While we weren't playing for sheep stations, $4 would have bought me burger and chips or six litres of gas. This kid had to be dealt with. I threw the cue stick on the table and tore off after him, with Woody in hot pursuit. Randy thought he'd got away with it and slowed to walking pace. He started to run when he saw us but got a bit of wheel spin on the wooden floor, enabling me to grab him by the shirt.

Woody and I looked at each other and a wicked twitch of Woody's eye gave a clear indication of what was needed. Woody had Randy by the belt and I had him by his arms as we dragged him into the men's toilet. This precocious little shit was going to pay dearly for his stupidity. Woody kicked the lid up on the toilet seat with his foot while pulling at Randy's belt and I dragged him kicking and screaming into the cubicle. It took about three attempts but we finally had his upper torso and head pushed into the bowl. I used my right elbow to operate the flush button and the sweet sound of water splashing up and around Randy's head was music to our ears.

'Fuck you guys!' he yelled at us when we finally decided to release him. He scuttled out of the urinal like a freshly released baby fish. We laughed and returned for the re-match with Gregg Hansford.

From Wellington it was a race by car, van or truck to Timaru, halfway between Christchurch and Dunedin. The racetrack was situated out next to the airport in a paddock, offering no protection from the föhn winds that rip through the Canterbury region. It was like being in a blast furnace. It suited the smaller bikes here and John had set the outright lap record on his modified RG500 Suzuki. Doing wheelies and the rough street circuits had taken its toll on my bike. The rear wheel bearings collapsed and I became a spectator.

The final round in Christchurch featured an annual raft race down the Waimakariri River, for all competitors. In mid-summer the river is benign and offers more than one tributary to navigate. Most riders used the inner tubes from tractor tyres to make a raft. We set off, some of us armed with makeshift oars with nails poking out the end to fend off the competition. Along the way we waved to shipwrecked crew stranded on gravel islands in the middle of the river, with their rafts now looking like discarded condoms.

5

BONJOUR, MONSIEUR AND COBBER! 1977

BATHURST AND 6 HOUR, 1977

The superbike arrived back on Aussie soil needing repairs and maintenance. Ralph did the work, which we used to good effect in races in Queensland, NSW and Victoria in the early part of the season.

Corky must have lost his marbles, because in an uncharacteristic fit of madness he offered to build me a production bike for Bathurst. 'Now listen, Bottle, I've found a write-off at the auctions and I think it might have enough k's on it to make a good Bathurst bike. Do you want to ride it if I build it up?'

Corky and Charlie needed to talk about this, as they were in partnership and it was going to be costly for the company. A few weeks later Charlie was walking past the Z1 as another ex-pat Kiwi, Garry Ellison (Frizz), was fitting the final parts. 'How long before this thing's going to be ready for the showroom, Frizz? I might have a couple of punters for it when you've finished.'

'You can have it after Bathurst, Charlie, once Greenbottle has done with it.'

Charlie looked perplexed. 'Like fuck! He's not going to be riding it at Bathurst — that bike's good saleable stock!'

Frizz said he'd better talk to Corky about this. Charlie turned and walked off; this was the first time he'd heard of this arrangement. He found Corky and within minutes Charlie could see the benefits of having a bike at Bathurst and agreed to support the plan.

With Bathurst looming, Ralph had the superbike ready to go. Corky had finished repairing the Z1B 900 and he had tuned her to perfection. We hired a caravan and set off for Bathurst at Easter, along with my mother who had arrived to watch the race. I'd scraped together $380 and paid for her return ticket from Auckland. It was her first and only international trip and she thoroughly enjoyed the three days at Bathurst.

The Superbike race resulted in an easy win for me with no one remotely challenging. However, in the production race I had to settle for second place behind Jimmy Budd on a similar Z1B when he snuck past me with a lap to go.

I had been hanging out with Peter Campbell, who had an engineering shop down the road. I pestered him and his partner Chris Dowd constantly as they tried to work a normal day. Chris had made a 125 cc Honda and asked me to have a ride on it at Oran Park. It was fun; Chris was adjusting and changing bits and then I'd go and have a ride and report back. It all seemed backwards to me because most guys were starting on small bikes and moving up. Here I was zipping around on a tiny little bike with two hands on the clutch. If it had seized it would have been goodnight nurse.

I took the Z1 up to Surfers Paradise for a non-championship event. I borrowed Corky's car and Chris threw the little Honda 125 cc on the trailer and away we went. Coming through Tweed Head just before Surfers, the red light came on. The alternator was poked. We drove on, intending to make the racetrack and deal with it there.

In the main street of town we stopped at a pedestrian crossing. Chris was driving and stalled it. It didn't have enough kick in the battery, so I got out and started pushing. A nice man in a flash business suit offered us a hand and helped push the car with the trailer. I was pushing on one side of the car and he pushed on the boot area. Chris dropped the clutch and the car fired, lurching forward. Remembering the trailer, I stepped away, ran forward and jumped in. I threw my arm out and waved to say thanks. Chris began laughing uncontrollably, gasping between breaths, 'Take a look, Croz!'

I turned to look out the back window. The poor bastard had forgotten the trailer and as Chris drove off it caught his beautiful Italian pants, leaving them in a ragged mess around his ankles.

'Do we stop?' Chris asked.

'No, we'll be late for practice. Keep driving.'

At an Amaroo Park meeting in Sydney I almost did a clean sweep, winning the Improved Touring race and the big feature race. I probably put a few regulars' noses out of joint in the process but it had a great outcome. Bel-Ray Oils Australia noticed me and decided to buy me a set of leathers and give Ross a few bucks to help with the costs of running the superbike.

With Rosko's bike I had a string of wins mid-year at both Amaroo and Oran Park. It was rare for me to fall off but when it happened it was usually because of an external factor.

We decided that the superbike needed a smaller wheel on the front so we could use racing slick tyres for more grip. Ross bought a special magnesium 18-inch wheel and we took the bike out to Amaroo Park to test it. I didn't know how the change was going to affect the steering. We fitted the smaller wheel and I went out for a couple of laps to run in the new tyre before giving it a real workout. On the second lap I went up the hill at Amaroo and was about to whistle over the top when there was a horrific noise and scraping as the bike bucked and kicked. I sat up and had the brakes on like a flash, not knowing what was happening. The whole exhaust system at the headers had come off and was dragging on the ground. It could easily have jammed the front wheel and I would have been history. I rode the bike back carefully to the tune of four burbling exhausts coughing out orange and blue flames.

Ralph was horrified when he saw what had happened. Someone had forgotten to fit the spring clips that hold the extractor system on. That was soon fixed and I went out again and did a few laps. Everything seemed fine until I gave it some but coming on to the front straight the bottom chassis rail touched, lifting the front wheel off the ground and down I went in a screaming heap. The bike slammed into the steel barrier and our new magnesium wheel disintegrated on impact.

As we pushed the remnants onto the back of the ute and headed off, I could feel the graze on my arm sticking to my shirt already. Ralph and I agreed on one thing: our testing of the 18-inch wheel was a failure and any further discussion on the matter must be carried out at the next pub.

Corky and Charlie had together tricked, cajoled or somehow convinced 2UE, Sydney's leading radio station, to contra some advertising for this year's Castrol 6 Hour race. For our part we would plaster 2UE all over a bike for the event. Clive Knight and I were entered for the race on our Z1 and poor old Corky drew the short straw and spent a week out amongst the flies and dust at Amaroo to get the bike scrutineered.

Under the careful eye of the chief technical officer he stripped the bike for checking, then reassembled it. He was not looking too flash by the time the race came around. We finished a disappointing sixth, covering 348 laps.

BOLT THE DOOR (Bol d'Or 24-hour, Le Mans, 1977)

Ross Hannan had big plans for our team in 1977 and this included an all-Aussie (with one Kiwi) assault on the French Bol d'Or 24-hour race at Le Mans in France. The race was to be held on the shorter 4+ km Bugatti course which uses the pits and the fast Dunlop sweeper coming off the main circuit. It's a huge race that doubles as a round of the popular FIM Coupe d'Endurance series.

Ross had seen the event before and decided that the bikes they used were in his opinion relatively slow and set up for fuel economy and reliability more than for outright speed. He could imagine the impact if we turned up with this fire-breathing Yoshimura superbike complete with its high bars and still looking like a standard bike. The Silhouette class would be easy for us to slip into because of the more standard regulations.

Ralph Hannan was at work when Ross walked in and struck up a conversation. It must have been a good one — it looked interesting even if you could only see the body language, with Ross bouncing from one leg to the other, arms waving with excitement and loud chuckles emanating. Ross finally left to go upstairs. It was now Ralph's turn; he looked at me and said, waving his arms around, 'My fucking brother! Sitting at home, doing nothing and he comes into work and says we're going to the Bol d'Or. I told him "We've done the Europe thing, Ross." But that had fallen on deaf ears and besides, Ross had already arranged some sponsorship. He was like a dog with a bone.'

When Ross told me he had been talking to a few potential co-riders, one of whom was Mike Hailwood, I was blown away. *The* Mike Hailwood! Unfortunately, after careful consideration, Mike declined the offer so we turned our attention to Murray Sayle, presumably because he might have brought with him some of Neville Doyle's Kawasaki budget. I got all excited but by the time the dust had settled it was Tony Hatton who was persuaded to co-ride. He would be a bloody good asset and fun as well.

Planning for an event like this centred on getting the funding to be able to compete on a level playing field. In the Silhouette class we could compete successfully. We needed money, though, and lots of it. Everything was expensive — the travel, freight, hotels, even being at the track with food and petrol, rental cars and, of course, beer money. As we started planning, the list got longer and the costs rose.

Ross approached Qantas Airways for some help financially, or at least to try to cadge some free tickets, but we got knocked back due to the potential bad press. If one of us got killed or had an accident and the bike was photographed with Qantas logos, it would not look good. We understood the reasons but Ross was tenacious and managed to convince them to help us with freight for the bike. The best way to handle that internally for them was to give us a cheque for a few grand and we would then pay Qantas freight to get the bike and spares there and back. We would use our own money to buy tickets from Qantas for Tony, Ralph and me. Others in the team, including John Galvin from Metzeler Australia, Peter Brennigan and John Fraser, would have to make their own arrangements.

Ross was always wheeling and dealing and he came up with a better plan. He had been talking with UTA French Airlines about getting some financial help. They were more responsive and said if we bought three tickets, they would send the bike free of charge. So we used the Qantas money to buy three tickets on UTA. We were told to deliver the bike, spare engine and tools down to the UTA freight depot, and our equipment would be flown to France and back.

Ross had some extra luck scratching together the odd thousand bucks but at some stage we just had to push the 'go' button and cut our cloth accordingly. With Ross carefully looking after the team administration he seemed confident and determined we were going to Le Mans. 'Mate, she'll be right on the day,' he would assure us. I hoped he was right and although I could afford a few beers, this involved thousands of dollars.

Bel-Ray came through with oil and some money and I scored big-time when Jim Davies agreed to pick up the costs for a new set of leathers. They had the Bel-Ray logo and they fitted and looked great.

'Don, what type of leather have you used to make this suit from?' I asked as his machine zipped along stitching the last two pieces together. Being a nice guy, Don Pollard looked at me thoughtfully, paused for a moment and said, 'For you, son, this is my finest leather.'

I ran my grubby oiled hand over the fresh-smelling hide. The leather was strong and thick. Just the thing I needed. 'Don, I reckon you've made these from old elephants' kneecaps.'

I finally tucked them under my arm, bid Don farewell and off into the world I went, confident that my elephant-skin leathers would protect me if on an odd occasion I just might slip off the bike.

Ralph had the bike looking sharp; the last thing to do was to fit the gas tank. Without spending much money he had welded a section on top of the tank to give us an extra 10 litres. It looked a bit strange but it worked. We planned to do a few laps at Oran Park one evening to simulate a night race and to check everything was OK. The headlights and spotlight were the biggest problem. Because we had mounted them on the handlebars they had to be adjusted at all sorts of odd angles so when you were leaned over in a turn you could see the road ahead. As soon as you stood the bike upright again the spotlights shone to the stars and into the black hole we went. 'Bang another one on here and point it up about this high; there, that'll fix it,' Tony suggested. Ralph threw another one on and we could see again, just like daylight. By the time we'd finished playing around and I had got giddy doing laps, we found we were on the lap record — according to our watches anyway.

We were all excited at the prospect of our 28-hour flight to Charles de Gaulle Airport in Paris, with stops in Singapore and Bombay. The feeling was short-lived, though, as we went to the check-in. We found no plane had arrived and all the booked passengers were being transferred onto a Lufthansa flight leaving later that morning. The pub was open and we retired to the bar to await further instructions. Armed with vouchers supplied by the airline, we lined up the beers.

With our original flight scheduled for 9.30 a.m. we finally boarded at 6 p.m. in a rather inebriated state. We waited until we were last to board, knowing no one was behind us which gave us a pick of the seats. We all made beelines for any set of four empty seats in the middle. Most of us made it but Ralph had spied this beautiful Indian girl and after stumbling around the cabin, plonked himself down right next to her in the unoccupied seat.

Ralph was pretty to watch as he worked his magic on her and she appeared to fall for his charm. However, within moments he was seen with his head back snoring and dribbling from the corner of his mouth. The alcohol had finally taken its toll on him. A few hours later he had recovered enough and with another Fosters in hand he began all over again. This cycle would continue all the way to Paris with Ralph using his charisma to pique this girl's interest, only for her to find her travelling companion had passed out again.

Our detour to Frankfurt on Lufthansa meant we arrived in Paris half a day later than expected and missed out on our first practice session. Our hotel was not far from the action and we decided to check out the Champs-Élysées. Despite our bravado we all began to fade and with our eyes on dip we retired to the hotel. Our little Indian girl was still with us under the care of Ralph.

Tony and I figured that Ralph might like some assistance with his little friend and we knew he would have locked the door. We figured the balcony might be the best way in. Up the wall we shimmied using an old grapevine for grip. It was a long way up. Over the rail we climbed, then bang! The lights went out and we couldn't see a thing. Ralph had pulled the circuit-breakers on the switchboard and we were left to exercise our Braille skills trying to get back down safely. It was clear that he needed no assistance from us that night.

In the morning we met for breakfast and out came the first bottle of Beaujolais, followed shortly after by another. With Ross away at the airport to attend to customs clearance for the bike, we were stuck in the hotel until we could pick up our cargo.

The hotel was located beside the Paris ring road and out of curiosity I walked over to the hedge and peered through. There were cars I didn't recognize and little scooters zooming about everywhere and on the wrong side of the road too. I don't know what came over me but I pushed through the hedge and waved down a man on a little Motobecane scooter. Surprisingly, he stopped and I gestured to him that I wanted to try it out and even more astonishingly he agreed. I hopped aboard the scooter and raced off down the highway, joining the ring road traffic. I had only gone about 400 metres when common sense kicked in and I did a U-turn, riding back against the traffic and handing his beloved scooter back to him. Eyes still wide open in disbelief, he picked his jaw up off the kerb, climbed back on his bike and disappeared, looking totally confused. I rejoined the breakfast table to cheers and clapping in appreciation of my stupid performance and we toasted our first day here — 'Vive la France.'

Our well-oiled teamwork swung into top gear when Ross walked in. He had picked up a small Renault car and at first I thought he might be suffering from the shock of driving on the wrong side of the road, but he was looking stressed. He walked with his characteristic hunch and that slight limp, clutching a bunch of paperwork. He grabbed a bottle. I reached for a glass. Tony pulled a chair closer to the table. Ray waved his arm to get the attention of a waiter. John Galvin brushed away the breakfast bread crumbs from where Ross was about to sit. As Ross reached the table I noted that I had just witnessed a slick example of our team at work. *Very impressive!*

Ross slouched low in the chair, heaving a big sigh. 'Guys,' he blurted, 'you wouldn't believe this.'

We would.

'But you know what these stupid fucking Froggies have done?'

We'd all guessed there was a problem …

'The idiots have off-loaded our bloody bike in New Caledonia or somewhere because of some weight restriction,' Ross sighed again. 'The guy at the airport said we might get it tomorrow! "Might," he says. He wouldn't know his arse from his elbow. So now we have to wait around here until the bike arrives.'

We were supposed to be practising yesterday ...

'Oh and guys,' he went on, 'listen to this. He doesn't even know what time the plane arrives tomorrow, let alone if it's got the bike on it!'

So no practice today either and we would not get there till late tomorrow at the earliest, so we'd better make the most of what practice time was left and at least get it qualified. The waiter arrived with another bottle of the Beaujolais and we didn't move again for another three hours. There was no need to move because we had nothing to do. We weren't prepared for a holiday in Paris but we were in need of rest so we made the most of it.

The following morning Ross arrived back from the airport, this time in a different mood. 'The bike is due today about 1 p.m. and by the time it's cleared we can be on the road by say 3 — might even make the night practice.'

We signed off our hotel bill and piled into the Citroën van and with all our bodies and luggage inside, it was clear with the bike in too it would be a tight fit. Then it began to rain. I began to get nervous ... I knew what was coming next. 'Croz, can you ride the bike to Le Mans?' Ralph asked.

'Yeah, no worries mate,' I heard myself say, looking over at Tony. I could have kicked myself. Tony had clasped his hand over his mouth in a feeble attempt to prevent a laugh. 'Bastard!' I thought.

Ross had done all the paperwork and the bike was ready to go. The packing crate was thrown in the back of the van and I was sent off to get some fuel for the ride to Le Mans. The route would avoid the infamous Le Périphérique and take us right through the centre of Paris and out the other side down to Le Mans. That's all I knew, other than it was about a couple of hours southwest.

With the rain steadily falling I reached over and flooded the Keihin carburettors, slipped it into gear and gave a mighty push. I swung my butt onto the seat and let out the clutch. The motor barked into life and I wobbled off down the road in pursuit of the van. The bike had a close-ratio gearbox giving me a very high first gear, making it quite hard to negotiate the inner streets of Paris. It had slick tyres that served only to protect the rims as they didn't work too well on the cobblestones. Constantly slipping the clutch and wheel-spinning my way, I was glad when we finally made it to the motorway where I could safely go faster. I could now relax a little and give it a few squirts of power. It seemed to run well for most of the way but at about 80 km from Le Mans I noticed a slight tightening-up of the engine. 'Oh shit!' I thought and instantly grabbed at the clutch. Coasting to a stop on the side of the motorway, I sat on the bike as Ross and the crew, dry and warm, trundled off into the distance oblivious to the fact I had ground to a halt.

I waited for a few minutes to allow the engine to cool a little and tried again. Although it fired up easily I could hear that telltale rattle indicating a seized piston. I took it easy and slow the rest of the way, found the hotel and Ralph soon had his sleeves rolled up and a screwdriver in hand in preparation for an engine transplant.

Before we began the surgery I stole the keys to the Renault and Ralph, Tony and I went for a drive around the old circuit. The Mulsanne straight was indeed long and tree-lined. I shifted my foot across the floor and pinned his foot to the gas pedal. Ralph was driving and it became a Mexican stand-off as to who would do what. The speed increased, the rpm increased, helped by being still in third gear and not top. Was I going to take my foot off his? Or would Ralph switch the ignition off? As the car sped along at well over 120 kph in third gear with the engine screaming in protest, it had finally had enough and popped a valve. We limped back to the hotel on three cylinders. 'These little blighters aren't very strong, are they Ralph?' I said as I tossed the keys to Ross.

With the practice engine fitted we set off to go through technical inspection, do the paperwork and get our pit area set up. David Dixon, who had been handling Yoshimura parts in the UK, had most generously lent us a caravan so we could have a place to rest and relax. It was parked directly behind our pit. Michel Rougerie was right next door. He'd been a multi-time French champion and a winner of the Bol d'Or back in 1969. His team looked well organized with massive supplies of race tyres, refuelling equipment and spares, and complete with this very tasty-looking young lady with dreadlocks who was playing the part of the perfect French racing mascot.

Ralph had a little trouble getting our bike through the technical inspection because of a rule regarding lighting. We did not have two separate wiring circuits for the two tail-lights. We had both on one circuit, so a quick-thinking Ralph and rather slow-thinking inspector resolved the issue with Ralph tricking him into believing we had two complete wiring circuits as per the regulations. All Ralph had done was to cut one wire and then reconnect it when he was instructed to. Job done and we received the official technical sticker of approval. It was show time.

I did a couple of laps, then came in to hand over to Tony for his mandatory few laps. I mentioned it was wobbling a bit at high speed. No problem really, it was probably because we didn't have any good rear shock absorbers, just the standard ones, and it was no worse than back home. It just meant that with the longer straights I had to hang on to it for longer. Tony came in complaining of a bad handling problem and I thought he was joking. He reckoned he couldn't hang on to it under full power. Was he talking about handling or just the plain old normal wobbling that every bike I rode seemed to have? 'What's wrong with the old bloke?' I thought. Tony went into a huddle with Ralph and Ross and I went out for a few more laps.

'Oh shit! Not again,' I murmured as I pulled in the clutch and coasted to a stop. This one was a little more serious and I pushed the bike back to the pit area to be met by Ross, Ralph and Tony. Ralph flew into his work. An hour later Tony exited the pit lane again with a new piston fitted and his mind firmly on trying to fix our handling problems.

This time it was Tony's turn and he came in with a terrified look on his face. The bike had wobbled badly and the engine had locked up on him. Ralph fitted the last of our spare pistons and we were now in a desperate state, with only one final practice to go. We grouped and reached a consensus. 'I'd say we're fucked, guys!' I blurted out. Hatton, though, was still convinced he could make it handle but conceded that something had to be done.

Ross's brother-in-law had arrived by this time and joined in. His V12 Ferrari was in sharp contrast to our team's appearance. Its beautiful clean red lines and sexy curves did not blend in well with a handful of Anzacs with their arses hanging out of their pants, all of us on bended knees assembling an engine on the dirt floor. We were surrounded by engine parts, an old tool-box, two tyre levers and a 12-pack of French beer. Not quite the Ferrari's typical photogenic accessories. Terry listened and casually asked what fuel we were using. Ross explained that the deal he had arranged with Esso before he left was for free racing fuel. For some reason the local agents weren't co-operating. They were saying we needed a special card or something. Terry asked again what fuel we were using. Ross explained that we'd seen this really nice Elf billboard opposite the airport and it had Phil Read sitting on a MV, 'so that's what we're using, Elf fuel'.

Terry, who had lived in Italy, was an ex-racer and suggested that we should dump the fuel and use some from his Ferrari. He added that his fuel was a higher octane than we were using so it might assist with our engine problems. It certainly couldn't be worse. Somebody found a hose and my expertise at siphoning fuel came into play as I sucked out about 20 litres of fuel from the little red Ferrari. Press, competitors and spectators all scratched their heads when they walked by as the donor Ferrari performed its fuel transfusion with our bike. Terry had also found some shock absorbers that might work.

With the day's work all done and no practice to worry about till the morning, we set off to find ourselves a 'jambon sandwich' and a few more French beers. About six beers later, as we walked over to the toilets, Ralph had an idea. He remembered years ago when he was here working with Ginger Molloy that the toilet block was built on a slope and thought he would try an old trick that he'd seen done before. He gathered some paper from a rubbish bin and waited until the topmost toilet was free, then in he went, bunched up the paper, set it alight with his cigarette lighter and dropped the flaming paper into the bowl.

The toilets didn't flush individually but every few minutes a gush of water would flow down the drain under all of the toilets, effectively cleaning them as it went. Ralph came out to watch the commotion as the flaming paper quietly floated down the drain. In each toilet downstream you could hear the yells and screams as the flaming ball of fire passed under each unsuspecting poor sod who perched there doing 'the business'.

The last day of practice dawned and with the bike ready to go with fresh racing fuel, Hatton was first out. After completing the few laps necessary to qualify, he handed over to me. The bike was a missile, finally, and I could get down to doing some fast times. Within a few laps I had taken our previously wounded and injured old superbike, now transformed into something of a weapon, and put some blistering times on the board. We had arrived.

This did not go unnoticed as bunches of journalists, whose curiosity had got the better of them, came sniffing around. What they saw was a feral team of Aussies having fun riding what looked like a production bike. They soon figured out we were serious but underfunded and this would make quite a story. The Le Mans paper that day carried a piece about our bike, complete with a front page picture captioned *'Les Tres Rapide Kangaroos'*.

The race started in front of what I calcuated was about 200,000 people but more than likely was around 30,000. From our qualifying position near the front I flew into action from the 'Le Mans start', sprinting across the track and leaping aboard. I began carving people up and out-braking them as I moved through the field. I concentrated on chasing whoever I could see in the distance and worked away at nailing them one by one. We had no team tactics — we just had to go hard from the start and see what happened. Tony and I soon got into the swing of it, sharing the riding duties with alternate hours.

A few hours after the start I was noticing that the little French mascot from our adjoining pit had been hovering ever closer to our pit wall. Unexpectedly, I made eye contact and I got a very warm and sexy look back. I thought about going over and having a little chat to pass the time while waiting for my next ride but I was due out soon. I kept looking at her as she leaned oh so sensually against a tool-box. I could see myself getting punched on the nose by a jealous Froggy shortly, so I backed off. She would have to wait.

I went out to do battle with the beast for yet another long hour. In the distance I could see a rider who appeared to be holding his own on me and no matter how hard I tried I just couldn't close the gap. A crash in the infield soon gave me an opportunity and I closed up on my prey. 'Bugger me days' if it wasn't Phil Read on the works Honda. A couple of laps later, the debris had been cleaned up on the track and the rider was pushing his damaged bike back to the pit area. I found myself tucked in behind Phil, thoroughly enjoying watching his display of beautifully smooth riding. He certainly had style and rode some wonderful lines that were different from mine. I noticed that his racing lines were all the very traditional type. Along the front straight he would move slowly towards the edge of the track to the braking point and then under brakes finally drop down into the apex and then accelerate out, ending up hugging the edge of the track again. He was conventional, traditional, smooth and fast.

I had had enough of looking up his exhaust pipe by now and the annoying harmonic noise created by our similarly powered engines running at similar engine speed became unbearable. It's the same noise that a twin engine aircraft makes when the engines get out of synchronization. The 'WAA-WAA-WAA' noise began to really piss me off.

I was fairly close in behind Phil as he headed off down the straight on his RCB Honda. I tucked my head down between the tachometer and speedometer, peering out over the top and moving in and out of his turbulent slipstream in hot pursuit. He wasn't leaving me behind but I was thinking about this torturous noise and how it happens when suddenly Phil sat bolt upright, using his body as an air-brake, and I could hear his Honda neatly being slipped back through its gearbox under brakes. I must have experienced brain fade or something, missing the braking point completely. I recovered by slamming on the picks and the front wheel screamed in agony under the forces. The back wheel skidded a few times, throwing it out and into a slide as I aimed for the apex. I managed to get the old girl into a gear that would work for the corner and with the rear wheel drifting sideways I wound on the throttle. The rear wheel slide continued but converted to a wheel-spin as the power came on. In a full cross-controlled side-on drift with smoke pouring off the back wheel I held the power on until it ran out of torque, allowing the grip to return. It was nearly a classic high-side crash but I recovered and continued, too scared to look behind.

On the corner where I had passed Phil, I noticed that a big black telltale line had appeared, showing evidence of my cock-up going into the turn. A corresponding thick black arc was also visible coming out of the corner with its characteristic huge hooked end where it nearly tossed me off. I pitted shortly after that and my mind immediately switched to the thought of the little French girl next to us.

I entered the pit lane and came to a halt. With the change of riders complete, I could now contemplate an hour of serious lusting over the French girl, but she was too busy next door packing everything up. Apparently, the team rider had crashed and the bike had been withdrawn from the race. They were going home. It wasn't long before it was my time to go out again but just before I was due to go I mentioned to Ralph to keep an eye on my friend next door for me. 'Oh, shit. Now it's you as well as Hatton,' Ralph laughed and straight away I knew Hatton had been checking her out too. There was a flurry in our pits and next thing I knew I was back out amongst the traffic. This time it was a case of getting rid of an hour's worth of fuel as quickly as possible so I could foil Hatton's attempt at getting any further with our favourite French femme. Eventually, the 'Pit In' sign was shown and I came in. Tony was ready and a quick refuel saw him heading out into the dwindling late afternoon light.

The French girl had now joined our team in the pit and was standing back out of the way leaning up against the fence. I walked over to her, making a mental note not to scratch my bollocks under any circumstances. 'Bonjour,' I said in my best practised voice, deliberately an octave or two lower than normal. 'Comment allez-vous?'

'Ça va,' she replied in a soft husky voice and continued talking in French, losing me completely.

My eyes glazed over a little as I listened politely before interrupting her to say, 'Excusé moi, non parle français.' She smiled and shrugged her shoulders enough for me to understand that she didn't speak English either. Then she began speaking to me in French and using hand signals and I responded in broken English as well.

I hadn't even taken my suit off and was still holding my helmet when Tony came back in complaining of bad handling. We needed another tyre and fitted a new Michelin but when he went out again, it had no grip. We inspected the tyre and found that it was not wearing but in fact picking up used rubber off the track.

The challenges of long-distance racing began to be evident as soon as the 'Lights On' sign was illuminated at the start-finish line. Our lights came on, then off, and then on again intermittently but luckily there was enough night light so we were not too badly affected. It was a loose wire somewhere and it took time to find it. We had also developed a small fuel leak in the tank up near the steering head. Murphy's Law came into play. We found the leak and the loose wire connection — it was in the same place. 'Handy,' I thought as I raced down the main straight with sparks flying out from under the leaking tank. The lights were still flashing intermittently. I made yet another pit stop and a hurried repair took place before I was pushed back out again.

In what seemed a short space of time, Tony and I both suffered crashes. I simply lost the front end on an infield corner behind the pits and slid to a stop. In that crash I bent and jammed the rear brake pedal solid. I ran back and got a spanner, removed it and restarted the old girl, then carried on. Tony had a similar incident but did a lot more superficial damage. This one took time to fix and I retired to the caravan away from Hatton with my new friend in tow to wait it out.

Someone gave the caravan a big thump on the outside, frightening the hell out of me and I was dragged out to find the bike all patched up and ready to go. It was getting cold as the night set in and without a jacket I was going to freeze on the bike. Our little French girl motioned to us that she would lend us her jacket so I slipped it on, knowing that it was in fact Michel Rougerie's personal jacket. I knew he wouldn't mind us using his jacket but he might balk at lending his girlfriend as well.

At one pit stop I was flagged down by an official. I stopped and, with the bike idling away in its lumpy, noisy manner, sounding as if someone had thrown a bunch of gravel down the carburettors, I tried to listen to what he was saying. He was raving and becoming quite animated, with his arms pointing in every direction. I guessed he was trying to tell me something. Using the classic Marcel Marceau mime technique, eventually he was able to get the message across that he thought I was riding like a circus clown. I promised I would tone it down a bit. I lied.

I had now become quite good at pulling wheelies out of the hairpin and a huge crowd had gathered to egg me on. I could almost hear them cheering and yelling over the noise from my exhaust. Before long I was due in to the pits again to hand over to Tony. Once again a quick change and he raced off out into the distance, the old girl sounding crisp in the night air. I could hardly wait to get back to the caravan. Ralph had said that Tony and I were playing like a tag team but I hoped he was just winding me up. I was looking forward to having a back rub and of course to continue with my French lessons.

Tony had borrowed the French girl's jacket as well because of the cold and that was the first thing I noticed as he pushed the broken bike into the pits. The jacket was torn to shreds with an arm hanging off. There were scuffmarks right up across the back. The zip was ground away and the pockets hung semi-detached from the side of what was left of the jacket.

Tony laughed as he explained that the flag marshals watched him skating up the road spread-eagled as the jacket was being ripped to shreds. It contained quite a few coins which were being scattered out along the track as the pockets were ripped open. He had picked up the bike and leaned it against a straw bale then went back out on to the track to pick up all the French coins. They didn't know what to do.

I took a look at the bike and noticed it was in a similar state. Scratched paintwork, broken exhaust, handlebars bent at odd angles and the side covers worn away. The ignition units were swinging around on their wires and the wheel had a large dent in it. Oil dripped out on the ground. It looked poked beyond repair but Ralph was busy assessing it and told me to go and take a rest. I almost ran back to the caravan to continue my private conversation.

The banging on the caravan was the last thing I expected. 'Come on quick Croz — the bike's ready. Hurry! It's been fixed. It's fine. It's all ready to go. Come on. COME ON. Let's GO-GO-GO!' Ralph was yelling.

'Bloody hell,' I thought, jumping off the bed in a mad panic. I slipped my leathers over my shoulders, zipped up, 'Oh shit, bloody hell!' I screamed as I caught a huge chunk of pubic hair in the zipper. I quickly managed to slip both boots on and made a lunge for the caravan door. As I burst through the door I was still trying to zip up my suit in preparation for racing. With the door now wide open, I stopped abruptly.

The whole team had gathered around the door and stood there. They all had beer bottles in their hands and all of them were laughing and pointing at me. 'Gotcha!' Ross roared. The bike still lay there, broken and irreparable. The bastards had set me up a beauty.

Our race was over. We returned to the hotel and continued the party. We reflected on what had gone wrong and how we'd do it better next time. At least I'd learned some French.

6

LIFTING MY GAME, 1978

NZ 6 HOUR AND MARLBORO SERIES, 1977/78

I figured that Tony and I had worked quite well together, with him doing all the technical set-up and issuing instructions to me on how to ride. We had a trouble-free run to win the New Zealand Castrol 6 Hour for the third year in a row but two laps down on last year's count when I rode solo. I might have to have a talk with him about upping his game next year.

Back in Sydney, Rosko picked up the new Z1R from Kawasaki and instructed Ralph to transform it into a modern version of our old superbike. It was different and handled slightly better. I wouldn't have a clue if it was technically any better but it looked nicer and after a few trial runs was proving a lot quicker.

With the Marlboro Series looming, I went home to Auckland to wait for the arrival of my new Z1R. Tony Phillips had loaned me his Holden Belmont and a trailer, which I took out to Auckland Airport to pick up the bike with. I saw the bike sitting on a pallet in full display. Three rear slicks and a pair of wet racing tyres sat beside it, secured with 100 mph duct tape. The Customs officer led me over to the bike, clutching a handful of paperwork.

'So this is it eh! Nice looking bike. Are you the rider?' I replied that I was going to race it over the next month, then send it back to Australia.

'Have you been racing a long time?' I thought what a strange question to ask; is this a wise guy or what? As I approached the Z1R sitting on its crate, I noticed a number of messages written on pieces of tape attached to it. 'TURN THIS WAY TO GO FAST'; 'TURN THIS WAY TO GO SLOW'; 'PULL THIS TO STOP'; 'LIFT UP HERE TO CHANGE GEAR'; 'PRESS THIS FOR BRAKING'; 'OIL THIS WAY'; 'GAS GOES IN HERE'.

Ralph had given a list of instructions on how to ride the bike and the Customs officer was laughing his tits off at my expense. He called a few other cargo handlers over and they all inspected it and kept looking at me as if I was the dumb shit who needed instructions on how to race a bike. I loaded it up and took it straight out to Pukekohe to test before the first round of the Marlboro Series.

I didn't win any races but repeated what I had done previously — entertain the crowd and have some fun. Best of all, I stayed upright.

BATHURST, 1978

Bathurst to Australians is like the Isle of Man is to the English — the mecca for motorcycles. People came from all walks of life as if it were the only outing in the year for them. Up on the mountain the crowds began setting up their tents, caravans and vehicles. Tarpaulins were jury-rigged between trees, resembling a gumdigger's camp from a bygone era. These camps usually had a huge central fire, and the inevitable portable coolstore on the back of a ute. Their camping spots were fiercely fought for and aggressively defended. Drinking would start on the Wednesday and continue unabated until Monday. This was a hard-arsed crowd but they were certainly enthusiastic fans.

Only the NSW police could ruin such a party atmosphere, which if left alone would probably self-regulate. But no, the coppers had to come in heavy-handed, cajoling and baiting people. It was the only way the politicians had of cracking down on the violence. Send in 'the

Squad from Sydney' that seemed to be made up of thick-skulled and narrow-minded coppers chosen to intimidate and ruffle the feathers of any normal fun-loving citizen.

Then there were those males who came to chew the fat, have a party and brag about all the shagging they claimed to be doing lately. It was safe to do this within the confines of this male-dominated sporting occasion. But there were also the families who came to Bathurst, happy to go camping with Dad and allow him to indulge in his only passion — motorcycles — for the one weekend in the year.

And then there were the experts — the columnists and other media people and their hangers-on. They all met here as if it were an AGM, mixing with marketing managers and sales co-ordinators for the major motorcycle manufacturers. Most had healthy egos and were opinionated, especially about the direction that the sport should take in Australia. Some took side bets on the outcomes of the various races. Unbeknown to me, I was the Achilles' heel for a lot of these guys.

I easily won the Superbike race, romping away from the opposition and posting a lap record in the process. I finished half a minute ahead, giving me about a five seconds per lap advantage. The new Z1R was working well and even the old superbike I had used earlier in the year took its new owner Mick Hone into third place.

Myles Stivano from Kawasaki NSW still wouldn't give me a bike when Ross asked him for one to use at Bathurst. We had already built up my Z1R superbike but I don't know what Myles was thinking when he refused to give me a standard bike for the production race, especially knowing how important such exposure was for sales. He knew best apparently and gave the new Z1R to his mate Alan Hales from Sydney. Jimmy Budd was amongst a horde of Suzuki GS1000 punters, and Yamaha's new XS1100 was also making a showing. By contrast, Corky's three-year-old Z1B looked a bit shabby but he assured me it had good bones.

I was fired up for this Bathurst and with a record attendance it was usually the production race that drew everyone's attention. On paper and according to Myles this should have been a cake-walk for Alan Hales on the Z1R but after the race started it became a battle between me on the old Z1B and Jimmy Budd on the new Suzuki GS1000. As the skies threatened and the first raindrops fell around lap 15, I knew I was in the pound seat with the Metzeler tyres John Galvin had supplied. Jimmy was on Avons and although we were fighting it out on the track, Avon and Metzeler were at it hammer and tongs in a scrap for tyre supremacy. My Z1B was running about 144 mph regularly down the straight, no faster than the previous year, and I had just taken the lead when Jimmy slipped off unhurt at Hell Corner in the rain during the last few laps, giving me the win. I had broken the lap record by 2.39 seconds and the race record by 19.5 seconds on Corky's old Z1B.

I thought I might be a bit cheeky and also enter the Unlimited race but the small fuel tank on the Z1R called for three stops, killing any real chance of a good finish. I was surprised to find out I was sixth overall as I crossed the line.

AUSSIE TITLES: ORAN PARK, APRIL 1978

'Hey Croz, about time you got on something a bit better than Rosko's old superbike for a change. I've just had Scaysbrook on the phone asking me to get someone to ride his TZ350. So d'you want to have a run at Oran Park on it in the Aussie titles? Mate, you'll kill 'em!'

Coming from Tony Hatton, this was a compliment. 'Hatto, I don't know; I haven't ridden a TZ much, but yeah! We'll give it a go.'

I didn't know what I'd let myself in for. I remembered Keith Williams' modified R5 that I rode at Baypark with a flat tyre. I had seen these at just about every race but I tried to steer clear of them. I had seen too many crashed TZ's and broken riders and knew they could bite just as hard as a superbike.

Ross had the Z1R back up and running again from our Marlboro

Series trip to New Zealand and the engine had been refreshed after Bathurst. Ralph met me out at Oran Park. Hatto was already there, cocking around with the TZ, mixing fuel and checking chain adjustment while I went out and did a few laps on the Z1R. I came back and swapped to the little TZ350. I was impressed at how easy it was to ride. The owner Jim Scaysbrook had gone off to the Isle of Man TT races with Mike Hailwood, leaving the bike in Tony's care. It was painted up nicely with a picture of a caped man called Captain Snack across each side of the cowling.

The 350 cc race almost started without me, as I was left on the grid struggling to get away. Up in the press box there was some interest in how I would fare and the Editor of *Revs* magazine began taking bets on who would win. Although he couldn't get a bid for me, I worked my way through the pack. Boulden, Ogilvy and McGregor had shot to the front but there was a cloud of dust which turned out to be McGregor getting a case of gravel rash. I must have had a rush of blood to the head as I zipped around the track ducking and diving, inside and outside of the riders in front of me. By lap four, Roger Hayes and Lee Roebuck were battling it out for the lead and by lap six I had come up behind, found a gap then continued on for the win. My best time was a new class lap record.

The Unlimited race on the Z1R was a case of win the start then play defensive to preserve any placings. I just didn't have the outright speed of the big 2-strokes to keep up with the leaders. I knew that was always going to happen but still finished sixth.

For the 500 cc event I used the TZ350. Despite another slow start, I raced through the field as quickly as last time. That's when I thought I could go around the outside of the leading rider on the last lap. I almost made it but as I swooped down into the corner and around I applied power and the back stepped out momentarily, re-gripped then flung me off like a rag doll. Surprisingly, it didn't hurt much but it was so spectacular that the crowd clapped and cheered.

A reporter approached me when I got back to the pits. 'Croz, what a great ride in the 350 cc event, and a new lap record too. And I just heard you've broken the 500 cc lap record as well, golly you were going so well and that crash — did you hurt yourself? What happened?'

'Yeah! I trowelled the model, I thought I would give it a go, bugger eh! But did you get it on TV?' The interviewer cracked up to think it might be more important to me that TV got the footage than if I'd done any damage to myself. I learned something that day. To be successful and interesting when being interviewed, you have to be animated and almost overdo it. A boring monotone in front of the camera only guarantees you'll only ever get one hit at it. Being loud, controversial, enthusiastic and excited will bring them back time and again.

The crowd apparently had been on their feet in the 350 race as I made my dash through the field. They cheered and waved again as I went out in the Improved Touring race on the Z1R and took an easy win by a big margin. I was expecting that anyway, as my bike was fast and relatively unchallenged in its class. I pulled wheelies down the full length of the front straight and only put the front wheel down to get around the corner. It must have looked spectacular as the white puff of burnt rubber streamed out the back like an aircraft landing.

On the victory lap aboard the Oran Park ute I was stopped at the first corner by a spectator who gave me a few cans of beer. It started a wave of people all clambering over the protection fences offering me hundreds of beer cans. By the time I had finished the victory lap, the ute's tray was filled to the brim with a combination of Tooheys New and Reschs cans.

I wondered if Captain Snack would mind if I took him down to Adelaide for round three of the Australian titles. I'd ask Tony — I'm sure he wouldn't mind. A few weeks later I was off to Adelaide to ride the Captain Snack bike which still had its Oran Park gravel rash damage to its cowling. When Jim Scaysbrook had left Tony with the bike he had just fitted a new set of fancy Electron carburettors so Tony was to look after the bike. He knew a lot more than I did about them so he threw the TZ on his trailer, along with his own little Honda 125.

It was the Australian titles and as he had his own bike to ride he basically left me to it. I ran the TZ350 in practice and the engine felt really quick and crisp and with a new set of tyres it handled nicely. The Z1R went OK until the ignition failed.

I was feeling quite confident on the TZ and as part of the normal set-up phase I had done a plug chop and was looking at it carefully, studying the colour. It looked fine and I went out in the 500 Senior preliminary race and finished way down in 13th spot. I came in and had another look at the plug colour. Hmm, I was scratching my head, remembering that Tony had given the jet needle a twist to lean it off a tad so I thought I might do the same. However, the Electrons I was playing with were the latest model and a full turn was like going down four normal jet sizes. I gave it a full turn, thinking it would only lean it off marginally.

The Australian 350 Junior title race started and I almost stalled. By the time I got away and on the chase I couldn't believe how well I was going. Even with my poor start I screamed past the others as if they were standing still. I ran out of time to catch the leaders but a third place wasn't bad and, I thought, I still have the 500 Senior title.

The Ultra Lightweight race was won by Tony; however, Ralph had brought a Moriwaki 125 4-stroke down from Sydney and during the early laps he lost it in the Bowl and head-butted a wall. The bike slid in behind him, puncturing his lung and he was carted off to hospital to spend a few days recovering.

I used rational thinking and figured that if a twist made it go that much better, I could give another twist of the jet needle and I might get a bit more power to be able to compete with the 500 cc bikes. Well, it was fast all right — it took off like a missile and suddenly without warning I heard 'ZONK'. The engine had seized solid and I was flicked off unceremoniously and dumped onto the track, landing on my left shoulder. When Tony found out what I'd done he was fairly critical but also understood, knowing how different the new Electrons worked. It didn't stop him giving me a ribbing every five minutes, though.

The pain was excruciating but I knew nothing was broken. I must have aggravated a recent rugby injury to my shoulder, as I was still playing New Zealand's national game in Sydney. I was out for the day and watched the remaining races instead.

ADELAIDE 3 HOUR, APRIL 1978

A few weeks later it was back to Adelaide again for the Advertiser 3 Hour race. Corky loaded the two Z1B's onto the trailer in his driveway and secured them. I had been relieved a long time ago of those duties, ever since he caught me arriving at Amaroo Park with the race bike on the trailer laying over at an odd angle and not tied down. Corky was there when I arrived and was watching as I pulled up to a stop in a cloud of red Amaroo dust. He was wearing stubbies, thongs, a yellow T-shirt and an angry face.

'Greenbottle, didn't you notice the tie-downs had come loose?' His shoulders were hunched over and his fists clenched. He set about ripping into me for not checking they were tight and secure. I had almost got over that one when he caught me again, this time with another bike about to fall off the Bankstown Honda ute. I was given another tongue-lashing and from then on he supervised or insisted on doing it himself.

It was a long trip again down to Adelaide and certainly not a successful one. It was a full car with Corky and his son Mick, Frizz and Graham Keys and me. It was a big race and well supported.

I had just passed the riding duties over to Tony after a refuelling stop about an hour into the race. He wasn't on the bike long when the crowd all stood up, craning their necks to see what had happened.

When the dust finally settled it was Tony who had crashed going into the first corner. He had clipped another rider at the end of the straight and lost the bike at a very high speed. Luckily, he wasn't hurt too badly and he managed to get the broken bike back to the pit area. It was knocked roughly back into shape in a matter of minutes and I re-entered the race. Mike Hailwood was circulating fairly quickly on his Ducati and I got in behind him. I had just lapped him but we spent the rest of the race in close company, often only millimetres apart and having lots of fun. I could pass him in a couple of areas and then he would pass me back again, showing me a pair of fingers at the same time.

The crowd loved the close racing and probably thought we were going at it hammer and tongs but we were just having fun. In the course of our playing, though, I pulled back two laps to finish sixth. Our team's other Z1 didn't fare so well — it nearly made it to the finish line in one piece but Graham Keys almost totalled it in the closing stages. The classic high side got him and flattened all the instruments. Corky tied both bikes back on the trailer after the race and we headed off in the direction of the Adelaide hills. It had been a tiring weekend and we wanted to be back on Monday morning but we still had over 1000 km of driving ahead of us.

7

WHICH WAY DOES THE TRACK GO AND WHAT'S THE LAP RECORD? 1978

SUZUKA 8 HOUR, 1978

Talk about being excited by the thought of going to Japan; I was rapt. During my high-school days I had done a geography project on Japan and enjoyed learning about the lifestyle of its people, their culture and religions. I had been invited to Japan to test a Moriwaki Kawasaki and then race it in the inaugural Suzuka 8 Hour on Honda's own circuit at Suzuka. Although the course had been used for a few international events in the past, the Honda Motor Company had decided to put it up as a round of the FIM Coupe d'Endurance championship.

None of us had any idea what to expect in Japan from Moriwaki. We knew that apart from the four major motorcycle manufacturers in Japan, the Moriwaki and Yoshimura companies were the highest-profile racing parts manufacturers. Earlier in the 1970s Hideo Yoshimura, whose nickname was Pops, had done a lot of work on motorcycles and the S600 Honda sports coupe. He had met Mamoru Moriwaki who was also racing an S600 Honda and was a user of the Yoshimura racing parts. They started an enduring relationship and Mamoru got to know Pops' daughter Namiko. They married and formed a very determined and strong team, eventually moving to

Suzuka in Mie Prefecture near Nagoya. They began producing racing components including camshafts, pistons, valves and exhaust systems under the Moriwaki brand.

Both the Yoshimura Company and the Moriwaki Company began to grow quickly in Japan. However, Pops saw his business future in the mass market of America and went off to California to set up his operation there. The two family manufacturing businesses subsequently became well known on both sides of the Pacific. For the riders and the racing fans, and even people on the street, there grew an immense admiration for their spirit of competition.

Moriwaki Engineering, with their base at Suzuka about 4 km from the track, was strategically well placed to keep an eye on Honda's racing development. These were exciting times as Honda, which had a manufacturing plant at Suzuka, had only recently made its return to racing in 1976. It had been nine years since they withdrew from international competition. They re-entered racing internationally with an RCB1000. It had a twin-cam head with four valves per cylinder and a gear-driven primary drive. It also had sand-cast crankcases, which presumably meant lightweight magnesium alloy. The RCB had dominated the FIM Coupe d'Endurance European series in 1976 and '77.

Honda probably saw the Suzuka race as being relatively easy to win, especially as continued development on the RCB had produced a formidable bike that had been virtually unbeatable to date. Charlie Williams and Stan Woods from the UK were going to be riding one RCB, but the main riders and favourites to win were the French duo Christian Leon and Jean-Claude Chermarin. They were scheduled to ride the other RCB. The RCB's lap times were so impressive in practice that Namiko had been relaying the information about its development back to America where Pops was based. The information he was receiving almost daily only served to fuel his desire to beat Honda at all costs. It was well known that Honda and Yoshimura did not see eye to eye and Pops could see that a perfect opportunity was presenting itself.

He had been working with Suzuki Motor Company and entered a highly tuned GS1000 superbike with the Americans Wes Cooley and Mike Baldwin as its riders. Moriwaki, on the other hand, had his own aspirations and built a Z1000 Kawasaki superbike which was also highly modified and extremely powerful.

Brenda and I were met at Nagoya Airport by Namiko Moriwaki and one of her workers, a short man with an enthusiastic nature and an infectious smile that revealed a huge set of white teeth. He was fun, laughing at just about anything we said. Although he didn't say much himself, he was nodding and evidently understood our every word. It turned out that he couldn't speak one miserable word of English. So feeling inclined to at least to teach him a few words, I started.

'OK, Hara-san, listen carefully,' I said. 'Do you know Mr Hatton?' A blank look came over his face, while his eyes probed me for assistance.

'Hatton. Hatton,' I repeated. 'Do you understand Hatton?'

'Ah Hatton, hai,' he replied.

I then said, 'His name is Fuck-face Hatton. Mr Fuck-face Hatton.'

'Ah soo, desu ka!' he replied, which I knew to mean 'Is that so?' It took some doing but I finally made him understand. I now had Tony Hatton renamed Fuck-face Hatton. Hara-san would meet Tony and hopefully say, 'Welcome to Japan Mr Fuck-face Hatton,' and I nearly wet myself thinking what it would be like being a fly on the wall at the airport. I felt a bit like a theatrical director setting the scene for a comedy. Hara-san takes up the story:

> 'I couldn't believe that Graeme was only 22 years old because he appeared so tall and confident. We had given Graeme and his girlfriend Brenda the VIP room in our factory. At first Graeme stayed around the factory, helping

us to pack camshafts and just wandering around … very quiet. A few days later, they asked to have a look around Suzuka City so we gave him a Kawasaki Z650. The Kiwi couple got on the bike and wheeled off down the road. I wasn't familiar with such riding back then and was very surprised, although Brenda wasn't — she was smiling and waving at us.

'At the weekend, we were planning to take Graeme out for his first test ride at Suzuka. I was worried he might be nervous but he just wheelied through the pit lane as he headed out onto the track. Only the western track was available in the morning and it was crowded. There were two Kawasaki factory KR350's on the racetrack just like buzzing bees and behind them was our big Moriwaki Z1. Coming out of the hairpin corner, Graeme lifted the front wheel and almost hit the back of the Kawasakis. Mr Moriwaki was smiling and nodding.'

Before leaving for Japan, I had studied the Suzuka course, more out of curiosity because on paper it was a technical-looking track. The Suzuka circuit is actually a figure-of-eight track with a flyover bridge so three circuits could be used — a western, an eastern and the full course that, at just under 6 km, was long. We arrived at the western track for two short practice sessions of 20 minutes each. There was a rough temporary pit area at the hairpin with no facilities other than a Japanese toilet.

I asked Hara-san, 'Which way does the track go and what's the lap record?' There was some confusion as to what I had said but I was here to have some fun. Hara-san scratched his head. A mechanic who spoke a little English asked again what I had said before he too began scratching his head. I had to resort to sign language to get my point across. Finally, everyone knew what I had asked and, straight-faced, they all got into a huddle and one mechanic came out pointing and said, 'That way, Crosby-san' and stated a time he thought was the record.

My first few laps had me trying to figure out where I was on the track. We were using the flyover bridge and it took me a while to get orientated. But once I had done that I found the bike very powerful and I could easily do wheelies out of the hairpin, and surprisingly it handled, steered and braked nicely. This gave me a lot of confidence. After the first session I was only a split-second off the best time, which I bettered in the next session. Hara-san remembers:

> 'We got to use the full Suzuka circuit the following day and after just two laps, we saw Graeme slide his rear wheel at the end of the 'S' Corner. He quickly counter-steered and managed to keep the bike on the track before returning to the pits. I thought he was scared and wanted to stop for a while. In fact he came to the pit because the handlebars had broken. While they were being replaced, Mr Moriwaki told Graeme, "Stay in fifth gear when you come down around the last corner. Nobody has ever done it before but I know you can."
>
> '"Do you want to kill me?" Graeme was saying, laughing as he headed back on to the track. After two more laps he was coming through the final corner in top gear.'

From the first lap on the big circuit I knew I would just love this track. Sure, it was long and fast but it suited my riding style. The bike went well and all the Moriwaki staff were talking about how fast I had gone in practice. In fact I felt a bit like a superstar.

'Was I pleased to get those two days of practice over and done with!' I told Brenda. Mainly because I was under a bit of pressure to perform and to ride fast enough to make Honda aware of the potential of our bike. It may have not looked pretty like their fully faired RCB's but our bike was raw and ultra-fast. I knew Hatton would like it too. Hara-san:

> 'I went out for a drink with Graeme and Brenda that evening. A tipsy Graeme told me about the promise he had made to Mr Moriwaki. He had asked Mr Moriwaki to buy him a watch if he qualified in 2:22 or less. That was an almost impossible lap time for me to comprehend but Graeme was already looking at the watch catalogue, telling me which one he was going to get. He looked happy. "Two minutes 22 seconds and I'm getting this watch," he said, jabbing at the catalogue with one hand and holding a beer glass in the other.'

Just as Moriwaki was keeping tabs on the RCB's progress, Racing Service Corporation (RSC) officials had been checking us out. George Payne from Honda Australia had been in contact with RSC over a technical parts enquiry when he was asked a strange question. 'Who is this Graeme Crosby?' Honda asked. 'He has just turned up with Mr Moriwaki and went incredibly fast on his first outing at Suzuka.' George told them that I was an 'OK' rider and left it at that. Intrigued, RSC then came back and asked George about Crosby's co-rider Tony Hatton. 'Who is he and is he any good?' the telex asked. George responded by saying 'please understand that Mr Crosby is only Tony Hatton's "apprentice" rider'. At that stage Honda may have begun to get a little worried.

Hara showed us a few of the seedy areas of Suzuka. At one bar we were treated to a humorous impromptu show that had us in stitches. We were the only ones in there, other than a younger worker who looked after the bar while 'Mama-san' was dancing. At first we thought she was alone, when suddenly a huge puff of cigarette smoke poured out from under her arms, indicating that a man was on his haunches under her billowing dress doing god knows what. Intermittently, he would draw on a cigarette that glowed from underneath the dress, then the smoke would pour from every orifice in her garment. He eventually emerged to stand face to face with the two foreigners. I have never seen anyone so apologetic and embarrassed as he bowed and retreated to the door.

The young girl at the bar laughed loudly and we became great friends. We went back to that place several times until one day we discovered she had set up her own bar near the Suzuka Grand Hotel. I decided to call it 'Mama's Bar'. That bar became a meeting place for all the foreigners who were racing at Suzuka and it quickly got a reputation for the fun we would get up to behind the closed doors. The first time I went I'd had a few drinks prior to arriving and needed to have a pee. No sooner did I have everything unzipped, out and ready, when a hand appeared from around my back, grabbed my 'old fella' and ensured that I was not missing the bowl. I got one hell of a fright. On reflection I thought, 'Now, that's service!'

It was usually me who arrived with a bunch of Australians and their mechanics and hangers-on. A quick nod by me was all that was needed to get her to follow after anyone who wanted to relieve themselves. The reactions were amazing — screams of delight and laughter. I loved to see the expressions on their faces as they returned to the bar. Most sat back with their mouths open still trying to 'get to grips' with what they had just experienced. She even had a collection of clean knickers behind the bar in a cardboard box. When the place was full of guys all drinking and laughing and having fun I would climb down behind the bar and come up with a pair of her knickers on my head and begin serving beers.

After a few nights of partying hard I realized that if you were last to leave it was likely that you would end up paying the bills of all those who had walked out without paying their share. I thought this was not a fair situation and decided to implement a 'foreigner's payment policy'. From that day on it was pay up first and you get your drink — no using the tab system for us foreigners any more.

The Yoshimura team arrived a few days before qualifying started and began setting up in an area set aside for their use by Moriwaki. They had driven down from Atsugi, just outside of Tokyo, to do the final preparation work for their assault on the Suzuka 8 Hour race.

It was the first time I had met Pops Yoshimura and we got on like a house on fire. He swore and cursed and I laughed at his use of English terminology. But man was he serious about beating Honda; you could see it in his eyes.

I had a little time one day when things were quiet to talk to him about his life during the Second World War. He had become a flight engineer on the Japanese equivalent of the C-47 or Douglas DC-3. He told me of one flight delivering freight for the war effort in Java. It was under Japanese occupation at the time and regular Japanese Air Force operations were being conducted to supply arms and food to the army.

'We were flying at about 3000 metres approaching Java when these three P-38 Lightnings attacked us,' Pops told me. 'On the first attack a bullet smashed through the cockpit, killing the pilot and cutting my face.'

Pops' hand moved up to indicate the scar across his face. 'I had blood everywhere, the co-pilot took over and dived into a big cloud and began circling inside the cloud. After about an hour the P-38's had to return for fuel and we were able to continue on to finish our flight.'

Pops continued:

> 'After the war was over I had no job but I became interested in motorcycles so I set up a repair shop and soon all the GIs were coming to get work done on their

bikes. The GIs set up a drag racing strip on part of the runway and we started racing there. That's when I learnt to "hot" them up, basically making them breathe and fit bigger valves which I could make from used aircraft valves. It was good-quality metal. Through the 1950s and early '60s I tuned up those English bikes. When the Honda CB72 arrived it looked interesting and although many of the GIs had drifted back to the USA I was still getting orders for parts.

'I saw the Honda Sport car and did some work on that and soon my engines were winning the Japanese championship for four straight years. Even Honda's own race cars could not beat my Yoshimura-powered cars. Honda started making parts hard to get for me. I got so angry. Then Honda had the CB750 and I tuned some engines that won at Daytona in 1971. But again Honda gave me trouble about parts supply, so I got really mad. I tried Kawasaki and their engine was good, but I was making a fast engine and the frames were junk. So I changed to Suzuki and it was a good move. I have a good relationship now with Suzuki. So that's why I want to beat Honda.'

Hara-san had been dispatched to pick up Tony. Hara-san asked, 'Are you Fuck-face Hatton?' Tony broke up laughing and Ralph Hannan, who had accompanied Tony, couldn't believe his ears. RSC had their representatives at the airport to pick up their own riders. Tony noticed how they were all pointing and bowing and acknowledging him. Then the penny dropped: the apprentice might already be in town but the master had now arrived.

Hara-san recalls another favourite story. 'On the night before the official practice, Graeme was out late drinking with his friends. Mrs

Moriwaki came to get us, telling Graeme, "Do you know what time it is? You have the qualifying session tomorrow. Now, go back and get some sleep." Graeme adjusted his watch and said, "It's too early," and gave her a wink.'

It was a hot time in late July and the rainy season had just finished. It was very humid so Brenda and I spent a lot of time relaxing by the hotel's outdoor pool between practice sessions. I dived in, only to find it was the shallow one for kids. I took a knock to my hand and it began to swell. I thought I might have broken it. That night I bought a big jug of cold beer and spent the night with my hand in the jug to reduce the swelling.

The following day in the first practice session for Group A riders, I was approaching the big fast downhill right-hander that leads on to the straight when I saw a fireball rolling along the top of the steel Armco barrier. I slowed and as I went past I saw the battered wreck of a works Kawasaki still engulfed in flames. The rider appeared OK but the bike had exploded on impact with the safety barrier. The machine had been torn apart and was now engulfed in a fiery ball.

Tony had witnessed it too and as we discussed the last corner, I told him I was using top gear onto the straight, by instruction of the boss. I wondered if the Kawasaki rider had been trying my fifth gear trick as well. 'Bugger that, Croz,' Tony commented, 'I'm going to start using second gear from here on in.' We looked at each other, shaking our heads.

I had no idea how hot it could be in Japan but these temperatures were well above my own comfort levels. Ice was used by the truckload to prevent dehydration and to keep the riders cool during our stints on the bike, which were generally about an hour long. I became aware that we were subjecting ourselves to acute heat exhaustion. I was worried about the possibility of losing concentration during my time on the bike through excessive loss of body fluids. Hara-san:

'When the night qualifying session started, Graeme's fingers were still too fat to fit into his glove so Brenda had to cut the glove with scissors to make them fit. But despite his injury and all that drinking, he easily lapped in under 2 minutes 22 seconds. He wanted to go out on the track and try again after David Emde on a TZ750 and the Yoshimura team posted faster laps, but he didn't get the opportunity because Tony also needed to qualify. Graeme had made 2:21.2, putting the Moriwaki team in third position.'

The night before the race I was checking out the town for action and was blown away by the sheer numbers of people sleeping on the street, in the backs of cars and anywhere they could find space. In the extreme heat and humidity I noticed just about every male wore a T-shirt with the short sleeves rolled up and a small white towel around his neck.

Rather late, I arrived back at the workshop where our apartment was located and although I tried to sneak in, I was spotted. I walked into the workshop and was confronted by mechanics and helpers doing last-minute preparations to our bike. Pops was there and his Suzuki was in a million bits. There were parts strewn all over the place and I quietly asked what was going on. I knew they had experienced clutch plate problems in practice, brought about by the high rotational speed of the clutch outer that was smaller than our Kawasaki's. I thought they might be replacing it before the race. Pops looked stressed as he stood by, picking his fingernails on both hands. His dark-rimmed spectacles were perched high up on his head. His eyes were alert and every now and then he barked an order that started another round of action.

Pops had qualified his bike ahead of the first French-ridden RCB and probably felt the strain of having to back up the qualifying time next day with a sustained high-speed run ahead of the RCB's. I was mentally prepared for the race and although I was apprehensive about how we would go, I went to bed thinking about picking up my new watch on Monday.

It was 37°C on race day and a huge crowd of 70,000 people had gathered for the spectacle of the first Suzuka 8 Hour race. Hara-san remembers it well:

'Getting the watch wasn't important any more; Graeme had earned it. He may not have been happy with the time; however, he knew what he had to do for the race. His friend Ralph was optimistic, saying, "You've got eight hours — don't worry about the qualifying time. Even the Hondas are behind us on the grid." Ralph didn't know what Mr Moriwaki had told Graeme. Although the Hondas didn't qualify as they were expected to, RSC weren't worried about the result. They believed they could win the race just like they had in Europe. And they were not the only ones who believed they would be victorious. The media were still saying that the RCB was the strongest contender, even after the poor qualifying session result ... but not Mr Pops Yoshimura. He knew how nervous the Honda riders were and he was confident that RCB would not be able to keep up with Yoshimura.

'Since the arrival of the Yoshimura team, we had barbecues almost every evening, prepared by Moriwaki staff members. We got together and had a good time, more team-mates than rivals. The Yoshimura team was working on their machine using space on the Moriwaki factory floor. The night before the race, I was at the Moriwaki factory instead of going to the bars in Suzuka.

Moriwaki was preparing three bikes. Graeme and Tony's team on a Kawasaki 1000, Renny Khoo from Malaysia and Tetsumichi Sanada on another Kawasaki 1000 and Masaharu Kasuno and Toshimitsu Sho on a Moriwaki original-frame Z650. I thought we would have another sleepless night, and Yoshimura members would probably finish their work by 1 a.m. because they had only one bike to take care of.

'But there was something going on at the Yoshimura team. Pops had come down to the factory floor in his pyjamas, listening to his team. He looked at the cylinder head and said something to his staff. Suddenly, the Yoshimura team got really noisy. Pops changed back into his clothes and started working on the bike. It was 5 a.m. by the time they finished. They said that the inner valve spring was broken. It cost them the whole night. Both the Yoshimura and Moriwaki teams left for the circuit that morning without any sleep. Their expectation of beating the Hondas was so great that their tiredness was never visible. They were confident, because they believed in the words of Mr Moriwaki and Mr Yoshimura:

"Honda will run an endurance race. We are going to run a sprint race, and if we make 190 laps, we can win. We've got tough riders who can make over 200 laps and they won't crash. That's the advantage we have, and our engines will endure, leaving the others behind. The TZ750 will not survive eight hours. Only Moriwaki or Yoshimura have a chance to win the race! Be confident in yourselves."

'These ardent messages from the two team leaders meant that the 8 Hour endurance race would be turned into an eight-hour sprint race. They were hell-bent on beating Honda.'

I prepared myself for the warm-up lap to check everything was working well but I was still concerned about losing fluids during the race. I had found some salt tablets and took a few. The bikes had been sitting on the grid for some time before the starter signalled for the warm-up lap to commence. I didn't see the flag being waved but instead heard another of those English phrases buried deep in the Japanese language: 'WARMING UPPU LAPPU!' I pushed off and it fired up, sounding strong and crisp. As I rode off to the first corner a nauseous wave hit me and I knew I was about to chuck up. I made a mad dash across the grass to the infield steel barrier. I stopped the bike and quickly released my chin-strap and ripped my helmet off. I'd just got it clear of my head when my stomach erupted in a series of projectile vomiting spasms. I gave my face a wipe with my glove and put my helmet back on. A little push and the bike fired again and I rode around to take my place on the grid. The course commentator had been describing my little spew act and had not been able to work it out. On the grid I explained what had happened and I saw the signs of relief on everyone's faces. I was ready for action.

I had done a wheelie somewhere out on the track and Mr Sato from the Motorcycle Federation of Japan (MFJ) wanted me to do another one down the start-finish straight to entertain the massive crowd. When asked, Mr Moriwaki politely refused his request. Naturally, I would have obliged.

With the time slowly ticking by, the riders were asked to move across to the other side of the track and get into position for the Le Mans start. It was a nervous time and getting hotter as the sun beat down. Standing in my position at No. 3 we were ready with 10 seconds to go. I began acting out the pre-fight ritual of a sumo wrestler. I thought it was amusing, but those in the grandstand were staring at me in disbelief. After all, this was a motorcycle race. Hara-san picks up the story:

> 'At 11.30 all riders ran to their machines. The Yoshimura and Moriwaki teams both started smoothly but one of the Honda RCB riders was having trouble starting his engine. He eventually got going but had lost valuable time. The TZ750 went past on lap one with Wes and Graeme following side by side. Then we saw white smoke coming up from the last corner and all the spectators got to their feet. It was the other RCB sliding into the safety zone. Now, Honda had put all their hopes on the remaining RCB that was trying hard to regain the ground it had lost at the start, but the gap with the top riders wasn't closing. The TZ750 was gradually losing its pace as well. Yoshimura was now leading the field, followed by the Moriwaki team.'

Tony and I alternated the riding duties, an hour at a time. It was extremely hot out on the track but the heat soak we suffered when we came into the pits for fuel and a rider change was unbearable. Each stop was the same, with me getting off the bike, pulling off my leather suit and lying down on a stretcher bed with cold wet towels draped over me to get my core body temperature down as quickly as possible. There was also a portable air-conditioner that was being ducted directly on to me. Tony would have the same treatment. On standby was a bloke who massaged my neck, feet and head. In broken English during one stop he asked me if I liked beer. I said 'Yes I do,' half-expecting him to hand me a can of cold Kirin. 'I know too,' he said. 'I can tell, I am trained in shiatsu massage and know these things.' 'Shit,' I thought, hoping he wouldn't say too much to Moriwaki.

Hara-san:

> 'Four hours had passed when one of Moriwaki's bikes suffered a problem. It was Kasuno and Soh on the Z650 and we could see smoke coming out of the exhaust. They were around eighth position but had to retire because of engine trouble. Soon after, we heard the screaming of Mishina, the Suzuka circuit commentator. He was telling the crowd that the RCB rider was pushing his bike at the 130R corner. The spectators were looking towards the last corner, patiently waiting for the RCB to appear. The rider had the top half of his leather suit hanging around his waist, and eventually made it back to the pit. He said something to his mechanic and that was the end of RCB.'

While I don't like seeing anyone crash or suffer misfortune, the sight of the RCB grinding to a halt was a welcome turn of events for us. That was one less competitor to worry about. As I sped around the circuit passing slower riders, I spied a rider ahead who was going pretty damn quick. I began concentrating and my lap times improved with the challenge of wearing him down, even if he was a lap behind. The faster riders may have been only marginally slower and it took a few laps before I could get in behind them. But once I was up close they would be aware of me because of the acoustic harmonics that produce a strange noise as both our engines go in and out of synchronization. If they were Japanese riders, I found I didn't have to rush to get past. I just had to wait behind them for few corners and they would get flustered and start taking different lines and eventually would make a mistake, invariably running wide while I whistled through. I figured out that most Japanese riders became uncomfortable leading a foreign rider, so I used this technique for the rest of the race.

There were four laps or about ten minutes to go before Tony was due in and I stretched my aching legs and arms before climbing into my leathers. I fitted a new darker visor to help with the glare of the late afternoon sun and found a new pair of earplugs. Reporters and photographers were busy doing their jobs, taking notes and clicking away with cameras that had lenses like rocket-launchers.

The pit suddenly came alive with activity and everyone began staring at the closed-circuit TV monitors for a sign of Tony. He had not come around. Seconds passed and soon we realized that he must have stopped. My heart sank. Mamoru spat out instructions as mechanics prepared for every type of emergency — wheels, chains, a horde of spare parts, ignition units, batteries, a set of handlebars ready to swap if necessary. Tony was pushing the bike back to the pits from Spoon Corner. Time seemed to slow down while we waited. Whatever the problem was, I was ready to go.

Hara-san:

> 'The commentator Mishina was looking through his binoculars for Tony and saying, "He's pushing the machine on the grass, running toward the pit." A few moments later, all the spectators in the grandstand started applauding Tony who was coming into pit lane, having taken only 15 minutes to push his bike from Spoon Corner. Later he said that when he was pushing the bike, he was thinking about those Moriwaki staff who had prepared his bike without any sleep, and he didn't want to let them down. He handed the machine to Graeme with an empty fuel tank then fell on the ground.

At the last refuelling, the air in the tank wasn't properly expelled and the bike had gone back out without a full load of gas.'

I rode like a demon possessed, trying hard to make up the lost time. I settled into a quick rhythm that saw me cut back my deficit by a substantial margin. I was un-lapping myself and moving back up the leaderboard. My lapboards were telling me lap number, lap time and position, plus time to the next rider in front of me. We were six laps down on the leader but with our lap times being so close it meant that while I was gradually closing in on them, I wouldn't be able to make up all those lost laps.

Finally, I saw the 'Pit In' sign and made my way in, slowing and unzipping my suit to get a final blast of cool air before the heat soak got to me again in pit lane. I stopped and went to lift my leg off the bike and was immediately pushed back on. Within a couple of seconds I was back out again. 'Fuck! What happened there? It was supposed to be Tony's turn,' I thought. I realized I would have to finish this race myself. So much for the cold beer I'd planned for that last stop.

The air temperature began dropping in the early evening and the horsepower increased dramatically as a consequence. The bike was back to its best and everything felt good. I saw a couple of 2:21 laps and thought how easy it was. The circuit got darker and I finally saw the 'LIGHTS ON' sign at the start-finish and flicked the toggle switch on the handlebars that turned on the front and back lights. It was getting difficult to see and I finally figured out why. My dark visor was not what I wanted now. With the minimal circuit lighting, the oil slicks became visible. Huge slicks deposited on the track during the day shone at night, making them easy to spot. These were evidence of engines that had haemorrhaged during the day.

With just a few laps to go, I heard an odd exhaust noise. It was getting louder, which made me think I was losing a header pipe. I managed to lean over coming out of the hairpin and take a quick look. I was amazed to see the disc rotors glowing dull red in the night air and the exhaust headers were cherry-red with heat. One had come loose. The last laps ticked by, then suddenly the safety lights flashed on, indicating the race was all over.

Hara-san:

> 'Wes Cooley and Mike Baldwin won the race for Yoshimura, followed by Isoyo Sugimoto and David Emde, whose 2-stroke Yamaha TZ750 survived the eight hours, with Graeme and Tony third on the Moriwaki. Yoshimura had successfully challenged Honda, and finally defeated them on their home track.
>
> 'Pops' wife Namie was alone in the US because they couldn't afford her flight to Japan for the event. Mrs Moriwaki called Namie with tears in her eyes. It was not difficult to imagine how a mother felt about her family's achievement after all the hard work.
>
> 'After the finish, Mr Nishiwaki, the chief machine technical inspector from MFJ, ran to the Moriwaki pit. His eyes were moist with emotion. "It was unfortunate for your team but I was moved by your race effort. Your two Moriwaki riders did great work. I am sure all those people who couldn't leave their seats until the Moriwaki machine passed the finish line would share my feelings."'

I downed four cans of Kirin in quick succession and talked to Tony about his race. Either he or I was out on the track and never had time to talk during the race. He told me he was too worn out to do his last stint. I told him I totally understood and we all lay down on the concrete to watch the most amazing fireworks display. We had to walk back to the Moriwaki workshop amidst a sea of spectators and we were stopped and asked to sign autographs. I would sign anything, but by far the most pleasurable were the women's T-shirts. I took great delight and a long time to gently sign on the breasts. We made it back to the factory where the victory party had already started. I was not surprised that most of the staff members had finally succumbed to fatigue as soon as the Moriwaki bike had crossed the line. Frozen in time, they had literally fallen asleep where they had been working.

As riders, Tony and I felt we owed this group of dedicated people for all the work and effort they had contributed. Of course we were both also very happy that we had been part of this prestigious race and had performed the way we did.

Hara-san wraps up:

> 'The following morning, we checked the machine's cracked exhaust pipe. We also found that the down-tube of the chassis was broken. It couldn't take Graeme's fierce riding style. For a long time Mr Moriwaki had planned to make his own chassis but he hadn't had a chance to develop it. He thought that Graeme would go to a factory team soon or later, but hoped he would stay with Moriwaki for one more year so he could realize his dream of building his own chassis. Mr Moriwaki went to his desk imagining Graeme riding for Moriwaki next year.'

A prize presentation was held at the circuit on the Monday. It was all pomp and ceremony with ribbons and speeches. Although we had already been on the winners' rostrum after the race, this was like getting two bites at the cherry. It was a time to reflect on our performances and gladly pick up the one million yen prize money in cash.

8

I CALL AUSTRALIA HOME, 1978–79

AUSSIE HONDA CASTROL 6 HOUR AND NZ 6 HOUR, 1978

Back in Australia, I was still a free agent when the Castrol 6 Hour race came around again.

'Hey Croz, you haven't signed up with anyone yet, have you?' Tony was asking me for a reason. 'Honda have the new CBX1000 coming out and I reckon it might be half a chance for the 6 Hour — big tank, plenty of grunt with six cylinders but it looks like it might have heaps of clearance. If you're interested, I'll talk to George Pyne at Honda Australia — they've got a few bucks too.'

Tony had got stuck a few years ago riding a CB750 which was not that competitive, but this new CBX sounded as if it would work and as I knew Hatto would make sure it was properly prepared, I agreed.

I picked one of the two bikes Honda had given to Tony to prepare and put about 700 km on it, riding down to Goulburn and then up to Newcastle. I was impressed but even more so when I took it out to have a run around Amaroo Park. My first lap on the bike told me this was a great bike to use around Amaroo because of the ground clearance, which was always a problem.

I put the bike on pole, half a second faster than the next rider. The joke was that the bike was so wide no one could pass me anyway. We think this was the first time a CBX1000 had been raced anywhere in the world, but that counted for nothing as we lasted only 20 laps before retiring when one of the six pistons seized as a result of poor fuel. When I was shifting down, the rear wheel began locking up and I was getting good at being crossed up for a lap or two before common sense prevailed and I pitted, thinking it was a rear brake dragging. We checked and found no problems with it, which led to our diagnosis that our engine was probably poked. It was, and the next day Tony confirmed it as being fuel contamination.

Our luck was not much better back at Manfeild, when Tony and I rode a Kawasaki Z1R in the New Zealand Castrol 6 Hour event. We knew there was going to be some serious competition this year, with more Aussie riders entered. The lap scoring was a shambles and from lap one nobody had a clue exactly where everyone was placed. Tony and I rode steadily and found ourselves leading with half an hour to go. Fate intervened when the muffler fell off a few laps later, causing it to hole a piston, handing the win to Suzuki.

BOL D'OR, PAUL RICARD, 1978

Rosko was at it again: the Bol d'Or 24-hour race was back on his radar screen. This time, though, he assured us, his nemesis was going to be tamed, Rosko-style. He said he had learned something from last year's Le Mans race and was prepared to make the appropriate changes. Quietly, he commissioned his friend Ray Brennigan to build a chassis that would take his powerful Moriwaki engine. This year it would be held at the ultra-fast Paul Ricard circuit in the South of France where all that power would be needed.

We went through the same process of scratching around to find a few bucks from here and there to make the numbers work. Bel-Ray again came to the party with some cash and John Galvin from Metzeler Australia paid for Tony's airfare. John had a few Metzeler endurance slicks to test which could work for us and be cheaper than buying any. Ominous cracks started appearing in the plan when the bike failed to arrive in time to be set up properly before being put on a plane. When we saw it we laughed until the tears ran down our faces. Not at the overall build job — that was a great piece of work — but at the Second World War triple-split windshield and hand-beaten aluminium cowling. It was similar to what you would expect to find on a German Messerschmitt ME 109 fighter plane. Ross had arranged with Moriwaki to supply a spare engine. Mamoru would not only help but agreed to bring it with him to Paul Ricard as hand luggage.

The first few practice sessions were taken up with making adjustments that should have been done before the bike left Australia. Tony and I were wondering who would be the first to be spat off, as it handled so badly. Ralph wanted to know when it started wobbling out on the track.

'Mate, it starts wobbling at about the same speed as a walker does when he breaks into a jog,' I said, adding, 'and there's never going to be a chance of breaking a throttle cable in this race. In fact the cable will probably rust out before it ever wears out.'

'We haven't even got off the pilot jet yet,' Tony added. 'It was that dangerous and at the speeds we were going we probably could have done the whole race with only three stops, and one of those would be after we went across the finish line.'

We needed a quick fix. Mamoru had the answer. He binned the mono shock, welded some lugs onto the swing arm and chassis, pulled out two racing shock units from his travel bag and fitted them. At least it went in a straight line now. It began to handle reasonably well and other riders stopped referring to us as a mobile chicane. Unfortunately, we lasted only a few hours in the race before an engine haemorrhage forced us to the showers early. It was exciting while it lasted, though, and we learnt a lot in short time. Maybe we'd try again next year.

Our hotel was in a quaint fortressed town called La Cadière, a medieval Provençal village not far from Marseilles. It's a charming and beautiful place with a restaurant overlooking the vineyards. Our little room high up in a tower had a huge bed, a stunning view and solid wooden shutters. One of our crew fell in love with the gorgeous hotel owner and we had to leave him there after he refused to come with us. Full of testosterone, he reckoned he might stand a chance if we stopped heckling him.

We had a look around the South of France before heading off to Brands Hatch for a local endurance race. I had never been to the UK before but we had used our time at the Bol d'Or to make contacts with other riders and check out what was happening across the Channel. I met an English bloke who had entered Brands and for some reason he was short of a rider. I volunteered without hesitation.

'We are a laid-back team Croz, so don't expect too much, but we enjoy our racing so see you there before practice.' It was that loose but I was happy to be offered a ride.

That race at Brands had no meaning for me other than it was a round of some endurance championship. When I turned up I was shown a Peckett and McNab Kawasaki endurance racer. When it was my turn to ride, I jumped on and promptly went to select first gear but put the rear brake on instead. I looked down. 'Shit, it's got the gearshift on the wrong side,' I said.

'Yeah, that's the way it is. Don't you ride that way?' the mechanic asked.

'No, I ride with the brake on the right but don't worry, I'll get it sorted.' As soon as I said that, I regretted it as he pushed me off down pit lane. I rode for about six laps, getting quicker each time, with only a couple of hiccups. Not only was the brake on the wrong side but the shift pattern was upside-down compared with what I was used to. A couple of times I down-shifted when I should have been up-shifting and jammed the rear brakes on inadvertently. The first problem I fixed by placing my foot under the brake pedal so I couldn't apply the brake. Then I ignored the rear brake — it was safer that way.

The main rider did the first 50 or so laps then I jumped on and brought us up from about 16th to 5th, then handed it back to him. He worked his way back down to about 16th again then I went out and dragged us back up to about 8th. I could see a pattern had been set.

I had been looking at a pile of beer cans gathering in the corner over the last few hours and when I came in for a change, the main rider was just draining another can. I remembered what this guy had said about being laid-back. It wasn't serious racing for these guys but even I drew the line about having a beer between stints. We finished the race in about seventh place eventually and I think I may have completed more laps than my team-mate, but by the time the chequered flag fell he couldn't have given a toss. It was time to go home and get back to some serious racing.

SWANN SERIES, 1978

Back in Australia again, with the demise of the New Zealand Marlboro Series, Swann Insurance stepped in and put up a $10,000 prize pool and ran a three-race programme. Oran Park was the only track where I had a real chance but even then I kept getting passed on the straight and as a consequence worked my way backwards to finish down the field.

Surfers Paradise and Melbourne's Calder Park proved more of a handful for me, as I realized that while the show I put on was exciting for the crowd, it wasn't doing me any good. I needed more horsepower or a better-handling bike with a little more grunt to counteract the faster 750 cc racers.

Jeff Sayle and his mechanic Mick Smith put four straight wins together to take the series, with Jeff's big brother Murray second and Gary Coleman third.

TEAM KAWASAKI AUSTRALIA CONTRACT, JANUARY 1979

I had all sorts of options open to me now but apparently the only person who knew fact from fiction was me. I had read conflicting newspaper reports that had me signing with Honda Australia but it takes good investigative journalism to root out the whole truth. That old phrase 'don't let the truth get in the way of a good story' applied. That was my situation as the New Year arrived and I looked at my options for 1979.

I had a quiet word with George Payne about Honda's racing programme. He talked mainly about production bikes and the introduction of the new CB900's but fell short of saying 'Croz, we want you!' His good friend and contracted service provider, Tony Hatton, had a more liberal approach and I used his ears to give me an insight into the politics of Honda Australia. He was a visionary when it came to analysing what Honda should or shouldn't do with their racing programme. Undoubtedly, they had the financial clout to get what they wanted, but you can't buy the passion or determination of an individual with his own goal.

I couldn't see the merit in changing camps to ride for Honda; there was no clearly defined future other than production racing domestically with them in 1979. Using Ross's superbike, to date I had never finished second to a Honda anyway, but I was getting a little tired of being passed by TZ750's and RG500's in the Open class. Despite putting up brave and flamboyant performances, often leading in the early laps, I was always destined to be overhauled and finish lower down the field. I wanted something more competitive.

Ross Hannan had something to do with the process of how Neville Doyle ended up talking directly with me over my plans for the 1979 season. Team Kawasaki (TKA) had had a three-member squad of Gregg Hansford, Murray Sayle and Rick Perry the previous year. However, Neville had international plans again for Gregg and for whatever reason, Murray Sayle was not going to be in the picture this year.

So, domestically, Neville had to field a team to contest the Australian championship but with Gregg away in Europe, the gap had to be filled. Firstly, he wanted to lock in a rider capable of winning the Aussie 6 Hour and the Adelaide 3 Hour races, which were important for the domestic road bike market. He was even considering running a Z1300 but I was a little dubious about the prospect of riding that monster. Secondly, Neville had already been assisting Ross with our superbike effort so he considered that area covered and to give a spare KR750 that was lying around plus parts on a private basis to Ross was probably a good move on his part to secure an already close tie-up.

For me it was the perfect arrangement: I retained a superbike ride, I had security in the knowledge of getting a Z1R for the 6 Hour, and as a bonus I could play with a KR750 in the Australian championship. It all made sense but when the sum of $10,000 was mentioned the deal was sealed tight.

Ross had been approached to run our Z1R at Symmons Plains in Tasmania in early February but with our old superbike desperately in need of an overhaul following the Swann Series it was just too tight. Neville contacted us and arranged for me to fly down and run the KR750 instead at the Australian Unlimited championship event.

Symmons Plains is just out of Launceston and it was a stinking hot February day. The KR750 turned out to be a dream to ride. It had raw horsepower and a fair amount of torque and surprisingly I quickly settled into the groove, putting up some respectable lap times in practice. However, the race was over for me about midway while I was lying third. I went down in a screaming mess in front of everyone at the pit corner. The rear aluminium disc rotor had literally disintegrated, locking my rear wheel in the process and I went 'tits-up'. It was not a good start but I was relieved when Neville pointed out the damaged disc. 'Interesting, that's the first time that's ever happened,' he said. I felt a little better knowing it wasn't my fault but pissed off about the crash. Rick Perry on the other TKA

Kawasaki went on to win in impressive style.

Once back in Sydney I was invited to Mick Smith's birthday and going-away party. It happened to be his mother's birthday as well and they had set up a marquee outside. He was off to Europe with a bunch of Aussie riders but mainly as a spanner man for Jeff Sayle. I was explaining to a few guys what had happened in Tasmania when Jeff interrupted.

'Yeah! Right! He says that all the time … it wouldn't have happened on Gregg's bike, you can bet on that, your bike was probably thrown together out of old parts anyway.' Jeff had had a few beers already and when the 'Sailor' had a few he could be quite direct and an expert in the Aussie national sport of sledging. For some reason he must have been bitter with Neville, but listening to his side of the story I could understand where he was coming from. Gregg was regarded as Kawasaki's future in international racing, having been at the top for many years locally. Neville and Gregg were a close-knit team, and like many successful partnerships each brought his own skills and collectively they dominated their sport. So I guessed he was defending his brother Murray who had been a team member with TKA in '77 and perhaps felt that the scales were not balanced. Why Jeff had a downer on Neville at the time I don't know, but he was giving us Kiwis a roasting. Then he started on me about my chances of winning Bathurst.

'And what's more, you won't see which way Boulden goes on that TZ750 at Bathurst. He'll blow the doors off ya! If you think that old nail that Doyle's given you will compete then you're a wanker!'

I was tiring of Jeff's bolshie attitude. I could feel my face becoming a little flushed. Then, before it could develop into anything, Mick parked his large frame between us. Like a referee he split up the warring factions and told us to knock it off. But I had been told — I may as well stay in Sydney for the Bathurst weekend. However, before I could focus on Bathurst, I had other business to attend to in Adelaide.

ADELAIDE 3 HOUR AND BATHURST, MARCH 1979

Rosko called me to say that Kawasaki Australia had sent new a Z1300 to his shop in Sydney. I should swing by and pick it up and then get some miles on it before we took it to Adelaide. We'd planned to run the bike in the Adelaide Advertiser 3 Hour production race prior to Bathurst.

Frizz was on the case already and had got his hands on it. He decided that a few modifications had to be done to the front and rear shock units to lift it up a tad so it would give me some ground clearance. It weighed over 320 kg and lacked clearance when cornering, so he had machined up some spacers for the front springs and modified the attachment points of the rear shocks to provide the extra clearance.

I rode the bike around the streets of Sydney, up into the Blue Mountains and even down to Canberra. I clocked about 2000 km to loosen it up a little but from the outset I had my doubts that this was going to work on the racetrack. I had been playing around doing wheel-spins outside our house and had got really good at it. Lighting up the back wheel and zooming off down the road with just a little front brake on, I could do the entire length of our street.

White smoke and big snaking black lines covered the street by the time I'd finished. It was a way of getting to know just how far I could push the bike and I realized that it would be better off drag racing than road racing, as it was just too big and cumbersome. I also concluded that the rear tyre was unlikely to stand up to the rigours of circuit racing. 'Do you know how heavy that thing is?' I asked Ross. 'With me on it, and a full tank of fuel, it's just under half a tonne.'

'Croz, try it at Adelaide at least. If it's not going to work then flag it. The thing will fly down Conrod at Bathurst, though,' he laughed.

'Yeah, and you get to watch from the pit lane while I'm trying to hang on to this whale.'

We all met at Corky's place at 6 p.m. on Friday and had a few beers while we waited for him to arrive home. The familiar sound of the 253 Monaro in the driveway signalled time to pack and get on the road. Corky got his kit together, then loaded both the Honda and the Z1300 onto the trailer. As usual it was a rotational driving effort with Corky taking the first stint through to Bathurst. Then it was my turn, just when it got cold and foggy, through Cowra and out onto the Hay Plain. At least this time it wasn't raining.

Frizz was always talking ten to the dozen about how to make things go faster. He thought a few hundred more kilometres at speed might do the Z1300 some good prior to the 3 Hour race. In the middle of the night it was dragged off the trailer and for the next few hundred kilometres we took turns fanging it up to maximum speed across the Hay Plain. We would have been thrown in the slammer if we had been caught but fortunately the Highway Patrol was not on duty at that time in that remote area.

Later, as we cruised into Tailem Bend on the Murray River, we thought about what we'd just done. In the early morning, kangaroos often feed on the fresh grass at the roadside. We could quite easily have been cleaned up by one. As we approached the Adelaide hills, Corky got going with his rendition of the poem 'My Country'. He began, 'I love a sunburnt country, A land of sweeping plains, Of ragged mountain ranges, Of droughts and flooding rains. I love her far horizons.' OK, OK, enough!

Mick Cork broke in to tell me a couple of stories about Peter Campbell. 'Mate, I don't know if you've heard this one, but a couple of years ago PC and Chris Dowd were coming down to Adelaide for a race and they were in the old Humber Snipe with its alloy V8 Valiant engine. It was pretty bloody quick and cruised at 100 mph easily. They were towing a trailer with the sidecar on it and had four drums of avgas racing fuel tied on the back. One came loose and fell off but it was still attached by a bit of rope and was being dragged along behind the trailer.

'You can imagine on the Hay Plain in the middle of the night, just cruising along listening to a Seekers song on the tape deck, when this drum exploded, trailing flaming fuel out the back up the highway. The sky lit up like someone had turned on a halogen light. If the drum was still attached and they'd stopped, the whole trailer and the other fuel drums might have gone up as well, so they kept driving until it burnt out.'

Frizz chipped in, 'And, did you hear the one about PC and Dowd again crossing the Hay Plain? They were in that Humber and PC was asleep across the back seat. They hit a kangaroo flat-out at about 100 and the thing went right through the front window and ended up in the back with PC. He woke up with the thing thrashing around in its final death throes with blood and guts everywhere. He didn't know it was a 'roo initially and thought he'd been involved in an accident and was looking at his own guts, intestines and blood.'

We got into Adelaide at about 8 a.m. and stopped for gas. After paying for the fuel, Corky started to drive off and got about five feet before there was a loud bang as if the trailer had caught on something. We looked around to see the nozzle still in the filler and a length of fuel line draped across the forecourt. It had been ripped out of the pump but luckily the auto shut-off valve had worked.

Corky got out and walked back to the attendant, holding the nozzle with a five-foot length of hose trailing behind him. We all laughed until he got back in the car, when it suddenly seemed inappropriate to make a sound until we got the racetrack.

It took me only a few laps of the track before I decided that the Z1300 was a dead duck — just too big and heavy for throwing around a track like this. I did some fast times but it was clear that we were going to be limited by tyre wear. When I pulled the bike from the race I could hear a sigh of relief from many people. But I didn't want to waste my time driving down from Sydney for nothing and took up the offer of a Kawasaki Z1000, riding with a local.

After we got back to Sydney, Neville had the bike picked up and it went off to Gary Thomas to ride at Bathurst. 'What are you riding that big whale for, Thomo?' I asked him.

'Mate, around Bathurst this thing will be a flyer — just you wait and see.' I had to give him credit for taking on such a big bike. It was risky but I couldn't argue with his decision. I had already made mine. My two rides would be on the KR750 in the Unlimited preliminary race on Saturday and the 20-lap Australian Grand Prix on Sunday. And I would use the Z1R in the Superbike race.

When you race at Bathurst, that first run down Conrod Straight is awesome. It is just one big long downhill stretch with two large humps and then a 90-degree corner. The old nail was being timed at around 265 kph in practice but just keeping it on the ground proved a problem with the aerodynamics. I had to pull myself up on to the tank and climb up under my screen in an attempt to shift as much weight forward to prevent the wheel from coming up. Having it in the air momentarily isn't an issue but it must stay straight while it's up there. There was no guarantee that the bike would behave, so everyone used the same technique.

I should have thought of Jeff Sayle when I crossed the line after Saturday's preliminary race. The KR750 went like 'shit off a shovel'. I blitzed the competition and was credited with breaking the lap record. There seemed to be an element of disbelief in the timing by some people. Just because the terminal speeds are high doesn't necessarily mean the lap times are fast, because my KR750 was no slouch across the mountain, making up for the lack of top-end speed down Conrod.

The sight of Gary Thomas on the Kawasaki Z1300 six-cylinder around Bathurst was breathtaking. He rode the wheels off it in the production race, finishing second to Tony Hatton on a Honda CB900. His 255 kph on the last lap down Conrod on that new Honda was impressive. A few people questioned if it was standard; in fact, when *Revs* editor Mike Esdaile pulled out his cheque book to buy 'that bike',

Honda's George Pyne apparently got the speed wobbles and began stuttering, saying he could have a new one on Monday but not this particular bike. This only served to create more suspicion.

I watched from the pit wall and was slightly embarrassed, knowing it should have been me out there. Now Gary was making me feel like an idiot for rejecting this beast at Adelaide but I decided that I was in a better position watching over the fence feeling like a wally than flapping off the handlebars, trying to hang on to that monster.

Then we heard that a rider had crashed on the mountain, apparently coming out of the Dipper in the 500 cc race. The news filtered through that he had gone over the fence and hit a tree. It was Ron Toombs, the ex-Team Kawasaki Australia rider who had been out racing again for the first time in a few years. He had been taken to hospital but his condition was not known, except that it was serious. Everyone hoped he would pull through and then they turned their attention back to the racing.

I leapt aboard Rosko's superbike for the 3-hour Arai race. On the surface we were looking in good shape and I was the fastest out there in practice. But this was also the first event entered by the new Honda Australia Racing Team and they had flown two superbikes over from Japan for it. Tony Hatton had tested them at the Suzuka circuit and recommended changes. According to George Pyne, they had to come up with something special to match our superbike, which had been unchallenged for a few years now. He didn't like the way we were monopolizing these events and with the new models coming out he was keen to get them out on the track. Practice had shown that Honda still had a long way to go and Tony Hatton was getting frustrated.

Unfortunately, the expected showdown didn't quite happen as my superbike rolled to a halt in the early stages of the race with a dead ignition. It was disappointing, as I had been leading. But we had thrown the cat amongst the pigeons by the way the Honda team cheered and jumped for glee and congratulated one another when

I pulled out. The Japanese racing bosses were present and in Ross's words 'They had more budget for meals than we had for our whole Bathurst effort, but I guess the wankers from Newtown and the Kiwi were starting to be taken seriously.'

The main event was the 20-lap Unlimited Australian Grand Prix. From the start it was a three-horse race, Boulden on his superfast Yamaha TZ750 tuned by Warren Willing; I was there battling it out on my old KR750 and so was John Woodley on his modified RG500. The three of us went at it tooth and nail for the entire 20 laps, passing and being passed, all trying desperately to make a break. We all had areas that we excelled in and exploited them to the max. Whether it was brakes, handling or speed, each one of us had our special talent. So the crowd was treated to a brilliant demonstration of close racing that would go down in history as one of the classics. I managed to pull a slight lead going into the last lap but coming down the chute Boulden came past like an arrow. I don't want to admit that he 'blew the doors off me' down Conrod but it was true. I crossed the line a close second, with John hot on my heels to take third.

Out of two races, I had won the wrong one. The winner of the 1979 Australian Grand Prix was Ron Boulden. I was expecting Jeff Sayle to turn up at any time and cringed at the thought of having to admit defeat. To Jeff's credit, we did catch up and he was full of praise and genuinely thought it was a great race. He still had a dig at me about my lap record, but then it wouldn't have been Jeff if he hadn't.

Just when you are enjoying everything and savouring the moments of victory, fate intervenes and delivers a blow. The tragic news came through that Ron Toombs had died from the injuries he'd sustained in his crash at Bathurst's Mt Panorama circuit.

9

GOING GLOBAL, 1979

ISLE OF MAN — MY FIRST LOOK, 1979

I was excited to be on the famous island at last. I was pleasantly surprised when the Isle of Man Tourist Board invited me to go over and familiarize myself with the TT course. They were paying for the airfare and accommodation and I tried to work out why. I thought I had the answer when I learnt that most local riders usually rode the Manx Grand Prix to get experience before entering the June TT races. We had a letter sent from Australia, penned by Mike Hailwood, supporting my application for a start. It had been accepted and as a consequence I didn't have to race the Manx Grand Prix. However, some wise person suggested I should at least be brought over to get some time on the mountain course prior to racing. I accepted the gracious invitation and Wally Radcliff was waiting for me at the airport when I landed.

The Isle of Man for a first-time visitor is unique in a number of ways. I couldn't care less what all the tourist companies had to offer, I was here to learn and wanted to get on the circuit as soon as I arrived. My first sighting of the circuit proper was at Quarter Bridge. It was exactly what I had imagined from those discussions years ago at the Auckland Motorcycle Club.

I asked Wally if we could do a lap. It was his job and passion to provide assistance to young riders and newcomers here to race the TT for the first time. Being a local, Wally was very knowledgeable about the TT and he also knew all the riders who had competed in the event over the years. He carefully drip-fed the basic information I needed, then described the idiosyncrasies of the TT that he felt I should know. What was coming through loud and clear was that as a newcomer I was expected to ride safely and within my capabilities. If I treated it like a high-speed tour I would be fine; he repeated this advice over and over, making sure he had drummed the message in.

Wally swung on the wheel and we drove out towards Braddan Bridge. The stone walls were suddenly on my radar and the high kerbs were jutting out. As the circuit opened out on the run towards Union Mills I began to comprehend just how fast this circuit was. At a shade over 60 km, it would take 20 minutes for one lap, averaging 180 kph. I was far from ready to do that. The open road past the Highlander pub was extremely fast and took you all the way through to the first real corner at Ballacraine. I made a mental note that this spot should be the end of section one.

The rest became a blur as I tried to cope with the continuously changing scenery. Wally explained that Laurel Bank had claimed a few lives, including that of Tom Phillis from Australia. Then we drove through beautiful Glen Helen and up to Sarah's Cottage, all familiar names to me. It seemed to go on and on from one historic place to another. I was surprised how narrow the main street of Kirk Michael was. If you lived there you wouldn't want to put your milk bottles out on race day for fear of being T-boned on your doorstep by a leather-clad gladiator on a race bike doing 230 kph. The street looked no more than four metres wide. That would be the end of section two.

Wally drove me to Ballaugh Bridge, where we stopped. The smell of garlic on the run-up to the bridge serves to identify where you are located on the circuit. It is one of the most photographed sections on the course. Taken in second gear, the bikes literally take flight over this humpbacked bridge before scorching off into the distance.

We continued on amongst the tree-lined roads and along Sulby Straight. I was imagining myself trying to hold on to a bike at speed along this stretch. I would soon find out just how bumpy it was. Later we slowed to a more considerate pace and entered Parliament Square at Ramsey. For me, that would be the end of section three.

Wally dropped into his house for a few minutes and introduced me to his wife, who appeared to be genuinely supportive of his role as a mentor for newcomers. What really surprised me on that first lap was the remoteness of the mountain once you have climbed up to the Gooseneck from Ramsey. It is high country from there on, with only scrub and peat fields bordering the road. It can be bleak and unforgiving in bad weather but the road across the mountain remains smooth and fast. There are no run-off areas for those unfortunates who make a cock-up, nor are there any safety fences, only ragged edges and drop-offs to catch you out if you are not concentrating. It would be a long, lonely, fast ride across the mountain, but after doing a few laps I realized it gives the riders respite from the stone walls and kerbs that begin to appear as you descend off the mountain down past Creg-ny-Baa and on to Signpost Corner.

Although it's only a few miles to the finish from here, the slowest part of the track has yet to be negotiated, at Governor's Bridge. With such high overall gearing on the circuit, this section by contrast is so slow that you need to take it with the clutch in before letting loose down Glencrutchery Road to the finish.

Wally left me to continue familiarizing myself with the track. The next day he arranged for a local Suzuki dealer to lend me a GT550 to do some more laps. I was asked to do a promotional photograph at Ballaugh Bridge. I obliged them by zipping across on the GT550 about three feet in the air.

I spent as much time as possible, both day and night, lapping the course, remembering the things Wally had been impressing upon me ... 'Don't concentrate entirely on the road in front but work on situational awareness — that's how to learn where the track goes. Once that's done and you feel you know the way around, then and only then start looking at the finer points ...'

When I got back to London I told Ross what I had seen and done and he reiterated those same words I would hear over and over: 'Treat it like a high-speed tour and you'll be all right.'

BRANDS HATCH, 27 MAY 1979

'Six hundred quid start money!' I said to Ross, 'Hell, that'll pay for the hotel and maybe a tyre or two plus a few pints.'

Ross looked at me and giggled. 'Keep the wheelies up and we won't have to worry about front tyres for a while — and what's more there's another £600 for the post-TT at Mallory if we do it. Now get out there, Croz, and do some practice.'

I fired up the bike and went looking for the gate to get access to the track. I lifted up my UV-cracked visor with my right thumb. 'Which way does the track go and what's the lap record?' I called out over the noise of the valve gear rattling and clanging between my legs. The flag marshal's eyebrows raised in disbelief. I could see him muttering, 'And who the hell do you think you are — Mike Hailwood?' I laughed and roared off down the track.

I knew Ross had been talking to Chris Lowe, the promoter for both the Brands Hatch and Mallory circuits. I just can't imagine what Ross had said to Chris to get money from him for us to race at Brands — or both events, for that matter. I'd heard through the grapevine he was a difficult person to negotiate with but he had a job to do and we knew it wasn't going to be easy. It still felt quite strange to me that organizers paid money for riders to turn up, when in all my previous racing I'd had to pay entry fees to the organizers. Ross reminded me that this is how it was done over here and unless we were paid we would not race. And more importantly, once we accepted a small amount of start money then it became a benchmark for future negotiations.

We had originally planned to do only two races but we could renegotiate our terms if we elected to stay for Mallory. 'Old Rosko, you cunning dog,' I thought. 'Eighteen hundred quid in the bag once the races have been completed, and there's prize money too.' When you looked at it that way, any prize money would be a bonus, or beer money I would call it.

Mamoru Moriwaki had generously sent two bikes for us to use, and a Japanese mechanic to look after them. I had stopped off in Japan to do a few laps of testing on his new TTF1 machine and although it was really good I still thought the old 8 Hour bike with its upright riding style would work better for me, particularly on shorter circuits. The testing at Suzuka must have been successful because the Japanese *Auto-By* magazine carried 20 images of me in just one issue. Originally, we had planned to bring only the TTF1 bike but I was glad he had sent both bikes. We planned to run them both in practice so I could choose the best one for the race.

The old 8 Hour bike looked and was a bit worn out but it created a lot of interest in the paddock as it leaned precariously on a nail box. Battle-scars from previous races showed by the way the tank, cowling and paintwork were all scratched, chipped and dented. This bike was by true definition an Australian superbike and was well suited for scratching around short circuits. We couldn't have cared less what people thought of our bike's rugged looks; sure it lacked that glamorous styling but it was fully functional and it was really a fun beast to ride.

On the grid it was a different matter because it stuck out like a dog's balls as I lined up for the first Forward Trust/Motorcycle Weekly F1TT race. I had already tried the F1 bike and tossed it away going into Paddock Bend, probably because of a cold tyre. There was no damage but we decided to park it up for the TT. While I felt totally comfortable aboard the Moriwaki superbike, there were a lot of people thinking it was not really the type of bike to compete head-on against the Honda factory with their very special purpose-built Formula One bikes.

The start of the race was hectic and I was a little way back but gradually reeled in Ron Haslam on his factory Honda. Coming out of Druids Bend I picked up a wisp of smoke and realized Ron had missed a gear. I surged past him but he regained the lead a lap or so later and I ended up running second, scoring 12 valuable points. While the race wasn't full of superstars, there was enough talent out there and I had created enough interest to make it exciting. The sight of my blue and yellow standard-looking Moriwaki Kawasaki Z1 with its 'sit-up-and-beg' high handlebars created a lot of attention. As a consequence of my unexpected second placing, I had apparently surprised the fans and the establishment and, if the truth be known, probably myself too. It was a pity I was hampered with a sticky throttle but I did enough to make people notice. A few began questioning how much of the performance could be credited to the bike or the rider.

The British public had no idea of my history but they soon began referring to my bike as the 'Sit-up-and-beg Moriwaki'. I had already ridden it to a creditable third place at the Suzuka 8 Hour endurance race in Japan the year before and I knew it was quick and had some advantages over other bikes. The bike stood out, but for a good reason. I dared to be different and I think my timing was right for the British public who were looking for something to spice up the TTF1 series, which on paper looked destined to become a Honda benefit.

Though the old girl had started life as a Z1B, little remained after its chassis was discarded and a new one built by Moriwaki using lightweight tubing with various strengthenings around the steering head, down-tubes and swing-arm pivot areas. The steering geometry and triple clamp off-sets were changed slightly to assist in steering, which provided a very stable platform. The Moriwaki 998 cc engine produced close to 125 hp.

The TTF1 rules at the time meant we were stuck with standard

Mikuni 28 mm carburettors but in Open class races I could change to the 31 mm smooth-bore Keihin race carburettors. It would give me a few extra horsepower and using the longer air funnels it produced strong torque and was easy to ride, providing of course that it was jetted correctly. There was no benefit to be gained by revving it past 9300 rpm, other than to hold or avoid a gear change. If you missed a gear, though, it was quite easy to clip a valve.

The cylinder head was ported and flow-checked. Big valves were used with 6.6 mm valve stems. Z650 upside-down valve buckets and lightweight shims were also used. The cams were Moriwaki special and matched perfectly with the lightweight thin-wall steel 4-into-1 exhaust system. It had a total-loss ignition but that did mean carrying a fully charged battery. A small cowling provided some wind protection and limited aerodynamics for those high-speed circuits and the high handlebars gave an incredible amount of control at slower speeds. The bike was certainly different, I was having fun and the crowds were enjoying my performances.

'Hey Croz!' I heard the voice of Bob Aldridge, whose cheerful mole-covered face I remembered from Auckland a few years ago. I wasn't aware he had settled back in the UK.

'Croz, it's bloody good to see you mate,' he said in his South African accent. I told him we were here just for Brands Hatch, the Isle of Man and Mallory Park, then we were going home. I explained that we hadn't planned to stay long but things were changing so rapidly I might be in need of a base to work from if we stayed. Being the typically generous person he was, Bob gave me instructions on where the key to his flat was kept in Surbiton. I was told to make ourselves at home; he said we didn't have to pay a thing. Bob's flatmates co-incidentally turned out to be Mick Smith from Australia and Dozy Ballington. Most likely Mick and Dozy weren't told of Bob's generous offer until Brenda and I arrived a few days later to plunder their sacred beer fridge.

Their flat was above a Ford dealership, right up against a railway line. Our address was 'The Mews', a term I'd never heard of before. More importantly, it was directly opposite a pub.

ISLE OF MAN TOURIST TROPHY MILLENNIUM, 2 JUNE 1979

We picked up an additional Japanese mechanic from the airport and drove our van up to meet the Manx ferry at Liverpool. On arrival at Douglas we drove straight up to the start line. It was my turn to explain the circuit to our two Japanese mechanics, and Rosko and Brenda. I had a captive audience and gave them a commentary on what I'd heard last time I was here. Within a mile Brenda said that it looked awfully dangerous. It may have coincided with a sudden lurch of the van.

'This is the bottom of Bray Hill,' I called out. 'The bike will bottom out here on the suspension.' Our Japanese mechanics looked at me in amazement.

'Ah soo, desu ka!' Sato replied.

'Yeah it's known to have broken a few frames all right,' Rosko said. He continued giving us a running commentary about his terrible experience last time he was here when they tried a mass start. 'They won't do that in hurry again,' he sniggered.

I probably didn't want to think about it, but as we passed the area called Snugborough where his accident had happened I couldn't help but reflect on the fact he was one lucky man to be alive.

I did a lap and then went and found our digs. I left Brenda and the Japanese there and returned to the start line. The track looked much better prepared than when I was here a week earlier. I ran into Charlie Williams, who without hesitation took me out for a lap. He told me what the dangers were and what to look out for. I was a sponge for knowledge. It had been a dream of mine for such a long time to ride the TT and here I was being guided around by probably the best TT rider in the world. Charlie wasn't trying to frighten me; he was just pointing out as many items of interest to give me an appreciation of the circuit. I was a willing listener. We had met during the New Zealand Marlboro Series and he remembered my performances on the big Kawasaki. Charlie made it clear to me that respect for the circuit was paramount.

That didn't mean I couldn't have some fun, though, and I ended up with Dennis Ireland and Graeme McGregor in a car that I happened to be driving. We went out to the airport to pick up Vaughn Coburn. Eager to show Vaughn around the circuit, I threw his bags in the back and away we went.

As there was no speed limit on the course, I was able to give the rental car a fairly demanding test drive. After the Glen Helen section it winds up a bit and with Vaughn getting a bit green around the gills I started down the Cronk y Voddy Straight. It's long and fast with a long downhill slight right-hand kink then a medium left, then a short straight to a special section called 'the Hole in Wall'.

If you'd not been round the course before, one look at the end of the straight tells you it's a dead-end road finishing straight into a huge stone wall. Vaughn had his feet up on the dashboard and his eyes were as big as dinner plates as we approached the wall at about 130 kph. His mouth dropped open even further when he realized I was not going to back off. As the wall loomed up he was suddenly speechless for the first time. Without a word I flicked the car left then right without backing off as we negotiated the high-speed chicane. The bushes on the left side obscured the road veering off at an angle. He was not amused but we all chuckled at Vaughn, knowing the boot was now on the other foot for a change.

I collared Alex George the next day and asked him to accompany me for a lap. Although the stories were similar, Alex was a little more feral in his description. We went around looking at the circuit from his perspective. 'Matee, be extra careful through this section or you'll be going home in a box,' he said in his Scottish accent. He had my undivided attention from there on.

'Oh shit Croz! Don't do anything silly here, you'll be meeting your maker if you do.' He was not kidding as he pointed to the rocky wall.

'OK Alex, I understand it can bite so I'll be extra careful,' I said.

'Nay it won't bite ya Croz, it'll fucking well kill ya, believe me!'

Both Alex and Charlie provided me with the most valuable asset you can take on board at the TT: I had been told to listen, learn and respect the circuit. This year marked the celebration of 1000 years of the Tynwald or Manx Parliament — the millennium year — but I had no idea about that kind of stuff. I made a note to find out about it because I figured there had to be more to the Isle of Man than just the TT races.

We had hired a house near Governor's Bridge where Moriwaki and his boys could work on the bike. Mamoru Moriwaki had arrived from Japan only a few days before and he spent some time refreshing the spare engine, working in the single-car garage. Straight off the plane from Japan, they couldn't deal with the English food. A pot of rice simmered away on a small gas burner in the garage. He had brought with him some spares and a new cylinder head so we could build a fresh engine for the race. Inside the packaging he had stashed packets of Japanese noodle soup and rice crackers.

Moriwaki Japan was not a rich company and the air tickets were expensive. Without an international racing budget to draw from, he had to use the Soviet airline Aeroflot from Narita via Moscow to London to save a few yen. He told us about his flight. The hostesses aboard the plane were all stone-faced and ugly with fat legs. He sat opposite one flight attendant on take-off and although her two inner thighs were touching, her feet and knees were still wide apart. I suggested she was there to manually kick-start the jet engines in case they didn't fire up normally. Early in the flight everyone moved up near the front of the aircraft, as close to the cockpit door as they could. He reckoned the cockpit was the only area in the plane that was heated.

Practice was a series of laps just to get used to the sustained high speeds. I found the section from the start to Ballacraine the quickest and all my pre-practice tension had gradually eased by the time I got there. I was given a hi-vis orange vest to wear, signalling to all other riders that I was a newcomer and to be cautious when overtaking me. This had an amazing effect, because I was inundated by well-wishers pointing out where I was going wrong. I took in what I needed and discarded the rest. I listened, learned and the respect came automatically.

We struck a small problem with grounding out the cowling on some sections but during all the practice sessions I had only one frightening moment. When I came around Kate's Cottage on the last practice lap, the left handlebar broke clean off in my hand. I was left holding a clip-on with the clutch lever and cable still attached. It was rather difficult steering it back to the pit area one-handed. Within minutes Mamoru had the clip-on re-welded, this time with strengthening on both sides.

I was tense and excited as I pushed the Moriwaki bike to the line for my first TT start. I had lots of riders ahead of me. Sitting astride the bike and waiting with my visor up, I noticed a familiar face. It was 'Skins' Scanlon from back home. His reputation and name had been built on his multiple crashes on production bikes. Every time he crashed, about a metre of skin would be stripped off his body, leaving him with multiple scabs and bleeding gravel rash. There has probably never been anyone in the history of motorcycle racing who has lost as much skin as 'Skins' Scanlon.

'Hey Croz, good to see ya mate!' He meant it too.

With no time to talk, I indicated he should drop by after the race.

'Hey, you be careful out there, Croz, you could easily kill yourself,' he said before giving me a big smile and the thumbs-up sign. I glanced again at my friend, remembering the last time I had seen him, covered in bandages from head to foot after he had crashed his

RD350 in a road accident while wearing shorts, thongs, a T-shirt and no helmet.

'Gee, thanks for reminding me Skins,' I said under my breath before pulling my visor down and moving to take up my starting position. Once under way you feel quite lonely out on the road, as you leave behind a start line full of well-wishers and hordes of riders and their mechanics all racing around putting final touches to their bikes.

On the first lap I missed a few tip-in points and ran wide a couple of times. By slowing down and riding more smoothly I got to grips with the circuit and recorded a lap speed of 109 mph. It turned out to be the second-fastest time by a newcomer, behind Pat Hennen.

There was quite a contingent of Australians gathered at the TT, many for the first time. The calibre of riding was outstanding, with brilliant performances from Graeme McGregor and Jeff Sayle in the Junior TT. While McGregor came in second, Sayle ran short of fuel, just making it over the line in fifth. Even Peter Campbell had made the journey across with Dick Goodwin and ran a strong seventh and eighth place in the two sidecar races. Peter was faced with a chassis failure during practice and had to cut up one of his chrome moly crutches to strengthen that part of the frame. Peter suffered polio as child, resulting in crippling deformities to his legs.

The Classic race was different and after fitting a set of 31 mm smooth-bore carburettors, I thought it might work quite well for me. However, it holed a piston up on the mountain and I managed to coast back down to the Creg pub where an on-duty policeman bought me a pint. I learnt two things that day: always break down near a pub and take a few pence in your suit just in case a bobby isn't there to shout.

I wasn't expecting miracles in my first TT year but I was pleasantly surprised. It would take a few more years accumulating experience before I could possibly win a TT. It was a fulfilling experience and I was glad to have finally ridden on the world's greatest true road race circuit.

Apparently, my ride on the Moriwaki bike was impressive enough to get me noticed. I had just run second to Ron Haslam at Brands and shown some style and flair that the British public had not seen before. I had more to give and looked forward to my next race at Mallory Park. The press ran some nice stories about Moriwaki and, with lots of pictures of me, we got our share of coverage. I did heaps of interviews, each reporter trying to find out where I had come from and details of my racing history to date but in the hard light of it, I had just arrived unannounced and put a couple of good performances together. I was seen as a fresh face with potential to liven up a TTF1 series that might otherwise have been just drifting along.

MALLORY PARK, 10 JUNE 1979

'Looks as if it's got bugger-all corners on this track, Rosko,' I said as I craned my neck to get a better view.

'Croz, it's a loop around the pond over there, down the back straight and around there and back again onto the front straight. That's it — how simple can it be?' We had parked the van at the hairpin gate, champing at the bit to get in and have a look around.

'Gates won't open till 8.30,' we were informed by a grumpy unshaven old man. He wore a grubby Belstaff jacket, which reminded me that I should look for my jacket. It was misty and quite cold. Ross was wearing his yellow NGK jacket and looked warm and toasty. As we stood behind the fence looking over at the track, I was casually checking its surface and noticing hundreds of black marks on the entrance to the hairpin. Countless cars and bikes over many years had left their indelible marks on the track. This was evidence of an imbalance in brake bias or just a plain old-fashioned cock-up under brakes; more brain fade than brake fade.

The Belstaff-jacket man opened the gate and a dozen little vans and the odd caravan trundled in to establish a good spot for the weekend. I soon began to recognize some of the familiar names:

Potter, Sheene, Marshall, Haslam, Grant, George, Williams, Woods.

By the time I'd done a few laps of this circuit in the first practice session, I discovered it wasn't as simple as Ross had made it out to be. You needed a lot of time on brakes and the big right-hander at the end of the straight goes on forever, so I decided it might not be about horsepower after all. This was all about short circuit scratching and I was learning that you need to be forceful and decisive. By the time the TTF1 race started I had been carved up, chopped off, ridden into and around and almost over by any number of competitors. I soon learnt that I had to be just as hard, up the inside at the hairpin and deep under brakes going into Gerard's. Devil's Elbow required a couple of deep breaths before going quickly through it, but it paid off with a good turn of speed down the straight.

The response from the crowd when I went out on my Moriwaki bike was amazing. The sight of my blue and yellow monster howling around Mallory Park at speed with me flapping from the handlebars was one thing, but dicing with the likes of Grant, Haslam, Williams and Rutter on a production bike only added to the excitement. The crowd warmed to me because I dared to be different and people love the underdog. It was a pity that the gearbox broke on the first lap and I had to pull in with a DNF.

Rosko had been busy, 'working on a few deals,' he said. By the end of race day at Mallory Park he had sold me off to the Donington and Snetterton promoters. It looked like it would be some time yet before I would be heading back Down Under.

DONINGTON, 8 JULY 1979

I might have been getting ready for Donington but Ross had disappeared. He was crucial to organizing everything for me — mentoring and planning was his bag. The week before, Moriwaki and Ross had talked about leaving the bike in the UK to contest more races. I was keen and Mamoru even offered to bring another mechanic

The perfect way to unwind from racing. After all, it had been a long day at the office! - *Croz Archive*

The little A7 Kawasaki 350 twin gave me an insight into racing and, despite its age, it performed really well. - *Croz Archive*

Cocking about on the ill-fated triple-cylinder S3, a time-wasting experiment. - *Croz Archive*

With its very narrow power-band, riding this 1970 model Kawasaki H1R-A was certainly exciting — real hand-on-the-clutch stuff. - *John Liddle*

Eric Bone and a very young Croz at Pukekohe for the One Hour race. We won and it was Eric's shout! - *Dennis Burley*

The rough old Kawasaki 750 H2 showing scuff marks along the mufflers after I decided to part company with it at speed during the Marlboro Series at Gracefield. - *Croz Archive*

A few laps on a Suzuki TR500 frightened the hell out of me — boy, was it quick! - *Croz Archive*

More brake adjustments on our H2 during the Castrol 6 Hour, 1973. - *Croz Archive*

Following Ginger Molloy aboard his Z1 900 during the Castrol 6 Hour, 1974. - *Bob Stevenson*

A defining moment, when at last I managed to beat Eric at a Hamilton road race. - *Croz Archive*

Leading the pack at Gracefield during the Marlboro Series, 1977. - *Croz Archive*

Finally, a trophy that had a real diamond set into it. You needed a magnifying glass to see it but it was there, honest! - *Croz Archive*

It looked like a production bike and handled like a rollerskate in a gravel pit. I had to hang on tight when street racing. - *Croz Archive*

My little stable of Kawasaki racers — not exactly a works team but fun nevertheless.
- *Dennis Burley*

The cowling looked a little odd. It went better without it on. - *Shigeo Kibiki*

Move over, I'm coming through! Production racing Aussie-style during the 6 Hour race, 1977.
- *Derek Hanbidge, www.Deejay51.com*

Don't you just love those railway crossings, straw bales and exposed concrete kerbing? Street racing at Wanganui in New Zealand, 1977. - *Croz Archive*

Corky and Charlie's trusty Z1B 900 took me to many production wins. Here we are at Bathurst enjoying a gallop on it. - *Croz Archive*

The team at Moriwaki Japan enjoying a day off after our third place in 1978. - *Croz Archive*

Sato-san and Namiko Moriwaki share a joke with me during an 8 Hour training session, 1978. - *Croz Archive*

Our 24-hour Kawasaki race machine in action at Paul Ricard. We were a bit behind the eight-ball from the start and never really caught up. I wonder why? - *Shigeo Kibiki*

It's fairly hard on the equipment when racing over railway lines, especially in the wet! - *Greg McBean*

The crowds may have loved my wheelie displays but truth was it saved tyre wear. - *Croz Archive*

The CBX1000 was wide enough to act as a mobile chicane. Try to pass me if you dare! - *Greg McBean*

One of the sweetest-riding street bikes I have ever raced. The CBX1000 proved quick and light but a dose of bad fuel took us to the showers early. Seen here is Ralph Hannan, Croz, Tony Hatton and George Pyne from Honda Australia. - *Derek Hanbidge, www.Deejay51.com*

The Australian Grand Prix at Bathurst was one of the best races ever. John Woodley (35), Ron Boulden (59) and I (4) battled the entire distance. - *Greg McBean*

The world's best four-stroke tuner in his day: Hideo (Pops) Yoshimura. - *Croz Archive*

Having fun entertaining the crowd … until the clerk of the course got a bit tetchy and threatened me with exclusion. Hee hee! - *Croz Archive*

Footloose and fancy free at Bathurst. Showing off with a huge lead, I was having fun! - *Greg McBean*

Wet and wild was OK but the straights at Bathurst were too long and the GP bikes were just too fast down the straight.
- *Croz Archive*

The Z1R Superbike of Ross Hannan was streets ahead of anyone for power. That was handy for me! - *Darryl Flack*

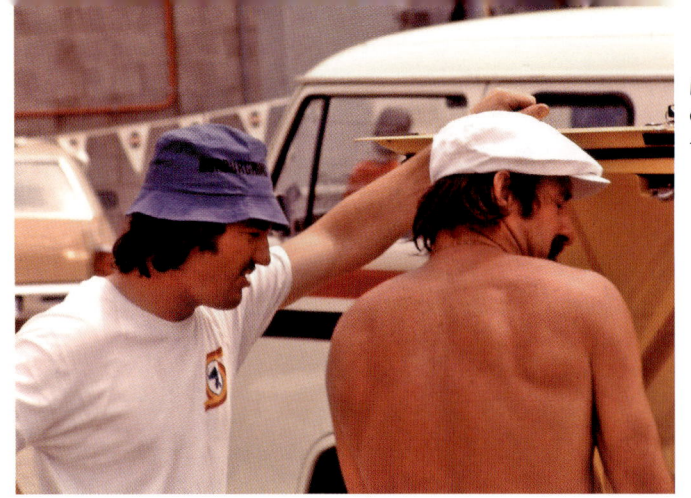

Mike Hailwood and I in discussions at Adelaide, 1978.
- Croz Archive

Team Kawasaki Australia rider Rick Perry and I on our KR750's getting ready to go out at Bathurst. - Croz Archive

I needed a Japanese phrase-book to communicate with my co-rider, Kiyohara-san.
- Derek Hanbidge, www.Deejay51.com

Discussing race tactics before the 1979 6 Hour with Kawasaki factory test rider, Kiyohara.
- Derek Hanbidge, www.Deejay51.com

Ross Hannan and I asking Charlie Williams which way the track goes and what the lap record is.
- MCN UK Bauer Media, www.actionlibrary.com

The Ulster Grand Prix, on a street bike? - *Croz Archive*

It might not look pretty but it went like a scalded cat. - *Croz Archive*

A cold and miserable Ulster day as I get ready to go out into the murk. - *Croz Archive*

The Moriwaki Kawasaki had style, with its high bars and sit-up-and-beg appearance. - *MCN UK Bauer Media, www.actionlibrary.com*

Plagued with brake problems, I lost valuable time as the brake rotors buckled with the heat and lost effectiveness. - *Croz Archive*

It was a bit tatty and used-looking but very effective on short circuits because of its handling qualities. - *Croz Archive*

First stop on arrival in London — a pub! - *Croz Archive*

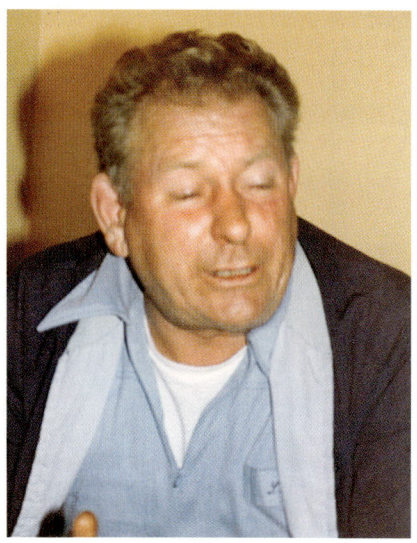

Aussie wharf worker Wally could talk without moving his lips and snore like a draught horse, as we found out in 1979 at the Ulster Grand Prix. - *Croz Archive*

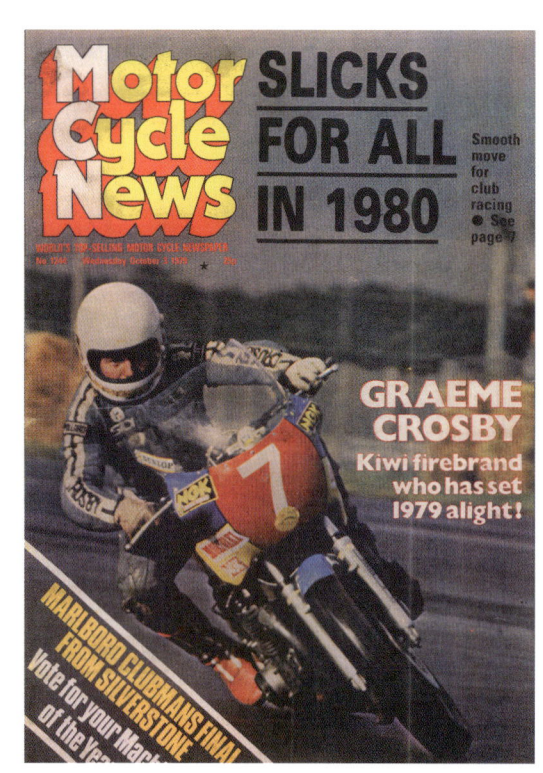

Captured on film, I nearly lost it but regained the front end in the wet. It was a close call. - *MCN UK Bauer Media, www.actionlibrary.com*

Pushing the Moriwaki Z1 through the crowd to find space to start the old girl. - *Jim Hughes*

On the way to my first world championship TTF1 title at the Ulster GP, 1980. - *Croz Archive*

The Suzuki XR34 500 cc Grand Prix racer. - *Vic Barnes*

Marco, Randy and myself. Our new Grand Prix team meet up during testing at Suzuki's Ryuyo testing circuit in Hamamatsu, Japan, 1980. - *Croz Archive*

Perks of the trade, working with fabulous models in a photo shoot with photographer Vic Barnes. Check out the chassis. - *Vic Barnes*

Here I am taking the piss out of the Brits by trying to be a bit English. Tea, vicar? - *Vic Barnes*

Well, I had to have a go at looking like some famous superstar. However, I did manage to keep most of my clothes on during the 1980 Suzuki race team PR shoot! - *Vic Barnes*

The Aussies never miss a trick when it comes to glamorous babes and bikes. *Revs* magazine carried this nice shot after I won the Daytona Superbike race in 1980. - *Revs magazine (Australia)*

over to give Kensai Sato a break. It wasn't difficult mechanically to look after the bike, but it required regular checking of the valve gear which was particularly sensitive.

I didn't mind staying on for more races because nothing was happening back home and I was enjoying it here. On the other hand, Brenda decided that following me around the place was not that exciting and she wanted to return to work in Sydney.

Ralph was busy on the phone trying to locate Ross, calling home and everywhere he thought he might be. We knew he'd gone to Italy to see his brother-in-law Terry, who had helped us at Le Mans with the Ferrari fuel. Terry confirmed Ross had been there but was on his way back to the UK. It was unusual not to hear from him, as it had been a week.

Meanwhile, the Sherpa van Bob had lent us needed to go back to its owner and I asked Bob to get the invoice so we could pay the rental charges.

'How much?! Bloody hell, I don't want to *buy* the fucking thing, Bob!' He was visibly upset. He had led us to believe it was going to be a lot cheaper. I looked at the bill again and noticed it covered only the first couple of weeks through to Mallory. He had been sitting on it for more than a month.

'Bob, if we'd known what the daily rate was I could have found something else cheaper.'

'Leave it with me boys, I'll sort it out. Let's go over the road for a drink.' This was Bob under pressure. Bob was good at striking up conversations with young ladies and had a fetish for big-bosomed women. Mick, Dozy and I were gathered at the bar while Bob worked his magic on this pretty dark-haired local girl who would have weighed at least 105 kg. About half an hour later we noticed Bob had gone and there was no sign of the girl. Good old Bob, we all commented, he's finally been able to pull one after all this time. He had been unlucky in love, so perhaps this might be his night. We had thought he was all talk and no action but it appeared he had come up trumps at last.

We finished our last drinks and headed for the door, across the road and into the alleyway that led to the back door of our flat. Bob was upstairs, armed with a small flash camera and busy taking pictures of this rather buxom woman who by now had stripped to the waist. She was obviously enjoying all the attention being lavished on her until someone pointed out that the camera had no film in it.

Bob kept saying, 'Guys, please! It's only minor details — I've never put a roll of film through this camera, but it does work.' We all laughed as she hurriedly gathered up her big floral blouse and scurried away down the main street.

A few nights later I asked Bob about the hire van. 'I think I can lose it in the system, Croz, so don't worry, just keep driving it. She'll be right, I'll sort it, don't give it a second thought.' I was getting worried after listening to him assuring me he would sort out this 'minor detail'.

The Donington circuit was quite new and a real departure from the style of circuits England had become accustomed to. This was a great example of a new-start project being driven by Tom Wheatcroft. It was built with passion and pride and as competitors we were made to feel really welcome.

The TTF1 race again became predictable with another close race between Haslam, Grant, Marshall, Moyce, Rutter and me, complete with my Moriwaki 'sit-up-and-beg' Kawasaki. A good second place ahead of Mick Grant on the works Honda made more heads turn.

SNETTERTON, 15 JULY 1979

A week later, and still with no word from Ross, we were getting concerned. His wife Carmen said she hadn't heard from him either. We packed up the old Sherpa van again and headed out of London for Norfolk. The circuit was about 10 miles from Thetford. I was thinking of the war and how Britain came so close to losing it all. The surrounding countryside was just like you would expect to see in a war film and you could imagine aircraft littering the skies as dogfights played out. I looked at the passing traffic and realized just how far we had already come technologically.

I thought the circuit was cool, particularly because it was built on an old wartime fighter base. The straights used the old runways and taxiways became part of the circuit.

Once again I scored another second place behind Ron Haslam. I wasn't too far down on top speed but while the bike was still performing well, it was getting time for another overhaul. I recorded the fastest lap of the race at just over 103 mph. Peter Clifford, editor of the *Motocourse* annual, asked to do a few laps on the Moriwaki so he could write a race report for a magazine. He probably didn't know what hit him when he threw his leg over the bike for the first time. He didn't look all that comfortable while riding around. His straight-back style needed to change to a more hang-out method to better exploit the handling characteristics. I was intrigued to find out what he really thought, so I made a note to keep an eye out for the report. We left Snetterton Sunday night for London with another 12 points in the bag for the championship.

I had a busy schedule to look forward to over the next few weeks. Tomorrow I would board a plane for Japan and then get myself down to Suzuka for the 8 Hour. I'd been partnered with an unknown Japanese rider. Then I'd head back to Sydney for the NSW and Australian championship race at Oran Park on the KR750. Then another long flight back to the UK for Silverstone. All this in the space of just three weeks.

10

MORIWAKI KAWASAKI AND THE 'SIT UP AND BEG', 1979

SUZUKA 8 HOUR, 29 JULY 1979

Tokyo was experiencing a torrential downpour when I arrived. The rainy season was due to finish and I hoped it would be gone by race day. By the time I boarded the bullet train I was ready to relax for the rest of the journey to Nagoya. I was carrying only a small bag with my Bel-Ray leathers, a helmet and some light clothes.

Recalling how hot it was last year, I needed only shorts, a T-shirt and sunglasses. I arrived at the Moriwaki factory and settled into the special guest room above the workshop. It was close to the Moriwaki family home, so I had to be quiet coming and going in the early hours when everyone thought I was asleep. Our bike was being prepared and I was really impressed when I saw it.

I dropped in to Mama's Bar and left late after enjoying a few handles of Kirin. I thought of Mama's Bar as being my after-dark Japanese office. The next day I was introduced to Akitaka Tomie, my co-rider for this year's event. He came highly recommended so I would have to wait and see how he went in practice. It was a big event and I hoped he wouldn't get carried away with the occasion and do something silly. Although we struggled to communicate, I knew he would do the job well.

In qualifying I went out and set a time that was unbeaten, taking pole position. My time of 2:17.3 was almost two seconds quicker than the factory Kawasakis in second position and nearly four seconds faster than Tony Hatton and Mick Cole on their Honda RCB. Hatto was running around complaining that he couldn't get tyres and his bike was slow.

It wasn't long before he came sniffing around our pit after we pulled out with an oil leak on the 52nd lap. He was after a rear tyre that we had not needed, so we gave it to Tony who went on to win on his works Honda.

It was a disappointing show this year but Moriwaki would use the information gathered to good effect and be back next year. The race was getting bigger each year, with crowds of 86,000 this time. By the time I got back to the Moriwaki factory I felt as if I had signed a thousand T-shirts. It was good money for Moriwaki and I made sure that if I wasn't riding, I was at least signing shirts in the Moriwaki PR booth.

By the Monday morning I was back on the train heading for Narita. This time my flight was going south to Sydney for the Australian titles race at Oran Park.

ORAN PARK, 5 AUGUST 1979

The contract I had with Kawasaki Australia was not actually as a TKA member but more as a privateer receiving a factory bike out the back door via its Australian distributor. I had a few races to do to fulfil my contract with Kawasaki. Oran Park was one of those, and luckily it fitted smack-bang between Suzuka and the Silverstone Grand Prix where I was scheduled to compete in the TTF1 support race.

I needed to concentrate on the NSW round of the championship. Garry Ellison (Frizz) had the KR prepared and ready to go when I arrived. I had some unfinished business with Ron Boulden because of his last-lap win at Bathurst and I knew the KR was pretty damn good around Oran Park. I got my revenge. There were no long straights for him to zoom past me and I beat him fair and square along with Greg Pretty, who had been on a winning streak until then.

Although it was great to be back catching up with my friends again, I sensed I was moving on in my own life. Perhaps it was the realization my mates were content to be doing the same old things, day in and day out. By contrast, my life had been on the go since well before I'd arrived in Sydney back in 1976. I'd been bouncing and bumping along an undefined road that from time to time had thrown up opportunities. If it looked good and seemed right at the time, bugger it, I would just do it. I had no idea where this road was going to take me, but one thing for sure was that I loved the lifestyle. Not having a family or physical base of any substance also meant not having lots of assets either and the true measure of where I was in life was the contents of my packed suitcases.

Once again I was back on the plane to the UK and looking forward to that Heathrow immigration man who always seemed to be waiting to process me. He was a Sikh, complete with his 'turbine' as I called it. He looked resplendent with his traditional waxed moustache and his Indian accent. 'Welcome to the United Kingdom my friend.'

SILVERSTONE, 12 AUGUST 1979

To say I was feeling jaded by the time I arrived in London would be an understatement. The round trip to Japan and Australia had knocked me. With nothing to do but sit there twiddling my thumbs for eight or more hours at a time, I would walk around the cabin and talk to the crew. A full bottle of chardonnay followed by a couple of liqueurs usually put me to sleep for a couple of hours but I always woke up feeling lousy. The combination of alcohol, low humidity and cabin pressure makes you dehydrate rapidly. I decided to accept the headaches and treat my jet lag as an occupational hazard.

We still had no word from Ross other than a whisper that he had been locked up in the Bastille for some transgression. It sounded strange but, with Ross, anything was possible.

Jumping back on the Moriwaki bike again after riding the F1 machine at Suzuka and the KR750 at Oran Park was like being reunited with an old girlfriend. Throwing a leg over it was just not the same any more — it lacked a bit of zest and didn't quite feel right. It felt tired and loose and in need of a lift, but it had to do for now because we didn't have a new set of pistons or a new complete head. That was due soon.

I thought Silverstone would be a difficult track. It was open and fast and as I didn't have a fairing to hide behind, I guessed I'd be at a disadvantage speedwise. In typical English weather conditions it was a damp practice when I nearly threw it away big-time. If ever there was a time when I should have gone down it was then. I was in a high-speed right-hand corner and felt the telltale unload of the grip on the front tyre and my handlebars began folding under. I was on the way down.

For some inexplicable reason I eased the bars back as if to lean further into the corner and it gripped again, but ever so slowly. I felt myself saying, 'Am I going? Yes I'm gone! — No I haven't! Yes ... no,' and finally it gripped long enough for me to regain complete control. *Motorcycle News* carried a full-colour front page photograph showing me with front wheel all crossed up.

I was right about the lack of speed. However, I tried as hard as I could but didn't quite have enough horsepower to catch Alex George, who took line honours with me second. With another 12 points, I was beginning to think I might be the bridesmaid and never the bride.

ULSTER GRAND PRIX, 18 AUGUST 1979

I agreed to let Wally come to Northern Ireland with us in the van. He had been pestering me about tagging along to the Ulster Grand Prix ever since we first met up at Assen. He was no spring chicken but this was his first overseas trip from Melbourne. He was following his hero Neville Doyle, the man who looked after Gregg Hansford's European Grand Prix effort. Apparently, Wally just turned up out of the blue at Assen one day to watch the Dutch Grand Prix. Neville found him a pass and gave him a bed in the caravan awning. Gregg and Kenny Roberts were good friends and within a few days Wally was everyone's mate. He had saved enough money from his job as a dockworker to make the trip.

Arriving in Amsterdam, he got buses and trains and somehow got close to Assen. We couldn't figure out how he managed because when he spoke he didn't move his mouth at all. Every sentence he said needed repeating because he mumbled.

'Did you have any trouble getting here, Wally?' Gregg asked.

'Not really but hardly anyone understands English.'

'Most people over here speak English, Wally, so why did you have a problem?' Gregg asked.

'Mate, I asked the taxi driver at the train stop if he spoke English, he said yes! Lying bastard. I told him I wanted to go to Assen, but he finally said he couldn't understand me at all,' Wally complained.

'Wally, *no one* understands you. I don't even understand you most of the time — you have to open your mouth when you speak to be understood.' Gregg detected a small twitch of Wally's top lip. He got the message.

Kenny Roberts asked Wally if he would mind his motorhome on Saturday night while he went into the town for a meal. He left Wally in charge of the TV remote and told him if he wanted a beer to help himself. Later that night Kenny arrived back to find Wally asleep with remote in one hand and an empty beer bottle in the other. The TV was still blaring away and a huge pile of empty beer bottles surrounded him. He had emptied the fridge.

I thought it would be entertaining to have Wally with us. Kensai Sato would not worry about him tagging along. The Sherpa was loaded up with the bikes and off we went to Liverpool to catch the ferry to Belfast. It was getting dark when we docked and I was a little unnerved by the presence of police. The high wired fences around the police stations and evidence of civil unrest were plain to see. I did something that in hindsight was foolish. I turned into Falls Road in County Antrim for some unknown reason. I had heard of this road and how the Catholics and Protestants tossed bombs at each other and I was curious to have a look for myself. I drove about 80 metres down the road and stopped. It was too eerie for me, so we did a U-turn and hightailed it out of there.

We made it out of Belfast safely and were out on the country roads trying to locate a home-stay that had been arranged for us. We were suddenly flagged down by what looked like the British Army. This was completely foreign to me and when the soldier poked the barrel of his assault rifle almost up my nose, I almost wet myself. I could smell the cordite on his breath as he asked, 'Is this your van?'

'Yes,' I replied respectfully.

'What's in the back?' he asked.

'Two motorbikes and my mate Wally,' I said, beginning to shake.

'What are they and are you going through to Dundrod?'

I told him two F1 Kawasaki bikes and yes, to the Grand Prix. He withdrew his smelly gun barrel from under my nose and signalled for me to move on. 'Good luck', I heard him say.

We found our digs eventually and had a couple of whiskies courtesy of our host, then we headed to our bedrooms. Brenda and I had a bedroom next to Wally and it was a restless night. I'd never heard such a racket. We had to get up several times and turn him over to stop his snoring. After the last attempt he briefly awoke, let out a loud fart, rolled over and went back to sleep, snoring loudly again. Next morning he was given instructions to sleep in the garage on the workshop bench. Wally was so apologetic and embarrassed when we told him of his performance.

That night we were taken on a pub crawl. Hector Neil knew most of the publicans and I got a glimpse of what Northern Ireland was about. The pubs were required to close at a certain time, after which a squad car full of police drove around making sure the proprietors were obeying the law. However, the tom-toms worked well and while I was sitting at the bar in a pub, the phone rang and the owner answered. A minute later all the lights were out and we stood in the darkness in the kitchen. When the coast was clear, we went back to the bar and continued drinking.

When we got home, Wally immediately grabbed a few blankets and disappeared outside to the garage where he curled up on the workshop bench and slept.

'Is that Wally I can hear? Oh no! Bloody hell, he's in the garage and we can still hear him.' I got up out of bed to find my earplugs.

I got a shock the first time I went around the track, as it was extremely fast and quite narrow in places. It would suit my Moriwaki but Haslam's works Honda had the legs on my unfaired bike in the race. Tony Rutter rode a superb race on another Honda to finish second, with me tucked up his exhaust pipe for third. Fourth place at the TT and a third here was enough to put me third in the TTF1 world championship, though it was made up of only two rounds. During the race I did a couple of wheelies coming out of Leathemstown Corner and soon the crowd was egging me on and getting me to pull more wheelies. They must have thought I was a loose cannon but I had connected with them. The spectators really appreciated my style and the bike.

OULTON PARK, 27 AUGUST 1979

Living in London over the last few months had been fairly hectic and the social life was getting better by the week as we got to know the locals. Even Bob finally 'got lucky' and achieved that without his camera for a prop this time. Racing during the weekends and partying during the week was fun but the reports going back to Japan must have been telling another story. I must have been sailing fairly close to the wind and urgently needed to be pulled back under control. Judging by my off-track antics and fearing a meltdown in my private life, Moriwaki had decided to fly Brenda back to the UK in secret to provide that stabilizing influence they deemed necessary.

Out at Heathrow, on the pretence of picking up another Japanese mechanic, Mamoru and I stood waiting in Terminal 3 watching the travellers feed through the arrivals gate. I was expecting to see a Japanese man when I turned to Mamoru and casually pointed to a woman who looked a bit like Brenda. As she got closer I finally recognized her. I couldn't figure it out until Mamoru explained. Of course I was very pleased to see her and Mamoru deserves credit for helping me avert a disaster in my private life.

One morning the phone rang at the flat. It was Ralph with some news on Ross. It turned out that Ross had been staying at his wife's brother's place in Italy and had two appointments for Moriwaki in France. He had been working on one guy who was building some Kawasaki chassis and also another Frog who was building an endurance racer for Marty Lunde. They both wanted to buy a few Moriwaki engines.

Brother-in-law Terry had just got a Porsche 3-litre turbo and he offered it to Ross to take it to Paris, thinking it would be a great drive for him. He had booked into the Hotel California on Rue De Berri close to the Champs-Élysées. Apparently, the next day a guy sideswiped him. It was the other fellow's fault and — shock! horror! — he even had insurance. Ross called Terry, who told him to take it to the Porsche dealer and get a quote. The shit hit the fan at the dealership when they discovered the car might have been nicked. Ross told them he'd bought it from a guy in a bar. However, the Froggy cops arrived and they checked him thoroughly. Ross didn't have a police record anywhere, so they knew he hadn't nicked it as he wasn't even in the country at the time. One of the cops took him aside and said, 'I know you know a lot more than you are telling us, so if you let us know everything then you can go.' But Ross, being an old Newtown boy from Sydney, kept his mouth shut, saying nothing to anyone.

The law in France and most of Europe is that you are guilty until you prove your innocence. Ralph told us Ross might be there for five months while they investigated the situation. So that's where he was, in the Bastille eating croissants.

Oulton Park was a long drive from London for the eighth round of the TTF1 Championship. I had heard that Sheene was going to ride the Paul Dunstall Suzuki with a Yoshimura engine but I didn't expect him to go as well as he did. Haslam picked another 15 points, narrowly beating Barry, who promptly decided that he preferred not to ride 4-strokes at all. Mick Grant, Alex George and Stan Woods followed, with me in sixth. The old girl was suffering again from brake problems but at least I crept home for a few miserly points.

SCARBOROUGH, 9 SEPTEMBER 1979

Scarborough sounds like a nice place, I thought. Soon I found myself singing the famous tune of 'Scarborough Fair', which got irritating after a while as I only knew the first few words. I had heard differing opinions of Scarborough. It was tight and dangerous and Phil Haslam had been killed there in 1974. That's why his brother Ron refused to ride here. And then there was Barry Sheene who, along with Mick Grant, had been rumoured to be getting huge appearance money from the organizers. Mick I could understand, because he raced on dodgy circuits but at speeds he was comfortable with and what's more he made no noise about it. But Barry Sheene had been critical of many dangerous circuits in the past, particularly the Isle of Man TT. So it seemed rather hypocritical to me that here he was slipping and sliding his way around this dangerous course. It had to be the money, I decided.

I walked past Barry's pit area and saw Mick Smith, who motioned me over, asking me how I was doing. We started chatting and he told me that Barry had not yet signed a contract for next year with Suzuki, and although negotiations were ongoing it was not a done deal. In fact Suzuki was actively looking for replacement riders. 'Oh,' I said.

'Mate, we've put your name forward — they want someone to race the new Formula One bike and a 500,' Mick said, then added, 'If you look around, who is there that can do the job?' We talked about John Newbold and Roger Marshall and other English riders and Virginio Ferrari plus a bunch of Americans including Mike Baldwin, but it always came back to me, with what I had achieved and my association with Yoshimura. I was looking like a good bet.

I had hoped to hear from Ross because this was one time I could use his help. He would be great to bounce things off if this deal went any further. Mick was the first one to put a sensible spin on why I should be given a 500 cc works ride. I had experience on the 4-strokes and had created quite a storm this year by racing my Moriwaki and getting great publicity. I knew Pops Yoshimura and that would help my cause. I would race at the TT and the Ulster plus my performance on the KR750 hadn't gone astray. I began to put it all together and it made sense.

I had a few more races to do before the end of the year and I thought, wow! I had suddenly realized that I never planned for the future — it's not my style. I had been falling in and out of piles of shit for years now but had always come up smelling of roses. I might have the odd dream about racing Grand Prix bikes but I had now realized I was racing from one track to another with no long-term planning. In fact I had not even thought about next year. The idea of getting a factory ride for 1980 was just too much for me to contemplate. My mind was spinning, thinking of what it would be like. At least I was on Suzuki's shopping list of potential riders.

'Get your mind back on the job, Croz,' I told myself. I had a TTF1 race to do and this goat-track kind of suited the bike. It was bloody narrow and tight in some places. I even had to slip the clutch in first gear to get any drive out of the two tight hairpins. So it would be new clutch plates as well after the race, I supposed. The circuit was only two and a half miles around, but the braking was really hard. My front discs were already buckled and warped but luckily I was not getting any pad knock-back so I should still have brakes, even when they were glowing red hot.

The crowd at Scarborough was crazy and enthusiastic, so every time I did a wheelie the spectators stood out on the side of the track cheering and yelling. I played up to it a bit and the more I did it the more they lapped it up. Organizer Peter Hillaby had paid me £600 so he was getting his money's worth. I had heard a report that I was bringing in more than 3500 extra spectators and if that was correct then I must have been doing something right.

The race started and was pretty much over for me within six laps, but not before dicing with Roger and Mick in a frenzied fashion. My brakes were poked and had begun fading as the lever disappeared into the handlebar. I had far too many hairy moments for my own liking around this tight and narrow track, but trying to stop the old girl at the tight hairpins was another story. My front disc rotors heated up so badly they bent like a saucer, rendering them virtually useless. I had to take a third place and 10 points and remember that this track might require more respect in the future. But this was Roger Marshall's home turf and he pedalled his Honda around the track like a maniac. Without Ron Haslam in the race, Mick Grant picked up second, showing me just what a great rider he was.

The after-race function was one big party with Sheene and Mick Grant making an appearance. Up on stage the two were engaged in a conversation with the compere but the crowd all began chanting for me. 'We want Croz! We want Croz!' I must have made an impact. I knew being different was the answer.

CADWELL, 16 SEPTEMBER 1979

After such a successful Scarborough outing, especially with the crowd's response, I was now sure that whatever I was doing was actually working. I was 'out there' being different, I was having fun and I was getting some serious results. Looking at that combination, it wasn't hard to see how I was getting so much press. My story was fresh — I was the new kid on the block and those who took the time to dig deeper found more perhaps than they had expected. My previous racing history was slowly being unearthed or exposed to the public through interviews and newspaper articles that were interesting to the reader.

I possessed neither airs nor graces, owned no fast cars and there were no *Vogue* models at my side, nor was there a choreographed PR machine busy sweeping a pathway to success for me. What you see is what you get with me — feral and raw but honest. The choice of machinery and my carefree attitude to life gelled with fans. Rough as guts on the outside but skilled enough on the track to make it work.

I had made a note to get my front tooth fixed so I could at least smile without being embarrassed. I had it pulled out a year ago because I could not find the money for the dental repairs. However, now I might just be able to afford a bridge if I could win some more prize money. The plastic temporary denture I had with its single tooth attached to the end of it had been stood on, dropped in a pan of oil and had even gone missing for weeks on end one time before it turned up in the bottom of a valve shim box.

We drove up in the Sherpa to Cadwell Park. Bob still hadn't come clean about costs but we were getting to the end of the season. I thought Cadwell was a bit of a goat-track at first but that's probably quite strong coming from me. I'd ridden on some outrageous tracks but I just couldn't get it together around there. I was hoping I would be able to perform well enough that Charlie the organizer wouldn't renege on his promise of £500. Mick Grant and Alex George ran first and second on their Hondas, with me taking third ahead of Ron Haslam and Steve Manship.

Only one more race to go at Brands in that series and it would be all over for the year.

DONINGTON AND IMOLA AGV CUP, 23 and 30 SEPTEMBER 1979

The Italian Imola circuit organizers came up with a cunning plan to put on a race series, one that repeated the successful AGV Nations Cup of the previous year. This international event was designed to get five teams together, comprising the four major motorcycle racing countries — Britain, France, Italy, USA — and one further team to represent the rest of the world.

Split over three venues — Paul Ricard, Donington and Imola — it had attracted the interest of the elite Grand Prix stars. The format was team match-racing, giving the public a chance to see multi appearances in a series of short races. Surprisingly, I was asked to join the Rest of the World team for the Donington and Imola rounds, using the ex-Hansford KR750 I had ridden in Australia. I talked with Neville Doyle and he agreed, even arranging a 'Carnet de Passage' for the bike. This is an international shipping document listing every item to facilitate transiting through border control in various countries. As long as all the items were present and matched the list, it was signed by Customs at the entry point and no taxes or duty would be paid. Going out the same applied, so it was important to ensure you kept every item listed.

It was getting towards the end of the season and the team managers were finding it tough trying to get a good-quality team assembled. The Italians had Lucchinelli, Rossi, Uncini and Pelletier plus a few weaker riders; the French were headed up by Pons, Sarron, Fau and Estrosi. The USA team was also strong with Roberts, Mamola, Aldana, Cooley and Schlachter. Our Rest of the World team consisted of Hansford, Hartog, Van Dulmen, Sayle, Coulon, Dennis Ireland and me. The Brits turned up with probably the strongest team with Sheene, Parrish, Marshall, Potter, Haslam, George and Grant.

Frizz had been responsible for looking after the KR750 and he volunteered to escort the bike over from Sydney. Brenda and I drove to Heathrow and collected both Frizz and the KR750 and made our way up to the East Midlands. I had been allocated £500 start money for Donington but George Beale reckoned if he could do the negotiation on my behalf for the Imola round, he could get three times that amount.

A disappointingly small crowd turned out, possibly because of the early morning rain and that this type of event had not gained in popularity as it had in Italy. But racing started and those who attended witnessed some great tussles. It wasn't truly a team's race but more of a series of personal match-ups between competitive riders. Sheene and Roberts were the top billing. I even had my first match-up race with Gregg Hansford. He beat me in one race and I beat him in another but it was enough to get Neville and Frizz excited. Frizz was I think expecting to get some additional help from Neville in the form of a new cylinder or exhaust pipes to give our ageing KR750 a long overdue boost in power. It was quite the reverse, because our old KR750 was as quick or even quicker than Gregg's bike.

Frizz and Neville were deep in discussions about what main jet sizes each one was running. We had a considerably smaller main jet and Neville thought we were sailing too close to the wind, particularly with the poor fuel. Frizz bent down and plucked a bottle of illegal octane booster out of the spares box he'd got off Wes Cooley. Neville looked at it with a chuckle and, shortly after, a 20-litre tin of fuel appeared from somewhere for Dr Frizz to administer his medicinal fix. Neville swung by a little later, wondering if anyone had seen his tin of race fuel. We showed him where it was and off he trundled. As it wasn't an FIM event we bent the rules just a little.

I certainly didn't disgrace myself at Donington but in a strange way I was able to show those who were watching that not only did I have the ability to ride the Moriwaki Z1 but I was also equally at home aboard a proper racing bike, even if it was old.

It was shoulder to shoulder at the Red Gate pub, noisy and smoke-filled with pints of beer being sloshed about the place. I'd got the beers in and was making my way back through the crowd. I had been slapped on the back and my hand was sore from all the handshaking. 'Good on you, Croz, well done and I love that Moriwaki bike, how much power do you have?' was typical of the comments and questions. I always tried to answer them and make a joke, or just take the piss in a nice manner.

I had pushed my way past a few more of the crowd and found Frizz and Brenda. Apparently, a guy had made a pass at Brenda and was still having a go at her when I walked up. Seeing what was happening, I interrupted and said something polite, nice and quietly to him, like 'Fuck off, you big git.' He was quite drunk and took a step towards me in a threatening manner but his balance was completely gone and he stumbled. He fell backwards, dropping his pint all over a young girl and her boyfriend. The boyfriend stood up and within seconds a brawl had broken out. Punches were being thrown, along with bottles and pint glasses. I got the hell out of there as soon as I could.

I turned to Frizz on the way out and said, 'Did I cause all that?' He nodded as we walked away, leaving the fans to sort out the mess.

We shared transport with Wes Cooley and his mechanic for the trip down to Imola for the final round. Our KR750 was back to being slow again as we had no more octane booster and had to install fatter jets to preserve the engine. The whole day I would rather forget as I rode my heart out going backwards. Struggling around at the back of the field was not me. We talked to Neville about what we should be doing and were given some even bigger main jets to use. Hmm! Frizz and I looked sideways at each other at this gesture. I recalled what Jeff Sayle had been saying about Neville during a party we went to in Sydney earlier in the year.

'My brother Murray was always given second-rate equipment and Harry always got the good bits. If you think that's going to change you'd better think again, Neville looks after Harry all right so don't think you're anything special — you Kiwis are all the same.' Jeff was very critical of Neville. It could have been just sour grapes; I didn't know because I was not privy to what actually happened, but it made me think long and hard.

Frizz decided we should instead swap to our fresh engine and between races carried out the complete engine change in 20 minutes. It was a waste of time, though, as it was still over-jetted. With the events all done for the day we lined up at the race office to pick up our start and prize monies. We all stood in the pay line waiting patiently. This was usually a good time to catch up with everyone else and listen to their stories. Some riders wanted to head off straight after the race so this was their final stop before driving out the gate.

The line wasn't moving much at all and soon a message came through that there was not enough cash to pay out everyone and we would have to come back the next day. We knew it was a small crowd and the weather had not been kind but we all wanted our money so we could drive home. About an hour later and after a series of typical Italian yelling sessions the owner or organizer found someone with the keys to the local bank. It was opened at about 10 that night and he came back with a sack full of money. George Beale had done a good deal for me in organizing the start fees and I pocketed the equivalent of £1700, all in 100 lire notes.

With the van loaded up it was back to the UK as quick as we could. Wes and his mechanic had a flight to catch back to the States so we drove through the night. We decided against paying the huge fee for the Mt Blanc tunnel and went the slow way over the Alps. To avoid boredom I thought it might be fun to switch off the van's ignition in the tunnels, pump the throttle, then switch it back on again. The resulting backfire was deafening. After the umpteenth time the muffler finally split, rendering the radio useless with the noise.

Back in England, Brenda and I needed to organize a flight to Sydney. It was inconvenient but as I had a contract with Kawasaki Australia to ride the Z1R in the Castrol 6 Hour and as I had already spent the 10 grand anyway, I had to show up. But it wasn't as if I was being dragged there kicking and screaming — we stood a good chance of winning.

11

UNEXPECTED FACTORY RIDE, 1979

CASTROL 6 HOUR, AMAROO PARK, 21 OCTOBER 1979

I had forgotten how feral Amaroo Park was on my first day out there. The battle with the officials had begun all over again as the bikes were being stripped, checked and measured. It was a robust contest between the technicians who were invariably 'trying it on' in some areas and the scrutineers who were making sure everything was as it should be. It was a production race and if you made it through the inspection process in one piece you felt like you had already achieved something.

Our Z1R flew through the inspection and was ready to go when my co-rider Akihiko Kiyohara arrived from Japan. I had met him back at my first Suzuka 8 Hour appearance. He was riding a factory KR350 and unwittingly had shown me around the short course during training. He was always laughing and seemed a genuine guy; however, the boot was on the other foot this time with him not being able to speak any English. I had been practising this little bit of Japanese for a while so I took him by the arm to the pit wall, leaned over and pointed up the hill.

I told him, 'Torakku wa kono yoo ni ikimasu. Rappu-rekoodo wa gojuuhachi-byoo desu.' He took one look up the hill then followed the track with his eyes from the tight top corner around through the bend and onto the straight. He turned to me, slapped the steel barrier and said something I couldn't understand, then laughed loudly. I guessed he was commenting on how close the steel barrier was to the track, laughing in disbelief. I had just told him in Japanese that the track goes this way and the lap record is 58 seconds.

He was under pressure from the start but put in some decent lap times and soon got used to zipping around the track doing a lap every minute. During qualifying, Dennis Neill on a Honda CB900 set a quick time of 57.3 and later that day I equalled it. Because he was first to set the time, he won pole. Initially, I had a good run at the front of the field then handed over to 'Kiyo'. After a few laps settling in, he got caught out on the other side of the track and the Z1R spat him off in royal style, damaging the bike superficially. When he finally made it back to the pit area he was looking decidedly second-hand and extremely sore. He couldn't continue riding, so we got the bike hurriedly fixed and I went out and circulated, just for fun.

I was back on a plane the next day bound for London and Brands Hatch to finish off what had been a brilliant year.

BRANDS HATCH, 28 OCTOBER 1979

Mamoru decided it was pointless bringing the old Z1 back to its birthplace in Japan after the season. It was worn out anyway and he sold it to Gordon Pantall for two thousand quid. It would have cost £500 to send it back home, so everyone was pleased. Gordon picked up the bike after Cadwell and brought it to Brands for me to race before he would take it to its new home.

'Hello, boyo!' I recognized Welshman Gordon Pantall's voice soon after arriving for the Brands meeting. The last time I had seen him was at his shop in Wales a month previously. I hadn't a clue how we got there but as we were leaving he took us next door for a cup of tea and a pie. The pies might have been regular issue but when the café owner asked if I wanted it heated I said yes and carried on talking. I glanced across to where the coffee machine was making the hissing noise and saw the café owner with his hand around my pie and the steamer nozzle stuffed right inside it.

'Is that normal?' I asked. Gordon looked at me a little bewildered, as if a difficult mathematical question had been put to him. 'You wanted it hot, didn't you? It won't be long,' he said, and carried on talking, oblivious to any health concerns.

'Hey Gordon, the bike looks good,' I told him. He had been looking after the old girl while I was in Aussie. It must have kept him out of the pub because it was a hell of a lot cleaner than I had seen it for a long time. Now that he was the new owner, Gordon had proudly painted PANTALL on the tank. Our Japanese mechanic had stayed on with the bike and had given it the once-over for its last official outing.

Gordon and I talked, then he asked if I had seen Ross Hannan. We had recently found out that Ross had been let out of the Bastille. He had waited the five months and had been to trial. He knew they couldn't drop the charges otherwise they would be liable, so they sentenced him to the five months for driving a stolen car. Not 10 minutes later, Rosko appears and walks up to us with his characteristic limp, all bright-eyed and bushy-tailed.

'How are you going Croz?' he said as we shook hands.

'Oh, you've finally turned up have you? How was the Bastille?' I joked.

'I wasn't in the fucking Bastille as you've been telling everyone. I spent my time at Fleury-Mérogis south of Paris and it was brand-new, just like a hotel, with no convicted people there. So I didn't get raped once.'

I believed him, then smiled, winked and called him a 'prison bitch'. He blew me a kiss; it was good to have Rosko back on deck.

Another familiar face at Brands was multi-world champion Phil Read. I had run into him at the first race meeting at Brands Hatch.

We had already come up against each other at the 24-hour Le Mans in 1977. I was on a similar bike with high bars and I remembered the incident well. I had dived past him out of control in a two-wheel slide going into the first turn and only just managed to hold it together, got it under control and exited leaving this huge black rubber mark out of the corner before slowly drawing away from him. It was an endurance race so I didn't expect that he was riding ten-tenths, but he had noticed me. So at Brands this time he offered to give me £20 to buy a pair of clip-ons to fit on the Moriwaki Kawasaki.

'Phil, I'd rather spend it on food; sorry mate,' I said. I didn't have the heart to tell him that my bike worked for me and I wasn't going to change it.

We took our old girl onto the grid for the last race in the F1 Championship. It was only 10 laps and although the pace was quick I cocked up a couple of laps from the end and finished in third place behind Ron Haslam and Roger Marshall, scoring enough points to finish second overall for the year. Not a bad effort on our part, and we were happy.

The final race was a toe in the water attempt to provide some excitement by matching the TTF1 bikes against the American superbikes. The organizers billed it as the 'British against the Rest' challenge. I was in the 'Rest' team and I called it a straightforward trouncing. I won my last race of the year from Dave Aldana and Wes Cooley.

I rode the bike back to the pit area and handed it over to Gordon. He was over the moon about his bike winning; in fact he was so emotional I thought he was going to burst into tears.

'Hey Gordon, you might want these as well.' I gave him a whole pile of spare parts that I knew he might need in the future. That night we had a barbecue out the back of Marty Lunde's house and Ross brought us up to speed with his time in custody and in turn I related our year, race by race.

CONTRACT WITH SUZUKI FOR 1980

Although my name had been linked with Suzuki since Scarborough in September, nothing was said until I received a message a few days later via Mick Smith that Maurice Knight at Suzuki GB wanted to see me. Although it was the call I had been waiting for, when it came it was still a shock. I had to sell myself to Suzuki for a fee but had no idea how to approach the negotiations. All I knew was that I wanted a 500 cc Grand Prix ride and a TTF1 bike for the 1980 season.

When the boys back at the flat in Surbiton were told, everyone had an opinion on what I should ask for. Advice was coming thicker and faster as more beers were drunk. All sorts of figures were being bandied around and I kept hearing that Barry Sheene had got thousands of pounds as a sign-on fee the previous year. This negotiating thing was all foreign to me and it was doing my head in.

'OK guys, listen — so how much do I ask for?'

There was a muted silence. No one actually knew what I was worth to Suzuki. Eventually, we all figured it must be an amount somewhere between two and twenty thousand quid. I wasn't used to talking those kinds of numbers but for some strange reason the contract money was less important, because my focus was on getting my arse onto the seat of one of those works bikes. It dawned on me then that I was not primarily driven by money, but by opportunity — the money would come naturally as a consequence of my performances on the track. This was the time I needed Rosko to be with me to discuss my options and provide some clarity.

Mick Smith worked with Steve Parrish's bikes during the year and as I was living with him in the flat, I felt I had a slight advantage. Mick was careful to keep me up to speed with what was happening and I could gradually see a cloudy image emerging, one that connected Suzuki and me. Martyn Ogborne had been a staunch supporter too and he had been dropping hints and suggestions on how to deal with Maurice Knight.

In the back of my mind I had been quietly hopeful that Kawasaki could come to the party with a 500. Neville Doyle in Australia was giving me all the right vibes but nothing had materialized. The 500 was unlikely to be ready until June, just in time for the TT. He had also talked about Daytona and some endurance events but, again, nothing concrete. Kawasaki was drifting along, perhaps constrained by budgets and were unable to finally commit to a race programme for 1980.

There are always going to be more arses than seats available and the game of musical chairs is almost inevitable. Riders tend not to leave the security of an existing team until they are locked into another more desirable seat. To give him credit, Neville had kept me up to date but I needed a deal now. Gregg Hansford was still in the picture but he had taken a strong stance on his belief that the World Series might actually come to fruition and he sat on the sidelines waiting for something to happen. Dozy Ballington had also provided me with sufficient negative comment about Kawasaki's plans that I could not afford to wait any longer.

As I saw it, there were two opportunities at Heron Suzuki within the race team. The first was to introduce the TTF1 GS1000R and win both the world and British championships. That would include competing at the TT and on a couple of those other dodgy circuits. No pressure — that didn't worry me.

Then there was the world championship 500 cc Grand Prix. I was bloody nervous about that because I had no experience at GP level and if truth be known, I felt I'd not earned the right to even ask for a 500 to contest the world championship. If I got offered the ride then I would have to fulfil the obligation of at least performing at the same level as other GP riders. I had no idea how I would fare if Maurice and Suzuki said yes. So what price should I put on my head?

The meeting with Maurice went well for both parties. He was a likeable man in a powerful position and from where I was standing he

UNEXPECTED FACTORY RIDE, 1979

seemed to be quite at ease. I was far from relaxed; I began fidgeting around, trying to look confident but my mind would not stop working overtime. Maurice had been in the motorcycle industry since the early 1970s and had cut his teeth on Lambrettas a few years before the Mods and Rockers generation were grabbing headlines in the 1960s. He knew what he wanted and I got the feeling I was there only to put the finishing touches to a plan he had already worked through.

It turned out to be the classic negotiation, lasting no more than 10 minutes. Maurice was complimentary about Barry Sheene and explained that Heron Suzuki wanted to take back ownership of the race team and invest in the new TTF1 programme. Barry had evidently become a little difficult to work with; this had become a case of the tail wagging the dog and it was about to stop. Barry was not comfortable about moving the race shop back to Beddington Lane and did not want to be riding 4-strokes, let alone competing at the Isle of Man. Despite all the publicity Barry generated, Maurice had had enough. He took the hard line and notified Barry that he would no longer be part of the Texaco Heron Team in 1980.

Maurice went on to say that it would be a fresh start for next year. A new transporter had been ordered and while some staff would stay, new ones were needed. It was positive and if his latest visit to the factory was anything to go by, Suzuki had some incredible equipment for us to play with.

He also explained that he was talking to other riders, which sent a chill up my spine. I knew Maurice had been in communication with Korky Ballington and I thought he would have done the deal by now. I'm not sure Korky had enough confidence in Suzuki to make the move but he felt Kawasaki were more committed. He was in a better position to know that than I was; better the devil you know than the one you don't. In any case we had jokingly argued about who was going to be the number one rider if we ended up as teammates. Other riders on the list were Virginio Ferrari, Mike Baldwin,

Randy Mamola and a handful of hopefuls. I thought about Randy and remembered that motel in New Zealand four years before, when all I could see were the soles of his feet as we flushed the toilet, holding his head down inside the bowl. That would be an interesting partnership, I thought.

I think Maurice's plan was for both riders to do virtually the same programme on both 2-strokes and 4-strokes. He leaned over the table, looked me in the eye and asked 'What did you have in mind, Croz?' I took a breath, bit my bottom lip, then replied, 'What do *you* think, because I really don't know. But I guess I would want a 500 and a bike for F1 rides.'

He said he was not prepared to pay a lot because Heron Suzuki was funding the new-look race team, but he could find a few thousand pounds. He had to confirm with Suzuki about the 500 but he agreed in principle. Great, I thought, at least he wasn't asking me to pay. Finally, we had a starting point; however, this turned out to be the ending point as well. Good old Maurice had changed the subject so quickly that we were now talking about the schedule of races. 'Wily old bugger,' I thought. But he got what he wanted and I got what I wanted.

Next year I would be racing the British and World TTF1 championships, plus the Shellsport 500 cc championship in the UK. I had also agreed to the Isle of Man, the Ulster Grand Prix, Daytona and Suzuka. On the 500 cc it was all of the 1980 Grand Prix races, assuming there were no major conflicting dates.

Although he had agreed to the few thousand quid, he also knew he had me over a barrel. He knew that I knew it as well. I had a factory ride with the new Suzuki XR34 and a pair of new Suzuki GS1000R XR69 4-strokes. Mind you, I would have signed on for nothing just to get the ride. After that I realized I really needed a manager for circumstances like this — someone who could go into bat for me and take the pressure off. But, for now, I had the equipment I needed for the next year.

I came away from the meeting a very happy lad. Looking back, it had been a rather fruitful season. My mind went over and over what I had just agreed to and I found myself talking out loud in the car as I drove back to Surbiton: 'Unknown New Zealander Graeme Crosby arrives in Britain in 1979 with all his worldly possessions in a carry-bag. His racing suit draped over his left shoulder, a scratched helmet in his right hand and with only £150 in his wallet, he is ready to take on the world. At the end of the year Croz picks up the currency from the foreign exchange booth at Terminal Three — a couple of thousand should do it until he gets home. He stuffs the US dollars into the new leather wallet that has yet to take up the shape of his bum. He reaches down to pick up his ticket. It's in the new Ralph Lauren bag, there, next to the big envelope containing his factory contract ...' Suddenly I was jolted back to reality. I was back home in Surbiton.

'Crosby you wanker, you didn't do the dishes this morning and there's no fucking milk in the fridge,' Mick yelled. 'And it's your turn to take the fucking rubbish out as well, tosser! Oh yeah and how did you go with Maurice?' he finally asked.

I was tempted to tell him Maurice couldn't make it because he had rubbish to put out, the cat to feed, and a hairdresser's appointment. But I couldn't wait any longer to tell someone. I looked at Mick, who had paused for a moment. 'A few thousand quid, three bikes and you as a mechanic for a whole fucking year, you wanker,' I said. We laughed, Mick congratulated me and soon the whole flat had decamped to the pub.

It was still up in the air who my team-mate was going to be. Ron Haslam had been mentioned but everyone was saying Honda wouldn't let him go. Mike Baldwin was still injured from a crash in the States and Virginio Ferrari was under a similar injury cloud due to his Le Mans accident, but he had been in negotiations already with the Olio Fiat Team Suzuki in Italy. However, he had refused a contract, presumably because of his reputedly turbulent relationship with team boss Roberto Gallina. Suzuki and Fiat supported the team and Virginio was forced to go direct to Suzuki in an attempt to get his own bikes. It didn't work for him.

I let Moriwaki know about the deal with Suzuki as soon as possible. He was happy, for two reasons. In his philosophical thinking he would see himself as a breeder of racers. He had given me an opportunity to showcase my ability and his machinery internationally. We both got the recognition and we both gained from it, perhaps in differing ways. Secondly, he would have liked it because Suzuki had such a close tie-up with the Yoshimura family group.

GOING BACK TO NEW ZEALAND, NOVEMBER 1979

What a season it had turned out to be. Arriving with essentially nothing and going home with a factory contract wasn't a bad outcome. Having finally agreed money and terms with what would be my employer and new home next year at Heron Suzuki, I turned my attention to clearing out the flat. A problem arose concerning reconciliation of the bills. Bob would have been the worst home economics student in the world and had no idea when it came to handling money.

With the bills laid out neatly on the table beside the eight cans of lager and a bottle of wine, it soon become clear that Bob had been spending our domestic expenses at the pub. We were behind in rent, the phone had been cut off and the power bill was now months overdue.

I should have been smart enough to pick up earlier on Bob's financial shortcomings. We'd had the use of the old Sherpa van through his work. We knew it was a hire deal but we didn't know the details. We had paid a nominal amount when asked months earlier but when it came time to hand it back it had accrued a debt of around £2400, which was a shock to us. Bob had insisted he had it covered and had told us not to worry about the hire fee. 'Don't worry about it, I'll s-s-ssort it out,' he assured us with his ever-present stammer. He then elected to do nothing about it. When the bill was eventually settled we suspect it was paid out of the flat expenses that were earmarked for the power and phone companies.

With my season ended, it was now only a matter of getting back to Sydney and shipping the KR750 over. One small problem remained — where was I going to find the money for the freight? Fortunately, Mike Trimby came to the rescue. He was the organizer of the motorcycle section of the Macau Grand Prix, working in that capacity for the Macau government for the previous three years. Mike and I struck a deal for me to compete at Macau on the basis that the KR750 was shipped on to Australia at no cost to me after the race. I also needed a mechanic to assist at Macau and Dave Cullen — 'Radar' — was planning to go home to buy a property on the Queensland coast and agreed to travel via Macau.

We had the KR750 boxed up along with our tools, leathers, tyres and spares. It looked a sorry sight, sporting a season's worth of battle damage. The advertising stickers were all faded and curled at the edges. The chain was hanging loose from the rear sprocket and I almost felt as if the old girl knew she was at the end of her useful life. We used the Sherpa on its last trip to deliver the crate to Heathrow for its flight to Hong Kong and on to Macau.

Macau promised to be a fun time with no one really expected to race balls-out. We knew it was a dangerous track but also understood that we would treat this as a paid holiday in the sun with a bit of riding required to meet the bar tabs that would be run up during our week in the Portuguese colony.

Radar and I took the Boeing hydrofoil from Hong Kong to find a filthy dust hole inhabited by what appeared to be millions of impoverished Chinese. The smell was atrocious. There were thousands of bicycles and old British motorcycles, broken cars and clapped-out taxis working the streets. Immediately, we thought of hiring a rickshaw and promptly bribed the driver to go as fast as he could to get us to the hotel. He was promised a few extra 'shekels' on arrival. By leaning back as far as possible, we soon discovered that we could almost lift the rider and his somewhat fragile bicycle off the ground, rendering his rear brakes and pedals useless. A big lunge backwards had the rickshaw charging downhill, with people scattering and chooks flying in all directions. Our driver managed to get things under control and was screaming something at me. He finally made me understand this was the end of the line.

We checked into the hotel and then went on a walk around the track in the blazing heat. I had no idea just how dangerous it was until then. Some sections were narrow, with huge potholes and uneven surfaces. The walls of concrete seemed like tunnels, allowing no run-off, or for that matter any margin of error. The slightest miscalculation would result in pain, so I told myself this was going be a 'race for show but not for dough'.

However, I was amazed at the potential for speed on this course. It wound down from the very tight hairpin at the top of the hill to the seafront, then followed the foreshore, opening up to almost motorway width, allowing a superfast run to the start-finish line. And that was just part of the first lap, before the riders headed back up the hill through the squalor of overcrowded residential areas.

We found a taxi to take us back to the area where our bikes had been stored and began the prep work. We started by cleaning and re-jetting the carburettors for the hot and humid climate. Although the KR was relatively easy to ride and maintain, the jetting was the crucial difference performance-wise. Initially, this was done by measuring both the wet and dry temperature and the air pressure and making the necessary changes. Although 2-strokes are not that hard to set up, a good 'plug chop' soon tells how close to the mark you are. With engine running at full power in top gear, you carry out a plug chop by pulling in the clutch and hitting the kill switch simultaneously, which leaves a pictorial snapshot of engine performance at full speed. By deciphering the colours and flow-marks on the tops of the piston, the jetting can be corrected accordingly.

Tyres were changed, balanced and refitted with the correct gearing combination hopefully chosen, based on experience. Although that part is pure guesswork, it's the first practice session that tells if a gearing change is required. It takes only a lap or two to get close to the correct gearing, then it's fine-tuning.

I heard that Steve Parrish had arrived here a few days earlier and let off some huge firecrackers he purchased from a local Chinese pyrotechnics maker. Somehow I found the same shop and bought an enormous roll of bangers. It seemed to be a fun thing to do at the time. Back at the work area, Radar was busy cleaning the bike and mixing fuel for the next day's practice.

My bag of firecrackers was full of big ones about 120 mm long and 20 mm thick. I laid them out in a long string and lit the end one. Like an M16 machine gun, these bangers made a deafening noise, sending showers of red paper debris into the air like a West Australian dust storm. The cloud of red paper could not settle fast enough for me. People began gathering and I had a feeling I might be asked to do some explaining.

Radar reminded me of the volatility of the fuel he had been mixing and pointed out it could have gone up in one almighty explosion. While he reminded me of my stupidity, what neither of us knew at that stage was that our makeshift workshop area was situated on top of underground fuel storage bunkers. I asked Radar later if it would have made a bigger bang than his 20 litres of racing fuel. He raised just one eyebrow and looked at me in disbelief before walking slowly away, shaking his head.

Despite my reservations about the circuit, the practice went well and I qualified a second or two behind eventual winner Sadeo Asami, who won both legs on his factory Yamaha YZR750. Race two was different, with Steve Parrish and me engaged in a battle for third for the best part of six laps.

Steve and I screamed down the hill and approached Fisherman's Bend, so-named because if you missed this corner it was straight into the tide. Peeling off and back-shifting down into third gear, we both ran through a line of engine oil left on the track by a terminally ill bike as it ground to a halt haemorrhaging oil. Steve and I both slid off ever so gracefully, one after the other. Leading the charge into the only piece of concrete in sight, I impacted the wall which conveniently had a foam mattress placed against it. This was in fact the only mattress that had been placed over this section of wall. Steve told me later that as he slid down the track he was anticipating smashing headlong into an unprotected section of the concrete wall. Incredibly, my crash had dislodged the mattress and miraculously repositioned it to provide him with the same softer stop against the wall.

Picking myself up, I went to drag the bike upright, intending to carry on, but as soon as I tried lifting the bike a pain shot through my shoulder like a red-hot poker. It felt like I had broken my left arm. The circuit ambulance arrived surprisingly promptly and in the company of two doctors we raced off with sirens and flashing lights to the local hospital. Although only a short distance, it was long enough for me to gather my thoughts. There was no way I was going to let the hospital operate on me if I could avoid it. I would tough it out somehow and get myself back to Hong Kong for treatment.

At the Macau hospital I was met by that horrible musty smell you associate with the old and dying. Its dirty walls and unswept floors only reinforced my view that the less time I spent in here the better. My left shoulder was X-rayed and it was plain to see that the staff were planning an operation on my broken arm. I was introduced to surgeons, nurses and an anaesthetist. An interpreter began explaining that I needed a pin inserted into my shoulder somewhere to allow my broken bone to heal.

'Whoa! Hold the phone,' I said, before trying to explain that the injury they were seeing on the X-ray was not today's. The only broken bone I'd ever had was five years earlier; the pain I had today was just bruising and not a fracture. Eventually, I convinced them to release me from hospital and I walked back to the hotel and began planning my trip home. Then I remembered I was due to go to Ryuyo, Suzuki's seaside test course near Hamamatsu, to test next year's Suzuki GP bike, the XR34-500 and the GS1000R XR69 4-stroke in mid-December, only a few weeks away. I had to be right for that visit, come hell or high water.

My shoulder was extremely painful. Alex George's wife advised me to get to Hong Kong as soon as possible and get a second opinion there. Hong Kong was run by the British, so I knew communication would be easier. The trip back across the sloppy waters of the Pearl River Delta on the hydrofoil was an uncomfortable experience but I was thankful I did not have to take the longer and rougher ferry ride.

Further X-rays confirmed nothing was broken. I got a booking on the next plane to Sydney, one that took me via Port Moresby. It was an Air Niugini Boeing 707 crewed by expat pilots and locals from Moresby. Before take-off I was surprised when passengers were served a bowl of what looked like liquefied mud and was probably kava. This was while we awaited the arrival of the Prime Minister of Papua New Guinea. His press secretary was seated next to me, a delightful lady and chatty too. We talked all the way to Moresby. The hostess had a head of hair on her about the size of a full-grown merino sheep.

Back home in New Zealand I got on with an exercise programme and caught up with mates, took flying lessons and generally enjoyed winding down.

12

MOVE OVER, HERE I COME, 1980

TESTING NEW BIKES IN JAPAN

On the 11-hour daylight flight direct from Auckland I found a green plastic tiki Air New Zealand was giving to its passengers. It dawned on me that I should be using this symbol to identify my country of origin. The tiki design can have several meanings, but I understood it as a symbol of fertility represented by the figure of a human embryo. I decided to apply it to my helmet, which would make a change from those tiresome line drawings of a kiwi.

I took a pen and traced around the outside of it. Sleep came easy for a few hours. Later in the flight I was treated to a flight deck visit at 37,000 feet and was invited to stay there until we landed. The crew and I talked cars, motorcycles and aircraft, as you might expect.

We were also discussing the longevity of long-haul flight crew and making a comparison with elite motor-racing drivers and riders. I thought about those who had worked their way through the ranks of amateur racing. Someone spots talent in the rider and thinks he can act as their manager. He takes charge, the doors open and earnings improve. Promising the world, these managers who have self-interest at heart thrust the riders into the hustle and bustle of a globetrotting lifestyle. The potential for making lots of money is there for a chosen few. Prize and start money for those who push themselves and deliver results can be substantial. But being offered a factory ride is the ultimate for any rider, because he has the tools for making the most of his position financially.

But what happens when a rider makes a wrong decision and in a split second the world as he knows it ends abruptly? Hospitalization, paralysis, infection and amputation are all possible outcomes but perhaps worst of all is head injuries. The world as the rider knew it suddenly stops. All the familiarities of a racing life are extinguished and exchanged for pain and an unknown future. Learning to be dependent on 'the system' becomes a reality. Despite all the promises, the friends you once had still follow the racing scene but slowly they drift away from you and some lose contact forever. That's the sad reality.

'I wonder if too much high-altitude flying can make you depressed?' I asked the captain. He glanced over his shoulder and made a flippant remark.

I then related the story about Pat Hennen and how I felt he was a prime example of this horrible scenario when his world almost ended prematurely at the Isle of Man TT in 1978. Crashing at high speed at Bishop's Court during the run from Rhencullen to Ballaugh Bridge, he sustained severe head injuries, ending his career and earning potential from racing. Faced with a long recovery and rehabilitation programme, he began the journey back from the edge and eventually was able to lead a full life again. He was an example of a highly skilled and ambitious rider who was destined to be a world champion. By now the discussion on the flight deck had got a bit heavy and as the pilots began their preparations for final approach I got the signal for no unnecessary talk below 10,000 feet.

I marvelled at how the seemingly carefree attitude of the crew at cruise altitude changed as we began our descent. They had instantly morphed into a highly professional and efficient team to bring this huge jet down through the clouds and line it up with the runway. At 340 feet a mechanical voice called out 'MINIMUM, MINIMUM,' from an overhead speaker, alerting the crew to the minimum height preset for the approach. Shortly after there was a slight bump as 18 big wheels kissed the tarmac.

I took a bus to my hotel in downtown Tokyo just after dusk. This trip was torture — the driver took the bus to its legal speed limit then used the throttle to control the speed. I got off the bus almost suffering whiplash from the constant on and off the gas. I thought he must be doing this on purpose.

Next morning I bought a rail ticket to Hamamatsu. I would repeat this routine with monotonous regularity over the next two years during my time with Suzuki. Arriving at Hamamatsu by the Shinkansen (bullet train), I was met by a Suzuki representative and taken to the company's head office nearby. I was greeted and politely offered green tea. I would have preferred a Kirin beer but he didn't offer. There was the usual small-talk and the customary exchange of business cards. I had learnt the protocol of taking time to study the card and not just flip it into my back pocket. Then it was off to the race shop, which I was really looking forward to. I had visions of complex testing equipment, radical engine layouts, and chassis of varying configurations waiting to be engine-fitted.

I also expected Suzuki to have security cameras and guards at the door. Their racing programme is important in showcasing their products but I was to find out it didn't matter a toss, as the whole factory was in effect a work-in-progress on any number of bikes, engines and outboards.

In the middle of the room I saw our two bikes. In a corner were two similar-looking ones belonging to the test riders Hiroyuki Kawasaki and Masaru Iwasaki. These carried the livery of the Suzuki Motor Co and were used in the domestic racing programme.

A number of production racers were being assembled for delivery to riders around the world. All the bikes, including ours, were in the standard gel-coat white. Actual colouring would be the responsibility of the team to which theses bikes were allocated: Heron Suzuki in the UK, Team Gallina in Italy and Will Hartog's Team Riemersma Racing in the Netherlands. By the time we had tested our bikes and cut chunks and pieces out of the fairing to make things fit comfortably, it was hopeless to even consider any painting. In any case we had 'John the Paint' back at Beddington Lane ready to create the superb Texaco Heron Suzuki paintwork.

Both Randy and I had two bikes. These started out identical, other than rider-chosen modifications such as seat and handlebar or clip-on position. Randy had elected to use heavy steering dampers while I chose lightly damped ones to increase feel. Interestingly, each bike would feel quite different when ridden in anger. It might be only a footrest that was 2 mm higher on one side or one chassis that was slightly stiffer than the other. Although I was expecting a high-tech race shop, in effect it was merely an assembly point for race bikes, both the production Mk10 and the works XR34's.

The race shop staff consisted of only four people, as most jobs were done within the factory walls by people who probably did not even know what they were making, just another widget or gadget. Rotation policy in Japan meant that a car mirror designer could well be transferred to design cowlings in the race shop. My worry was that an ashtray designer for the Suzuki Swift might end up in the race department making pistons. The design department would be working on any number of projects, of which only a handful might go into full production. This included design of our race bikes. A visit to the design department showed this policy in action, as one designer was drawing up a headlight bracket while the guy next to him was working on my TT Formula One chassis.

That night we were taken out to dinner with Mitsu Okamoto and Tadeo Matsui, the men who would be alternating over the GP season as guests of either Heron Suzuki or Team Gallina. We ended up in some bar drinking whisky and water in the early hours. I considered it essential to get to know what makes people tick. On the way back from a sordid bar, Mitsu used his cigarette lighter to jokingly light a colourful paper floral lei I had nicked from some poor unsuspecting street vendor. Within seconds I was engulfed in flames and the skin on my neck began blistering. The paper lei was in fact a synthetic material and proved difficult to extinguish. Eventually, it was ripped from my neck, leaving a severely burnt ring around my throat between my collar and chin. I knew the pain would get worse but, being the gentleman I am, I shrugged off any hint that I was in agony.

Mitsu was mortified that he had caused me to get burnt and was very apologetic. I didn't want to take it any further, half-hoping I might have an opportunity for some leverage when special parts were needed. Although this socializing gave me an insight into the character of my Japanese hosts, unfortunately the reverse also happened. Everyone knew I had been on the town partying when I was injured and a trip to the infirmary at Suzuki headquarters proved this. 'Crosby-san, please don't drink any beer tonight,' the Suzuki team boss Mr Yokouchi requested next morning. He knew already what I was like because of his friendship with Yoshimura. Pops no doubt had told them stories of my beer-drinking antics. Meantime I had already spied a few very interesting little bars that deserved a late night visit.

The testing sessions were a mad rush and seemed to always be last-minute efforts. The bikes, fuel, tools, tyres and spares were loaded onto the back of a very small Suzuki truck with a tray about the size of a beach towel. Piled up high with our expensive race equipment, we headed off to the countryside in search of the test track at Ryuyo on the Pacific coast, about 40 minutes from Hamamatsu.

Test time was limited and we were joined by Masaru Iwasaki,

one of the test and development riders for the RG programme. He was quickly out on the track while we were still doing some setting up on our bikes. I heard the XR34 winding up from the hairpin up and into the 170-degree corner leading onto the front straight. When it came into sight I could feel the wind pressure and rush of turbulent air as he whistled past us, followed by its crisp exhaust note. It sent a shiver up my spine. 'Shit,' I thought, 'what the hell have I let myself in for?'

Then it was our turn, so Randy, Will Hartog and I rode a few laps getting used to the circuit, which I thought was surprisingly dangerous. Its high speeds made me focus on the proximity of the steel barriers and tyre walls that were very close to the edge of the track. I could see only a couple of flag marshals; that made me a little worried but I knew as we raced around the track we were in constant view via CCTV monitors that were set up at the pit area. We hoped they worked.

It was a good session, providing us with a baseline to work from. We all posted reasonable lap times and noted the changes we wanted made. These 2-stroke GP bikes were new to me, and I felt I was out on a limb with no capability of providing quality feedback. I also knew I had no experience to work from with these bikes. Based on lap times, Randy performed better than me, as I had expected him to. He had had GP experience and time on production RG's the previous year.

I preferred the whirling clatter of a 4-stroke valve train complete with its gutsy, throaty exhaust note. I now had to adapt to the more refined 2-stroke engine. Lack of engine brake and its overall lighter weight made braking more critical and I had to quickly learn to manage its lighter inertia. Being heavier in mass, the 4-strokes were slower to move from side to side and much more predictable under brakes. It didn't matter too much if you were a few hundred revolutions either side of where you wanted it to be, as it would still pull away with its ample torque. However, riding the 2-strokes meant you needed to be on your game constantly and be ready to ensure engine rpm delivered the power as required. Being a few hundred revolutions ahead or behind the optimum can mean losing precious seconds on a racetrack. Having a smaller window of power to work with, I had to learn to use the expertise around me and not to try to ride through any problems.

I had my first look at the GS1000R Suzuki that arrived later that day. The seat rail needed to be lengthened by 40 mm so I could fit my big arse on it and still be able to lie flat across the tank. I was used to having the high handlebars with its associated elevated views from above on most of the big 4-strokes I had ridden in the past. Now I found myself in that classic head-down, arse-up pose I had managed to avoid for so long. I remembered my discussion with Phil Read at Brands the previous year, when he offered to buy me a set of clip-ons, and had a quiet chuckle.

Coming off the GP bike and onto an F1 bike was also like chalk and cheese, something I would have to get used to, and quickly. My schedule this year called for a lot of race meetings where I would be jumping from one onto the other. It would be like going from a heavy truck to the finesse of a highly tuned sports car. I would have to learn to cope, though. Randy had signed to do the same programme of 500 cc and TTF1 races but I had heard he thought it would distract him from his GP duties. I couldn't have cared less; in fact the more races the better it would be for me.

We attended a post-testing session meeting with Suzuki's race team boss Etsuo Yokouchi and the design team. Generally, everyone was happy with Suzuki's 1980 package complete with the new technology engine and its cassette side-loading gearbox. There was some concern about delivery timing and additional parts that were still in test mode. But all in all it was a successful first-time test. I retraced my steps to Narita and caught another Air New Zealand flight back to Auckland.

SUZUKI, MY NEW HOME, 1980

With my holiday in sunny New Zealand over, it was off to London again in February. At Beddington Lane I went straight to the race shop and spoke with Rex about plans for the season. He explained that the Venezuelan Grand Prix at San Carlos had been cancelled. It was going to be a late start to the season.

The entries had been put in for the opening Grand Prix events but I was not on the FIM grading list so we would just have to wait and see. I was worried about the list because it gives automatic entry to a Grand Prix for those on it. If your name is not there, the organizers usually reject your entry. I thought a factory rider should have automatic entry. Instead, I had to play their silly waiting game just like anyone else.

The opening three rounds of the TTF1 championship all clashed with the first three Grand Prix — the Austrian on 20 April, the Italian on 11 May and the Spanish on 18 May. Luckily, it was the best eight results that counted for the TTF1 championship, which I thought might play into my hands if I had a good run at the end of season. In July I would also miss the Finnish Grand Prix because it clashed with the Suzuka 8 Hour race. It was going to be a busy race programme this year.

I negotiated a performance bonus with both Mick and Radar to give them 20 per cent each of any prize money I might make during the season. This was on top of Suzuki paying their wages and accommodation while away. I wasn't sure if it was the going rate but I kept my word religiously and paid them in cash straight after the racing finished and well before I got sidetracked with partying. I confirmed the rate was at the top end by asking a few discreet questions of other riders. If my rate was more generous it suited me, because I felt I would get a greater level of support and commitment from the boys if they were happy.

I was in Belgium as a spectator in 1978 to watch the World F750 round at Nivelles. On the way I dropped in to the Bruges Hospital to say hi to Ray Quincey, who was recovering from a crash at an international race and had suffered some form of paralysis. A lot of Aussies had turned up for the Nivelles race and I thought it would be nice to show up and support them. Thur Cohen from Bel-Ray Oils had generously invited Brenda and me to stay in a hotel near Antwerp. Bel-Ray had its European offices in the hotel, so the room was free for us to use. He also loaned us a little Renault car that we took to Nürburgring the following week to watch the German GP.

The first day we drove directly to the track and found the Aussie contingent having breakfast. Plain white bread rolls being washed down with Belgian beer seemed a little strange but I quickly realized that funds were short in the camp. Mick Smith was a larger-than-life character who had taken time out from his job in Australia to mechanic for Jeff Sayle at some European events. It was a kind of working holiday and everyone knew it wasn't going to be easy.

A series of mechanical failures and poor finishes had eaten up their cash reserves, but the team was being held together by the brave Aussie wives and girlfriends who were used to this. Their last few dollars had become the focus of their attention. It was settled virtually by decree as Mick Smith walked into the Aussie camp carrying two dozen bottles of beer. He had taken it upon himself to treat the boys — after all, it had been a long, hot day. The funding problem would have to wait.

We returned to the hotel determined to ensure the guys would at least have some breakfast next day. Brenda and I casually drifted into the restaurant next morning, not wanting to draw attention to ourselves. We were blown away by the array of food set out in true Continental style. We set about discreetly filling bags with food for everyone back at the track. Our nervousness began to show so we called it quits when we had three large bags containing assorted bread rolls, cold meats, cheese croissants and other goodies. Then we scurried off to the track. Our 'generosity' was greatly appreciated and we were able to do the same thing the next day. It was a reminder of just how hard it was living on the smell of an oily rag.

So it was great to have Mick on board with us at Suzuki, especially having witnessed first-hand how he survived in 1978. He had gone home to Australia at the end of the year, got a job and saved up some more money. He returned in '79 with Jeff Sayle, who had found a generous sponsor who provided them with a transporter and a caravan for the season. It was good at the start until all the friends and family started arriving, when it reached bursting point. He didn't want a repeat of 1978 and picked up a job spannering for Steve Parrish, a rider in the Texaco Heron Suzuki Team. He stayed for the rest of the year.

My other mechanic was the Aussie 'Radar', who had competed in motocross until an incident while mucking about on his dirt bike sent him over backwards, with the resulting impact leaving him with a cracked vertebra. When doctors advised him to take an extended break from racing, he packed his bags for Europe. After purchasing a Transit van in London, Radar set out on his big adventure, but he had no firm plans and drifted around the UK, eventually finding a job at Suzuki GB working on Mike Hailwood's bike at the TT.

Rex told me he had organized with Vic Barnes, a high-profile London photographer, to do a pre-season photo shoot with a new 500 and he was planning to drape a beautiful model over the machine. 'Hmmm,' I thought, 'this could be nice ... this is what being a factory rider is all about ... photo-shoots, sexy models ... it's a tough job but someone's got to do it.' I drove into Kensington to a studio where a mocked-up bike had been delivered.

Vic had me doing all sorts of silly poses for a couple of hours. The purpose of the shoot was twofold. One was a normal PR exercise for Suzuki; the other, I needed to address the British public on why Suzuki GB should be hiring a Kiwi over the local British talent. Vic and I decided that I needed to take a humorous approach to the issue. Last year I had already been seen wearing my favourite T-shirt, which featured a tin of Kiwi shoe polish and the words 'The English might have the culture but Kiwis have the polish'.

We set up shots of me with a bowler hat and a teapot, and even holding a pint of Guinness just to make the point that I was at least trying to be English. Then I had a few shots done by myself and even some without my shirt on. That had me worried but I wasn't about to take my pants off; I drew the line at that. Then the model arrived and, well, that's another story.

DAYTONA, 7 MARCH 1980

With Suzuki Great Britain's contract safely tucked away and feeling semi-organized for the first time in years, I was able to begin focusing on the first race on the schedule for 1980. Daytona was important, not only for Suzuki America but for all the major manufacturers. Suzuki's racing activities were being run by Yoshimura R&D America, with Pops Yoshimura's son Fujio in control. I was asked to run one of their GS1000 superbikes in the Bell Helmets 100-mile event. Suzuki would also provide me a new GS1000R, designated the XR69, to use in the 200-mile event.

This was a complete turnaround because a few years earlier we had approached the American Motorcycle Association (AMA) for an entry into the Superbike race at Daytona. Pops had even promised us a bike. There was one big stumbling block, though: 'Yes, you can race but first you have to get an AMA licence.'

Not being sure of what impact this was going to have on me, Ross and I did some further exploration. We found out that I would need to hand in both my FIM and ACU (Auto Cycle Union of Australia) licences so I could be issued an AMA one, just for one race. Apparently, a rider could not hold both licences at once. However, once done, I would not be able to convert it back so easily, leaving me stuck with an AMA licence.

Daytona was sanctioned as an international event now and I could enter. The team at Daytona included Yoshimura R&D's rider Wes Cooley, whom I'd met back in New Zealand during the Marlboro Series. Wes had ridden Yamahas in those days but recently he had made a name for himself competing in the Superbike category on a GS1000. Along with Wes was Dave Aldana, the 'Mad Mexican'. Dave had lots of experience at Daytona and was one of those guys you knew was going to be extremely hard to beat.

The Suzukis of Cooley, Aldana and me were up against the Honda USA team. Manager and rider Steve McLaughlin with young 'fast' Freddie Spencer and Ron Pierce made up the team. Kawasaki fielded Eddie Lawson and Gregg Hansford. It was a talented line-up.

I landed at Orlando Airport late in the evening. I needed a rental car and being America the choice was always great, from a small compact to a huge Cadillac. The sales desk staff gave me the impression that as long as you could pay you could have almost anything. I selected one of those huge long continental coupés. It was like Boss Hogg's car from *Dukes of Hazzard*, minus the bull horns on the bonnet, or 'hood' as the Yanks say. I had driven only a couple of miles, just enough to get me onto the four-lane freeway, when suddenly I noticed there was no drive through the transmission. I coasted to a stop and parked this monster on the edge of the freeway. I locked the car and began looking for someone who could tell me how to get back to the rental company to get a replacement for my drive to Daytona.

It was getting late as I stumbled down from the turnpike where the car had finally come to rest. I spotted one of those Masonic-type lodges nestled down a bank beside the turnoff but with no windows it looked sinister. I could see plenty of cars outside so I bashed on the door and entered. I wondered what the hell I'd walked into as I looked around the room. I had never seen such a weird bunch of people. Everyone was wearing strange little hats with tassels on the top and communicating by secret hand signals. I was scared so I quietly asked to use a phone and retreated outside to await delivery of another car.

The car arrived and I was given a red Ford Mustang coupé, not bad I thought. With my gear now transferred I set off for Daytona. Arriving in the wee hours of the morning I found at my hotel a group of Irish lads partying and I joined them for a few beers. I was always amazed by the fun-loving Irish and was mesmerized by their accent. We decided to go out and find any old bar that was open because at that time of the morning it was probably going to be fun watching the locals.

At about 3 a.m. we were driving back to the hotel along the beach, which was legal as it was classified as a road. The sand was a little soft and the car struggled in places. I drove towards the water where I was expecting it to be a little firmer. It was low tide and the car began to labour in the soft sand, calling for more power. I stomped my foot on the throttle and within about 20 metres we were buried in sand up to the sills.

Despite using the foot-mats to try and get traction, we watched the car sink deeper into the sand. We made a call to a local tow company which arrived about 15 minutes later as the waves began lapping in over the door-sills of our nice new Mustang. The useless tow truck driver not only tied the tow-rope around one of the tie-rods and broke it at the first pull but also managed to get his truck stuck in the process. I think he may have been one sandwich short of a picnic. His eyes were too close together for comfort. Another tow truck was called and it pulled the first truck out and then our car, which now had no steering. The tide by this time was rolling in across the back seats. We walked back to the hotel wet and covered with sand.

Brenda was due to arrive from New Zealand so I borrowed a friend's car and picked her up at 5.30 a.m. from Daytona Airport. I had to explain how our rental car got stuck in the tide and was now absolutely rooted. Naturally, I blamed the drunken Irish for our predicament.

Faced with a car that bore more resemblance to a crayfish pot than a vehicle, I was in desperate need of help. A journalist, Bob Berry, who reckoned he had experience in dealing with the 'American way', insisted on showing me how it's done here in the USA. Embarrassingly, I left him to it. I was scared of the repercussions from the rental car company and had visions of being locked up for weeks and unable to race. But Bob soon turned up with an almost new Cadillac Eldorado rocket ship. His theory was that America is all about service, so he just demanded a new car to replace the one that got stuck in the stand, which he reminded them is after all an authorized roadway. To this day I still don't know how he got away with it. Go Bob!

I arrived at the racetrack and was amazed at the size of this superspeedway, which only days earlier had hosted the Daytona 500 NASCAR race. The circuit was littered with long black tyre marks and scrapes along the metre-high concrete wall. The circuit is a tri-oval with 33-degree banked corners. As a foreigner I was given the opportunity to look around the circuit with one very proud Daytona Speedway course marshal. He drove me around the circuit slowly and never went on to the banking. At turn one he stopped and challenged me to try to walk straight up from the bottom of the banking to the top but my ankles could not bend the required 33 degrees so I had to turn around and walk backwards up the slope. He then went on to explain that the motorcycles used the whole tri-oval but deviated into the infield as the speeds on the back straight were far too high for two-wheeled machines. A strategically placed chicane was used to reduce the entry speed onto the final high-banked corner.

The Yoshimura race team had already arrived and we exchanged pleasantries while I scanned the surrounding area for my bike. I spied it being wheeled out of the truck. It looked like a normal Yoshimura race bike — a little tatty. But after a quick check of Wes Cooley's bike, I realized both looked scruffy so I relaxed. I remembered having seen them before at Suzuka, and I knew that all the make-up in the world wouldn't make them go faster. In a crazy way I think that's always been one of Yoshimura's positive points — they spend more time, money and effort on performance than on presentation. As a rider, I felt it would have been nice to have a sparkling new race bike, one that you could put your arms around and feel proud of. After giving this some thought, I decided it's about power first, then handling. And the paintwork — well, who cares?

The Yanks had a system I was not familiar with, that allowed sponsors to put up independent prize money for riders who use their products and carry decals. At technical inspection and sign-on I was confronted with a potential sponsorship clash between spark plug suppliers. Which one do I sign — Nippon Denso Spark Plugs, sponsor of the Yoshimura Team, or Champion Plugs, which put money into Team Suzuki Great Britain? Randy's manager Jim Doyle marched right on in there and before long he almost had me watching the race from the sidelines. It was a deadlock, with both sponsors wanting representation. I had a Champion Spark Plug badge on my race suit and the bike had Nippon Denso spark plug decals. Champion's man on the spot had his views, as did the Denso representative, and both were quoting clauses in contracts and referring to possible penalties and consequences. Thank god common sense finally prevailed and in a show of gentlemanly diplomacy we all agreed to my covering up the Champion badge with race tape.

I was only the hired rider and wasn't forming any long-term connection with Suzuki America or Yoshimura. Politics stink, I told myself, but perhaps next year I would ride a diesel — it would be a lot simpler.

The first lap of practice made me forget about the appearance of the bike because it was a missile and handled like it was on rails. The boys at Yoshimura and Wes Cooley had done a great job setting it up. This was the best superbike I had ever ridden, smooth and predictable on the racetrack. I had to sit high up on its back but when

I tucked in behind its bikini screen, even at top speed it retained a satin-smooth grip on the track. I felt safe riding it. The track, though, was something else. Those first few practice laps at Daytona scared the shit out of me because of the combination of extreme banking and the high speeds that we were able to attain. I had never experienced the positive G-forces that exerted extra pressure on my head and probably doubled its weight.

I did some laps on the XR69 and although it was fast and handled great I couldn't really get to grips with it. Perhaps it was the Goodyear tyres we had to use. I thought they were as hard as Bakelite. It took about three laps to get any temperature into them and even then they provided little grip, particularly on the right-hand side, as there were only two right-hand corners. I'd need to spend some time on the bike, testing, to really unlock its potential. There would be little time to do that at Daytona. During the practice sessions we also experienced brake problems with fading and despite changing pads and other modifications it looked like I had to go into the 200-mile race with less than perfect brakes.

The circuit was a strange phenomenon for me because I had to quickly get used to riding high on the banking and knowing when to come down off the turn to get a good run down the straight. Too soon and you run wide; too late and the wall is there right in front of you. I practised counting the Daytona signs painted on the banking wall as they whizzed by and soon figured I could come off the banking on the third sign. I also figured that the fastest line was up high and hugging the wall only inches away.

Because of the number of entries, it was necessary to have two heat races to decide grid positions for the Saturday race. Although my heat was a short race I managed to cross the line in second position behind Dave Aldana. Both of us carried out plug chops to get a good read on engine performance at full throttle. The mechanics were then able to peer down into the cylinders and check the colour of the piston to determine if the jetting needed adjustment. We cruised to a halt, got off, and pushed our bikes back to the pit area.

The results of the heat races and qualifying positions were posted on the board in the afternoon, surprisingly showing that both Dave and I did not complete the heat race. According to the officials, in order to record a finish the rider must go past the timekeepers who were positioned on the infield straight, after the finish line. I was under the impression that a waved chequered flag meant the end of the race — wrong. Despite our protests, Dave and I were instructed to start from the back of the grid in the second wave on Saturday. My start position was 49th.

I was really pissed off to be relegated to the back of the field. So when the flag dropped and the first wave got away I still had to suffer the indignity of a further 10 seconds wait before we were allowed away. I had a huge amount of anger in the tank, so I shot away from the line, using the grass verge to pass every rider and lead the second wave into turn one. I had calculated that all the second-wave riders were slower than me and I would out-brake them going into turn one. It worked. Within four laps I had left the entire second wave behind, caught and passed most of the first wave and had the leaders in sight. Up front the battle was between Cooley and Spencer who had pulled out quite a margin on the field. In the early laps Honda had lost McLaughlin to an engine misfire, Hansford's fuel cap had come loose and he had to pit for repairs.

I could began to smell the kill just before half-time as first Cooley retired with a broken crank, leaving Spencer out front but realizing he was losing ground to me. He could do nothing as I gradually closed in on him. Ron Pierce then pitted for rear brake problems and refuelled but he was certainly not out. Spencer pitted for fuel on lap 11, giving me a break with a clear track ahead to put more distance on him. Yoshimura signalled me in for a very fast fuel stop and I re-entered the track just ahead of Spencer. It was a tough race for me, keeping him at bay, but I knew the last chicane on the back straight would be critical for the finish.

Wes Cooley had told me on more than one occasion that it's a bad situation to find yourself in leading on the last lap. This is because as you exit the last chicane before the high banking that leads to the finish line, it's really a drag race and using the slipstream of the leading rider you can easily pass him before the finish line. This was playing on my mind and in a concerted effort I tried hard for the last three laps and managed to pull a gap on Freddie that he could not make up. I whistled pass the finish line in just under an hour of racing to record a very satisfying win.

The day after, the *Daytona Beach Morning Journal* carried the headline 'A VIRTUOSO PERFORMANCE'. It looked like a good word so I had to ask what it meant. 'Oh yeah, that's me,' I told the girl at McDonald's as I picked up my pancakes and coffee. In the same article it quoted Freddie Spencer: 'When you ride in this league with riders of this calibre the slightest mistake is going to cost you.' I digested his statement, understood where he was coming from entirely, ordered some maple syrup and drove off down to the beach.

The 200-mile race on Sunday was shaping up to be a great event. A completely revised set of rules allowed the big factory 4-strokes into the race for the first time. Maximum capacity of 1025 cc up against the 2-strokes with their 750 cc limit and with carburettor restrictors and the unrestricted 500 cc machines. Daytona had had its share of controversial events in the past with Barry Sheene having a rear tyre blow-out at well over 170 mph on the banking and crashing in spectacular style. Stories of excessive tyre wear plagued Daytona and carburettor restrictors were introduced to reduce the usable horsepower. Purpose-built tyres had to be made for safety reasons. On paper this new formula seemed fair and was designed to avoid a repetition of the Yamaha-dominated race of the past. It was also intended to make the race better for the spectators, with more brands competing.

My qualification was less than impressive and somewhat disappointing for Suzuki and me. I had won the 100-mile race and this was an anticlimax. The bike had brake problems from the start and I retired early in the race. Coming off a great win the day before, it was hard to keep the momentum going when faced with a bike that wasn't quite up to it. There had to be a positive to take out of this and I identified the fact that we would need to be taking a long hard look at our GS1000 XR69 braking system when we got back to the workshop in Beddington Lane.

Having had to wait a few years to ride this circuit was well worth it after all, despite all the weird rules. When it came time to pick up my prize money, about US$12,000, the office at Daytona retained 20 per cent. This cut was apparently for some bloke named Uncle Sam, which prompted me to ask the cashier 'What does this Uncle Sam of yours ride anyway?'

I thought the Daytona weekend was a great start to the season. I knew this was a good race to win for a number of reasons. I had never ridden there before and to win gave me a lift in confidence. Hell, I would need all that confidence with the Grand Prix season starting soon. I had never raced a Grand Prix before, so my performance at Daytona should have proved the decision to let me race Grand Prix was a sound one. I was not frightened of a challenge.

We all had a few beers after the event, then along with Rex White and his wife Dorothy, I went in search of the biggest steak in Daytona, to be washed down with a few margaritas. It would be a great feeling going back to my adopted homeland with the spoils of war. The big Daytona Superbike trophy would be plonked in Rex's office in pride of place.

13

CRISIS OF CONFIDENCE, 1980

TRANS-ATLANTIC, 1980

Controversy surrounded the annual Trans-Atlantic Match Races in 1980, mainly as a result of the selection process. Much to the disgust of a few English hopefuls, I was drafted into the British team. I was a little embarrassed but what the hell, I was on an ACU licence and the rules allowed it.

Why I was picked for the British team I'm not sure but presumably it was because Team Heron Suzuki was British. I had heard rumours of Barry Sheene arguing for better start money for other members of the British team, so I was not sure who would be turning up. Some journalists thought it inappropriate to have a Kiwi racing for Britain. I had to remind them we had been defending British soil for years. 'Keith Park was a Kiwi, you know,' I said. 'He was the Royal Air Force Commander who defended you blokes from the Luftwaffe during the Battle of Britain. In any case I didn't make up the rules for the Trans-Atlantic.'

The British team consisted of manager Mike Hailwood, Barry Sheene, Mick Grant, Ron Haslam, Dave Potter, John Newbold, Keith Heuwen, Chris Guy and Alan Pacey. I had no idea about the match races and how they fitted into the Motor Circuits Developments programme and decided I would just go with the flow. The photo shoot I did with Vic Barnes portraying me as a Pom would come in handy when it was seen in a few magazines.

The races were being held at Brands Hatch on the Friday, Mallory on Sunday and Oulton Park on Monday. There were two races or legs each day and I had been given an XR23 to ride which I'd seen at Beddington Lane. Its big fat exhaust pipes poking out each side made it look like a whale but, according to those who knew, it went like a missile. It had started life as a 500 cc Grand Prix bike, then it was bored out to 653 cc to make it eligible for the Formula 750 class, which had just been dropped this year in favour of the TTF1. I got to use the orphan, which on paper looked impressive. Yet everyone I talked to about this bike said it was dangerous and it had hurt a few riders. 'Well, that's handy to know,' I responded. I began getting that 'I feel like a crash dummy' feeling.

Randy would ride his XR34 500 for the American team which was made up of a bunch of extremely competitive riders led by Kenny Roberts. The team included young Freddie Spencer whom I had already come up against at the Daytona Superbike race. Brands Hatch would be his first overseas trip and with him would be Erv Kanemoto, a brilliant engineer and Yamaha race technician. Dale Singleton, Richard Schlachter, John Long, Wes Cooley, David Aldana and Skip Askland made up the numbers.

Practice was a little unnerving as this was my first ride in the UK with Suzuki GB. Martyn Ogborne had me do some laps on the 653 cc just to check it out and casually mentioned that if I was to biff it away somewhere on the track to make sure I bent the chassis. Most things were repairable but Suzuki would not straighten a chassis. I was a little bemused by his statement as he continued: 'Look, Croz, the XR23 is an old bike and can hurt you as it has others. It's a powerful brute and bloody difficult to keep the front wheel on the ground. So be careful and like I say if you throw it down the road make sure you completely fuck it! We don't want to fix it again.'

I blasted off out of the pit lane during the last practice session. On the second lap as I sat up and pulled the brakes on going into the first turn, I felt that ever-so familiar release of the external pressures as the suspension unloaded. The front tyre had lost its grip on the slippery surface and I found myself skating up the road on my bum. The bike had come down on its side and ever so gracefully slid to a stop. I arrived in equally graceful style. I looked at my bike and could see nothing worse than scratches on the right side of the cowling, a bent handlebar and a broken screen. 'Sorry Martyn,' I thought, as I dragged it into an upright position. I waited for the crash truck to take us back to the pit area. 'You're gonna have to fix her again, Oggy,' I could hear myself saying.

I was met at pit lane by Rex and Martyn. They both looked at me, surveying my leather suit for any signs of blood or a glistening bone sticking through my suit. 'I'm OK Oggy, I lost the front end …' I began, but was cut off mid-sentence by Martyn.

'You silly prat', he said. 'I can see you're OK but did you fuck the bike like I told you to?' I laughed and promised I'd make a better job of it next time.

The bike was kicked back into shape and taped up for the first race. I was very nervous but I also knew it had been a cold tyre that had brought me down. We all had to contend with the dodgy areas on the track that the Formula One boys had polished smooth with the diamonds fitted to the skirts of their ground-effect cars. God help everyone if it rains, I thought, because there will be carnage. A smoothly ground mirror-like surface and rain is lethal for any bike and it was likely that with the first shower every rider would be doing pirouettes around the steering head trying to keep upright. I saw it as just another Formula One cock-up with no consideration shown to us motorcycle racers.

My mind went back to my first race at Brands Hatch, where close to a year before I had made my UK debut. Today I had no excuses because I was on a factory bike competing against a sampling of the world's best riders. I'd come a long way in a year, but today I would really have to prove myself.

In the first race I got a great start and led for three laps before Freddie Spencer came past. I was determined to hang on and managed a close second. I spent most of the race climbing up onto the tank to get my body weight over the front wheel. The bloody thing spent more time clawing at the air than on the ground. It was a great result for me, though, finishing ahead of Randy, Kenny and Barry.

Between both legs of the Trans-Atlantic was the first round of the British Shellsport 500 cc Championship and I had my first outing on my XR34 500. It was the first time we had lined up together on 500's as a team. Randy led for the first few laps until I got my shit together and passed him. I was putting some distance between us when I noticed water on the inside of my screen. The engine was getting hot and I had to back off just to make the finish. It was a satisfying start to the season and a good race, with Randy eventually leading me over the line by a couple of seconds. After the race, Radar found that the engine had blown a head gasket. We had the best bikes and were up against production racers, so it was not surprising that we finished four seconds ahead of third-placed Dave Potter on his Yamaha.

After a false start at the second Trans-Atlantic race, our British team had a few retirements with clutch problems; things were not looking too good for the overall points standing. I compounded the situation by retiring on lap three. My rear tyre had got covered in slippery oil from a gearbox oil seal leak and threatened to spit me over the handlebars. I retired to the safety of the pit and Newcastle brown ale. The day had shown the doubting Thomases out there that I could ride a Grand Prix 2-stroke competitively. My self-belief was growing.

The team made the trip up to Mallory Park for the Sunday and with the XR23's oil leak fixed I was feeling reasonably confident. A broken steering damper in leg one made life extremely difficult and I settled for fifth place. Roberts, Spencer and Randy scored all the points. Looking at the lap times, I was considering running the 500 in the second leg. It was a little down on outright power but its handling and nimbleness in traffic made me think it would be a wiser choice.

The second round of the British Shellsport 500c championship was another procession. This time I got the best of Randy and won by 0.7s. There was little in it between our best lap times with Randy bettering me by just 0.2s. It felt like a clean sweep.

I was only six laps into the second leg of the Trans-Atlantic race, trying to work my way past a few riders, when I exited the hairpin and the 500's front wheel climbed into the air. I short-changed into second then third, accelerating up to Devil's Elbow. I pitched it into the downhill left-hander, the bike settled and loaded up with G-force and I began winding on the throttle. I felt the telltale unloading of the back end and then the seat fell away momentarily before the tyre regained full grip. I was flicked off on the high side and the bike and I slammed into the metal crash barrier. It happened almost instantaneously because the barrier was so close to the edge of the track. I looked up from under my bike to see Mick hanging over the fence looking down at me. He had the sense to grab Brenda, who was right there at the point of impact doing timing for me. He pushed her away so she didn't see any of the blood or gooey bits. Mick told me that it looked bad — he thought I had broken my leg and a bone was poking out. I looked down and saw a puncture mark on the inside of my calf and blood oozing out through the hole in my leather suit. It didn't hurt at first but when I tried to stand up it struck me that all was not well.

The St John Ambulance guy arrived and tried to make me sit down until a stretcher appeared but I was able to hobble with support and was gently lifted over the crash barrier. I was now feeling a little light-headed and shock was on its way. I lay down on the stretcher and was whisked off to the medical centre. It must have looked spectacular because all our team were hanging over the fence watching as I slid into the wall below them. The noise was apparently horrific as the Suzuki slammed into the steel guardrail. I slid into the bike, impaling my leg on an aluminium footrest. I was lucky it didn't score a direct hit on the bone as it went into my leg and the damage was confined to the calf muscle.

After an assessment by the circuit doctor, he suggested I take the ambulance to the local hospital in Leicester. Reluctantly I agreed, and was lifted into the back and lay there while the driver negotiated the small country lanes amongst the busy Easter traffic. For once I was relaxed, knowing I would be out for a while with the injury. But, equally, I was disappointed in myself for crashing, pissed off that it was two crashes in two meetings, which was unusual for me.

I thought about Rex, who was busy consoling me by playing down the incident, but I knew he was also assessing his own predicament. It was the correct thing to do, to accompany me to the hospital. He would have to wait for me to be seen by a doctor, by which time dinnertime would have come and gone. He knew hospitals have cafeterias and they sell chocolate bars. His big bushy eyebrows twitched at the mere thought of chocolate. They twitched several more times before we arrived at the Accident and Emergency section of Leicester Infirmary.

In a strange way I felt rather good, a bit like a Boy Scout in that I was prepared. I had heard it said that you leave your dignity at the hospital door. But that morning I had washed, shaved, showered and put clean knickers on.

I sat in the emergency ward for a couple of hours and not one person came to see me. I was expecting that from the National Health Service. Finally, a nice-looking girl in a nurse's uniform came past and asked if someone had seen me yet. She asked a few questions and then had a look at my wound. She took a lead pencil out of her pocket and began probing in and around my open gash. As soon as

I realized what she was doing I said 'Whooo! What the hell do you think you're doing with that pencil? Get it out of there — I don't want a fucking infection you dimwit.' Without a word she walked away and I couldn't help thinking she might not have even been a nurse at all. I was perplexed by her actions.

A duty doctor came by with a clipboard and peered in, did some probing and asked a few questions, then said, 'It's not broken so I'm going to close it with a few stitches and then you can go.' Eventually, I was seen by an old matron who cleaned the wound using sterile equipment and bandages that at least looked new. Ten minutes later I stood up and hobbled off with the aid of Rex's shoulder.

I made the trip up to Oulton Park the next day just to cheer on what was left of a broken British team. The Yanks won the Match Race Series convincingly. Donington came and went as well with me sitting on the sidelines watching Randy win his third Shellsport race to take a handy lead.

The injuries I knew would heal quite quickly, but my right hand was another story when I sat on a bike and twisted the throttle. The first and second finger had no strength and I needed them to work the brake and throttle. I had limited time to get ready for the first GP.

AUSTRIAN GRAND PRIX, SALZBURG, 19/20 APRIL 1980

I was at Beddington Lane one afternoon waiting for Rex to go so I could use the phone to call home. Maurice Knight came down to the workshop and hunted me out. 'Croz,' he said, 'it looks like we have a problem with the Spanish organizers. They've turned down your start application so we'll send Randy to Spain and we want you to ride at Donington on the F1 bike instead.'

I knew Maurice was as keen as hell to get me out there on the F1 machine. Understandably, he wanted a good showing on British soil with the new bike because that's where Suzuki's market was. With us opting out of Scarborough in favour of the Austrian GP and with the following two rounds of the TTF1 Championship also clashing with the Italian and Spanish Grand Prix, we knew it was going to be difficult to make up for lost ground later in the season. I could understand his thinking but was still a little disappointed. I had yet to start a GP and already here I was being asked to skip a couple. I felt hopeless, my heart sank and I probed Maurice for the reason why I hadn't been allowed a start. I knew what his answer would be.

'You're not on the grading list so they won't let you start,' he explained. I struggled with his explanation and wondered if there was another that would prevent me from starting. Rex had already gone through this with the organizers at Misano and had managed to convince them to give me a start. I had two works bikes and no GP to ride them in. I understood the grading system but how do you get on it if you can't get a start? It was a catch-22 situation.

Rex began making calls to the British Auto Cycle Union (ACU), and the FIM and I made a call to the Australian Federation to request a document to support my application. Rex ultimately championed my cause and a clearance eventually came through, confirming a start for the Spanish GP.

With the Venezuelan GP already cancelled, our new team set off from the Croydon workshop for our first GP of the season at Salzburg in Austria. The Salzburgring circuit is nestled in a wooded valley near the beautiful city of Salzburg. Brenda and I had elected to drive there in our new car. A few weeks after I'd arrived in the UK, Stadium Helmets had approached me with an offer to use their crash hats for the year. Somehow I negotiated a deal with them and picked up a new 2-litre Fiat Ritmo as payment. This little 4-door hatch was Bertone-styled and was apparently built by robots. There's nothing like taking delivery of a new car — especially one with style. I also couldn't help smiling at the thought that I'd got more money from a helmet sponsor than I did from Suzuki. I was glad it was not public knowledge just how little I had signed on for with the Suzuki team.

During testing at Brands Hatch the previous week I had lost the front end again, going around the hairpin in what I thought was just a slow step-off, but I banged my right hand rather heavily in the fall. Later that day I discovered a rather large hard lump on the back of my hand. I made light of the pain and thought it would come right in a few days. While the damage might have been minimal, my pride was severely dented.

Our drive through Austria and into Mozart's hometown was just beautiful and left an impression that would stay with me for life. Salzburg is a fabulously elegant and sophisticated city surrounded by hills and with a real sense of its own history. I wanted to come back during the winter, when it would be romantic and magical.

The team was booked into the Gasthof Am Riedl at Koppl, close to the circuit. Each year Suzuki made a booking for the following year, so we were welcomed warmly. As we nestled into our cosy room I thought of the benefits of being a factory rider. The team management worked through all such arrangements when it had its pre-season planning meetings. I thought it would be a case of 'OK guys we're off to Austria — anyone know a good hotel?' This is where Rex White excelled. He introduced me to the best pork schnitzels I had ever tasted, washed down with a few large glasses of Salzburg Marzen Bier. Looking out across the valley with its exhilarating views, I wondered if life could be much better than this.

A private practice session had been arranged for Wednesday so we could at least get a few laps in on our new XR34's, which we thought were promising. That morning I walked out into the fresh alpine air and noticed a few snowflakes floating down. The sky was opaque, an ominous sign. Out at the track I studied the layout by driving around the ring road and peering through the trees. It looked fast and had Armco barriers bordering it. Although it did not look like a technical course with lots of corners, all racetracks usually have only one racing line, which I would find out soon enough.

Our new Team Suzuki bus looked slick and professional parked in a prime spot close to the Dunlop truck. Our team had signed a supply contract with Dunlop, whose technical manager Peter Ingley would keep our bikes shod with the very best and latest in tyre technology. In turn, we would provide Dunlop with a platform on which they could test and develop racing tyres, with the goal of winning the world championship. Eventually, the technology would be used on street bikes. It was all about marketing and branding I guess, but for Randy and me it meant we had access to Dunlop's best racing product, a factor we saw as giving us a huge advantage. The bus had been designed to function as a transporter, workshop, spares storage and hospitality unit. A large awning was attached to the side, providing both shelter and an external workspace area.

In the paddock Radar and Mick were preparing the bike for the first session. Randy's mechanics were in a similar position of readiness. I knew I needn't worry about being there all the time because that was their job and where their expertise lay. Radar once jokingly told me, 'Riders should be treated like mushrooms — keep them in the dark and feed them shit.' An old saying for sure, but I knew where he was coming from. I could easily have got involved rubbing shoulders and keeping an eye on things, standing over and checking my mechanics' work. But I had full trust in these two guys and the team management; after all, we were chasing the same thing. All of us wanted to win races — for the riders, the team and for the factory's sake.

To assist our team mechanics, Martyn Ogborne was on hand with his invaluable file of data that had been compiled from a number of riders over the years. Both Randy and I benefited from the previous year's data. In this case all of Barry Sheene's race records and settings were neatly recorded and could be pulled up at any time or phase of a GP. This was to be one of those times as we checked for overall ratios and, once fitted, we were to be almost on the money from the first lap.

This year the bike was considerably different from the previous year's. We now had a cassette-type side-loading gearbox, allowing us to change internal ratios independently and without having to split the crankcases. Each of the six gears had between three and five optional ratios and simply by changing two cogs, the rpm at a given speed could be altered. This was all new to me so I spent lots of time studying the speed and gear charts to come up with a solution to a problem, though I think unless the bike is at its maximum performance you could easily go backwards if you get it wrong.

I got on the paddock bike and did a lap of the track. It was extremely cold and I hated the cold, as my blood seems to go real thick then the circulation slows. I looked down at my hands and noticed my fingers were all white on the tips. I knew I would get in only a few laps before having to come in to warm up.

As soon as Radar pushed me off for the first sighting lap and I tested the steering damper, I knew I was in trouble. The fact that my vision was being impaired with the snowflakes on my visor was the least of my problems. My right hand had not healed quickly enough, rendering me as useless as tits on a bull. Under brakes I was in pain. In an effort to minimize the pain I tried bracing my legs against the tank under brakes to take the weight off my wrists. The steering gave a flick coming out onto the front straight and gave my wrist a real tweak. I was in trouble. My leg had not really got back to full movement and the grippy seat pad made it rather awkward to move around from side to side as I changed directions. Nothing seemed to be working and luckily the test session was called off due to the snow. Secretly, I was pleased but played the game and acted disappointed. Maybe it would all come right tomorrow.

After a debrief following those few laps, it was decided we had achieved little of value, so it was off to the hotel for another beer and one of those schnitzels. On the way I made a detour to find a doctor and reluctantly asked him to give me three cortisone shots directly into my damaged hand. I was wary of having these shots because I'd heard there was a risk of damaging your eyesight over time. The doctor gave me three jabs, then relieved me of all my funny-coloured Austrian money.

We awoke the next morning to a strange peacefulness. It was eerie, almost surreal, and deadly quiet. I pulled back the blinds and opened the shutters to find about two metres of snow in and around the hotel. My first thought was, Great! — another day to allow my hand to heal. There would be no practice today.

The snow continued falling during the morning and the gossip was that the Austrian GP might be cancelled. I could not race and expect to do well — my hand would not allow it. Then we heard it was official; none of us would be racing here this year.

Randy had parked his brand-new motorhome in the hotel car park that night. We all made the customary visit to check it out and agreed this type of accommodation was the way of the future for GP riders.

The crew had settled down to some serious drinking at the hotel bar and the stories were flowing. Then, KAWOOOOMF! A huge explosion was heard, the windows shook and glasses rattled, followed by total confusion. We all rushed to the door. Randy's motorhome stood with its interior partially exposed to the night air. It had literally exploded, peeling the roof back and splitting three sides. We thought Randy must have died, as no one could survive such a destructive force. We rushed over and were relieved to find he was not in it. Going out for dinner that night had saved his life. He was sure in for a surprise when he arrived back at the hotel. We figured it must have been a gas leak and with gas being heavier than air, it filled up until the level reached the heater pilot light and up she went.

On Monday we all set off for Italy to get ready for a private testing session at Misano. I had not ridden there before, so it would be valuable to get some experience and to set up the bikes going into my first Grand Prix.

TESTING AT MISANO AND BRANDS

We had a few days up our sleeves with nothing to do but wait until our scheduled two days of testing at Misano on Tuesday 29 and Wednesday 30 April, followed by another scheduled test session back at Brands on our new XR69's. I was beginning to feel nervous. Other than the Trans-Atlantic races in early April, we had yet to fire a shot in anger as a team. I looked at the race schedule again to remind me of just how much racing was in the pipeline. I just wanted to get on with it.

The private testing at Misano presented me with a problem I had never had to face before. I had developed a mental block about my riding ability and I could see no way around it. I had allowed self-doubt to get the better of me. That seed had probably been sown by the murmurings in the paddock about why I had been given a works Suzuki.

To the European press I was an unknown, someone with no experience who had somehow been given a works bike. I had no history in Grand Prix racing, so why was Suzuki wasting their time and money on me? They could easily have had Virginio Ferrari or any number of experienced riders but instead potentially the best bike in the world was handed to some guy from New Zealand who rode 4-strokes.

The process of losing my confidence possibly was compounded when I started floundering around trying unsuccessfully to produce lap times of any significance. Over the next few days there was no appreciable improvement in my lap times. The stopwatch is ultimately the sole indicator of a rider's ability and the results reflect that, but the more I questioned my ability, the worse my performances became. The stopwatches kept recording faster lap times for everyone except me. I felt like I'd hit a wall, embarrassed by my inability to connect with this bike. I went in search of a silver bullet.

After testing was over on Tuesday afternoon I slipped out of my racing suit. I was feeling really despondent. I wasn't looking forward to the trip to Brands Hatch for another two days of testing; I just wanted to find a hole to crawl into and die. Reluctantly, I packed my suit and helmet into an overnight bag. We couldn't catch a flight that would work, so Radar and I were dropped off at the local train station at Rimini. We would take a train to Pescara further down the coast, then connect with another train direct to Rome to overnight. We had booked an early flight from Rome to Gatwick so we could make Brands Hatch by 10 a.m.

We couldn't speak or understand Italian but we gathered that we would be stopping at a station long enough to get some food. Radar and I jumped out, picked up a sandwich and a few beers then jumped back on the train. About an hour later Radar began looking at his watch. He was thinking we should have been at Pescara by now.

Finally, Radar asked a passenger how long it would be before we reached Pescara. In his best English, he quietly informed us we'd passed through Pescara over an hour ago and it was another 30 minutes to the next stop. By the time we backtracked to Pescara and caught the last train to Rome it was just after midnight. We found a little hotel close to the station and went exploring, ending up in a bar full of beautiful women.

We made the early flight to Gatwick and by 11 a.m. I was out on the diesel doing laps at Brands Hatch, fine-tuning the suspension and happy to be on a bike I felt comfortable with. The testing turned out to be valuable because we discovered a problem with the valve-to-piston clearance. The engine had great power and torque and the carburettors worked well, making it easy to ride, but if you over-revved it past 9400 rpm the valves clipped the piston and power was lost instantly.

If you really got it wrong and mis-shifted badly, the engine might destroy itself and rattle to a stop. I learnt over the next two days to avoid using revs that high. Our new 4-stroke team was led by Dave 'Junior' Collins with Steve Moore backing up in a part-time role. It wasn't a 20-minute job to replace a bent valve, so I had to be extra careful. It was important to know the limits of the bike, especially how far you could go before you risked bending a valve.

ISLE OF MAN PREVIEW, 3–4 MAY 1980

With the successful testing session over at Brands Hatch I caught a flight to the Isle of Man. I was pleased to be getting a couple of days on the Island to reacquaint myself with this tortuous track. I needed to make as many laps around the circuit as possible before this year's event.

The previous year I'd been lucky to come away with a good result but this year I could feel the pressure building. I arrived at the airport and went to hire a car and to my astonishment I was turned down. My reputation had preceded me and I found there was a ban on the 'Croz' renting cars on the Isle of Man. This year was to be different and I had to work hard to find anyone willing to lend me a bike or perhaps a car to do some laps. If I got desperate I might have to catch a bus.

A call to my friend Wally Radcliff at Ramsey seemed to do the job. He had given invaluable assistance to the 'newcomer' the year before. He must have had confidence in me and knew what larrikins we racers could be, given half a chance. I was only here to re-learn the circuit, with no distractions to lead me astray. I promised not to do anything crazy and Wally was able to get a car for me. I did about 20 laps to get a feeling for the course again, then went in the opposite direction around the track. It turned out to be a novel way of improving my circuit knowledge. Most of the laps I did, however, were on my intended racing line which quite often had me on the opposite side of the road. This was purely to simulate where I would be on the track during the race. It would also help me to become more familiar with the corners, exit points and those little bumps that act as memory joggers during the race.

I also rode a few laps at night and stopped at just about every pub, just to see what the locals were up to. I sat there sucking on a pint of local ale, just waiting for the opportunity to start a conversation. I would carefully steer the conversation to the subject of the TT races and found I got tips about the course from all kinds of people. Most of them related how good they thought Joey Dunlop was around the track. 'He's flat on the tank around this bend ... he doesn't back off at all around that bend ... he's by far the quickest through this section' ... and on and on it would go, story after story. 'Hell,' I began to think, 'do I need to be here listening to this?' Maybe I should try the Crosby Pub next, it might be different, I thought, picking up my pint and draining the last few drops before leaving.

Tomorrow I would be on the plane back to Gatwick to connect with another flight back to Italy. I hoped that my few days here would remain etched in my memory banks. I wanted to be able to retrieve it all in a split second if need be.

Riding at the TT can also have a negative effect on your racing. The TT is a place where you can ill afford a mistake and the little man in your head talks constantly of being smooth and fast. Over-riding can only lead to dire consequences, but on the short circuits of the UK a more aggressive style is needed. It takes a whole race meeting to get back up to speed if you have just come off the TT where high-speed touring is recommended. It's just one of the anomalies of road racing.

I dropped off the undamaged car at the airport and made the plane for Gatwick, happy that the time spent here had been fruitful. Later I boarded another flight to Firenze where I was picked up by Martyn and taken to Rimini. Weather permitting, the Grand Prix season was about to get under way.

ITALIAN GRAND PRIX, MISANO, 11 MAY 1980

It didn't take long for me to realize that I had not shaken off my demons. It was becoming clear to many that perhaps I hadn't earned the right to have my bum on a factory bike. Luckily for me the press had focused on the story about Virginio Ferrari's plight as it developed with his new sponsor Zago.

Virginio had burnt his bridges with the Gallina team and lost any opportunity of getting any factory support. He was given an RG Suzuki by Zago who had provided Suzukis for Mike Baldwin and Randy Mamola the year before. Virginio arrived at the circuit ready to race and the Italian press were all excited by his presence. However, his bike was impounded by the Italian police following accusations that money paid to him by Bieffe Helmets had ended up in Zago's bank. How individual sponsorship works in teams varied a lot, but perhaps Zago thought he had the right of access to it. Whoever was right or wrong didn't matter to me as long as the press kept their eyes and poison pens pointed in another direction, away from me.

Another source of distraction for the journalists was the development of the breakaway World Series. It had been festering on the sidelines, slowly gathering support and threatening to derail the FIM Championship. The original concept was to gain better conditions by forming a new World Series. This was the riders' reaction to what they felt was the organizers' failure to heed the groundswell of dissatisfaction. The riders who supported it still retained that passion and drive for change but the new World Series lacked specifics and failed to get momentum, leaving riders with no choice but to return to the FIM-controlled championship.

Fundamentally, the World Series was still active and being orchestrated by a small band of believers who would not go away. Since plans for a World Series had leaked out at Silverstone the year before, it was only a matter of time before the FIM recognized the problem and tried to block any advance by this bunch of freedom-fighters. During the off-season some circuits had agreed in principle to run World Series races but the whole programme needed time to get bedded down and to do this all within a year was unrealistic.

However, in a show of strength the FIM contacted all circuits, informing them that if they ran a World Series event then they would not be allocated any FIM races. The small, dedicated group behind the World Series, led by Barry Coleman, had been fighting for better conditions for the riders and had indirectly achieved some good results. As if to placate the riders' demands, the FIM announced that prize money would be increased, but the starting money system was to be abolished.

My self-confidence was still a problem, but while I knew I was having trouble, Mick and Radar were quite relaxed and understood the pressure on me. They insisted things would come right but it was proving a painful experience for me. Worst of all, Randy had set an unofficial lap record in practice, making me look slow by comparison. Finally, after all the qualifying was over, I had recorded my best time at 1:24.6, a full 2.2 seconds slower than Marco Lucchinelli but surprisingly only 0.1 seconds slower than Sheene. It didn't matter that I was slower than Barry but being 16th on grid behind lots of privateers really made me feel sick.

Looking at the company I was in at my first Grand Prix, it was a pretty damn good line-up, making me further question whether I deserved being here. 'Am I good enough to mix it up with them?' I asked myself.

My leg had been giving me a lot of pain but I couldn't blame my poor performance on that. Demoralized, I lined up on the grid for the race and became a DNF statistic, along with five other factory bikes. Mine locked up on lap 12 as a result of an ignition problem but most likely it would have run a bearing like the balance of the factory Suzukis. Each of them rumbled to a halt at various stages of the race, all with collapsed main bearings. It was not a good start for the Texaco Heron Team. The only saving grace for the factory was that Graziano Rossi actually managed to get his Gallina Suzuki to make it across the finish line for third place and 10 points.

SPANISH GRAND PRIX, JARAMA, 18 MAY 1980

Brenda and I drove off in the direction of Madrid for the Spanish Grand Prix at Jarama. We stopped in Barcelona and drove around Montjuic Park, wondering how they could possibly run a 24-hour race on a street circuit like that. I was so happy not to be involved in those 24-hour marathon events.

I recalled talking with Radar about his last trip to Jarama when he stopped to buy food halfway across the barren land between Zaragoza and Madrid. He spotted a nice-looking salad with what looked like macaroni pasta wrapped in a large lettuce leaf. Back in the truck he started picking at it and couldn't quite recognize the taste, so he peeled back the lettuce leaf to expose part of a sheep's skull. What he'd thought was macaroni turned out to be sheep brains. Radar biffed it out the window in a second.

The Japanese technicians were also on the road and we ran into them about 100 km from Madrid. They had stopped at a roadside café which sold all sorts of weird things and I spotted a decorative goatskin bag. It was full of the local red wine and came complete with a shoulder strap, which caught my interest. I bought it and threw it in the car along with a few sandwiches and cold drinks. We agreed to meet each other down the road at a lay-by where we would relax and eat our lunch in the hot sun.

I opened and tested the wine bag. It was horrid and dry but when I passed it to Okamoto-san he gulped it down, muttering to me 'Crosby-san, this is local wine and is very good for you — try some more.' I did and it was still bloody horrid, so I passed it back. Soon Okamoto-san had told us his whole life story and in the process he became less and less coherent until finally he fell asleep. We left him flat on his back in the afternoon sun while his Japanese mate snoozed nearby.

Randy's first M1 chassis arrived at Jarama just in time to get it ready for qualifying. Hartog and Rossi got theirs as well but it didn't bother me because I still felt slightly guilty that I might be taking the place of someone who could do the bike justice. I was half-expecting to be dropped in favour of some up-and-coming youngster.

I found out in the first few laps that my front wheel had a patter — an uncontrolled bouncing of the front wheel — that I put down to a lack of dampening. Nothing I tried worked. I spent long hours studying the suspension charts, looking for a magical solution. I spoke at length with our suspension man from Kayaba but all he could do was produce more bloody charts to study. I didn't want charts, I wanted action. So far it had been a turn here and a twist there on the dampers, which had produced no noticeable improvement and out of desperation I finally asked Mick to do something drastic. I needed a hole drilled in the front damper tube so I could get some feel into the front end. It had to be done at night away from prying eyes and after the Kayaba man had retired to the hotel.

My low self-confidence since the Mallory Park crash hadn't improved any and now the problems with the bike's set-up exacerbated the situation. Mick and Radar ripped the front end out of the bike and pulled the forks apart. We drilled a 1 mm hole where we thought it might work best and reassembled it.

The first lap of the race I found it worked better but slowly things got worse as it heated up. Although still there, the wheel patter had almost gone in the front but reappeared in the rear with a vengeance. I must have disturbed the suspension balance of the bike and it was proving almost impossible to ride fast.

I had a battle staying upright but I was more fortunate than some. Randy had complained about the bike dragging on the ground through corners and it caught out both Rossi and Will Hartog. Kenny ran away with the race and Marco finished a great second with Randy third and Sheene fourth. Apparently, Barry had been pissed off that his new bikes didn't compare very well with the new Suzukis; if that was so, he must have been rueing the day he changed camps.

After the finish line I carried out the customary plug chop and pulled to the side. Barry was already on the side of the track pushing his Yamaha back to the pits. He leaned over to get my attention, asking, 'How did you get on, Croz?'

'I think 12th — not too good eh?' I replied.

'Mate, it's a fucking long way to come for no points,' he said, as if to rub it in.

I was furious, knowing he was absolutely right. I went back to the paddock one very disappointed and depressed factory rider.

FRENCH GRAND PRIX, PAUL RICARD

It was getting worse for me every race. I loved the circuit at Paul Ricard with its long straights and open corners. But right from the first practice lap I was slow, almost lethargic and definitely lacking in self-confidence. I couldn't seem to shake it. I went from one problem to another, unable to clearly define what it was or how it should be fixed. I was well behind the 8-ball in my lap times. The days of having fun, just turning up and blasting around the track with a few minor changes had long gone. Racing now had suddenly became one hell of a lot harder and I was appreciating just how well Kenny and even Randy handled the difficult task of setting up bikes with only minimal track time.

I was also discovering that the privateers had become good at turning on the tap when required, leaving me floundering around. I was lost and needed help. I had no one to turn to for support other than Mick, Radar and Brenda. I had gone off the rails completely and was scrambling to get a foothold to stop my world from spinning away from me.

Perhaps I had taken on too much this year. The TTF1 championship continued rolling along, despite my not being there and now I was also missing critical points in the Shellsport race at Brands. I was starting to think that I should have stayed in the UK and ridden at Brands instead of toughing it out here and getting myself stressed.

Some press reporters were able to rationalize the situation I found myself in. They had seen what I was capable of and some had commented that my recent performances were uncharacteristic of me. Something was going to happen to shake me from this depressed state. Bloody hell, being 20th on grid was not exactly what I had in mind; in fact I'd never been so far back on any grid, ever.

When the race started Kenny, Randy and Marco disappeared off into the distance, leaving me with a bunch of privateers battling it out for minor placings. Randy had his new M1 going great guns but his Nava helmet continued to plague him with fogging problems. My helmet fogged up regularly but never as bad as Randy's. This time he possibly lost a place through not being able to see clearly. I got locked into a private race with Barry Sheene and we spent the whole time swapping places. Towards the end of the race, making the turn on to the front straight, Barry got it all wrong and lost the front end. As he crashed, his little finger must have got caught under the bike as he slid down the road. It was a mess requiring surgery, but the doctors managed to save it, using pins to hold it together.

Although I finished fifth I was less than happy with the result, knowing I could do a hell of a lot better. I just had to dig my way out of this hole somehow. I checked the race reports that Martyn had sent back to Japan. Randy's one had sections detailing suspension changes that he had made, speed trap times of 283 kph and performance reports on his Dunlop tyres. My report was almost devoid of information, as if to say there is nothing to report. Martyn was correct. It made me more depressed.

Gary Taylor, a PR man from London who had been helping the team, had asked photographer Don Morley to give me a lift back to Marseilles Airport as both of us were going straight on through to the TT from there. The first London flight didn't leave until Monday morning and as accommodation was tight we shared a hotel room.

As we headed for Marseilles my mind went back to the race. I never used to get too hung-up if I'd had a bad day. Until a few months ago those had been few and far between. Suddenly, it dawned on me: I had never really been pushed personally to perform. If I looked back on my career to date, I had always been challenging in the tough races but I'd never doubted that I lacked skill. Virtually without exception I had always out-performed my equipment's perceived capabilities. Right back to the old A7 days — though it was ancient I'd wrung every ounce out of it. The H2 was also old but I rarely got beaten. Rosko's superbike — unbeaten again, and even with the Moriwaki bike in the UK the year before, I exceeded everyone's expectations. I had been on the move up and if I didn't win, it was normally not because someone was better than me, it was the result of a mechanical fault or I was riding a bike so vastly different that I wasn't expected to win. Until now I had never needed to look at me, the person.

At the hotel Don was trying to phone his wife Jo, who was going to meet us at Heathrow then join us to go to the Island. He also had to make arrangements for getting his French Grand Prix films picked up. Don picks up from here:

> 'I was lying on my bed with my back to Croz, desperately trying to hear and be heard, but conscious Croz kept asking me if I fancied a drink. I nearly collapsed laughing when I turned round to look at Croz, as rather than offering me a can or a bottle he was standing behind me with the hotel fridge held aloft for my perusal. And I should mention that this fridge until a moment ago had been tethered to the wall.'

14

RUNNING ON EMPTY? 1980

ISLE OF MAN, 31 MAY 1980

With my first few Grand Prix over I was glad to get back to the UK and eager to kick my depressed state. Don and I had arrived at the start of practice week and I remembered to say hello to the fairies under Fairy Bridge on the way into Douglas. Bizarre as it sounds, I did indeed greet them and will continue to do so, just in case.

The F1 team was already there and had set up camp at the Majestic Hotel. Everyone was excited about the prospect of this year's TT event. I had booked into a private house in Douglas for the fortnight at an astronomical cost but it gave me the autonomy I needed. My first designated job was picking up Pops Yoshimura and his wife plus mechanic Asakawa-san from the airport. These guys knew the meaning of hard graft: even Pops' wife had spent long hours polishing valves late into the night when their business was going through tough times in America. I had huge respect for the Yoshimura family. I was hoping I could deliver the goods just like I had at Daytona.

This year's TT programme would be hectic, with three races scheduled within a week. My XR34 and XR69 were perhaps the best bikes at the TT this time and I would need them to overcome my inexperience around the circuit. I had a great team around me but when the flag drops the bullshit stops, leaving me to prove my worth out there on my own.

As everyone settled in for the week and the journalists began arriving, the inevitable issue of track safety raised its ugly head. The same old topic questioning the suitability of the course as an international event was being regurgitated. Of concern was why the ACU and the Manx Government should shell out a whole lot of cash to lure Grand Prix stars to the TT. The feelers had been put out this year but there was little interest shown and it failed as a recruitment process. So again this year it would be left to the TT stalwarts who regularly came over and enjoyed what TT supporters claim is the best event in the world on a true road racing course.

A few months earlier I had organized my starting arrangements with the ACU. I'd discussed it with a few close friends, so when Vernon Cooper from the ACU called me and offered me a guaranteed £6000 for the event, I agreed. I would pocket that sum win, lose or draw. Converted to Kiwi dollars at an exchange rate of 28p to the dollar, it was looking rather nice. I just had to make sure I remained upright and walking when it came time to collect.

I enjoyed the TT the previous year and would always justify its dangerous reputation by repeating what I'd been told: 'It's only a high-speed tour — treat it that way and you'll be fine.'

'Bollocks!' I could also argue that once the visor goes down and your eyes glaze over with adrenalin it really is a balls-out, as-hard-as-you-can-go ride, but it's the course that demands how fast you actually go, and that is balanced by your desire for self-preservation.

The senior practice was held early in the morning and for me it was just as easy to get showered and put on my racing suit before driving the short distance to the paddock. Martyn was already orchestrating proceedings, running around like a headless chook co-ordinating our team. Rex was also on deck but he was out on the prowl for a 'bacon buttie' sandwich and most likely a chocolate bar for dessert. Radar and Mick were making the final adjustments to my XR34 Suzuki. It looked ugly this morning, sporting a huge alloy tank that was used the year before on Mike Hailwood's bike. It was essential so we could carry enough fuel for three laps. No more climbing over the bike like a monkey — this would be racing in the traditional style, because the big tank would not allow much rider movement.

I pushed off from the start and accelerated down Glencrutchery Road, noting just how long the first gear ratio was. It seemed to go on and on forever.

'Shit it's high — can I make it round without having to slip the clutch?' I wondered, remembering I had to negotiate the tight hairpin at Ramsey and the Gooseneck. I whistled down Bray Hill, where the G-forces really come into play, bottoming out the suspension, pushing a pressure wave of forces through all the chassis components. I hit the bottom of Bray Hill and the bike made its normal heavy shudder.

'Holy shit!' I yelled through clenched teeth. I was being electrocuted. My whole body reeled with the pain of 40,000 volts. Instinctively, I flicked my thumb to find the kill switch, then pulled the clutch in and calm was restored. I wasn't sure exactly what had happened, so I released the kill button and let the clutch out again and sure enough I got another whack. I quickly figured that the new tank must be touching a plug lead to send all that high voltage back up through the tank and into the chassis. Holding the handlebars and being wrapped around the tank, I really had been electrocuted.

Coasting to a stop, I lifted up the tank from its rubber resting pads and checked the plug cap ends. I could see where chaffing was present, most likely caused by the weight of the heavy fuel tank. It was about 38 kg under normal conditions but under G-load it was more like 80 kg, enough to bulge the bottom of the tank out and arc against the plug caps nestling below. The tank needed to be modified a little, so I pushed-started the bike again with the tank sitting loosely on the chassis and rode off the course and through the streets of Douglas back to the paddock. Radar and Mick had just sat down for a cup of tea and a bacon buttie when I rolled up. They looked surprised as I was supposed to be at least 20 minutes away — the time it takes to complete a lap. I teased them about how easy it was being a mechanic, sitting around drinking tea and feeding their faces. Then I explained the problem and they got back to work.

The tank was given extra clearance and I went out for two more laps. Although heavy at first, it improved as the fuel burnt off and the weight lessened. I felt good with the bike and the gearing at Ramsey Hairpin worked but only if I had a clean line and kept up the speed; otherwise the clutch would get a hiding exiting the Hairpin. I could try a lower ratio if it rained for the race. By the time the session ended, I was happy with my lap times but aware of the locals who had posted faster times. What they lacked in equipment they made up for with track knowledge and skill. Next Wednesday was going to be a tough race.

The last practice session for me was on the Formula One bike. I felt I knew most of the circuit reasonably well but there were areas where I lacked confidence. The best way to tackle the circuit, I thought, would be to tack onto someone who really knows the course. I went out with the expectation that someone would come past so I could do just that. In the final F1 session I knew Alex George was behind and I waited for him to pass me somewhere, probably before Ballacraine.

I set off down Glencrutchery Road, down Bray Hill to Quarter Bridge, getting the feel of the bike. It felt heavy and a little cumbersome with a full load of fuel but I had not ridden it for a while and within a few more corners I was getting into it, flying past the Highlander towards Ballacraine. After a long sustained run in from Glen Vine at full throttle, it's hard to judge a braking point at speed but I made a mental note of a low wall that ended just when my arsehole began to twitch and I had to go for the brake.

The dead flies were already building up on my visor and my new boots were slowly getting that small indent on the sole I needed; after a few more miles it would provide a foothold on the footrest.

I heard Alex coming out of Kirk Michael on my run to Rhencullen but knew I had to stay on line and let him do the overtaking. I was waiting for the 4-stroke resonance that would let me know just how far behind he was. I was slow coming off Ballaugh Bridge and he slipped by and pulled away. Everything went light as I crested the rise alongside Sarah's Cottage. I had left it a bit too late to tuck in behind him. Bugger, I'd better let him go. I followed him down Sulby Straight, one of the hardest parts of the circuit. The speeds are exceptionally high and it is critical that you are right in the centre of the road, otherwise you get kicked out of your seat with the bumps. I felt like wanting to turn the steering damper up two notches but I knew I would then lose the overall feel of the bike. I came across the newly resealed section at the end of Sulby just as Alex disappeared out of sight. I started braking for the Sulby Bridge corner and tipped the bike into the turn; exiting the corner I rolled upright and with the throttle on I came up across the bridge.

I was suddenly confronted by colours, marshals with hi-visibility vests and flags being waved. People were running down the side of the road. I approached Ginger Hall reducing speed and realized there had been an accident. I wasn't expecting what I saw, though. Straw and debris had been strewn across the road and those telltale fibreglass white scrape marks led my eyes to where Alex George's big Honda had come to rest. He was laying stationary on the kerb about 20 metres away from his bike. It was a horrific sight and my heart missed a few beats. I felt a large lump forming in my throat. My mouth went dry and I could hardly swallow. This was not supposed to happen, not to Alex.

I pulled to a stop almost before anyone had arrived and parked my Suzuki against the stone wall. I rushed back up to Alex, who initially appeared to be in a semi-conscious state. I quickly checked that he was breathing then turned my attention to his helmet, looking for scuffs or impact marks that would keep me from removing it. With no visible signs of damage, I carefully and slowly eased Alex's head from his helmet. I was very careful not to move his head just in case he had suffered spinal or neck injuries. I tried to put myself in his position and kept talking to him to keep him conscious and constantly reminded him that help was on the way. But no doctors came and the shock would soon be setting in. The nearest doctor was stationed at Ballaugh which was only a few miles back. I wondered if someone had a radio nearby but I couldn't see anyone using one. Apparently, the accident had been called through to race control via the telephone but whoever reported can't have stressed how bad it was.

With shock now setting in fast, his leathers would go some way to helping conserve heat loss. I had no idea of the injuries and knew only that a recovery position would be best for him. He struggled in our attempt to roll him onto his side and I realized he was trying to tell us to leave him in the same position. It was hard assessing his physical condition but looking at where he'd crashed, with the stone walls and cobbled kerb, it looked bloody menacing and unforgiving.

Making him as comfortable as possible, I then backed away to allow the marshals and a first aid person to do their job. The rescue helicopter had been dispatched and would soon be here. There was nothing more I could do. I felt sickened by what I had seen and perhaps the sight of Alex in this critical state made me take a step back and re-evaluate this event.

Pushing my Suzuki off the kerb and bump-starting it, I rode around the rest of the course and made for the pit entrance. My crew were surprised but happy that I had come back in one piece. They had been hearing stories from other riders who saw my Suzuki up against the wall and thought I had been involved in the accident. This was serious stuff and we all felt for poor Alex, hoping that he would be OK.

I returned to the track after a few minor adjustments to my bike and did two more laps. I tried to put the accident out of my mind. Alex's ashen face with sweat and dust in his nostrils remained vivid in my mind. Alex was unquestionably a very talented rider, who was perhaps nearing the end of his career. The Isle of Man rewards riders like him with all his years of experience. It is a case of the old bull and the young bull, where experience balances the odds and the older rider hopes for a big pay-day before going into retirement. This was going to cost Alex dearly, maybe even his life.

Back in the paddock a ground-swell continued to build about the lack of safety measures and concern that the TT was getting too dangerous for these big bikes. Some believed that limits should be imposed and all manner of people were putting their two pennies' worth in. I even suggested that a limit of 500 cc could be adopted. But I should have remained silent because I had not yet earned the right to comment on this circuit.

I kept checking on Alex after his crash but as usual I couldn't get a straight answer. They would say something like 'He's bad and we don't know if he'll make it.' I tracked down his wife and she thanked me for stopping and rendering assistance. She went on to explain the extent of his injuries, which included broken bones. She told me it was touch and go for Alex and that the next 24 hours would be critical.

Saturday's TTF1 race was first up on the agenda for me, to be followed by the 500 cc senior race on Wednesday and the Classic on Friday. The TT formula class was established a few years earlier in response to removal of the Grand Prix from the Isle of Man in the mid-1970s. It also served to bolster up the flagging Superbike class that was dominated by Yamaha and had been losing popularity. This formula allowed other manufacturers to participate and the rules were straightforward. Any chassis was permitted but the production-based engines had to retain the original cases and cylinder head castings and be no bigger than 1000 cc. The carburettors had to be the original size but as our Suzuki had an oval-shaped inlet we had to insert a special ring-type restrictor in the carburettor. The rules included a 24-litre fuel tank restriction.

On race day I awoke with the butterflies, that tight, almost nauseous sensation in my stomach prior to any event I was riding in. My appetite was zero. I always struggled to eat anything on race days. I arrived at the start line area and it was abuzz with activity. Martyn had been looking at the allocated starting numbers again. We knew already that our starting number was going to be contentious, but as a novice at the TT I could not understand why I had been given number three starting slot. Normally, it is given to the faster and more experienced riders to avoid getting tangled up overtaking slower riders. That made sense, but I certainly did not want to be setting off on the world's toughest racetrack in position number three with the works Hondas behind me. 'Bugger that for a joke,' I thought.

Martyn regarded it as a dangerous move putting an inexperienced rider like me up front, as it would cause too much pressure. He lodged a request to the FIM jury to consider a change of my starting position. The jury approved the change and we were moved to number 11, which by coincidence happened to be the same starting time as Mick Grant on the big Honda. I had wanted to be shifted back down the starting order a little, not specifically next to Mick. The spot was earlier allocated to Dave Aldana but when he failed to show up, the FIM jury allowed me to use it.

At first I was concerned starting against Mick with all his years of experience at the TT. But I guess it suited me to keep him in sight rather than trying to keep 40 seconds ahead for the duration of the race.

The entire team was present at the start except for those doing the signalling. They were already out on the track taking up their positions in strategic areas to provide me with an up-to-date picture of how I was performing. I needed to know where I was on the road compared with my competitors. I wanted a position and then a time in seconds in front or behind the next rider. That would give an indication of how far behind or ahead I would be. The latest times were broadcast by Manx Radio and we placed our signallers at Ballacraine, Kirk Michael, Ramsey, the Gooseneck and Creg-ny-Baa, all areas that were accessible by road from outside the course.

I had chatted with members of the crowd and well-wishers before going for a 'slash' behind the stands. Coming out and still zipping up my suit, I was confronted by Barry Symonds from Honda Great Britain who told me that Honda had protested the change of my start position and consequently I would have to revert to my original place at three. I saw red and thought 'fuck you guys', as I'd only just managed to get comfortable with my new starting position next to Mick. My mind raced and I felt hot and frustrated as I moved to take up my position.

We had already positioned ourselves on the sixth row. I didn't know what to do. Honda were saying I'd have to start on my original position. I thought we had made the change correctly and it had been confirmed. It must have been a ploy to unnerve me. Well, it worked all right. Three minutes before the start of the race, I decided 'fuck them, I'm staying exactly where I am'. The countdown began and then at 10-second intervals I could hear the bikes revving up before they shot down Glencrutchery Road.

I was watching the starter drop his dinky little flag. He got prodded on the shoulder by a timekeeper just to keep the intervals correct. Exactly 50 seconds later it was my turn and both Mick and I got away cleanly. Mick apparently had some problems with a carburettor and it was misfiring. He didn't get the jump on me that I think he was looking for.

My visor was prone to fogging up with the cold. It happened religiously, despite all my experiments to prevent it, including using 'Fairy Liquid' and other anti-fogging chemicals. I could usually deal with some fogging but as my visor didn't fit perfectly it allowed air to come in. It's the wind rushing in that makes my eyes water, causing the problem. The drops formed and hung on the end of my eyelashes. It was like being in a goldfish bowl — my vision became blurred, making reading the road difficult. A few miles out from the start the flies arrived. They were splattering continuously onto my visor. But it was the big fat bugs with yellow guts that got me. I knew to expect about 10 per lap. When one hits you it's like being struck with a duck egg. Your vision is instantly restricted and the first instinct is to wipe the visor with your glove. I have only done that once, luckily in practice. In a desperate bid to clear one of these bugs the previous year, I tried wiping the fat yellow thing off my visor and it just smeared its horrid yellow gunky entrails all over the visor and I had to pull up almost blinded.

I followed Mick for a couple of laps and he gradually got away from me, a few seconds at a time. When I went in for fuel at the end of the second lap I lost track of him completely. I couldn't make head or tail of my signals and rode the rest of the race oblivious to the fact Mick had stopped only once. On the last two laps I tried to make up some time but crossed the finish line in second place, only 12 seconds behind Mick.

When I crossed the line Mick had already done a U-turn and was trickling back up Glencrutchery Road to the paddock. I saw him bashing away at the tank of the big Honda with his fists as I flew by. Stopping and turning back up the road, I could still see him from behind bashing away. I thought I knew why immediately. There could be no other reason than to deliberately reduce its volumetric capacity. It was not being done as an expression of elation, that's for sure.

I arrived in the winner's enclosure and my bike was immediately taken into a secure area. Gordon Pantall congratulated me, reporting that the Honda had made only one stop. He also told me he thought they had used a big tank.

'Well, Gordon, I just saw Mick bashing the hell out of his tank just back there,' I replied, but by now the crowd had grown and I was being pushed and pulled away to the press area for photographs. I could see Gordon's face livid with rage as he put two and two together. He had been discussing the strategy with our team well before the finish and debating whether a protest should be made. My ears were ringing and hands still tingling as I slipped out of my helmet. Camera shutters clicked away as I was being slapped on the back and congratulated by the hordes of fans. When Martyn arrived I told him what I had witnessed. He hurried off to find Gordon and a protest was written up, but by the time the protest had been registered the Honda was nowhere to be seen.

Eventually, it was located and the tank inspected. It was larger than the allowable 24 litres and Mick admitted that the capacity would have been 28 litres, but as it had plastic bottles inserted the capacity was brought back to 24 litres.

As I had witnessed Mick's attempt to reduce the tank's capacity, I figured it must have been larger than the rules allowed, otherwise his actions would have been meaningless. The protest went to the FIM jury and was controversially thrown out a day later. Honda may have got away with it, but in doing so a shadow was cast over their sportsmanship. My name was mud to some TT supporters and the whole affair became divisive, splitting the Honda and Suzuki fans.

A few days later, with all the aggro over the F1 race slowly dissipating, I focused on the Senior TT. I had the only true Grand Prix bike in the race, but the local riders had the advantage of local track knowledge. My race plan was to go as hard as I felt comfortable with, then see how things developed. If I had to, I might give it a bit more but it was a six-lap race. The 240 miles of racing puts a lot of strain on equipment and sitting on the start line I felt comfortable knowing we had prepared ourselves well.

I started fairly quickly but was lying fourth on the first lap behind Cull, Guthrie and Ian Richards on his RG500. I felt if I rode consistently smooth and fast I would do all right here, but realistically I needed another year's experience before I could think about winning it. By lap two I was up into second where I stayed for the next three laps. The bike performed flawlessly but we had fitted a new screen before the race that turned out to be almost impossible to see through because it badly distorted the view. I spent the whole race looking over the screen to save accidentally running up a kerb.

My fuel stop was lightning-fast and I pulled 27 seconds back on Ian Richards. By lap four I was only five seconds behind and on the following lap I took the lead, two seconds ahead of Ian. Fortunately for me he then suffered a broken gearbox at Ballacraine, leaving me with a 52-second advantage to cross the line for my first TT win. Afterwards I was informed that I was only the third factory Suzuki rider to win the Senior TT, after Jack Findlay and Mike Hailwood.

The prizegiving during the week ended in a shambles as I was chastised and booed off the stage by a very vocal and rowdy Honda crowd. My team were forced to form a guard around me and they escorted me from the function just like a professional boxer. I was disappointed at the poor sportsmanship shown by the crowd and it took away the opportunity to savour the moment when I was presented with the huge solid silver Senior TT trophy.

Alex's condition gradually improved until finally it was announced that he was out of immediate danger.

The phone rang late at night. There was a bang on the door and a voice called out 'It's for you, Graeme.' 'Croz, its Charlie, we've lost Corky.' I was confused, 'What do you mean?' I asked. 'Mate we've lost Corky, he's gone, he had a heart attack today and he's gone.' I felt my mouth go instantly dry. 'Jesus Charlie, what happened?' It was beginning to register but I needed time to take it in.

Charlie continued, 'Corky had said to Shirley he wasn't feeling well and went and sat on the couch. Then he just slumped forward and that was it, gone!' I tried some small talk and it didn't work so

I thanked Charlie for his consideration in thinking to call me with this sad news. My eyes welled up and I began to cry softly. This was all new to me. I crawled back into bed and explained to Brenda what had happened. I spent the rest of the night lying there in disbelief that my good mate had gone.

My mind raced with the thoughts and feelings I had for this energetic man who was now no more. All I could keep thinking of were those crazy times we enjoyed together, including the day we were in a sinking boat on Auckland's Waitemata Harbour and I found out Corky couldn't swim.

I thought about Corky and how he always portrayed himself as a staunch and solid Aussie male, so it came as no surprise that he wouldn't have sought medical advice. At such times you think not only about your friend's family but about your own mortality. I went to sleep knowing that at least I had given him a smile when he heard I had won the Senior TT.

After my race in the TTF1 event, Pops and his boys (Asakawa, Junior and Radar) quickly replaced the cylinder and pistons in the Majestic Hotel garage to increase its capacity to 1084 cc. Then it was loaded into the back of the team van and taken up to Jurby Airfield so it could be checked and run in.

'Croz, can you get out to Jurby?' Martyn asked. 'We need to run in the big motor.' It was absolutely pissing down and I didn't want to go anywhere.

'Anyone want a ride on the F1 bike?' I was hoping some silly bugger would volunteer. Ray Battersby from Suzuki GB had his hand in the air before I had finished asking the question. Despite the rain, the airfield still had 30 or 40 hopefuls riding up the left side and back down the right side of the airstrip doing checks. Water was bouncing off the surface and the spray and mist formed by the motorcycles hung in the air like a fog.

Later Ray told me his story.

'I took up the offer of running the XR69 at Jurby. I watched closely as Pops' mechanic Asakawa-san hunched himself over the tank and push-started the big Suzuki. Once under way, he handed over the bike to me and I hoisted my excess baggage over the tank, selected first and dropped the clutch, changing up to second and then into third gear. I thought I could use a bit more throttle and before I knew it, the thing screamed away as the revs hit the sweet spot. I shot to the back of the seat and my arms were like ramrods, hanging on for dear life as the front end went light.

'I couldn't close the throttle because of the tension in my arms and I couldn't heave myself forward either. I couldn't see with all the spray and I was frightened to make a steering correction to the left because the surface was like a shallow lake. I was very conscious of aquaplaning if I crossed the sheets of water. Eventually, I managed to slow the bike down and even turn it around, then joined the other lads on their TZ350's returning to the start area. I put on a matter-of-fact face as I nonchalantly approached the van and passed the riding responsibilities over to another willing helper. Pops asked me what revs I had done in each of the gears. He then told me I'd been doing about 140 mph. That was the fastest I'd ever travelled on land.'

The Classic event turned out to be a disappointment. All the testing I had done previously had identified the only weakness in the big Suzuki: if you missed a gear and it over-revved, then you would probably bend a valve. On the third lap I mis-shifted and the tachometer needle shot up past 10,500 rpm. I knew straight away my race was over as the engine took on a new and unfamiliar note. It sounded sick, so I returned to the pit area and suggested an electrical failure as the possible cause for our stoppage. I jokingly blamed Ray for all the abuse he had given it at Jurby during 'his' test session.

The win in the Senior TT and my second place in the F1 gave my confidence a much-needed boost. Now I could look forward to the post-TT event at Mallory Park.

15

KNOCKING OFF THE SHARP EDGES, 1980

POST-TT, MALLORY PARK, 8 JUNE 1980

For different reasons, Randy and I were brought back to reality at Mallory Park for the post-TT event. Randy rode the XR69 for the first time in anger and promptly decided it was not what he wanted to do. I could understand that he wanted to concentrate on the Grand Prix events and we all knew he didn't have his heart in racing the big 4-strokes.

For me, it was the problem of getting back up to speed after riding the TT course. The continuous high speeds at the Isle made me ride differently and when I got back to Mallory it was a shock. Now it was back to the 'balls-out' riding style that has you teetering on the edge of crashing, lap after lap. It took a while to get back into that mode. Other than testing at Ryuyo in Japan and at Brands a few times, the Isle of Man was the only track where I had raced the XR69. We were concerned about the crankshaft being strong enough and the suspension needed work to get it to turn in correctly. Mallory became a testing session for us but the unexpected failure of an ignition unit meant we came away with no points. Our race programme for the TTF1 series was not looking particularly promising, although everyone would be able to drop their two worst rounds. I had already missed four races, scoring no points and even with a second at the TT, I was way behind.

DUTCH TT, ASSEN, 29 JUNE 1980

The Assen circuit at nearly 8 km around is one of Europe's best. It winds its way through a network of country roads and could be guaranteed to always produce a great race. The weather generally becomes the dominating factor and it has to be considered when setting up for the race and making tyre choices. The track may be fast, narrow and crowned to disperse water but the surface is smooth, offering plenty of grip.

I struggled with brake pads that refused to behave properly and ended up reverting to the Japanese pads for the race. With this change came the soft lever and I found myself pumping the master cylinder to get any pressure. Getting the carburettors to work coming out of slow corners was driving me mad. We changed pilot jets, made air screw adjustments and finally fitted different slides in an attempt to get drive out of the turns.

It was turning into a mess again and I started the race in the middle of the field. Once again I couldn't understand how Jack Middelburg was riding so fast. He had a good but not exceptional bike, but for some reason he just flew around this circuit. My performance was again dismal and embarrassing, but with other riders experiencing mechanical failures I inherited eighth spot and took three points to at least maintain my position in tenth place. Whoopee-do! I felt like handing the keys back and apologizing for taking up everyone's time. Although far from pleased, I was learning how to get on top of the set-up quickly, and actually looking forward to Belgium the next week.

BELGIAN GRAND PRIX, ZOLDER, 6 JULY 1980

My motorhome finally arrived in the UK from the United States. It was sitting on the docks in Liverpool, waiting for its new owner to pick it up. My friend 'Pan Am' Peter Defty had been left $10,000 to buy me a motorhome from my Daytona winnings. He found a nice 28-foot Itasca 'C' Class motorhome with a huge gas-guzzling V8 in it. It had travelled only 8000 miles and was in great nick.

I made a mad dash to Liverpool to pick it up, then drove it straight through to Zolder, arriving a couple of days before my birthday. It took all of 50 km for the nylon tyres on the motorhome to become smooth and round again after coming off the boat. The trip across the Atlantic had put flat spots on all the tyres which vibrated horrifically, sending anything that was not tied down crashing to the floor.

Arriving at Zolder, I was finally able to relax in my own space and in some respects it served to divert my attention from the crisis I was feeling as a rider. In practice things started coming together as I got the suspension working. My times began coming down; perhaps I had turned the corner at last.

The Professional Riders Association (PRA), led by the small core of 500 cc Grand Prix riders (notably Kenny, Marco, Rossi and Randy), had been talking about how many starters were being allowed for the 500 race. After practice had finished, the group decided to lobby the organizers on behalf of the 500 cc competitors, to reduce the number of starters from 35 to 30. It seemed strange that the PRA took this action while not considering the other classes.

Some privateers thought the idea stunk and even Barry Sheene excused himself after qualifying at the back of the grid. His damaged finger from the French Grand Prix made racing here too difficult and he left before being told he had missed the cut.

At Zolder a major problem arose when the timekeeping equipment failed to provide accurate results, leaving the organizers without certified FIM-approved qualifying times. In an attempt to placate everyone, they increased the number of starters to 40 per class. Then the PRA lobbied even harder and had the 500 class re-classified back down to 30.

Imagine if you awoke on race morning to find that the starting line-up had been reduced to only 30 and you were number 32. A few guys were indeed gutted, amongst them Stu Avant and Dave Potter. The PRA had shown its true colours — it represented the interests of only a few selected 500 cc riders and its fragile credibility began to fade.

My performances were improving and on this occasion I posted a time just over two seconds slower than Randy, who was on pole. My Suzuki felt good and we even tried a new rear brake torque arm in an effort to keep the bike from pitching too much under brakes. By fitting an extra brake calliper to one front disc and having it connected to the rear brake, we figured it would prevent excessive pitching as well. It was discarded after testing but assessed as being worthy of future work. After each practice or race, it is imperative for the riders to carry out a plug chop. To date, we had been looking at plugs in the normal way but now our Suzukis needed the heads taken off after every run, checking for detonation, or pre-ignition, which was quite prevalent with the vastly differing quality of fuels.

The race provided me with a real shock at the start. No sooner had I pushed the bike a foot or so when I dropped my chest onto the tank and simultaneously dropped the clutch. The engine fired and away I went, leading the Belgian Grand Prix. It's such a great feeling knowing that your engine has fired up first and you have a clear track in front of you.

'Holy shit, what the hell do I do now?' From my position of ninth on the grid I had ridden right through the leading bunch. It didn't last too long before I was passed by only two or three riders. I was maintaining my place and towards the end of the race I thought I might just get past Kenny, as his suspension called enough, but he hung on and crossed the line just ahead of me in third spot. I was rapt with my fourth place finish and the eight points it carried, but it was Randy who collected the full 15 points for the win.

We had a big party that night in the paddock. I felt I'd now got rid of the monkey off my back. My confidence had returned and best of all, it was great picking up my prize money. It wasn't about the cash for me; it was the thought that I could reward my two guys who had been doing a great job putting up with me floundering around at the back of the field. I counted out Radar and Mick's share in colourful Belgian francs and set off to find them.

SNETTERTON AND SUZUKA 8 HOUR, 20 and 27 JULY 1980

My race schedule this year had worked out quite well with only two real conflicts on dates and that was the French Grand Prix and the Finnish Grand Prix. The Finnish clashed with the Suzuka 8 Hour race in the last week of June. I had no option but to do the 8 Hour, which was by far the most important race in Japan. It was also a round of the FIM Coupe d'Endurance championship. I was excited about my prospects for Suzuka, not only because I enjoyed the long technical circuit, but because I had built up a collection of friends in and around Suzuka city.

Meanwhile I had to get Snetterton over and done with safely and with wet conditions forecast I needed to be especially careful. I could just imagine the reaction if a telex needed to be sent to Japan informing them I had stepped off injuring myself and wouldn't be making it to Suzuka.

The circuit near Thetford in Norfolk was wet all weekend and though the surface was like glass in places, I got through practice unscathed. Randy, on the other hand, would have preferred to stay in the bus rather than come out and play in the wet so it gave me a distinct advantage. I still faced stiff competition from Mick Grant, Ron Haslam and the usual bunch of tough-riding Poms who seemed to excel when the conditions deteriorated.

Having missed the first three rounds of the TTF1, I felt I had already left my run a little late in the title chase for the championship.

I had given away too many points already and was well behind, scoring only 12 points at the TT. I needed to get on a winning streak, and fast. My position in the Shellsport Series was marginally better but would have been healthier if I hadn't crashed at Mallory Park and missed two more rounds as a consequence. I was still in fifth place but with only 27 points I was a long way back from Randy.

Race day was bleak and miserably cold, and my feet stayed freezing all day. Both the TTF1 race and the Shellsport championship race were run in the rain and I won both relatively easily, bolstering my position in both championships. I jumped to second-equal with Stan Woods on 42 points, leaving Randy still leading on 67 with three more races to go. Keith Huewen on his Yamaha 750 beat me fairly and squarely in the Race of Aces. Whether I had my heart in it was debatable.

Straight after the race finished I threw a couple of cans of beer in the car and made my way back to London. I had a plane to catch the next day. My flight took me from Heathrow direct to Moscow on an old Boeing 707. On the climb-out we hit an air pocket and dropped what felt like 3000 feet. I was surprised just how many things went flying — bags and bottles that were not secured floated in mid-air for what seemed an eternity. At last the aircraft gave a solid shudder, signalling a return to normal flight and I ordered a red wine and settled back in my seat. On landing in Moscow we had to walk about 50 metres from the plane to the terminal. It was freezing cold so I bought a bearskin hat and drank four local vodkas. At least I think it was vodka; it tasted more like kerosene. When I re-boarded the flight I was seeing double and fell asleep for the final sector to Tokyo.

Arriving at Suzuka, I checked into the Suzuka Circuit Hotel as I was not going to be staying with the Moriwaki family this time. I went straight round to the Moriwaki workshop to see my friends. The place was a hive of activity with foreigners coming and going. Mamoru Moriwaki had enlisted Dave Aldana and David Emde to ride, plus Marty Lunde and Mike Trimby. They also fielded four entries with Japanese riders. It was going to be a big effort keeping all six bikes going for eight hours.

Our Yoshimura team appeared more focused, with only two bikes. I was riding with Wes Cooley on one of two XR69's and Mick Cole and Richard Schlachter would use the other. Kawasaki had the usual factory test riders entered, plus Gregg Hansford and Eddie Lawson. Honda put their effort behind the UK team of Ron Haslam and Roger Marshall. Additionally, there were two French Honda endurance teams with Hugeut and Hubin on one RS1000 and Fontan and Moineau on the other.

The hotel at the Suzuka circuit had just finished building extensions and it was pretty flash. We all received meal vouchers for various restaurants in and around the circuit for our stay. All meals were supplied and the evening meal vouchers would buy you an expensive dinner of teppanyaki steak. If someone was not going to use their voucher, I made sure I got it. These could be exchanged for jugs of cold Kirin beer and as the temperatures during the day often exceeded 35°C, they were prized items.

We got through practice without any major problems other than adjusting the suspension to suit both riders. And for most of the day the paddock restaurant was where everyone congregated out of the heat. The air-conditioners buzzed away, barely able to keep up with temperatures in the high 30s.

We got into the habit of cooling off at night in the hotel's outdoor swimming pool, jumping the fence then racing to be first in. Security must have turned a blind eye, as the pool was officially closed at that time. Thursday after evening practice I got called over by a group of mechanics and private riders from the UK. 'Croz, you coming swimming tonight?' they asked. I was known by the staff and my Japanese, limited as it was, would probably be enough to save them from getting locked up if caught.

'OK, see you guys at the fence at 10.' I couldn't pass up this opportunity and made the rendezvous. Stripping off all their clothes, the guys plunged into the warm water, naked butts dancing in the moonlight as they splashed about. I made sure I was last to start getting my gear off. Instead I stopped short, gathered all of their loose clothing and did a runner up and over the fence, leaving them to find their way back to the hotel naked. Next morning I heard all the stories of the naked foreigners creeping around the hotel grounds looking for a way in past the front-desk staff.

On race day over 100,000 spectators were present to watch the start in sweltering heat. The rainy season had just finished and humidity was extremely high. The mercury was at 35°C. It was going to be very sticky and almost unbearable out on the track during the one-hour stints. Plenty of fluids were needed, so I topped up on an isotonic drink named Pocari Sweat. A strange name, but it worked well keeping me fresh and alert.

Our Suzuki was quick but surprisingly fast was the Moriwaki Kawasaki with Aldana and David Emde. Less than one-tenth of a second separated us by the time qualifying was over, but it was our Suzuki on pole position.

Namiko Moriwaki had asked me on behalf of the organizers to say something in Japanese to the crowd before the racing started. I agreed and then spent a few hours learning a sentence or two. I was introduced to the crowd and began my little Japanese rendition of the statement, basically saying that I am going out to do battle and will do my best. The only thing I missed saying was a big 'BANZAI!'.

With the fanfare and formalities completed, the race started. I was doing the first hour and we would alternate the riding duties through the other seven. As usual with this race, the crashes came thick and fast with bikes and bodies soon littering the track. Handing over to Wes for his turn meant I could relax in the pit area and try to cool down. In the heat of the day the actual riding wasn't the problem — it was when you came in, purely because of the heat soak. When I saw the pit-in sign after 22 laps I carefully unzipped my racing suit to allow the air to rush in and cool me. Coming into the pits, I had to stay on the bike while it was refuelled and the tyres changed. This is done for safety reasons because if fuel is spilt it will be on the rider coming in and not going out. The heat soak really set in at that point while I sat astride the hot motor in 37°C heat, in direct sunlight.

Wes slipped his leg over the bike once I was clear and was off for his stint. I was really exhausted with the heat and stripped myself free of my leather suit. In our pit we had a stretcher and a fan that was directed onto me. I lay down and gulped three more isotonic drinks while the cool air slowly brought my body temperature down to a more manageable level.

On hand was the team's physiotherapist to give the riders a massage. In typical Asian fashion they tend to work with pressure points. I had other ideas and preferred the soft-tissue massage which his pretty little assistant could have easily administered. But no, I had just jumped off a bike from doing an hour's hard graft and this bloke had a hold of my foot and began massaging vigorously, unaware of the excruciating pain he was inflicting.

The team manager came over to let me know I had five laps before Wes came in. I already knew that and had been constantly checking progress as the race was developing. We were in a strong position but needed to keep up the speed and put as much time as we could between us and those following. Wes and I continued exchanging riding duties as the race progressed.

At about the six-hour mark I was looking for that first pit-in sign that would tell me I had only two laps to go. I came in and Wes went out, the bike was working perfectly and the engine seemed strong. I noticed Pops and Asakawa feverishly punching numbers on the calculator and I guessed they were working out the strategy for the last two hours. Asakawa came over to me. 'Crosby-san, ah! Can you do two sessions? Wes has blood trouble.'

'What's the problem with Wes?' I asked.

'He has diabetes and his blood is no good to race,' Asakawa replied. 'You have to do two sessions.' I knew Wes was diabetic but I thought if you took pills or jabbed yourself with insulin you'd have things under control. He was out there racing around in this heat and he was in danger of passing out.

I was in the pit area for only a few minutes when chaos erupted. The place became a hive of activity as the refuelling equipment was dragged into position and new tyres placed near where the bike was to come in. I was told to get ready and as I slipped my helmet on, Wes appeared on the bike. After fuelling up he nearly collapsed as he was dragged from the bike. I was on, out and into it within seconds. No tyre change, only fuel and a rider this time. I circulated and got a call to come in at the 22-lap mark. Wes was ready and we did a quick change before he escaped out of the pit lane.

The calculators were out again and I soon discovered the reason why. Despite being sick, Wes had been sent out to complete the minimum required number of laps for a co-rider. I had to finish the race by myself but the rules meant I could not ride more than 70 per cent of the race. Pops and Asakawa-san were busy working out how long we had to go and if I was OK doing the rest of the race.

The Kawasaki team of Gregg Hansford and Eddie Lawson had caught up and were right up our exhaust pipe. Beside us in the paddock Neville Doyle was busy doing his calculations too, checking that Wes made the minimum time. I am sure he was preparing to protest if we got it wrong. Pops was looking worried and began picking his fingers nervously. Not a good sign, I thought, as I asked him what he was thinking. It all depended on when I crossed the line because it took over two minutes to do a lap. He wanted me to arrive at the start-finish line just after seven o'clock. Otherwise it would be an extra lap and I would break the regulations and be disqualified.

Wes came in after doing his minimal stint and I went out with fresh tyres and full fuel. About an hour later I had to come in again but was out in a flash, maintaining a 12-second lead over Hansford on the Kawasaki. My lap times got faster as the night wore on. The track surface was shiny in the night air and our lights were on. Here I was howling around just waiting for the last lap signal. Finally, as I crossed the finish line amidst a barrage of photographers' flashes I knew I had done enough to hold off the challenge. Only 23 seconds separated first and second after eight hours of racing.

I thought about the 1 million yen prize money in 10,000 yen notes, all wrapped up in a nice fawn envelope with a pretty bow tied around it. I could picture it being handed to me by an official. It would have to wait, of course, and as I rode back into the pit area, Pops was ecstatic. Suzuki had won the 8 Hour race, and on Honda's home track.

The garlanding ceremony was over and I was on my fourth Kirin beer when the fireworks began. The highlight of any Suzuka event was the fireworks display. Following that I made a trip to Yoshimura's sales booth on the inside of the circuit and signed T-shirts and souvenirs late into the night. I finally ended up in the Log Cabin bar at the hotel, partying until the early hours.

Monday morning it was back to reality with the prizegiving ceremony, then I was on the train to Nagoya to catch the Shinkansen to Tokyo. I reached around to check my wallet — phew! My million yen was safely tucked away.

SILVERSTONE, 10 AUGUST 1980

It may have been my home Grand Prix but by hell that wouldn't make it easier. The heat was on Kenny to beat Randy decisively to take the championship. I was more worried about getting valuable points to hoist me up the ladder and to show the form I knew I possessed.

The practice and qualifying went well on the 500 and I began to get some confidence back but my half of the team was left to carry on pretty much as we pleased. The pressure was focused squarely on Randy. Doyle had turned up with his trademark Suzuki cap with its 'scrambled eggs' braid. Thinking it was a bit over the top, I took to wearing the same type of hat but I advanced its design by incorporating a rasher of bacon drooped over the peak. It was purely aimed at taking the piss out of Doyle; it worked and the journalists loved it.

I had two jobs to do at Silverstone this weekend. One was to get some points under my belt in the 500 race and the other would be my third outing on the TTF1 machine. Looking at how the TT Formula One race had shaped up points-wise, we needed a plan that would ensure Suzuki would win the TTF1 championship. Doing the maths on the possibilities, I calculated that not only did I need to win the race, but I would have to do so by a considerable margin. Following the Isle of Man TT, Mick had 15 points to my 12. If I beat him at Ulster and he ran second, we would be tied on 27 points. It would then go to the time differentials, where Mick had 11 seconds on me. The pressure was on me, not him. He could sit in behind me all the way, as long as he finished within 11 seconds of me.

So I needed to win the Ulster Grand Prix and finish ahead of Mick by 12 seconds, or have Mick finish third. It was a tough call, so the guys back at the office called Joey Dunlop and offered him my spare XR69. He could ride it at Silverstone and then use it at the Ulster Grand Prix. Joey knew what was being asked of him: it was down to team tactics and, faced with the same problem, Honda would do likewise. Consequently, Joey Dunlop was at Silverstone ready to try out his new XR69.

'Hi Joey, how's it going? I asked.

'Dead on,' he replied with the faintest hint of a smile.

'Well, these are the terrible twins mate, take your pick,' I said, pointing to the pair of F1 machines. 'They're both the same and have been set up the same so I don't mind which one you have.'

He said he didn't mind either. I wanted him to choose so there would be no argument. Eventually, he got the message and pointed to the bike nearest him. He raised an eyebrow and with a muffled voice said, 'This one will do.'

Our session started and I went out and set a time, came in and checked how I was compared with the opposition. I was happy with the time until Joey went faster. He came in and it appeared he was happy with his mount, but I wanted to know how he felt on my bike as I had done all the settings and was curious to gauge his reaction.

'Dead on,' he commented. I was expecting something else, so I probed.

'Is there something that can be done to make it better? Does it over-steer or under-steer? How are the brakes — do you want more or less pre-load on the front?' I quizzed him.

'No, it's dead on,' he said. I loved the Irish accent.

I went back out and posted a better time. I came in to find Joey had gone faster yet again. 'Jesus, Junior, I can't have that,' I told him. Junior showed me his lap times. We were faster than the Hondas but I had been forced to extend myself, and by my own team-mate. Out I went again and this time I put in a lap that Joey couldn't beat — but by god he came awfully close. After it was all over, I asked again if there was anything he would like changed. The same answer: 'Dead on.'

'Joey, don't you know any more English than "dead on"?' He looked at me with a smile and said, 'Yeah, are you getting the next round in?' I knew we would be good team-mates.

I liked Joey for his attitude — no airs or graces, just a no-nonsense approach to racing. Joey possessed a reservoir of untapped potential which we had witnessed at the TT back in June when he did a 115 mph lap around the TT course holding onto a loose fuel tank.

Getting a good start is imperative to winning races and my starting technique on the 500 was a reliable and easy way to get the bike fired up. I rocked the bike back and forth in gear to find a compression stroke; no matter how small it was, I knew it would help. On the drop of the flag or lights, with first gear engaged I pushed only a couple of steps and leaned on the tank, at the same time letting the clutch out. My secret was to crack open the throttle so the slides of the carburettors were just slightly open. This would ensure that the mixture was correct for the low airspeed entering the carburettors in the start-up phase. I could then apply power and throw my right leg up and over the seat, the sheer acceleration literally dragging me aboard.

It rarely failed me and in the race I again found myself leading into the first corner, away from the dangers of the midfield mayhem where every rider jostles for position. I had qualified fifth on the grid which was about where I should have been, given the stiff competition. The tide had begun to turn and my dismal performances in the first few Grand Prix were looking like a thing of the past.

The race up front was again between Randy, Kenny and Marco and I was left to battle it out against Will Hartog and Graziano Rossi, both on works Suzukis. I had the measure of Rossi and was in a position to make a move when I felt an unstable feeling creeping into the bike. I had had flat tyres before and knew almost instantly that I was in trouble. Unable to keep the pace up and with only a few laps of the race left to run, I decided to nurse the bike home in the hope of at least collecting some points. The chance of points gradually faded as rider after rider slipped by, pushing me back to eventually finish 13th. I rode into the paddock disappointed at getting a flat tyre but quietly confident that my performance was good enough to take a bit of heat off me and banish the blues. Mick took a look at the rear tyre and found a piece of fencing wire poking out.

The British Grand Prix this year also sadly claimed the lives of two characters of the sport. The likeable French racer Patrick Pons crashed his 500 cc in the race and was hit by a following rider and sustained fatal head injuries. Mal White lost control of his sidecar and was killed in the sidecar race. He was passing a slower outfit and collided with another competitor at the entrance to the ultra-fast Woodcote Corner. Two deaths are two too many in any sport.

To take anything good away from the day, I still had the TTF1 race to do and although I faced a strong challenge from Honda I was amazed at how well Noddy Newbold rode on his Harris-framed Suzuki. I had been extended in practice by Joey but the race was even faster and I had to really concentrate to put some distance between us. In doing so I set a new lap record of 1:32.7. Joey managed to get ahead of Noddy and Ron Haslam was pushed back to fourth while Mick Grant had to settle for a fifth. Suzuki scored a one-two-three finish.

I had moved up the points ladder and with my two wins and a second I was in fourth place on 42 points.

ULSTER GRAND PRIX, 16 AUGUST 1980

I had had such a great time the previous year at the Ulster Grand Prix on the Moriwaki bike doing wheelies and generally enjoying myself that I genuinely looked forward to racing there again. Sure it was regarded as being potentially more dangerous than the TT by many people but at a shade under 12 km a lap the average speed was still close to 188 kph. The race would last about 39 minutes, whereas the Isle of Man was a full two hours.

You can't help but admire the enthusiasm of the Irish spectators and their passion for true road racing. Perhaps because Ireland lacked a purpose-built track of any note, it was left up to the various organizers to find suitable racetracks. Dundrod had been around for a long time but I had been shown some Irish tracks that were so bumpy I thought it impossible to stay on the bike. Irish riders had courage in abundance and no matter how good you might be on the mainland, there was always someone over here who would make you look silly. Call it madness or stupidity, but the level of talent or skill the Irish riders showed on the open roads was simply remarkable. They were virtually fearless.

The gloves were off when our team turned up. A true battle had developed between Honda and Suzuki. Our 12 points against their 15 meant I had to win. Joey was brought in to help make that happen but Honda had also enlisted the help of Sam McClements, a local rider who knew the track. With a factory Honda under him he stood a good chance of negating the Joey Dunlop factor. I had to contend with Ron Haslam and Alex George, also on factory bikes, as well as Roger Marshall and Chris Guy. I felt I was ready for the final of this two-part series.

The flag dropped on a damp track and instantly Joey Dunlop disappeared into the distance, as only he could do, leaving me to fend off the Honda challenge. Ron Haslam and I battled it out for second and third with Mick sitting back in fourth. All I needed was for Joey to slow down and let me through so he could split up Mick and me. Honda had a few problems with Sam McClements stopping with clutch trouble and Marshall had suffered brake problems, so it became a four-way race. Haslam finally got by me to claim second on lap six, then near the end of the race Joey eased his pace and dropped back to third behind me, leaving Mick in fourth. Two second placings would see me win the world championship by a single point, as long as Mick finished fourth.

When Ron slipped off his bike at the hairpin, I couldn't work out if Mick was ahead or behind Joey. I crossed the line unsure of whether I had won the world championship. As I slowed down, first Joey then Mick tore across the finish line. Luckily for me, Joey had kept Mick at bay and Ron had re-mounted to finish fourth. I had done it — with Joey's help. Justice had prevailed and I felt like it was payback time for the tank-bashing fiasco back in June. It slowly sunk in that I was a world champion and a part of me thanked Pops Yoshimura for all the work he had done over a long period. I thought of his wife toiling away long into the night, grinding and polishing valves. I knew she would share in the happiness of this day.

I wasn't really motivated to race in the Unlimited Classic later that day but then thought I might go out anyway and see how I felt. Without any team orders Joey let rip on the Suzuki. To give him credit, he was bloody fast and I wasn't going to get into a dogfight with him. I did a few wheelies and before I knew it I could see the crowd all moving up closer to the edge of the track as I zoomed by on one wheel. When the starter showed me a black flag I knew I was in trouble but pretended not to know why.

I came into the pit lane next lap to be confronted by a couple of irate Irishmen. One clasped a clipboard as he yelled into my ear above the clattering of the valve gear. 'Mr Crosby, you've been shown the black flag because we think you're riding dangerously and we don't appreciate you doing wheelies out on the track.'

'OK, I'll behave myself,' I said and he motioned me to continue back out. I stopped doing wheelies down the straight in front of them, but continued pulling monos as soon as I was out of sight. The crowd loved the show — it had become my trademark.

I was invited to a local nightclub and asked to judge the Miss County Dremora Destroyer competition which lasted until the wee hours. We went back to our digs and continued partying.

I was happy to have won but conscious that some people thought it was not a true world championship. They argued that you cannot have a world championship decided over just two races. I thought about that for a long time and could see their point; however, it was a TTF1 title, not a Grand Prix series event. The words 'Tourist Trophy' lend weight to the fact it is a title contested out on natural road circuits in the three classes — Formula One, Two and Three. I had won my title on two of the most dangerous road circuits on the planet. I was proud to be crowned world champion and as the race was open to anyone in the world who wished to compete, I felt like one.

16

TIDYING UP THE LOOSE ENDS, 1980

NÜRBURGRING, 24 AUGUST 1980

Peter Defty, the Pan Am pilot and friend of Jim Doyle, left me with his rental car to do a few laps of the 22 km Nürburgring circuit. He must have been either drunk or just downright stupid, and he should have known better. The car had plenty of fuel and new tyres. He eventually got it back with no fuel in the tank, tyres that had had the manufacturer's name 'Klebber' scrubbed completely off the sidewalls and the engine tinkling away with heat after doing a lot of hot laps.

I had just completed a series of laps with several groups of unsuspecting passengers, all believing I would take them on a slow lap around the course. Almost valve-bouncing the little red Opel, I sped up and down the hills and along the straights, always leaving the braking until the last moment, for good effect. I scuttled around the blind bends and drop-offs so typical of this circuit.

It was open to any traffic and with no speed limits it was a great way to get to know the flow of the circuit. I swear I saw Peter Campbell make a move in the passenger seat with his polio-paralyzed leg desperately looking for the foot brake. He had every reason to go for the brake, because fear is a powerful thing. I had the benefit of having done quite a few laps before he got in the passenger seat and I knew exactly where to brake.

Once strapped in, passengers were at my mercy. I gave them a running commentary of where we were on the circuit, taking great care to talk my way around the track. 'OK, over the crest of this rise that's coming up is a fast left-hander followed by a tight right so hold on,' I recited. I knew there was no left-hander over the rise, only another straight stretch of road. 'Oh! I got that one wrong, maybe it's the next rise coming up!' The look of panic on their faces was priceless. They were thinking I didn't know my way around after all, and the thought of disappearing off the track through the Armco barrier in a screaming mess now seemed a real possibility. Although it was fun at their expense, I was actually learning the track, looking for braking markers and objects I could use as reference points to keep me orientated.

As the practice sessions drew nearer, the PRA was still floundering around and it was creating problems for the organizers. Issues that should have been addressed by the FIM earlier when they had the chance were now staring them right in the face. The PRA through its core of vocal riders had identified two circuits, Nürburgring and Imatra, as being too dangerous and had asked them to be dropped from the world championship. The FIM had ignored the request and carried on as if they had no interest in what the riders thought. Barry Sheene decided that with where he currently stood in the world championship it was pointless going to a circuit he thought was dangerous, so he didn't show up. Most of the others had taken the view that pressure from sponsors and teams simply meant they had to race.

However, there was a division opening up amongst the riders as to just how dangerous the circuit was. Sure it was long and winding but I liked it and it was more akin to the circuits I had already been riding on, like the Isle of Man and the Dundrod circuit at Ulster. Getting good results on circuits like those and here in Germany was a sign of a well-balanced rider able to handle different tracks. Perhaps the drive to make every circuit safe meant the beginning of the end of the 'natural' tracks. We might be left with a small group of 'approved circuits' that suited one style of racing. To be a true world champion you have to race on circuits that are diverse in nature and have character. I considered the Nürburgring as a track with character — it would do me just fine.

The talk of walking out fizzled as soon as practice and qualifying started. The PRA had no teeth despite being slowly recognized as the elected representative body of a handful of privileged, mainly factory-supported riders, who were better off financially than the privateers.

How the hell was I supposed to react when faced with calls to join strikes and boycotts when the circuits so far were all still a novelty to me? I had not yet earned that right. I was one of the privileged few who didn't have to use the public loos or worry about standing in queues to use lukewarm showers in the paddock. What gave me the right to be judge and jury? I needed to be careful not to rock the boat and get offside with my peers. Relying on others' anecdotal evidence of previous years' experiences with some circuits meant I was not qualified to lend weight to an argument either way. I was sure something had to happen but not being up to speed with historical issues and complaints, I decided to vote with the majority, even if it seemed hypocritical coming from Croz, the Isle of Man and TT supporter.

Having finally learnt the 20 km track about as well as I was going to and listened to the criticism coming from other riders, I was ready to try to qualify. It was bumpy and in poor condition in some sections but perfection is hard to find. A bunch of disgruntled riders threatened to pull out if it rained; I was not going to have any of that stuff. I was here to race in the final GP. Emotions were running high and Lucchinelli and Rossi had even suggested they would do only one lap and pull in. Roberto Gallina was livid and threatened to fire them if they did.

The normal sequence of qualifying went without a hitch and I relaxed after the last session of the day with a bottle of red wine. The barbecue was fired up and it was our turn to cook the steaks. I was on my third glass and had gone off to check out the qualifying times. Seventh was not a great result but it was a new track for me anyway. At least I would get to start.

I heard my name being called out from the motorhome as I arrived back. 'Croz, mate, you got 15 minutes — we have those Q8 needle jets done and we want a plug chop, see you over there.'

'Holy shit! I've had three glasses of red wine and now I have to go and do a lap, it'll be a fucking slow one for sure,' I said to Brenda as I reached for my suit and helmet. I did one slow lap, a plug chop as I finished and then left the bike with Mick. I got back to find another glass of red had been poured and the barbecue was now up to temperature.

The race started with me in the leading bunch along with Randy, Kenny, Will and Marco all dicing for the lead. Marco and Randy built up a small lead over us and I was left battling it out with Kenny and Will Hartog. Randy appeared back in my sights towards the end of the race, his Suzuki obviously injured. The smoke trailing out behind him was evidence of an oil leak that threatened to spill onto his tyre. I passed him and managed to get some distance at the same time on Kenny and raced towards a second place finish.

I was rapt at my second placing and although it had taken a long time this year I finally felt I deserved a break. However, with the Grand Prix season over it was time for me to complete the UK race programme, which was far from finished.

JAPAN AND BACK, 27 AUGUST 1980

'Are you telling me, Rex, that Suzuki Japan want me to fly over and back just for a party this coming Wednesday night?' I could hardly believe what I had just heard. Perhaps I'd underestimated the importance of wining the Suzuka 8 Hour a few weeks before. I knew Pops was really pleased to stick one up Honda, but when Rex mentioned that Suzuki Japan wanted me to fly back to Hamamatsu to celebrate the win I was blown away.

'No problem, but if I leave on the Monday I'll have to miss Oulton Park.' We'd planned to rush up to Oulton Park for Monday's Shellsport race.

'The factory don't care if you miss that one, and in any case Randy will be there to wave the flag.' Rex was serious.

'Leaving on Monday I'll get to Hamamatsu on Tuesday, the party is on Wednesday night. Then I'll have to get back to Narita by Thursday night to make it to Donington on Saturday. Shit, it's going to be a bloody quick trip and I'll be poked by the time I get back.'

'Croz, they're sending you first class with Japan Airlines, and they have approved a sleeper cabin on the plane so you'll be in good shape when you arrive and when you get back.' I chuckled at the thought of sleeping all tucked up in a soft bed with 330 passengers below all tossing and turning, trying to get comfortable sitting upright.

'Can you do it?' Rex asked.

'Bloody oath.'

Flying first class on Japan Airlines to Tokyo was a brilliant experience, though it probably cost more for the ticket than my contract sign-on fee. It was a mad rush to Hamamatsu, where I met up with Wes Cooley who had flown in from the States. At the Suzuki party most of the speeches were in Japanese so I stayed close to Pops who translated for us. As the party drew to a close it culminated with the breaking of a ceremonial wooden sake barrel. I showed my appreciation by drinking my fair share. I witnessed first-hand the show of emotion that the staff of Suzuki Motor Company had in being winners.

Next day, feeling slightly seedy, I retraced my steps to Narita. I arrived back at Heathrow on a bitterly cold day. A heavy, overcast sky signalled the kind of weather I didn't want at Donington.

The beautiful JAL hostess personally ushered me off the plane moments after the pilot had switched off the engines. She thanked me for flying with JAL and said she hoped she would see me again. I thought that would be sweet but if she ever saw me on board again it would be because she had been caught doing something naughty and had been demoted to cattle class. I doubted I'd ever be able to afford to fly first class again, so I said sayonara to her.

I was brought back to reality with a jolt when I discovered my bag had failed to show at baggage collection. My suit, helmet and all my gear, including gifts and clothing, had gone. I filled in the forms and left with little expectation of getting my bags back. It was looking like 'sayonara' to those too.

DONINGTON, 31 AUGUST 1980

Those in the crowd at Donington could have been excused for wondering what the hell Randy was doing on my TTF1 machine. It may have looked like him but it was me wearing his spare helmet and race suit. There was no word of my baggage from Heathrow, which I had now renamed 'Thief-row'.

My fascination for aircraft and aviation continued to grow and with Donington Park being so close to the East Midlands Airport I used to sneak off and go exploring. The airport had no security gates so I was able to poke around and inspect the aircraft. I found a Mark 1X Spitfire just as it was being towed out for a test flight. The sound of that V-12 Merlin was just beautiful. I could have stayed there all day.

I also took a few flying lessons in a little Piper PA-28 that the Castle Donington Aero Club had for hire. Its registration number was G-AZYF and on my first flight I was shown how to do instrument flying. I had already gained my New Zealand pilot's licence, but lacked the experience that can only be gained through time in the air. The instructor took me up for an hour and I never saw a thing except the inside of cloud. My head was spinning with the concentration required to read and interpret the instruments while maintaining control. I had a lot to learn. The flying bug had bitten me and I knew I wanted more of this.

For some reason I had brought a bit of aggression back with me from Japan and rode the wheels off the TTF1 bike and in doing so set a new lap record of 1:16.4, almost half a second faster than Ron's record. I felt as if I had a fighting chance now after winning my last three outings. Joey Dunlop followed me home ahead of Mick Grant, while Ron had gear selection problems and missed the chicane completely, dropping further back.

Unfortunately, the same aggression wasn't there for the big ITV World of Sport race. It was probably asking a bit much of the F1 bike and I got blown off by the big 2-strokes of Barry Sheene, Dave Potter, Roger Marshall, Mick Grant, and Randy on his 500.

The 500 cc race was not part of the Shellsport series but it was still paying a few quid in prize money. I was more than happy to collect my second place winnings.

CADWELL PARK, 14 SEPTEMBER 1980

The fun and action at Cadwell Park was not about the racing this time — it was the mechanics' annual ride day. I wasn't worried about them riding the bikes; in fact it gave the regular riders a chance to take the piss out of the mechanics for a change.

As I was about to push Radar off on the F1, I lifted his visor and said, 'Can you only do two laps mate — it gets dark at 6.30.' The hands on my watch had just passed 12 noon. Mick Grant only let his mechanic Nigel Everett out on his 500 on the condition that he promised not to go as quick as him.

Barry Sheene's mechanic Ken Fletcher went out dressed in Barry's racing suit and came straight back in without completing a full lap, complaining that the rear tyre had gone off, the bike needed re-jetting and third gear was a tad low. I reminded Ken that a lap means one full lap and he's sounding too much like his employer. He did look sharp, though. It was a fun time and it served a useful purpose, to let the mechanics experience what they had been working on all year.

I had spoken with the Cadwell Park organizer Charlie about start money. He reluctantly agreed to pay me his standard amount of £800 for someone of my 'pulling power'. But Charlie also offered a little sweetener. He confided to me that if he got more than 12,000 paying spectators through the gates he would give me another £300. I am sure he used that line on all the riders negotiating a start fee.

It was Ron Haslam's race for the taking but he pulled up apparently lame, effectively handing Mick Grant the British TTF1 title. It looked like Honda had done all the maths and Ron had played the team orders game well, but in doing so denied the spectators an exciting finish.

I lined up with all the other placegetters of the day to collect my prize money and start money. Finally, the door to the little office opened and a rider walked out still with his leathers on. 'Next!' I heard. I walked in and sat down in front of Charlie as he thumbed through his little black book.

'Name please?' without looking up.

'Crosby,' I said.

'What class are you in?' he asked, still without looking up.

'F1.'

'Where did you finish?' I wanted to say 27th; that would surely make him look up.

'Hmm, so you had a good day then eh!' He started counting out the £10 notes, then pushed the wad carefully across the table at me. Still looking down, he picked up his little notebook again.

'How much did we agree?'

I saw my opportunity. 'Three thousand pounds, I think it was.' Just testing him.

'You thought wrong lad, I have you down at £800.' Still with his head down.

'What about the crowd, it was more than 12,000!' I knew only too well what the answer would be.

Finally, he lifted his head and peered out the window. 'Close today, but not quite — there were no spectators above that building and that's my reference mark. More like 8000, I'd say.'

He gave the pile a final shove across the table and said, 'There you are lad, now off with you. Next!' he yelled and out I went.

MALLORY PARK, 21 SEPTEMBER 1980

It wouldn't be Mallory Park without the bloody rain. Saturday was wet, cold and miserable but it was the same for everyone. I often thought that some privateers might pray for rain on big race days like this. The prize money is bigger of course than a normal club day meeting but with that bigger purse comes more competition and professionals with their superior equipment. Rain is a great leveller because in wet conditions power can sometimes be a disadvantage. It's then rider against rider and that's where local track knowledge can play a bigger part in helping to balance the scales.

On race day, Sunday, thank god it was going to be fine for my two races. I'd got the 15-lap Shellsport 500 race plus the big 40-lap Race of the Year. I had reservations already about racing here after I'd head-butted the wall earlier in the year. I didn't fancy another trip to hospital but all thoughts of crashing disappeared as soon as I threw my leg over the bike.

Radar handed the bike over to me with the engine running and temperature gauge sitting on 75 degrees. Selecting first gear, I rode off up pit lane, standing up on the pegs and pushing my shoulders forward to stretch the leather on the back of my suit. This action also had the effect of making sure my crotch was 'adjusted' correctly. Back on the seat again, I lifted one leg and pulled at the leather on my thigh. My boots relaxed as the leather slid up, allowing more freedom of movement. Repeating the same process with the other leg, I was now ready for action.

A quick check down either side of the cowling to make sure nothing was leaking, followed by another check of the water temperature gauge and finally a look over my shoulder for traffic. It would take two good laps to get the brakes and tyres up to working temperature. I did three laps without going too hard, just to 'bring in' the new front tyre. Our Dunlop tyres came out of moulds that had been coated with a releasing agent or gel. They were slippery at first but as the friction forces and braking action took hold, the temperature rose to over 70 degrees and they became quite sticky and grippy.

Just one lap around here always keeps me busy. Overall gearing has to be set so that I reach top speed and maximum rpm at the end of the longest straight. I want it to be 11,500 rpm with the engine gasping a little for breath. Across the start-finish line I have already changed into fourth gear, then fifth as I move across the track in preparation for my entry into Gerard's Bend. Approaching the breaking point, I look for that little scrape mark on the track and use it as my turn-in point. I am already back two gears into third, blipping the throttle to avoid rear wheel hopping and keeping the revs at or above 7000 rpm. The entry has to be under brakes and in a gear that still produces an engine-braking effect. That has to happen because it changes my castor angle and trail geometry. A gear higher and I'll under-steer and go wide. By holding a tight line it's now possible to accelerate gradually, balancing the throttle opening with the radius of the turn.

The bike is leaning over almost to its maximum design angle with the power being delivered through a small contact patch on the rear wheel. Looking up, I estimate that I can begin to lift the bike and start putting on more power. I select fourth and roll it upright, using the entire available track as I shift into fifth and then sixth gear. I look to see if I can reach that 11,500 rpm target and then brake again at my braking marker.

Back two gears in quick succession and I lean into the esses. Changing direction is difficult here due to the gyroscopic procession properties of our wheels and tyres. They weigh enough and the rotational speed is fast so there's a fair bit of inherent stability to overcome.

Exiting out of the esses it's up one more gear into fourth and I hold it, accelerating towards Shaw's Hairpin. By holding a tight line under brakes I minimize the risk of someone coming up the inside, but I can really feel the weight through my forearms. Hard on the brakes and back to first gear and at the last minute I slide my bum across the seat so I can lean into the corner. My knee goes out which helps move bodyweight inside the bike's centreline. Having the right first gear ratio is imperative because I still want that rpm as high as possible to enable me to have the power to exit cleanly. The corner is so slow that the revs drop back under 6000 rpm. The speed has gone out of the wheels and with it goes the stability.

I get the turn over and done with as soon as possible and start bringing in the power. It's clean on carburation and without a hint of hesitation; although not delivering heaps of power it does push me out of the turn. As the power band hits the sweet spot the bike literally climbs around the sprocket, power-lifting the front wheel about a foot off the ground. I short-change again into second to avoid an over-rotation and the wheel drops away. Second gear takes me towards Devil's Elbow, a blind downhill corner that takes me back to front straight again. I need to short-change again into third and take a swooping line as I go into Devil's Elbow because once committed I can't change gear. Leaning over and feathering the throttle at about 8000 rpm at the apex, I can tell it feels neither rich nor lean. And using the entire road available to me I accelerate, changing up into fourth gear as I zip by the start-finish line.

I did that for 15 laps in the Shellsport 500 race, and only finished third. Maybe I got it wrong somewhere as it was a lot of work for 10 points, being beaten fair and square by Randy and privateer Phil Henderson on his Suzuki RG500 production racer. I would have to sharpen up my act in the Race of the Year.

The 40-lapper Race of the Year had a big entry list, including Kenny Roberts on his 500 Yamaha, but the rest of the field seemed to be on 750's. I was only six laps into the race when I noticed water on the inside of my screen, a sure sign of impending failure. With another 34 laps to go I knew I wouldn't make it and pulled in. A blown head gasket caused the overheating and more-expensive damage would have occurred if I had continued.

17

SEE YOU NEXT YEAR — SAME TIME, SAME PLACE, 1980

USING MY HEAD, 1980

I had one last 500 Shellsport and TTF1 race to run at Brands, then it was all over for the season. The Kent weather turned sour on us with two wet races. Although Brands is known for being extremely slippery in the wet, I didn't mind because it was another opportunity to test Dunlop's new full wets. However, by the time the races were lined up on the grid everyone had decided on intermediates. My choice of tyres cost me points as the track dried, leaving a distinct line. My wets just couldn't hang in long enough.

We had done some experiments with the rear brake torque arm in an attempt to stop the bike pitching so much under brakes but in the wet conditions we reverted to the conventional torque arm. More testing on that would be carried out in Japan.

The 500 Shellsport race was won by Graham Wood on his Yamaha and he was welcome to it, though I managed a close second. That was enough to place me second overall in the series with two wins, three seconds and a third. My DNFs took a toll on the total points — Randy was struggling as always in the wet and finished a creditable fourth but he had already picked up the Shellsport championship with his five wins, several seconds and a few minor places.

The TTF1 final race was also run in wet conditions. I led Haslam and Grant home to make it five wins on the trot. Unfortunately, I came up four points short of winning the championship after counting my eight best races. If only I'd had one more race ...

Heading off to the pub sounded like a great idea to me. The one at Brands could hold a few hundred people and when I got there it was packed to the gunwales with drunken fans who had settled in for the night. I got a great reception when I turned up to have a few beers with the boys. I loved rubbing shoulders with the fans who paid to watch the racing and in effect paid me.

Unless you have a pit pass or paddock pass it is difficult for the public to get in and see the riders and their teams. Mixing with them in a pub can put you at risk, as I was about to find out. I thought I was safe with these rowdy fans because we were all passionate about racing. I fitted in well and began slurping back a few pints. Then a drunken fan poured a full pint over my head. I laughed and shrugged it off although I was not too happy about getting wet. About 20 minutes later the same guy came up and did exactly the same thing, rambling something about me being one of the boys. This time I said in a nice but firm voice, 'Pal, if you do that again I'll drop you, now fuck off!' Job done I thought, then pushed myself up through the crowd to the bar and ordered another pint.

On the way back the same guy did the same thing for the third time, so with the speed of Muhammad Ali I lashed out with a sweeping left hook that caught him flush on his chin and he fell backwards into his mates. I guessed he had been put up to it but I wasn't going to be staying around to find out. I felt like a presidential candidate as my bodyguards stepped in. Radar, Mick, Jeremy Burgess and even little George formed a guard around me before escorting me out the door. A huge fight broke out after we left and a knife was pulled and someone got stabbed. I would think twice about going into a pub full of drunken fans again.

I called Maurice Knight's secretary Mary to see if I could get an appointment to see him. She said to come on over and added that he was in a good mood. When I arrived Maurice asked what he could do for me. He bloody well knew what I wanted and would make me sweat. With the pleasantries over I plucked up my courage.

'Well it's almost the end of the year and I thought we might talk about next year's racing programme.' My hands went all sweaty.

Maurice explained that my name had come up several times with the Japanese factory regarding next year and although the 500's had been a bit difficult earlier on in the season I had performed when it mattered. Daytona, Suzuka and the Senior TT win were great results for Suzuki. In the TTF1 we were again a bit slow off the blocks and that fiasco at the TT on the F1 bike was unfortunate.

He didn't leave me to hang out to dry too long before saying, 'Croz, we would love to have you back next year. We enjoyed your company but if you are looking for shitloads of cash it won't be coming from us.' Oh boy, I thought I might have had a bit of trouble extracting a few quid out of him.

'So it's the same programme again, TTF1 and Shellsport 500 plus the Grand Prix?' I asked.

'Yes, plus the TT, Daytona and of course Suzuka again,' he confirmed.

'Great! Any chance of a little raise?'

'Not really, but we've earmarked a few more grand for you. How's six thousand quid sound?'

'Beauty, that'll do. I suppose you will talk with Mick and Radar, because I'd like them back again with me.' I had one more question to ask: 'Maurice, can you check with the factory to see if I could have my world championship bike to keep?'

I walked out pleased with my deal. It would have been nice to get more money but I rationalized that if I had the equipment the money would come.

A week had passed when Mick Smith asked if I wanted to do the Swann Series. Someone in Australia had contacted him. He was keen on taking 'the Diesel' out to Australia and showing its capabilities. I checked again with Maurice and he had just received advice that Japan would allow me to have the bike. That sorted the Swann Series, as they were paying for the bike to go from London to Sydney then on to New Zealand, where it would remain.

I had noticed that a lot of alpine skiers, winter sport athletes and some road racers were wearing the Kiwi-branded helmets. During the year I had driven past the factory near the Swiss border in Northern Italy at a place called Bellinzona. I contacted their product manager with the idea of using their helmets and emblazoning my own tiki design on it. After a quick trip to talk with them, I returned $10,000 richer and with a contract under my belt for the following year. Having my own Kiwi-brand helmet was something I knew was right. I quizzed them why the name Kiwi and they said it was difficult coming up with a four-letter word that meant the same in all languages. I could have offered them some alternatives but elected to keep my mouth shut.

TESTING IN JAPAN, HOME AND SWANN SERIES, OCTOBER 1980

Junior (Dave Collins) was rapt when he was told he was going to Japan with me to carry out testing on the new bikes. Both the new 500's and the XR69 would be available for a gallop around Ryuyo, Suzuki's test course. He hadn't been to Japan but had heard some of my stories about the antics I'd got up to over there.

He followed me as I negotiated our way into Tokyo from Narita and onto the Shinkansen to Hamamatsu. As we zipped along at 220 kph we had a few more beers, then Junior thought he might try some sake. I had one or two and he may have had four or five. They say never mix grain with grape, and Junior found out what happens if you do. He went from a cheerful person to a withdrawn and rather sickly looking individual. If it wasn't for me he would have missed getting off the train at Hamamatsu. I had to drag him away from the safety of the onboard loo.

Once off the train Junior was in damage control mode, more interested in sleeping than in attending the technical meeting. He wisely remembered it is better to remain silent and be thought a fool than to open your mouth and remove all doubt. He put on a brave face, smiling but not saying much. I felt a bit sorry for him as I was responsible in a way.

At the test track Randy and I rode the new XR35 which was a big improvement over the previous year's XR34. It was lighter and lower, with a new, smaller engine design. Our times were close to the mark and threatening the lap record. Randy concentrated on his job of making the most out of a short testing session while I devoted time to the XR69 which was sporting a new single-shock full-floater rear end.

At the technical meeting, attended by all the design team and race team leader Etsuo Yokouchi, the discussion surrounded making the XR35 smaller again and, as a result of Randy pushing for this change, Suzuki produced a prototype that was to be tested secretly in California. We had two engineers responsible for engine development and chassis design, Makoto Yoshida or 'Big Mac', and Makoto Hase. It was a big jump for me to be sitting around the table talking of design-build for next year's Grand Prix bikes.

The 2-stroke programme was clearly the domain of Randy but the F1 bikes were what interested me most. This was because I felt I was a part of the inner sanctum of development. The tight relationship that existed between Etsuo Yokouchi, who had been instrumental in the GS 4-stroke programme, and Pops was evident. The other Japanese XR69 chassis designer was Manubu Suzuki, a fun guy who had a crush on Pops' daughter Yumiko and loved drinking Scotch. She would cringe when I mentioned his name but secretly I think she quite liked the attention.

Often when we had spare time, Manubu Suzuki and I would talk candidly about the design and how to get the best out of it. We scratched it all out on a napkin with a pencil so we both understood fully. Ultimately, we had a great set-up that required little change at the racetrack — perhaps a slight difference in castor angle by slipping the forks through or up 5 mm was all it took to get it dialled in. The rear suspension was a little more complicated than the XR35 because of the extra space available for the rocker arms making it more progressive. The XR35 forks were used but required different springs because of the heavier weight. We returned to the UK pleased with what we had to work with the next year.

It was time to go home to New Zealand for the summer break. I packed my trophies into a steel Suzuki parts box a metre square and even managed to squeeze in a BMW R100 that I had bought as a write-off. It helped that the BMW had been crashed head-on into something so it fitted quite well. My solid silver Senior TT trophy would have to go as carry-on baggage. As it was insured for some horrendous amount I couldn't afford to have it out of sight. In London I picked up my 1980 FIM certificate from Ken Shierson, the general secretary of the ACU. Only then did it sink in just how much I had achieved that year.

Our trip back was literally the long way home, via Sydney, Brisbane, and Honiara in the Solomon Islands, where we had a long-standing invitation to visit my old friend Woody, who had taken up a contract with the New Zealand Government Foreign Aid programme, teaching boat-building skills on the remote island of Tulagi. When we arrived home at last we went out house-hunting, on the strength of the money I'd been sending home over the past year.

Being back in Auckland meant catching up with some old friends, including Max Farquhar and Brian Lawrence. We arranged to meet at a local pub. I had to deal with an issue that had been bothering me for some time. Inadvertently, I had promised each of them a

Champion Spark Plug jacket from Europe. They couldn't get the genuine article and the New Zealand ones didn't quite cut the mustard and they both wanted to show off their European jackets that I had personally brought back for them. The problem was that I had only one.

I soon resolved matters by cutting the jacket right down the middle and carefully folding each half so the sleeve would be visible on both when unpacked. After a few ales I presented them with a bag each and sat back to watch the reaction. Brian and Max were ecstatic with their new gifts and as if rehearsed, simultaneously they began trying on their jackets. Max had his left arm in the sleeve and Brian had his right arm in the other, then they both went looking for the other sleeve. I pissed myself laughing when finally they realized what they were doing and that each had only half a jacket. In true Kiwi spirit a deal was done a few weeks later and I saw Brian walking around proud as Punch with his now restored acquisition, complete with a neatly sewn join down the back.

I had one last engagement in November, racing the now 'old' GS1000R in the Aussie Swann Insurance Series. It was a four-round series, Oran Park in Sydney, Surfers Paradise on Queensland's Gold Coast, Adelaide and finally Sandown in Melbourne. There was some tough local competition on a bunch of Yamaha 750's and RG500's, but I went out on a limb by bringing a 4-stroke instead of the GP bike to compete head-on with Australia's best riders.

Oran Park was like a homecoming to me. Before I arrived I knew I'd end up at the Inn of Trees pub just down the road and it would be just like old times. When I turned up, Mick and Radar had the old girl out ready to go. It looked like it had done a few rounds over the past few months but it was in good shape. The 1000 cc engine would be good around here, although I had the big engine ready to go if required.

The track was going to be the short course but a surface problem meant the Grand Prix circuit would be used instead. I didn't care either way but I knew my appearance in this series got a few guys stirred into action. I was a target and a measure for others to judge their own capabilities by. If they could beat me fair and square here, they could be forgiven for thinking they would be able to perform at the highest level in the UK or Europe. If that's what it took to get them over to the UK then great, I would have been of some help. But first they had to beat me.

I was wary of a few riders before arriving here and Andrew Johnson was one such character. I had rarely come up against him in Australia but his reputation preceded him. This hard-charger with a never-give-up attitude would be a hard nut to crack. Unluckily for AJ and fortuitously for me, he biffed his Yamaha 750 away on Friday practice, breaking his shoulder and setting fire to his bike in the process.

When we lined up for the first leg of round one, a glance along the front row showed a huge depth of talent. Ron Haslam had come from the UK and Dave Aldana from the USA, but what worried me was that aggressive group of local riders. Sayle, Boulden, Coleman, Pretty, Trinder, Cole, Muir, Neill and Gardner were all capable of upset wins. The first race was a tough one for me, disposing of some tough challenges and leaving Trinder chasing me hard all the way to the finish. I set a new lap record on my way to collecting maximum points.

During the break I got a surprise presentation from Kel Carruthers. He had been to the annual FIM congress meeting in Malta and brought back my world championship FIM medal. I was stoked.

Radar, Mick and I went into a huddle discussing how to get better performance out of the bike and I made one critical change that we would pay dearly for. I thought that in the previous race I could have got away with a harder tyre so we changed from a 796 to a 784 compound tyre.

After spending three-quarters of the second-leg race in second place, sniffing around Ron Haslam's exhaust pipe and unable to pass, I finally overtook him but Steve Trinder followed me through and a couple of laps from the end he made a desperate move and got me on the inside. My tyre was sliding and I couldn't peg him back and he went on to win. We were now square on points.

That night I did in fact end up at the pub and had a cracker of a time catching up with everyone. Nothing had really changed but it felt like I'd been away for a long time. I had been a busy boy and today's race was my 28th race day for the year, excluding testing sessions. And I still had a further three to go.

Gregg Hansford had been doing some TV commentary work during the series and I spoke to him about his plans for 1981. He was hoping that a KR500 would be ready for testing any time now. He was getting a little anxious, knowing they had been working on it for some time. I was surprised he didn't try elsewhere for a ride. Neville Doyle had been working closely with the factory doing some development work but Gregg needed time on a competitive bike. Gregg was close to Kenny and I thought he might look for other opportunities, perhaps with Yamaha. The year before, Gregg got dicked around waiting for the World Series to eventuate, and he probably missed a few opportunities by remaining loyal to Kawasaki. Work on attempting to change or restructure the establishment should be done quietly by those championing the cause, while the day-to-day racing business must carry on. As professional racers we have only a temporary hold on our position; anything can happen so we have to seize the opportunities as they come along.

Surfers Paradise was another familiar track for me. I knew it was quite fast but I had heard rumblings that a 4-stroke couldn't match a TZ750 at Surfers, so my chances of an overall win were a little optimistic. I was cautious how I approached this for a change;

perhaps a couple of years at the coal face in Europe had taught me to make a statement with action, not words.

I told Mick we needed more power. Radar and Mick exchanged the engine for our spare 1100 cc version. I didn't like the bigger engines and on the very rare occasion we fitted it, both performance and reliability suffered. After some practice laps and a few changes to the carburettor settings I was pleasantly surprised how well it was performing, except that I still struggled to get the carburation to play ball. In a desperate bid to speed up the process we borrowed another set of carburettors from Ralph Hannan, and re-drilled the air-bleed jets out to compensate for atmospheric conditions by using a number drill to get the desired result. It worked and we went to the grid on pole position by a slim margin.

The first leg developed into a duel between Greg Pretty and me. At the start I allowed Greg to get a good three-second jump on me and I was stuck trying to get around Steve Trinder. Sadly for him a misfire developed in his TZ750. He'd thought it was a better choice than the smaller RG500 at Surfers and I agreed; I even sold him a spare Dunlop tyre. Luckily, he didn't use it to beat me. Once past him I set out after Greg and only caught him in the last five laps. With three to go I made a move, got past and stretched the lead but he came back at me on the last lap. We crossed the line with only one-tenth of a second separating us.

As I was changing back into my racing suit for the second leg, I felt a small lump under my arm. At first it didn't worry me, but later I found myself feeling and probing for the lump which was about 1 cm across and growing. I began to get worried that it might be a cancerous growth or tumour. I decided to find a doctor for an opinion.

The second leg was exciting for the spectators as Pretty, Trinder and I spent most of the race swapping the lead. It wasn't until the last few laps that things got a bit out of hand with some risky manoeuvres. We all had a go at various methods of shaking each other off our tail, until on the last lap I caught a note change in my engine and it dropped a few revs. Coming onto the straight for the final time I knew I had lost power and ultimately the race, as Greg sped past to win by less than a metre. I rode into the pit area and quietly told the boys our big engine might be poked and we'd need to get the old engine back in for Adelaide.

Radar and Mick quickly dropped the engine out and removed the cylinder head to check for damage. The valves had been just touching and it needed a new cam chain tensioner. Further inspection showed a broken ring. We had already ordered a new crank, so it would be good to get all the parts down here from Yoshimura in time for the next round.

Because both Greg and I had a win and second apiece, it was the winner of the second and final heat who took the overall victory.

'Shit Radar, I always win the wrong bloody race.'

I attended the prizegiving but the zing had gone out of the moment for me. I was focusing on this thing growing under my arm. It was too late to find a doctor that night. I had a few Castlemaine beers but my mind was elsewhere.

Next morning I found a doctor who checked me out and suggested carrying out a biopsy during the week. 'Fuck,' I thought, 'if he wants a biopsy then it's serious.' The timing was not going to work for me as I'd be in Adelaide, so I elected to wait until I got home to have the operation. It was going to be the longest three weeks that I have ever had to endure. I was being consumed by the possibility that I might be dying. I started having panic attacks and just could not believe my bad luck.

Brenda listened to me as I talked frankly for the first time in a long while. 'Look at me — I've just signed a new contract with new bikes, we have a new house back home and life is pretty damn good. I have a huge future ahead for me and now here I am at the beginning of this new life, a life most people would die for, and I'm thinking it might be me who's dead.'

With a serious expression Brenda asked, 'Have you got life insurance?'

'You'll be the one wanting life insurance if I can get a hold of you,' I said, which broke the ice.

Heading off to Adelaide, I had a five-point lead and needed that extra horsepower for the long straight that was similar to the one at Surfers. A few phone calls along the way to try to get a new crank out from Japan in time paid dividends. Mamoru Moriwaki decided to fly to Adelaide and bring a new crank with him from Yoshimura Japan. He arrived late Thursday night with the crank and some other spares. I went out on Friday and posted a 58.2 second lap. This was the quickest time but I sensed a note change in the engine. Having ridden so much I was really in tune with the sound and I knew that anything out of the ordinary required looking at. Mick soon found the culprit — a slightly bent valve.

The Adelaide racetrack was a combination of a road race and drag strip. The 'Bowl' was a slightly banked 180-degree corner that led onto the straight. It had no run-off, just a concrete barrier on the edge of the track. Clerk of the course Peter Sparks agreed with riders' concerns over safety and obliged us by lining it with straw bales.

By the time the first leg was ready Boulden, Muir, Trinder and Haslam were all only a split second behind me and the rest of field not far behind them in qualifying. Ron Haslam got the jump at the start and I followed but got tangled up, leaving me fifth on the first lap. I got past Aldana and chased Ron but I could see up front Muir was getting away and taking Pretty with him. Once past Ron, I chipped away at the gap. I approached a dust cloud and looked to see who had caused it. I couldn't make out who it was, so I got back to the job at hand and closed again on Pretty and Muir.

Coming off the front straight Greg got it wrong and speared off the track in another cloud of dust. I had Muir in my sights and could see he was struggling, so I got past as quick as I could then put some distance between us to win the first leg. Coming into the pit area I got off the bike, handed it to Radar, lifted my visor and asked, 'Who binned it over the back? It didn't look good.' Radar explained that it was Steve Trinder, who had been taken to hospital with a compound fracture of his leg.

Immediately, my hand went in search of the lump under my arm, hoping I wouldn't be able to find it now. It was there and still the same size.

One of the feature races was the B.O.S.S. Trophy. I hadn't planned on going out but thought why not? I picked up a win and the associated spoils of war — a silver plate and some cash for the party afterwards. The second leg proved to be a more convincing win for me as I took the lead from Ron Haslam the first time around the Bowl. I didn't look back and went on to win the race and take a commanding points lead with one round to go.

'So where's all your fancy 2-strokes now, eh?' I was so pleased that my decision was a good one to bring the Suzuki Down Under. On paper anyone would have agreed with my rationale. The Suzuki was quick, steered great and I had the track knowledge, having ridden the circuits before, so why wouldn't I be odds-on favourite to win the series?

Steve Trinder had a seven-hour operation that night on his shattered tibia. His TZ750 was reported to be completely poked.

Sandown Track in Melbourne was quick and would suit the big 2-stroke Yamahas. It was also a double points round, meaning I had to finish to stop anyone leapfrogging me in the points standing. The two Ronnies — Boulden and Haslam — joined me in a race-long duel and on the final lap I missed a gear, clipping the valves and had to limp over the line with my damaged Suzuki, but the third place finish was enough to give me a clear overall series win.

The presentation was done and I had a few beers with the boys, picked up my winner's silver platter and went back to the motel. According to a newspaper report I was the destroyer of myths — 4-strokes can and have beaten the 2-strokes finally. I checked and that lump was still under my arm.

Arriving home, I went directly to a doctor and he also recommended a biopsy, booking me in for a day operation at a local hospital. Two nervous days after the operation I went to see the quack with my chin down and heavy shoulders. He reported that there was nothing sinister in the results, suggesting perhaps it might have been just a lymph node fighting an infection. Or it could have been a swelling due to an injury or stress on my hand, or possibly a repetitive strain injury. Immediately, I felt so much better; my spirits were already rising and my sense of humour returned.

'Well, OK, doc, I'll cut back on the masturbation in future,' I said, laughing, and bounced out of there. Bring on 1981 — I was ready.

Over the Christmas period I took more flying lessons. My passion for aviation was growing even stronger and somewhere up ahead I could see it was going to become the focus of my attention. I got a message that our new bikes were ready for testing and this time it was a repeat of the previous year in most respects, except that Suzuki had been doing a shitload of work on the GP bikes and for that matter the F1 machine.

On numerous occasions Brenda and I had talked about getting married. Typically, this would happen over a bottle of wine in a restaurant, when we could relax and concentrate on our relationship for a change instead of dealing with the relentless day-to-day racing programme. We had been together since she turned 18 and she had put up with all my antics since then, good and bad. I felt there was no hurry nor was there a necessity to get married at all — this life in the fast lane was all about me; I was pursuing my goals through racing. Brenda was always there for me and formed a reliable part of my racing and personal life. She needed her own space and life, so we figured that as I was at last in a position to provide security, we could build our home together. We were not a strong church-going couple so we had a modest wedding at her parents' home and a function at a popular Auckland restaurant with 50 guests.

I had been married for only a few days before it felt like I was doing a runner on the poor girl. Almost without warning Daytona had crept up on me. I was due to fly out to America to start the 1981 season.

18

DÉJÀ VU, 1981

DAYTONA INTERNATIONAL SPEEDWAY, 6 MARCH 1981

Because the AMA rules this year were slightly different, I was to do only the one Superbike race and use an F1 to race in the 20-miler. I left Fujio Yoshimura to give me whatever he thought would work. We had stronger competition this year and Freddie Spencer was again being billed as the favourite to win on his CBF750-based Honda. In qualifying we found our Suzukis and the Honda were similar in speed but Wayne Gardner aboard a Moriwaki Z1 was showing ominous signs, posting some really quick lap times.

One bike magazine had been saying I'd 'blown the side covers' off the Americans last year. I was more circumspect this time about my chances. I hadn't forgotten how dreadful the qualifying system was the year before and had prepared myself for any absurd behaviour that might get in my way. I was effectively on loan to Yoshimura R&D to help win the Daytona 100 Bell Superbike race held over 26 laps on this high-banked circuit. Last year I was so focused and pissed off that I must have ridden like a demon to win, given the penalties placed on me prior to the start.

This year I was hoping for an easier time, but for the first half-hour Wes Cooley and I were locked in a three-way battle with

Freddie on bikes that were almost identical in performance. Midway through, Freddie made for the pits to refuel and his crew cocked it up completely, leaving him back in sixth. Wes and I refuelled without a hitch and continued trucking around at high speed with only inches separating us. It was going to come down to a last-corner effort to win. Before the race, Wes had been recalling duels that had been won and lost on this final corner. 'Croz, whatever you do, don't lead going into the last turn — they'll get on to your tail and slipstream past; it's happened to me before.'

With one lap to go and Wes leading, I had him where I wanted him. I was confident of being able to pass him on the run to the wire. The last corner was lined by straw bales to form a chicane. It was designed to slow the bikes down enough so they could re-enter the high-banked oval at a lower and safer speed. Wes went through, probably expecting me to slip by him just before the finish line. I followed close behind ready to pounce but as I wound on the throttle coming out of the turn the back wheel let go. It was just a slight rear wheel kick but I lost a little momentum. At that point I had to kiss goodbye to first place, knowing I'd run out of speed to make the slipstream overtaking manoeuvre. I crossed the line a split second behind Wes.

The disappointment was only temporary, as the following day my GS1000 failed to perform and I was classified as a non-finisher. Then I was really pissed off.

Brenda met me back in London where I was busy getting ready for the new season. The schedule was going to be a long one. We had been out cleaning the motorhome and discussing what we needed to buy and had come into the workshop for a cup of tea with Linda, Gordon and Rex.

The radio was on but we weren't taking any particular notice. Suddenly, we all stopped talking and listened as the announcer read the breaking news bulletin. Mike Hailwood and one of his children had been killed in a road accident. We were all stunned and saddened by the news and it took some time to sink in. It was one hell of a loss, and not only for the motorcycling fraternity, as he was a household name worldwide. I saw it as a mean Act of God that 'Mike the Bike' was denied the dignity of an exit more befitting of the person he was. To be killed in a road accident while going down to get fish 'n' chips for his family was a tragic and ironic ending to a true champion's career.

A NEW SEASON: CADWELL PARK, 5 APRIL 1981

I had been working closely with Rolf Munding of R.A.T. Motorcycles in central London, trying to get more Moriwaki parts sold in the UK. He had been importing parts and wanted to handle the whole range and act as the UK distributor. After discussions we set up a joint venture company called Moriwaki UK Ltd that would import and distribute Moriwaki parts. Because of my racing itinerary I couldn't play an active role in the day-to-day activities, so I left it to Ralph and his partner Andrew. I retained a shareholding and threw some seed capital in and left it for them to run.

I thought Moriwaki UK had a good future but just being able to get product for the UK market out of Japan was proving difficult. Moriwaki constantly looked towards their domestic market for the bulk of their sales. It was booming and they preferred to spend money on developing high-performance after-market exhaust systems for new models released in Japan. No one seemed to be looking after our orders that we placed for the older Kawasakis and the parts supply was drying up. Things needed shaking up so we could place bigger orders and be assured they would be filled.

Rolf Munding contacted me early in the 1981 season with a plan to form a Moriwaki team. I knew Roger Marshall was available because George Beale was pulling out of racing, leaving Roger high and dry and I knew he would be a good bet. Mamoru Moriwaki had been keeping an eye on Wayne Gardner, who had in effect followed my footsteps to the UK. Within a few weeks we had Roger and 'Digger' (Wayne Gardner) ready for the first race meeting at Cadwell, complete with a Mercedes van and a caravan.

Both Digger and Roger would race in the Superbike and TTF1 events. Since I had done my bit in 1979, the Moriwaki effect had diminished a little and to get it cracking again we needed this extra exposure. With a good showing at Daytona the boys seemed to be getting on well, with Roger looking after Wayne and his girlfriend Donna at his house in Yorkshire.

Our '81 team was assembled and we kicked off the season with a testing session at Brands Hatch. I got a heap of laps in on both my XR69 and the XR35. Other than a couple of niggling issues, it was judged as a success. The first race would tell just how much we had improved the bikes over the winter break. Mick and Radar plus Junior and Steve would be helping me out again this year and Randy's team had Jerry Burgess, who we called Blossom, and Little George. Martyn oversaw everyone, communicating with the Japanese and was on call for anything that was needed. The season opener was at Cadwell Park and we were up for it.

Cadwell Park was not my favourite track but I wanted maximum points in this first event, which featured both the TTF1 and Superbike championship rounds. It would set the scene for what we could expect this year.

We had our new XR69 with the full-floater suspension and an upgraded power unit but anticipated that Honda would have a similar set-up for Ron. I had more than a passing interest in how the Moriwaki team would perform. Mamoru Moriwaki would be getting into Roger's head, building up his confidence and self-belief. He loved this track with its changing contours and the little hill where the bikes get airborne. Mamoru had been building an aluminium chassis for Roger. Digger's Z1000 superbike was a big improvement over my

'79 version and one of his goals was to beat me outright in front of Mamoru. I was going to be under a lot of pressure.

The TTF1 race was tough and Roger proved from the first lap that he would be competitive on the Moriwaki F1. First time out he ran a close second to me, edging Ron Haslam out. Roger was so wired he could have been given a moped and got the same results. Wayne followed with an impressive ride in fourth place, holding out Noddy Newbold. I was rapt to win the race and to start the season with 15 points was a far cry from the position we had found ourselves in the year before.

I hadn't planned to do the Superbike championship but with only the one TTF1 race, it made sense to get some more track time with our F1 bike. The Superbike race turned out to be a thriller, with Wayne and I going at it hell-for-leather. He got the better of me in the last lap and I followed him over the line with Ron third. Wayne had assumed the mantle of an Aussie battler and became the underdog for the series, perhaps emulating me from 1979.

Mick Smith suggested that as a Moriwaki UK director I might have only ridden as hard as I needed, to let Wayne win and guarantee some free publicity. While the Superbike series held little interest for me, Mamoru Moriwaki was excited about Wayne's win, so Mick could be excused for thinking that.

DONINGTON PARK, 12 APRIL 1981

Our Suzuki team was at full strength for the two-day event at Donington. It was the second round of the TTF1 Championship, plus there was the ITV World of Sport race on Saturday and a John Player Gold Cup race on the Sunday. This was our first outing for our new XR35's.

It was drizzling on the Saturday, not unusual at Donington. The first race was wet and caused a few riders to come undone in the slippery conditions. Both Randy and I complained about our clutches slipping too much at the start. Randy, Kenny and Steve Parrish all crashed out on the second lap, which left me to fight it out with Barry Sheene, Kork Ballington and Keith Huewen. I had qualified fastest on a wet track with a time of 1:24. This was almost 10 seconds slower than in the dry and with Barry being in such good form he won the ITV World of Sport Challenge, with me taking second ahead of Kork. Our brake problems from the previous year were still causing concern.

It was dry on Sunday, which meant swapping suspension settings back to normal from the changes we had made for Saturday's wet conditions. In the TTF1 race I found my Suzuki to be quick. It performed flawlessly, enabling me to not only take the win but lower the lap record to 1:15.3. It wasn't much slower than the outright lap record; our new F1 bike was just a dream to ride. Roger followed me home on the Moriwaki just ahead of Digger in third place with Ron fourth. I had 30 points and counting. Race two, the John Player Cup, saw me follow Randy home and again the lap record was broken by a Suzuki.

Afterwards I was reflecting on our performances with Radar, Mick and Dave Collins. Both our XR69 and XR35 had come through looking good. Only the brakes needed attention on the 500 but I was pleased we had got rid of the single-acting callipers of the XR69 and were now using ones similar to those on the Grand Prix bikes.

Because it was a good pay-day with two second placings and a first, the following day I drove down to London hoping to find a VW Kombi van for my brother Steven and his wife Gloria. They had been saving up for a trip around Europe. I bought an old burnt orange van for £800, a steal because the Australian guy's girlfriend was sitting on the doorstep giving someone directions to Pamplona, presumably for the Running of the Bulls. I caught the tail-end of the conversation when she mentioned they were leaving on Wednesday and the van had to be sold. It was about 2.30 p.m. so thought I might wait it out for a while. An hour later the girl was still sitting in the van, reading a book. I asked her boyfriend how much, knowing full well he had a sign wanting £1500 or near offer.

'Hey, I've got £650 — will that buy it?' Naturally, he said no but added I could have it for £1200. I put my hands in my pocket, shuffled through the notes, then said, 'Mate, I can only afford £720.'

He came down again, this time to £1100. I turned to Brenda and asked how much she had. She shrugged and said £20. That was £740 he knew I had and he'd seen the colour of the money. I turned to walk away and was putting the cash back in my pocket when he made the fatal mistake of asking how much did I really have.

'Look, I think I can find another £60 so that makes it £800 all-up and I can't afford to buy insurance so it won't work.' I turned again, but this time I heard him say, 'OK OK, you can have it for £800.' Job done.

TRANS-ATLANTIC MATCH RACES

'The rotten bastards have changed the rules for the Trans-Atlantic races this year,' I said to Rex as he chomped on his lunch in the cafeteria. 'Last year it was OK for me to be a temporary Pom but not any more eh! You buggers are pretty good at knowing how to change the rules to suit yourselves. It's only when you get yourselves into a good old stoush, like a war, that you come looking for support, Rex, mark my words.'

The papers had just released details of the popular Trans-Atlantic Match Race series in April. Last year some British riders had given me flak over my inclusion in the British Team. According to the media, Dave Potter's sponsor Ted Broad had been given the job of managing the selection process and already the knives were out, with infighting about who should represent the Brits against the Yanks in the annual Trans-Atlantic Challenge. Mick Grant was given the red card and Irishman Joey Dunlop stepped up with his TZ750. Steve Henshaw was included and then it got messy trying to work out who should be invited. I wasn't on the list this year, so I would be spectating.

That left me to focus on the three Shellsport 500 cc championship races. There were no TTF1 races to do and after the first Brands Hatch round I was one up, with 15 points. Keith Huewen, Korky Ballington and Johnny Newbold followed me over the line, and on the Sunday at Mallory Park it was a repeat performance in a bitterly cold wind. Another 15 points in the bag plus another beautiful silver tray.

SALZBURGRING, AUSTRIA

My brother Steve and his wife Gloria arrived before our first Grand Prix and I gave them a quick run-down on the Kombi van. It was important to know all about how it works, just in case. 'Here's the keys, there's the van, Dover's that way and we'll see you in Salzburg!'

They were waiting for us when we drove into the Salzburgring. Already they seemed to be adapting well to life on the road. Then I noticed a wire poking out of the dashboard. It turned out to be a makeshift throttle cable. 'Didn't get very far,' Steve said. 'Halfway to Dover the bloody throttle cable broke, so I have to get a new one soon.'

What a ripper of a start to the season, achieving pole position at the first Grand Prix. I had been looking forward to the 1981 season since finishing second at last year's German GP at Nürburgring. After the qualifying results were posted for Salzburgring, a journalist asked me how qualifying had gone for me. I told him it was hard work but I did it by sheer guts and determination. Then I couldn't help myself and told him, 'Actually, pal, I slipped the timekeepers 10 quid,' and added, 'That's not bad for a 4-stroke rider, eh?'

Our new XR35's had been reworked over the latter part of the previous year at Hamamatsu, Japan. We thought we had the jump on the opposition. Randy was pissed off that the changes he wanted made personally to his bike were actually incorporated in all the XR35's and we all benefited. The new M-3 chassis worked a treat and the whole package looked better. Our team was a much improved

From last on the grid to first across the line, angry and fired up I won the 1980 Superbike race at Daytona in aggressive style. Don't mess with me! - *Shigeo Kibiki*

Pops Yoshimura and son Fujio in Victory Lane, elated at Suzuki's dominance of the 1980 Bell Helmets Superbike race. - *Croz Archive*

'Freezing bloody cold' but we still had to go out and test at Mallory in early spring. - *Croz Archive*

Martyn Ogborne, the consummate professional, prepares my Suzuki XR23 for the Trans-Atlantic races at Brands … I crashed it! - *Croz Archive*

Despite an early tumble in practice, I managed a second place behind Freddie Spencer in my first race. The XR23 was a real beast to ride. - *Chris Allen*

Ballaugh Bridge at the Isle of Man during my Senior TT win in 1980. - *Croz Archive*

Midnight refuelling practice with Junior, Radar, Mick, Martyn and Rex White. I was at the pub!
- *Croz Archive*

Following Kenny Roberts at Zolder, Belgium Grand Prix, 1980. A fourth place gave me a well-overdue boost in confidence. - *Croz Archive*

It was a tight race but a win is a win and I will take it, champagne and all. On the podium for the Isle of Man Senior TT race, 1980. - *Croz Archive*

Aussie's Jan and Arthur Blizzard assist me (a Kiwi) with the solid silver Senior Trophy. After all, I'd used an Australian racing licence so I was in effect an honorary Aussie. - *Croz Archive*

Joey Dunlop keeping an eye on what was happening as the race developed for the 1980 TTF1 World Championship between Ron Haslam and me. *- Croz Archive*

Controversy and Croz, never too far apart. Mick Grant proved a very slippery customer during the TTF1 race. *- Croz Archive*

Suzuki GB director Maurice Knight and his wife with Brenda and me enjoying dinner in Peel at the Isle of Man, 1980. *- Croz Archive*

Asakawa and Radar fitting the 'big' engine for the Classic race as Pops watches on, Isle of Man, 1980. *- Croz Archive*

The 500 XR34 being prepared by Radar, Junior and Rex in the hotel basement during the 1980 TT. *- Croz Archive*

In the hot conditions of Australia, a four-stroke finally beats the two-strokes during the Swann Series, Oran Park (Australia), 1980. - AMCN

Blue Lewis and I talk about his time as Jim Redman's mechanic back in the 60s. His van looks about the same vintage! - *Croz Archive*

My favourite T-shirt: 'The English might have the culture but Kiwis have the polish'. - *Croz Archive*

Team Suzuki doing some PR shots at Mallory in early 1981. Radar and Jerry Burgess play with the front ends while Martyn looks on.
- *Don Morley*

The Ulster Grand Prix in 1981 and more team orders. The Suzuki XR69 continued to out-perform the Hondas.
- Croz Archive

The great Stanley Woods with Bill Lomas and a new young test rider for Stanley's big Velocette. Jurby Airfield at the Isle of Man.
- Hugh Wilson

'Twenty-four litres of race fuel, thanks. Do you take credit cards?' A quick stop during the 1981 Classic TT race to refuel on my way to another TT win. - Croz Archive

Smiles all round for the winner.
- W. Gruber, Salzburg

The Suzuki TTF1 GS1000R XR69 in full flight at Silverstone. - *Croz Archive*

Down Bray Hill at speed, almost airborne. TTF1 race, Isle of Man, 1981. - *Croz Archive*

Getting ready for the 'off' — getting final instructions from Junior on the start line at the Classic TT, 1981. - *Croz Archive*

On pole position next to Barry Sheene for the British Grand Prix in 1981, a race I certainly won't forget in a hurry. - *Henk Keulemans*

The XR35 500 cc Suzuki Grand Prix machine. A delightful bike to race at a time when Suzuki almost had it right. - *Croz Archive*

I knew exactly what happened — I had the best seat in the house! British Grand Prix, Silverstone, 1981.
- *MCN UK Bauer Media, www.actionlibrary.com*

A wet start to the Dutch Grand Prix at Assen, 1981. - *Henk Keulemans*

Following those road-racing experts Jack Middelburg and Boet van Dulmen, Finnish Grand Prix, 1981. - *Henk Keulemans*

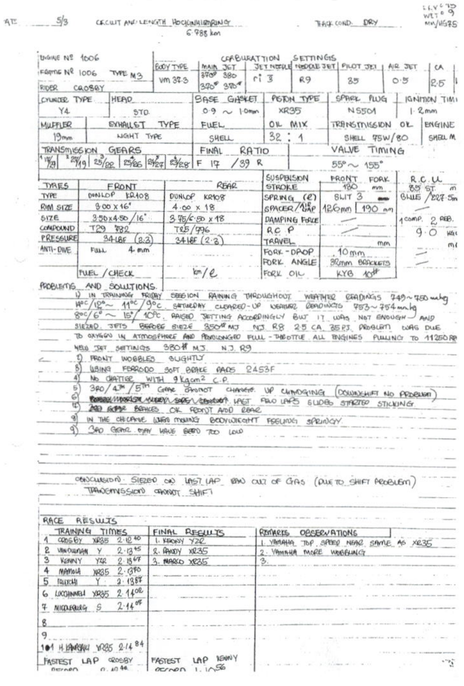

On the start line in pole position with a dodgy gearbox. German Grand Prix, Hockenheim, 1981. - *Henk Keulemans*

In a pensive mood prior to the start at Hockenheim, 1981. - *Henk Keulemans*

The 500 cc German Grand Prix race records with all the settings noting the transmission problems. Hockenheim, 1981. - *Croz Archive*

1981 Ulster Grand Prix, Northern Ireland. Out of sight of the officials. - *Croz Archive*

Agostini gives me a pep talk before a training session.
- *W. Gruber, Salzburg*

The factory Yamaha YZ750 that took me to victory at the Daytona 200. It was a real hare-and-tortoise race but the old girl keep circulating while those around fell by the wayside. - *Shigeo Kibiki*

Freddie Spencer watches as I grab hold of the big Daytona 200 trophy. It was a close call and the positions could have been reversed so easily if not for the tyre-wear factor. *- Shigeo Kibiki*

'Jumping Jack' Middelburg tosses away his chance of winning the Hengelo International. - *Henk Keulemans*

Trying on my new 1982 Yamaha OW60 with Radar and Trevor Tilbury. It fitted well and looked good but on the first lap we knew we were in for trouble. - *Croz Archive*

Doing battle with and getting stalked by 'King Kenny' Roberts. - *Croz Archive*

Radar with his hand on the throttle and giving advice on how to deal with a particularly difficult corner at Imola. 'Don't back off', he's telling me. - *Manfred Mothes*

Although a stopgap measure while the V4 was being built, the OW60 was a dream to ride. - *Manfred Mothes*

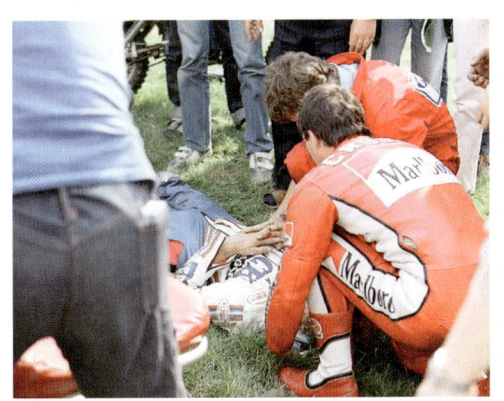

Rendering assistance to Jack Middelburg, who was involved in the horrific Barry Sheene crash, Silverstone, 1982. - *Croz Archive*

'Look, Ago, no skin on my hands.' I contemplate the use of touring gloves to make things a little more bearable. British Grand Prix, 1982. - *Volker Rauch*

Having a great ding-dong battle with Marco Lucchinelli on his factory NSR500 during the Imola 200. - *Henk Keulemans*

Roberts on the V4 (OW61), Sheene (OW60), and me following along as we round the La Source hairpin, Spa, Belgium Grand Prix, 1982. - *Henk Keulemans*

It's party time as I celebrate my birthday with Korky and Bronwyn Ballington, Trevor, Aussie's Lindsey Walker and Jimmy Scaysbrook plus a few others. - *Croz Archive*

A blistering hot start in the 1982 Yugoslavian 500 cc Grand Prix. Sheene, Spencer, Uncini, Lucchinelli, Katayama, Middelburg … oh yeah, and me! - *Croz Archive*

Leading Freddie Spencer and Barry Sheene around the Rijeka circuit in Yugoslavia during the 500 cc Grand Prix. - *Henk Keulemans*

Franco Uncini, Barry and I on the podium for the Yugoslavian Grand Prix. Run under extreme temperatures, it had everyone gasping for breath. - *Henk Keulemans*

Freddie Spencer, Franco Uncini and I after a hard-fought battle at Misano.
- Henk Keulemans

My last start in a Grand Prix. It ended up with me taking an unexpected visit to the local hospital. German Grand Prix, Hockenheim, 1982. - Henk Keulemans

Deblin, 18th January 2010

Dear Sir Crosby,

    I would like to start this letter by sending you my best regards. I am a big fan of motorcycle racing. I visit all important races in our country as well as in the neighbouring countries. For the long time I have been interested in this sport I have admired many riders. However, I grew fond of you because of your singular style of riding, achieved results and behaviour to your fans. I would like to ask you to send me your autographed photograph or at least to sign the card attached to this letter. Your autograph would always remind me of fabulous experiences I enjoyed thanks to your performances.

    Additionally, allow me to congratulate you on all your successes achieved both on home and foreign racing circuits. You rank among the best racers in history thanks to your results.

    I thank you beforehand for your gentleness and wish you good health, good luck and all the best.

Yours faithfully

Bohuslav Svehla

A sample of one of the many letters I have received seeking autographs, signed photos and memorabilia. They still keep coming!
- Croz Archive

A very special thanks to my wife, Helen — here with her 'assistant' Sophie-dog — who totally inspired me to put down in words my story, the way it was. - *Croz Archive*

My inspirational wife and our fur-child aboard Bessie the Harley. - *Croz Archive*

operation compared with the previous year's.

Although Yamaha had done some pre-season testing at Salzburg on a new aluminium-framed square-four, it looked similar to the Suzuki RG models but with an electronically controlled power valve system. It would be competitive in the right hands and Kenny Roberts would be able to wring every ounce of speed from it. At this stage there was only one available for Kenny, although in time Barry Sheene would get his. In the meantime he would have to make do with the older reverse cylinder YZ500.

The Yamaha and Suzuki teams had booked the Salzburg circuit for some early testing, though it was only needed for some fine-tuning. At least this could be done on a dry track and in normal temperatures. By the time qualifying had been completed I found myself on pole position.

Kenny had made a cock-up in practice and thrown his new OW54 away, damaging the forks and cracking his new aluminium frame. He was forced to quickly change to the spare chassis, which was not ideal. Randy got caught out with a cold front tyre and ended up on his bum sliding down the road and aggravating an old hand injury.

The race was run in dry conditions and although I got a great start and led for a few laps, Randy and Marco Lucchinelli got by. Kenny Roberts rode around with a misbehaving rear damper unit, retiring after a few close calls. Up front the boys got tangled and Marco ran off the track, ending upside down in the dirt. This elevated me to second and our guest factory test rider Hiroyuki Kawasaki claimed third, giving Suzuki a clean sweep. Throughout the race my front brake lever was getting soft and requiring two pumps before I could get pressure. I figured the calliper seals must be too tight and as the pads wore during the race they kept being pulled back to the original position instead of slipping through.

The year before, to get me on a TTF1 bike, Suzuki had also provided me with a Grand Prix bike. It was a compromise or trade-off in our negotiations but others I knew had seen it as a waste of a bike. Things had now changed and I was a competent Grand Prix racer who would be able to do justice this year to the factory XR35.

Unexpectedly, I was offered a new Mercedes E220 station wagon to use while in Salzburg by Mercedes-Benz marketing representative Wolfgang Gruber. I celebrated my podium finish by taking Brenda up into the mountains to a flash hotel high above the snowline, where we had a beautiful Chateaubriand, a bottle of fine Merlot and finished off with several cognacs.

GERMAN GRAND PRIX, HOCKENHEIM, 3 MAY 1981

If ever there was a track that sends shivers up the spines of mechanics then it has to be Hockenheim. The circuit takes a detour from a seated arena amphitheatre, with its tight corners, out into a heavily wooded forest and back again. The forest section is long and fast with a couple of chicanes to keep the speeds at a reasonable level. However, it's the oxygen and CO_2 levels that are constantly changing during the day that make carburettor jetting difficult and potentially expensive. It's a power-demanding track so getting the jetting correct is imperative. There is a need to err on the rich side to ensure a level of safety.

The changing weather conditions proved we were all not infallible and in one session I seized both of my bikes. It was as if the Hockenheim circuit was saying, 'Croz, don't think I'm going to roll over and make things easy for you. Watch your back!' It cost me a couple of new pistons and a cylinder plus some lost practice time. Throughout training and qualifying I had problems with shifting into third gear, a problem that wouldn't go away. As I was coming out of corners in second and accelerating hard, the shift to the next gear just wouldn't happen. I found myself almost head-butting the screen and my ankle soon tired with the constant gear-shifting attempts.

'Achtung Fahrerlager,' the paddock PA blasts out. We know it means 'attention in the paddock' but we have to listen in three languages. We are instructed to form up at the pit road entrance to be let out for practice. I sit astride my bike and next to me is Gustav Reiner, a privateer on a Suzuki RG500. He lifts a leg but he can't quite get his leg up and bent enough to go over the seat.

'This bloody knee of mine is pissing me off, I can't bend it enough. Shit! Graeme, can you hold my bike for me?'

'Sure, Gustav.' I lean over and balance my foot on his foot-peg and hold the tank with my right hand. He walks over to the edge of the bitumen surface and pulls back a knee protector to expose an open gap in his racing suit. I take a look at his knee. It's inflamed and swollen badly. He grimaces and then with a huge push between both hands his knee explodes with blood and pus. Three more times he squeezes and pushes and the poison oozes from his knee. He stops and flicks the knee protector back on and clips the Velcro back into place, stretches his leg then walks back over to me. 'Thanks, Croz, for holding my bike,' he says in a very matter-of-fact way. Then he throws his leg over the bike and sits down. 'I have to do that every time I ride. It will be OK after a few laps; the pain goes away!'

I dined out on that story many times, with people laughing or crying or throwing up.

After dodging showers on Friday I got myself together on the Saturday and posted a time again that gave me pole position. But not before some grief over the supply of a power-up kit that had arrived from Japan. It was handed to Randy's mechanics to fit to his XR35. Radar and Mick were furious that only one kit had been sent and a heated argument took place with the Suzuki factory representative Mitsi Okamoto. It was too early in the season to play favourites, we reckoned, but he was insistent that Randy got the first upgrade. This year was going to be a struggle if Suzuki thought there was only one rider in our team. Both of my guys took it on the chin, then in true Anzac DIY style went about copying the power-up kit. The cylinders and heads were modified late into Friday night and next day I put the bike on pole position despite the dodgy transmission.

The race was another story, though. I had the speed and lead on a number of occasions but the damn gearbox continued playing up. Before long I had lost the slipstream effect that's so vital at Hockenheim to stay with the leaders and then slowly drifted back through the pack to eventually finish 13th. Randy had suffered a similar problem in training as me but in the race he seemed unaffected. I was furious after the race when it was suggested Randy had been given different transmission oil to try.

ITALIAN GRAND PRIX, MONZA, 10 MAY 1981

The next GP was the Italian at the Autodromo Nazionale of Monza, north of Milan. It is without a doubt one of the most historic motor-racing circuits in the world. It had claimed the lives of Renzo Pasolini and Jarno Saarinen during a 250 cc race at the Grand Prix in 1973. I heard about the accident 12,000 miles away at the Auckland Motorcycle Club's Thursday night piss-up. This was a case where the crème de la crème of 250 cc GP racing were taken out in one accident. It was quite bizarre. What actually happened on that first lap of the race remains controversial. Pasolini's bike was thought to have seized, throwing him off; and Jarno, following behind, was unable to avoid crashing into him. The ensuing pile-up involved 12 riders.

The condition of the track on that day continues to be the subject of debate. Some have attributed the accident to oil left on the track during the 350 cc race when Walter Villa's Benelli began leaking engine oil on the penultimate lap. His pit crew encouraged him to finish the race in order to collect championship points and I would have done the same. It was argued that race officials neglected to clean up the spillage prior to the start of 250 cc race. One rider, John Dodds, made his concerns known to authorities, and was allegedly met with threats. However, my understanding is that Pasolini's fall and the damage to his bike were both consistent with the bike having seized.

There had been no motorcycle Grand Prix staged at Monza since 1973. The car guys had had a free rein to build their own car-friendly circuit with steel barriers very close to the track and their chicanes being slowly installed at the fastest parts of the circuit. Franco Uncini gave approval as the FIM riders' representative to include Monza as a Grand Prix venue again for 1981. Most riders still had concerns, not only about issues surrounding track safety but because the organizers were selling tickets to the paddock. Security and safety were again being compromised. The actual facilities in the paddock were abysmal but luckily we had our own motorhome and I could go and read the paper and relax there.

Our motorhome had sprung a leak in the roof after I had stored it outside in the UK over winter. Someone mentioned acid rain but if I was listening I probably thought it was a name for a new rock band. I never thought it was actually a corrosive atmosphere or that the aluminium roof would start corroding. The motorhome had about 80 litres of grey water storage, so I developed a system whereby I created a small leak that continuously dribbled out and downhill across the paddock. The effect was that we were able to extend our time between emptying the grey water out to five days — perfect for a GP racing paddock, providing no silly bugger decided to pitch their tent downhill from us.

Suzuki had arranged to privately hire the circuit for practice on the fifth and sixth, to test tyres and to set up and jet my own new sand-cast magnesium Mikuni 37.5 mm carburettors that had finally arrived from the factory. We had been using 36 mm Mikuni carburettors, which were relatively easy to set up and worked well. Temperature, pressure and humidity were calculated and the jets were selected based on atmospheric conditions at the time. The bigger carburettors were designed to provide a boost in power and I needed all the help I could get.

Throughout our unofficial practice sessions I was finding it difficult getting the engine to come cleanly out of the corners, particularly around 7200 rpm. The engine kept hesitating slightly and lacked grunt or power and as a consequence I was slower onto the straights. My lap times were disappointing. The inability to convey to my crew if it was lean or rich was getting me down but I had to persevere. I knew that with having a bigger size venturi, the airspeed was slower and more difficult to control, but potentially there was more power available to use. Despite many jet changes I still couldn't get it right. I was chasing my tail and felt as if I was letting the team down by not knowing exactly which way to go. It must have been frustrating for both Mick and Radar.

Steven and Gloria arrived later that day and, as promised, I organized to get tickets and a paddock pass for their Kombi van. That evening, not wanting to give up my prime site in the paddock, we decided to use the Kombi as the taxi for a dinner we had planned with some Aussie friends. Ten of us piled into the van and headed off to an Italian eatery. We ate well and drank copious quantities of the local house red, spilled litres of beer, and finished off with a grappa or two and a drinking competition. Not a sober soul in sight when we set off in the dark back to the paddock.

As we entered the paddock at speed, someone grabbed the handbrake as we rounded a corner behind the pit entrance and the old Kombi lurched up and teetered on two wheels, on the brink of rolling over. Luck was on our side that night, thanks to a larger than life Aussie character, photographer Lou Martin. He had the good sense to move a few feet to correct the centre of gravity and the old Kombi came crashing back to earth, right side up. Later Lou claimed he'd only moved to recover a bottle of beer.

The following day the problem with the carburettors was resolved in what was a bizarre turn of events. During the second session of official practice on the Friday I arrived at turn two, called 'Curve Grande', which my basic understanding of Italian told me means 'big corner' — and it was. I was on a hot lap and shifted down from fifth to fourth gear and then to what should have been third. A split-second later something literally erupted between my legs and a huge vibration immediately set in. 'Shit!' I thought and grabbed the clutch in an attempt to isolate the engine from the transmission. Looking down between the sides of the cowling, I noticed that a connecting rod had parted company from the crankshaft and it had come up and out through the engine casing. The motor was poked — the first big blow-up I'd experienced. With the clutch in I coasted to a stop beside one of the official flag marshalling points. Following much arm-waving and yelling, I left the bike in the care of a marshal and ran back to the pit area to complete the session on my second bike. Up until then my lap times were very competitive, with a best time of 1:54:37 which was close to Marco's best and pole-position time of 1:53:96.

That session ended with no improvement in lap time but I had a couple more laps under my belt. Radar was ready with the little yellow pit bike on completion of the session when I came in. I piled on behind him and away we went to pick up the expired XR35 which I guessed by now had finished giving up its last drop of oil on the grass embankment where I had left it. We arrived at the second chicane to find the old girl leaning against the fence. She was all alone — no flag marshal or official in sight. Radar was quick to notice that all that remained of the carburettors was the cables. Some rotten bastards had cut off all four special carburettors with side-cutters, leaving only the frayed ends of the cables.

The 36 mm Mikunis had worked really well up until now and I felt that although I had to settle for a little less outright performance for the race, it was not the end of the world. In any case I had no option as Suzuki only supplied one set of the bigger carburettors that were now subject to a change in ownership. I was really surprised that the bike was stripped of those carburettors because no one should have been aware they were a special size.

Despite all the problems leading up to race day, I managed to get a time fast enough to put me fourth on the grid. I was a little disappointed but happy to have a place on the front row.

Race day was gloomy with overcast conditions prevailing and it looked like we were in for a wet ride. The pre-race tension I always felt was not helped by having little to eat in the morning. My thinking was that if I needed an operation following a crash I would be better off with no food in my stomach. I was also wrestling with the difficult decision of which tyre to start the race with. The choice of tyres was always left to the last minute and while I had the ultimate say, it was usually a team decision. On the positive side, the prospect of a wet race always gave me a little lift in confidence, knowing that I'd had so much experience racing in atrocious conditions back home in New Zealand. While I was not frightened of a wet track, I also knew that the American riders were less comfortable. I was confident I had the measure of Randy on any track in the wet. Michelin full wets had to be the choice of the day if it was heavy rain but I also knew they didn't have the endurance of our Dunlops. Our intermediate tyres were better than the hand-grooved Michelins. So I wanted it to be either really pissing down or just slightly wetter than damp.

Races in poor conditions are usually the ones that take the longest to finish, and they can really drag out. There are additional external factors to contend with. Visibility and visor-fogging always posed a problem. The venting of hot air out of the helmet was a constant necessity, so I used a fine smearing of dishwashing liquid applied to the inside of the visor. This would work for a while but as my body heat and breath warmed, the visor usually began fogging up. Randy had bigger problems than me, which I blamed on helmet design. If I could only work out how to breathe through my ears everything would be sweet.

We were prepared for the inclement weather but the variable atmospheric conditions meant your strategy had to be flexible. I had chosen a set of Dunlop full wets that I had been developing during testing sessions earlier in the year. These were a hard compound for durability, and had a great tread pattern that provided the rider with good feel in heavy rain. What we lacked in our tyre armoury was a very soft full wet that could compete head-on with both the Michelin and Goodyear full wets. The soft compound gave exceptional feel in torrential rain but lacked durability for the longer races. In effect, once the track began drying, these tyres overheated and become almost useless.

I thought I was in the pound seat as we sat on the grid. Kenny had the Goodyear 'chewing gum softies' while Team Gallina had selected Michelin full wets. I calculated that if I could keep the leaders in sight early on, then as the race progressed and with the track drying I would be well positioned to take control.

The start flag finally dropped on the 500 cc race and with spray pumping out of the tyres we approached the two right-handers over the back — 'Variante della Roggia' and 'Curva Di Lesmos'. These corners were notorious for being almost impossible to ride around upright, let alone race around when it was wet. The large trees forming a canopy over these corners dropped slippery sap directly on to the track surface, making it treacherous. We were confronted with absolutely no grip and both front and rear wheels began doing the 'dance of the desperates' on the glassy surface. By the time I exited the corner rather gingerly with both feet down I knew I was one of the lucky ones who had made it. On the next lap around I saw the carnage and mayhem that had happened on that wild first lap. For the first eight laps it was as though I were riding on fingertips and toenails. I had a big front wheel slide and dropped back a few places; Barry Sheene got the better of me but I recovered and passed him again.

I then settled down to chase Kenny, who by now had managed to get a commanding lead that seemed to be opening up. His tyres must have been working well and my plan was not working, at least the way I wanted it to. A high level of concentration was required until mid-race, when the rain eased to allow a damp track and a dry line to develop. I knew I had to chase down Kenny in the closing laps. The last laps were done trying to find every puddle along the straights in an effort to cool the tyres and minimize the tread break-up. Somehow I ended up 'in the zone'.

For those riders who are merely going through the motions of a race it can be like drawing teeth; lap after lap can drag on until finally they see the chequered flag waving. Throughout the race you can retain virtually full recall of just about every aspect of each lap, corner by corner. You may be on the edge but ultimately you are not 'in the zone'.

Being in the zone is another step up and seldom attainable but once there it's a whole different story. I suffer memory loss when I'm racing to my ultimate potential, in the zone. When I am 'in the moment', it leaves me with no capacity in my memory banks to record what is going on as the race unfolds. There is plenty of time later to do a self-analysis and congratulate yourself and watch video replays but, for me, being in the zone involves a kind of time collapse, and the race can seem like it's over as soon as it has begun. I assume that having full recall of a race can only mean I was not 100 per cent focused on the job.

I knew Kenny was in trouble with his tyres being literally ripped to shreds on the drying track and he would be struggling to hold a competitive lap time. The lapboards confirmed I was closing on him. Using mental arithmetic based on my lapboard information meant although my tyres were worn badly, they were in much better shape to finish the race and, God willing, given a lap or two more I should have won my first GP.

19

CONTROVERSY AND CROZ NEVER FAR APART, 1981

CIRCUIT PAUL RICARD, 17 MAY 1981

La Castellet near Marseille is home to another of my favourite racetracks. At 5.8 km, the Paul Ricard circuit includes the long Mistral back straight. I loved the track, its facilities and the location. It rarely rains and on a good day speeds on the Mistral can reach close to 300 kph. With help from the Mistral tailwind and the slipstream effect when tailing someone, you have to be careful on the high-speed right-hander off the end of the straight.

Every race has its problems and this time everyone was focused on tyres. Both Kenny and Barry had been given new square four 500's by Yamaha but had taken different approaches with them. Compounding Barry's problem was his insistence on using Michelins following his horrific crash at Daytona while on Dunlops. Mind you, when it suited Barry he was capable of having a bet each way if he could see any snippet of advantage. He had tested his Michelins but decided the Dunlops had more potential. However, there was a complication. His new bike had a 16-inch wheel similar to ours. Suzuki GB was the only team contracted to Dunlop and our tyres had been working well, particularly on the new Gamma XR35. Barry asked Dunlop's Peter Ingley but was told nothing would be available. Our team had been working hard testing these tyres and I certainly didn't want anyone else benefiting, not yet anyway.

The new Yamahas turned out to be pretty damn fast, a good 5 kph quicker and it looked like Kenny had his tyre choice sorted. Goodyear had plenty of compounds and constructions for him to play with but time would tell if a combination would work.

Our practice was focusing on gearing to get the correct drive out of the corners but the conditions kept changing. A weak frontal system came through on race day and with the change in humidity our carburation ended up way too rich. Then the tailwind turned into a crosswind and we couldn't pull max rpm because of our reduced power. Randy and I slogged it out for much of the race with our machines coughing and spluttering coming out of corners. The Yamahas of Kenny and Barry slowly pulled away but Marco had joined them on his Suzuki, which was jetted differently, enabling him to pass and pull away.

Late in the race the inevitable tyre problems emerged. First Kenny then Barry lost ground and both Randy and I overhauled them to place second and third. It wasn't a brilliant ride given the richness of the engines, but we hung in there and collected valuable points. I felt as if I now belonged to this Continental circus and proved that when I was given the right equipment I wouldn't waste it. With two seconds, a third plus two pole positions, I felt I'd justified my place. I'd done my apprenticeship and paid my dues.

After the race had ended the Aussies and Kiwis slowly began making a beeline for the gates. A queue had formed in front of a coin-operated public phone box, where we employed a Morse code method to bypass the need for cash. Within a few hours of the race finishing, New Zealand had my scoop on what had happened. Max Farquhar was top of my list in Auckland. As an efficient spreader of news he was the perfect voice of Europe for me. The phone would ring: 'Croz here, Max, scoop, scoop, scoop!'

He would almost wet himself with excitement. 'What's up? Who won? Who crashed? How did you get on? How are the women in France?' I had to cool him down before giving him a brief report. He would listen carefully, ask questions and would promise to call my mother first then the others on his list. Then a banging on the outside of the phone box signalled my time was up. I would be replaced by another 'tapper' trying to connect with his home somewhere in the world.

Back at the pit area it was my shout for tonight's barbecue at our motorhome. Brenda and some of the girls had gone shopping and came back with huge steaks, enough to feed a small army of Aussie riders, their families and mechanics. Our steak was a big hit and everyone got stuck into it. Then a passing Frenchman identified it as horse meat. As most of us were hungry we kept chewing relentlessly until not a bit of the 'viande de cheval' was left.

The cold katabatic air had just begun rolling down from the north. We lit a 44-gallon drum and burnt an old race tyre to keep us warm. There was plenty of cheap red wine in plastic two-litre bottles. It was bought on the basis of the most wine for the cheapest price equals the best deal, also resulting in the biggest headaches some of us had ever suffered.

BRANDS HATCH SHORT CIRCUIT, 24 MAY 1981

After our celebrations at Paul Ricard, it was a slow trip back to the UK and that familiar English scratcher's circuit at Brands for round four of the Shellsport 500 Championship; and with three wins in as many races, I was well prepared for my next one. With a diminished competitive line-up I saw only Korky Ballington, Dave Potter and Keith Huewen as potential challengers. It was over almost before it began and in a blinding flash 12 laps disappeared without trace. I bagged another 15 points and another goddamn silver tray.

YUGOSLAVIA, 31 MAY 1981

Brenda and I had arranged to get our visas for the trip to Yugoslavia. The Grand Prix at Rijeka held some fascination for me because I'd not been to that part of Europe before. We booked a flight direct to Zagreb, picked up a rental car and drove the last few miles to the hotel at Split on the foreshore at Rijeka.

I was conscious that I had competed on the last 11 consecutive weekends and still had the Isle of Man to go the following week. I was not short on track time that's for sure, but running both the 500 GP and the British programmes was a tough call and I was thinking it might be too much for me this year. With no recovery time I felt I was just rushing from one event to another. It didn't help that one of the magazines came out with a headline quoting me as saying, 'British riders have it too easy.'

I had been discussing how much time I was spending on a bike, racing or training to the point where it became second nature. Apart from a few exceptions, the English didn't seem to be represented much in Grand Prix racing and I made a statement trying to explain why this was so. My take on it was that in order to have competition you need to go out and find it, not just be happy with turning up each week racing against the same people, as you don't learn that way. Pushing yourself hard and chasing better riders can only lift your game and increase your skill level. It's a soft option to stay at home and be content bashing around familiar territory. It's too easy for the English riders to stay at home and the price you pay for mediocrity is not having representation on the GP scene.

An exception was Keith Huewen, who was a prime example of an English rider who definitely had some spark. He had the get-up-and-go, always out there trying his best and reaping the rewards.

Once again we were up against it with the organizers not being on the ball safety-wise. Other people's interpretations of adequate safety levels often fall short of the riders'. Ultimately, we are the ones who pay the price and we were getting tired of confronting the same opposition time again. This time Rijeka had simply failed to ensure that the flag marshalling was up to standard. Jack Middelburg only made it out of the pit area before ending up in a tangled mess with stones from the edge of the track and debris scattered over the track. The accident was not attended to for some time and in the later practice another incident at the same spot left a rider lying injured for several minutes before help arrived. We needed swift action to rectify such shortcomings.

With our support, Barry Sheene demanded action and suddenly several ambulances appeared as if from nowhere. Apparently, the clerk of the course, who is responsible for the meeting, ripped into the flag marshals about how slack they had been.

At least in training and qualifying I kept my Suzuki upright while many around me fell, some with silly accidents but Korky Ballington's crash took the cake. He had a tyre delaminate at close to 180 kph and the bits that flew off locked his front wheel. Torn ankle ligaments and skin damage effectively ruled him out. He couldn't push-start his bike and withdrew from the GP.

This circuit was quite demanding with its banked corners, but what really takes it out of you physically is the high-speed changing of direction under full power. Our bikes were well set up but it took a lot of strength to hang on to them. Randy got rid of his 16-inch front wheel in favour of the 18-inch, which provided more gyroscopic stability for him, while I changed the triple-clamp off-sets from 30 mm to 27 mm to get more trail and stability; it became too heavy and I wished I'd still had a 30 mm set. Instead I elected to tough it out for the 32 laps.

The 350 cc race was always a good one to watch but on the second lap Michel Rougerie crashed and came to rest lying on the track alongside his bike. He picked himself up apparently uninjured and making a dash for the safety of the grass beside the track he ran smack into an oncoming rider. He was fatally injured in the collision. The accidents were becoming a regular thing, and when death strikes it makes you wonder who is going to be next. We expect to race safely and can take the odd tumble or fall in our stride, but the thought of death to me always seems a long way off, almost as if I were blessed with good luck. Plenty of times the hand of fate could have rested on my shoulder and I would have paid the ultimate price. Fortunately, it passed me by without even giving me a second glance.

I have never been that close personally to anyone who has been killed on the track to make me really question my mortality. Possibly it was because of my transient lifestyle, not staying in one country long enough to form a strong enough bond or a deep friendship. Sure I knew these guys, but not well enough to have had second thoughts about my chosen profession. You could call it thick-skinned, or just pig-headed.

I took my place on the grid at number four. It was the usual group of Randy, Kenny, Barry, Marco and me who escaped into the distance, leaving everyone else behind. I soon regretted not changing to an 18-inch wheel as my energy was being sapped. The twisty circuit demanded a heavy workload and I had my arse hanging out trying to keep up. I held on but just couldn't improve on fourth and settled for the eight points. My decision to run the smaller 36 mm carburettors had paid off. It was difficult riding but marginally easier by not having to worry about a flat spot coming out of corners with the bigger 37.5 mm ones.

ISLE OF MAN TT RACES, 6 JUNE 1981

With a break in the Grand Prix series for a couple of weeks, some of the international riders headed off for some R&R. The Americans zoomed off back to the US and their favourite McDonald's outlets. Some were nursing wounds from accidents in the first half of the season. Still in one piece, I was off to the Isle of Man for a few quick laps of the mountain course. I could already smell the garlic and salt air in my nostrils, and could feel that fresh morning chill on my neck when zipping past the traffic lights and down Bray Hill. I planned to enjoy my time this year on the island.

It had been strange negotiating start money this year with the ACU. Everyone knew I was contracted to race Suzukis at the TT — it was in my job description, as it had been the previous year. I was committed to go, despite my little white lie about retaining an option not to go if the money didn't stack up. Being paid to race was still foreign to me. I also liked it because, unlike Uncle Sam, John Bull didn't have his hand out for a cut.

This time I settled on a minimum start guarantee of £12,000. It sounds like an awful amount of money, but the truth is that it's actually a guarantee that I will earn that much in total when I walk off the circuit, win or lose. The first year I received a £600 guarantee and won more than that in prize money with my fourth place in the TTF1 race. Therefore I couldn't claim against the Tourist Board for a top-up.

The second year, with a £6000 guarantee, again I earned more in prize money with a win and a second place — no top-up. However, this year with a £12,000 guarantee I would have to do extremely well to avoid needing to make a claim. But the increased guarantee gave me more security, knowing I would earn no less than that amount whatever happened.

Other riders had been negotiating with Vernon Cooper from the ACU about start money. There was much dissension amongst the regular TT racers, some of whom probably counted on the guarantee to make it through the rest of the year. Vernon wanted new international talent but had struggled to attract any top-line Grand Prix riders to this treacherous track. What really got up everyone's nose were the high offers of start money reputedly being offered to lure new riders. Hard-charger Jon Ekerold would likely do well but American Dale

Singleton I thought was a doubtful contestant. Dale had recently won the Daytona 200 and was a funny and likeable character. I could listen to his Southern accent all day long, but would he come to race or just ride around and collect the money? Everyone had an opinion.

Brenda and I flew into Ronaldsway Airport on a bleak day, picked up our rental car and drove into Douglas, slowing at Fairy Bridge to say 'Hello' to the fairies. The importance of this tradition might be bound up in some local folklore but I was not going to query it. The true test, though, is at the end of race week when I'm still alive and kicking. 'Thanks fairies, you've looked after me,' I would say as I made my way back to the airport.

I spent practice week driving around and around the course. I took with me anyone who was remotely interested in doing a lap. Some wanted to be let out of the car within a few kilometres of the start when they realized I was going too fast, but with no speed limits the rental car got a thorough workout. I did so many laps that I was continually looking for gas stations. It was all about re-acquainting myself with each section, locating race lines and points of identification so I wouldn't get lost during the race. My commentary to my passengers would really be a set of instructions to myself: 'Coming up on the left is Laurel Bank, this is where Tom Phillis, the Australian rider, was killed in 1962', or 'You have to watch out here as the road drops away and the kerb sticks out a bit — Charlie Williams broke his ankle here.'

'Check out that rock wall there, guys,' I would say, pointing to a rocky outcrop. 'Mitsuo Itoh, the Japanese Suzuki rider, head-butted this wall back in mid-60s. He's still around and will probably be here watching the races next week.'

Brother Steven and his wife Gloria came over and shared a rented house with Brenda and me. The beautiful stone bungalow was a luxury we hadn't enjoyed for some time. Gloria had volunteered to cook our meals, a real treat for us. The house's proximity to the start line had its advantages, especially with the early morning practice sessions. As I walked past one of the ACU officials I joked with him, 'Hi Colin, which way's the track go and what's the lap record?'

He smiled and slapped me on the back. 'You take it easy out there, Croz. Don't you do anything silly.'

It was just getting light around 6 a.m. and the start line was a hive of activity as riders and mechanics did final adjustments before being let out on to the track. The travelling marshal had already been dispatched to ensure there was no livestock or traffic on the course. On the start line a blackboard was held up with the words FOG ON THE MOUNTAIN. Oh fuck, that's just what I didn't want to see.

As my bike was readied it was plain to see that a little fog wasn't going to stop practice going ahead. It was up on the mountain and, drawing on my interest in aviation and meteorology, I figured it was more likely low stratus cloud than fog. While I was waiting I drew an artificial horizon on the inside of my screen with a black marker pen, as if to say I was going to have to use my instruments in the cloud to navigate over the mountain section.

I set off into the early morning sunlight that had been working so hard to make its way through the clouds over Douglas. It was cold and damp and I had intermediate tyres on to build up temperature quickly, allowing at least some grip on the slippery surface. Making it through to Ramsey I started the climb up May Hill and into the fog. At first it was reasonably good visibility but soon it deteriorated into a thick pea soup. I arrived at the Verandah section confident that by holding a constant line through all three corners on the cliff edge, they could be taken as one.

It's different in the fog, though, and I set myself up on the correct line and allowed the centreline mark to move right to left three times under me while I kept the constant radius going. Halfway round I forgot whether I'd done two or three corners and froze in the thick fog. It was a big drop off the edge and I think it would have taken a week to find me if I had disappeared over the cliff. The fairies must have saved me this time, as the dense cloud suddenly parted and I found myself online, right where I should have been.

Instantly, I recalled the American term 'sucking vinyl'. My seat cover was made from a different material but I could still visualize myself having to stop and extract the seat cover from between my buttocks. It was so close, and it scared the hell out of me. Once back at the paddock I told no one of my experience and it remained a secret.

Mick Grant had left Honda at the end of the previous year, freeing him up for Suzuki GB to give him the use of one of my XR35's to use in the 500 cc Senior race and also my spare XR69 for the TTF1 race. It was quite a turn of events from the previous year's tank-bashing episode but it was in Suzuki's interest to win both races. Mick and I successfully tested and ran both the 500 and F1 bikes in practice, and as riders we got on like a house on fire.

It was Monday morning and the first race of the week, the Senior TT, was about to be run as the riders moved to the start area. The weather was atrocious and I didn't feel too keen about racing off down Bray Hill in the wet on a GP bike, especially with a heavy 9-gallon tank that we'd fitted so I needed only one stop. Six laps at speed around here in these conditions seemed ridiculous and dangerous. Visibility was down on the mountain, so the start was sensibly delayed.

An hour later the race was started but after a few miles I felt the engine tighten up and I stopped. The piston seizure so early in the race made me think the fairies were again protecting me. I found my way back, handing my broken Suzuki over to Radar and Mick who set about diagnosing the problem. A retirement in the Senior race effectively meant the bike was now finished with and could be loaded up ready for home.

However, with the race still under way and about midway through, it was red-flagged and stopped. No winner was declared and we soon found we had been thrown a lifeline, as the race would be re-run the next day. All competitors were allowed to restart, regardless of whether they had broken down. It was a mystery why the race was stopped, as a few laps had already been completed and the weather had not deteriorated further. From a safety perspective, the helicopter could not land up on the mountain and that was given as the reason for stopping the race. I agreed and in my position it was quite convenient for me to do so, as I would be able have another shot at it.

The next day was an exact repeat for me. I felt the engine momentarily go tight again just metres from where I had stopped yesterday. I pulled in the clutch and coasted to a stop with the engine only slightly seized. It could have been worse. On the positive side, it was a few steps closer to the Highlander pub where I threw the old girl against a stone wall and went in search of a beer.

Figuring that I was going to be stuck out here for a while, I tentatively restarted the bike and trickled back to the paddock in first gear, using the choke periodically to keep the lubrication up and the temperature down to avoid any further engine damage. Even before I had time to find Radar and Mick, I was informed by Lou Martin of the news that Kenny Blake had crashed a few miles out from the start. A few hours later the word was being spread around the paddock. Tragically, Kenny had died of his injuries.

'Shit, not Kenny, bloody hell, what happened?' I wanted to know all the details. Slowly, a picture began forming, based on the scrappy information that was filtering through. 'Skippy', as he was known, managed to get himself killed on a slippery part of the track. He was further back than where he should have been because of a problem or pit stop but as a consequence was seen by a few people to be riding far too quickly for the conditions. From a spectator's viewpoint the fastest riders are at the front and as the field goes by in 10-second intervals the racing speeds decrease. When Skippy came through that section he was observed going noticeably faster; this was lending support to the theory. No one would know for sure but it was a very quick, high-impact death. This was the first time I had lost a close friend in a racing accident. Last week it was Rougerie, a few weeks before that it was Sauro Pazzaglia at Imola, Mike Hailwood back in March, George O'Dell and now Kenny Blake.

I went over to see if I could find Rourg Murphy, his friend and travelling mate. He was not there; he might have been at the hospital or making the call that mothers dread to take.

Kenny's Hanomag Henschel van was parked in the school grounds. It had an awning attached to one side. Scattered around were all of Kenny's worldly possessions. Clothes hanging on a makeshift line, a small gas burner, a pile of rumpled-up bedclothes and a front slick tyre lying across it. This was a workingman's van, no sign of a woman's soft touch anywhere. Within the awning were two race fuel drums that were used as seats and a small camp table. That was it. It was as if these sad objects were waiting for their owner to come back from the shop. But this was the end of the road and come Friday night the van would still be parked there. The thought of my own mortality came over me and I felt myself shiver involuntarily.

Come Sunday we would be packing and moving on to the next race, just like a bunch of gypsies. Who would be left to look after Kenny's affairs? I supposed once we had all gone, a small, dedicated group of people would come around quietly to dismantle everything and sort out Kenny's personal effects and arrange for his body to be either repatriated or dealt with as instructed by voices 12,000 miles away. What if it was me, I wondered; how would Brenda cope?

The TTF1 race on Wednesday was shaping up to be a beauty. Suzuki had Mick Grant, Noddy Newbold and me, all on the XR69's. Honda had Ron Haslam, Alex George and Joey Dunlop on works machines. The Moriwaki team had Roger Marshall and Graeme McGregor on a pair of Moriwaki Z1's. It was a big field when the privateers were added to the mix.

The conditions were a bit marginal for slicks and we waited until the last minute before making the decision. Dave Collins had our spare wheel ready with a slick fitted and I made the decision to run the slick tyre in expectation of a dry race. Dave removed the wheel on the start line and fitted the new wheel with a slick.

'Oh shit,' Dave cursed behind me. 'It's got the wrong sprocket.' He raced off to get the correct sprocket to fit to the wheel. We checked with an official to ask whether, if we missed our start position, we could then start at the next available unmanned slot whenever it appeared. Yes, and luckily 40 seconds later a slot become available and I pushed the XR69 into position.

Colin Armes from the ACU, this time with his 'race face' on, was directing starting procedures and flatly refused to allow us to start, directing us to the back of the line-up of riders all poised to go. We had two sets of instructions contradicting each other now. I was forced to wait at the end of the queue until I was finally allowed to go. About six minutes after the first pair of riders had been let away, I got the old girl fired up and set off down Bray Hill.

Those first few kilometres provided all the surprises — a visor that was not sealed completely allowed wind to come in and make my eyes water. It's hard to see when you're looking through a fish bowl but this time it was also my visor tear-offs that were vibrating in the wind against my helmet. It was so noisy I couldn't hear the engine. I had a couple of goes at trying to stick them back but finally gave up and ripped them all off. I was suddenly at the mercy of those big fat yellow bugs. They arrived one by one as the race progressed, slowly turning my visor into a palette of multi-coloured bug guts and flattened fly carcases.

When my first signboard came up at Ballacraine I missed it completely, not knowing where to look, but I didn't miss the next one at the fast section exiting Kirk Michael. I still couldn't understand the numbers but saw a minus sign and a six or something, so I figured I must be six seconds behind whoever was leading. It stayed like that for the next two laps and when I pitted I had Martyn yelling in my ear about a protest from Honda and not to worry, just keep going and a second later I was off out again. Him telling me not to worry? Christ, he should have kept his mouth shut. I was the one now worrying what the hell was going on.

In the pit area Martyn had been handed a note from the race control saying that I had been penalized six minutes for being late for the start. Despite arguing our case with the messenger and realizing it was futile, Martyn then sat down to work out what it all meant. He looked at the penalty time imposed and quickly noted that it had been calculated from when the first riders left the start line. I was not scheduled to leave the start line until my allotted time about 70 seconds later. Therefore, even if we accepted the full penalty, it should have been only 4 minutes and 50 seconds. They had got it wrong.

Martyn did two smart things: firstly he advised Honda that we would be appealing the penalty and warned them not to take any notice of the time penalty. Secondly, he immediately protested the time penalty on the basis that the calculations were incorrect. Martyn hastily wrote out the protest on a Suzuki letterhead and went looking for an official.

It must have been like handing over a case of the black plague — no one wanted to know. The connotations of a protest between the Suzuki and Honda teams were disastrous, as the previous year had shown. Martyn was told Ken Shierson of the ACU was in the control box. He asked to see Ken but was told Ken wasn't there.

'Prats, I could see the bastard myself from where I was standing and here was this guy on the door refusing to let me in. So I pushed my way in and went up to him. He didn't want to know and then simply refused to take the piece of paper. I made a grab for his tie and as his hand came up I slipped the protest into his palm.'

With the protest duly served, Martyn went back to managing the team, informing Honda that we had protested and had done so within the 20-minute guideline. Out on the track I could still not make any sense of the signals I was being shown. The way I was reading them, I had picked up only a couple of seconds. The first sign I understood to be −6:0 so I thought that I must be six seconds, not minutes, behind. Over the duration of the race I closed on the leader by about a second a lap according to my signals; man it was hard work as the circuit still had many damp patches, just to make things interesting.

There was no indication of who was in front; it could have been Ron, Joey, Mick, Alex, Noddy or Roger. Flying blind, I had no option but to continue trying to close the gap. I crossed the line in third position on the road, glad to have the race over with. I was on an adrenalin high and confused when I entered the winning enclosure. Buzzing away in my head were the weird signals I had been receiving.

Martyn thought I had won the race but, with the protest still pending, the FIM jury had not yet met to decide on its merit. The garlanding procedure continued with Ron Haslam getting the win, Joey second and me third. I was still buzzing when everyone was slapping me on the back and by the time I got back to the paddock I realized it would be a wait before any decision was announced. Martyn took me through the whole race as he saw it and I finally clicked that the numbers I was chasing were minutes, not seconds. No wonder it was such a hard race.

'What happened to Mick?' I asked

'The silly fucker missed a gear and …'

I finished Martyn's sentence for him, knowing only too well that a missed shift on the diesel meant trouble: ' … a bent valve, I bet.'

'Correct,' he replied.

The official press officer Allan Robinson was a really nice man who had a soft spot for the Kiwis. We always got along fine; in fact he even liked the odd Aussie as well. It was his job to report any FIM jury decisions to the international media at the press office. He called a press conference to address the situation. He explained that the

TTF1 final results had been protested by Suzuki, members of the jury were now deliberating, and he would report back with the decision.

Likeable big Aussie journalist Lou Martin was always lurking around the press office, primarily because food and drink was provided free. Their phones were also available for the journos to file their reports back home to their papers, and in Lou's case, to his girlfriend as well.

Lou was walking past the FIM jury room just as it was finishing its deliberations when he heard Allan being briefed on the decision. Lou heard I had been credited with the win because the ACU was wrong in its calculation of the penalty. Instead of a six-minute penalty it should have been only 46 seconds, meaning I had won by more than two minutes. As Allan was busy writing this down to get it factually correct, his blood pressure would have been rising in anticipation of calling the world's media to attention before proudly announcing the winner of this year's TTF1 race.

Lou saw his opportunity and just couldn't help himself. He ran off to the press office and called everyone to attention. As the room instantly fell silent he jumped up on a table just inside the main door. Allan was on his way back from the jury room, preparing to make his speech and ready to field questions from the assembled press. At the instant he entered the room, he was confronted by Lou's backside and heard Lou proudly yell out, 'Ladies and gentlemen of the press, Croz has won the race.'

Allan was disgusted at what he heard and saw. His thunder had been stolen by this roughneck Aussie who had no authority to do what he had just done. If looks could kill, Lou's life expectancy would have been shortened in a tick.

I was both relieved and overwhelmed by what had happened. Not only had I finished the race in a quicker time than anyone, but in doing so I had lowered the lap record to 19 minutes 54.6 seconds with an average speed of 113.7 mph, and that was in patchy conditions.

Honda spat the dummy, complaining that they had slowed their riders down based on my time penalty. It was not a sound strategy, as they had been informed we would be protesting against the penalty. Gerald Davidson complained bitterly about the decision but to no avail. Ron Haslam and Joey for that matter must have felt cheated; I could understand that but I felt it would be pointless to discuss it with them.

News of the revised positions at the TT soon spread and emotions were running high, especially in the Honda camp. By the next day I was either hero or villain to everyone on the island. The words 'controversy' and 'Crosby' had become synonymous with the TT.

The rumours started going around about Honda's intended reaction to the TTF1 race. We heard they were planning to stage a protest in the Classic event on Friday. What transpired defied logic as Honda arrived on the start line with men and machines all dressed in black and devoid of any sponsors' names or stickers. This was Honda's way of showing everyone that the TT was antiquated. I preferred to deal with things on the track.

I thought Mick Grant was going to be the one to watch. Luckily, he was off a few seconds before me but with a dry track I was confident I could at least hold my own with him. I thought I had the measure of Ron but Joey Dunlop was another matter. Predictably fast, smooth and unflappable, he was dealt a bad card and given less fuel than was required to do three laps, so ran out. Ron Haslam retired with a broken engine and the steam came out of the race. Mick Grant had again mis-shifted and bent a valve, making it hard to restart after the fuel-stop. As he nursed his Suzuki around the course, I caught and passed him to complete a double TT victory.

I nearly didn't make it, though, because on the last lap I had a heart-stopping moment at Signpost Corner. It's only a matter of a few miles from the finish but I must have lost concentration. I whistled into the corner and straight away knew I was in trouble as I had missed my tip-in point. I was going to run wide, so I picked it up and used what was left of the available slip road. I ended up on a bank with the bike beside me, luckily undamaged. I quickly remounted, push-started the old girl and fired off in the direction of the finish line.

Coming back into the winner's enclosure I felt a huge sense of relief. I cast my mind back over the past three years. Eight starts, three wins, a second and a fourth; that was enough for me. The TT is without doubt one of the best events of its kind in the world and I felt privileged not only to have been a part of it but to earn the spoils of war in three separate classes. If I knew what fairies ate I would have made sure it was my shout. They kept me safe.

Unfortunately, there was no time to spend reflecting on the situation, and, equally, no time to savour the euphoria that victory brings. It was back to work at Donington next weekend.

'Hello fairies,' I said out loud as I passed over the bridge for the final time, heading towards the airport. 'Look after Skippy for us,' I added quietly to myself as I drove away.

20

ANY CHANCE OF A HOLIDAY? 1981

DONINGTON, 21 JUNE 1981

I'd arrived at Donington early after driving up from London. I was fresh from the TT but paranoid about being slow on the short circuit after all those miles of high-speed touring. It always happens when you get back on the short UK circuits — gone are the long swooping lines or three-quarter braking efforts. It's back to maximum braking, blocking manoeuvres, sticking it up the inside of someone, leaning on another or just plain hanging on to the inevitable uncontrollable slide and trying to remain upright.

We had three races over the weekend, the World of Sport Superbike Challenge and two other superbike races. Barry won two races and had a second, Ron won one with two seconds and I had two third placings but pulled out of the last race when the XR35 nipped up — again. By the end of the meeting, I felt I was back up to speed again.

DUTCH GRAND PRIX, ASSEN, 27 JUNE 1981

I loved riding the Grand Prix events and life on the road was fun. The Dutch GP at Assen is a prime example of a track that is great to ride and a sociable occasion. The year before we had stayed in a local pub and had a blast. This year we had our motorhome and I was keen to do a good old barbecue. With the arrival of a few new Japanese faces from Suzuki I thought it would be nice to invite them. Japanese people don't eat much meat because it's so expensive in their country. So I arranged to buy some steak locally and invited Suzuki test rider Masaru Iwasaki and Mitsu Okamoto plus a few others. The following day the Japanese had developed sore jaws from the tough meat we served and from that day on, everyone would make excuses when we mentioned a barbecue. I never told them they had eaten horse meat, though some might have guessed.

Thunderstorms were forecast for race day. The rain bucketed down after the finish of the 250 cc race. Once again we were inspired by hard-riding Aussie Jeff Sayle who had been locked in a battle amongst the top group, finishing fifth. I knew it would be a celebration that night.

Assen in the wet was not as bad as many riders thought. It was banked and therefore free-draining with a good surface. During qualifying we had trouble with changing direction under power, so we adjusted the offsets on the forks back to 27 mm. It stopped the wobbles but made it slightly heavy to steer. I was still struggling with brake problems and the lever again was soft and spongy, making it difficult to ride over a long period. It was getting frustrating.

I figured if it was to stop raining, a dry line would quickly appear and intermediates would be the safest choice. After the warm-up lap I thought we had made the wrong decision. Kenny was busy fiddling with the front end as the race was about to start. Just before the flag was to drop, Kenny's Yamaha was dragged to the side. His brake pad had been installed backwards and had welded itself to the disc on the warming-up lap.

After one lap I could see how the track was being blown almost dry with the wind pressure being created by our bikes. Randy crashed just after the start, and I led for the first few laps before Boet van Dulmen went past and I could see from the spray that he was on full wets. I looked skywards for any sign of sun. Nothing, but the track was slowly clearing. Marco squeezed by and I could only just stay with him. Then on lap seven I was approaching the first right-hand 90-degree corner behind the paddock. I pulled on the brake and went to shift down but the front end collapsed from under me, sending me skating down the slippery road towards the grass verge. It was as if I were in slow motion, so slow that I thought I could see worms looking up at me and they even had time to suck themselves back into their holes as I slid over the grass.

I thought I would be able to remount and tear off again in hot pursuit. I jumped up, did a bow for the spectators, then picked up the bike and push-started it. It fired up and I rode off relatively undamaged, but as I rejoined the track I thought about my dodgy front brake and looked down to see there was no lever. That fixed the problem with my front brake because now I no longer had one. So it was back to the pits for me to record another DNF.

SPA-FRANCORCHAMPS, 5 JULY 1981

I kept wondering what it would be like to have raced on the famous old Spa track before it was shortened. It claimed to have had one of the fastest lap speed averages over its 15 km length and even driving around it in the motorhome sent a shiver up my spine. I liked the new 7 km circuit that had been constructed. The only part that was a little concerning was the downhill off-camber corners but it would be the same for everyone.

I had just parked and hooked up to the water when the Swiss rider Philippe Coulon pedalled past on his pit bicycle. He stopped, we chatted for a while and the conversation turned to fishing. He knew of a trout farm nearby which he thought would be worth checking out for a possible midnight raid. We rode our bicycles out to the farm and did a reconnoitre for any potential problems we might encounter during our fishing expedition. We planned to carry out the raid the next evening.

I went into the toilet block and found a kid aged about 10 selling toilet paper for a few francs. I was so disgusted I gave him a pile of Belgian coins, more than he would have earned in a day, and sent him on his way with a directive not to return. Brenda and I bought a large supply of paper and left it in the loos.

The first practice session had me thinking of gearing and internal ratios to match the circuit. I spent far too much time cocking around with speed charts, graphs and carburettor data. Both Randy and I usually ended up fairly close on the overall ratios but we differed on our internal ratio choices. I was trying different second and third gears that I thought might be of benefit but in fact I was hopelessly lost. If the jetting worked then the ratios seemed to work but if the engine was a bit fat or rich I felt I needed to change a ratio to get the power back to where I wanted it. This was confusing and with the ever-changing atmospheric conditions it would be a lottery as to what I would use in the race.

Practice once again highlighted our brake problem, with the lever still coming in and requiring pumping a few times. Despite all the changes and modifications we did, we still could not find a solution. The engine had also developed a misfire towards the end of the last qualifying session, so I failed to record a good time and would be starting 10th on the grid. Something was drastically wrong and I didn't know how to fix it. I also had a mental block about the off-camber corners and perhaps this was where I was losing time.

I couldn't get into the groove right from the start. Before the race, I had lowered the pilot jet down to a #30 from a #35 and it was working fine in that range; in fact second was now proving too low. Up on the main jet it was still flat and I had no top-end speed. It was such a mess I thought a puncture would come in handy, just to put me out of my misery.

It rained, the sun came out, I even passed someone and then got passed again by three others in quick succession. I just wanted it all to end. During a heavy shower Gregg Hansford shot into the pits, did a wheel change and raced back out onto the track. During any wheel change the disc brake pads are pushed back and usually either a mechanic or the rider checks to ensure he has hydraulic pressure. For some reason this wasn't done and when Gregg went for the picks at the end of the fast straight, hello! — no one at home. He took the slip road at speed but some thoughtless official had parked his car across the escape road. Gregg hit the vehicle, breaking his leg again in the same place as at Imola, effectively ending his motorcycle racing career.

Marco won with Kenny second and Randy third. I struggled through the race while dealing with the misfire, all the time lamenting how I'd got it all so wrong. Finising seventh, I was now in fifth place in the championship, one point behind Boet van Dulmen.

SAN MARINO GRAND PRIX, MISANO, 12 JULY 1981

At least we got a result out of Spa when we ripped the 500 apart. Mick and Radar discovered a leak in the crankcase that had likely caused the misfire throughout the race. After the repairs were made, Imola seemed like a fresh start for us.

'I'm back!' I told Mick when the qualification times listed me as fourth on the starting line-up. Later that day a journalist asked me to describe the Dino Ferrari-Imola circuit from a rider's perspective. Here's what I told him:

> 'I suppose we must thank the Formula One car drivers for insisting on the building of good facilities but they've really screwed up the circuit with chicanes all over the place, especially the Aqua Minerale. We fitted small carburettors to the Suzukis to make them more tractable through the chicanes and mine had the same gearing as at Donington, which means it was doing 162 mph

flat-out across the start-finish line. Into the left-hander, I hook it back one gear. You could go through in top but you scrub off so much speed that the engine bogs on the way out. It's faster in fifth, revving hard at about 140 mph.

'I think it's an important section of the course and I felt pretty fast through there, holding it tight to the inside until about halfway round when I straighten up and get back on the gas. I change into sixth and heave into the right-hander then brake hard about halfway round. If you're on your own here you never brake in a straight line but curve right and then left into the hairpin, still on the brakes and changing down to second.

'If you want to get past someone, though, you can brake really late and stuff it up the inside going into the left-hand hairpin. It's not the fastest way round but you will take the other guy's line and by hooking back another gear you can get on the power and accelerate hard coming out.

'The next short straight leads over a brow and I could never get it quite right. You arrive over the hill heading for the grass on the right with the front wheel light just when you want to be getting on the brakes and peeling off into the left-hander. It's the sort of thing that gets the frame all knotted up. The left-hander is off-camber and therefore very slippery. It leads to the most useless chicane I've ever seen. You just bang it right and left and accelerate through the next right in third. The camber changes halfway through over a slight brow and the rear wheel spins, forcing you to change into fifth to keep traction. Then you hold fifth before braking for the next chicane.

'The exit here is a bit slippery and I was revving the engine like hell in second to save two gear changes before braking for the next chicane. Coming out of that one, the front wheel comes up and you change into third, fourth and fifth as you rush down the hill into the sharp left. Brake hard and back into second or maybe first, depending on traffic.

'Accelerate into third before the next double left which has to be the weirdest corner I've ever been round as the tarmac changes halfway through. It's a long corner for third so you've got a lot of revs on by the time you come out and change into fourth and fifth.

'I knock it back one going into the next right-left chicane; it's surprising how fast you can get through it. The final left and right are critical to the speed on to the start-finish straight and I found it best to hold the bike really tight in the left-hander so I could accelerate early going through the right and out onto the straight.'

Once again tragedy marred a good event when the Italian rider Sauro Pazzaglia was involved in an accident during practice on his 250 cc MBA. He suffered fatal head injuries, dying in hospital later that day. It was just another case of a senseless death that affects our sport all too often.

Despite all the good intentions, a race seldom goes the way you plan it. The skies looked menacing and I developed a knot in my guts in anticipation of the event being run with thunderstorms threatening. I watched for the temperature drop signalling the imminent arrival of a gust front that usually precedes a downpour. We had full wets ready to go if need be. In the dry, 21 laps of this track would be no problem but should it rain heavily, the normal race excitement would turn to panic, with each team working out a strategy for their rider.

We can't change tyres that quickly, so the time lost in the pits during a tyre change needed to be balanced against how much slower the rider is on the track.

Kenny Roberts was flattened by food poisoning and failed to show up on the grid as we formed up. Our team had decided on using slicks but I was very apprehensive at the decision. Marco pulled rank on his team and demanded that a cut slick be fitted, leaving us waiting for him. The race should have been started by now but, hey, this is Italy and what the hell.

When the flag dropped I got a blinder of a start and led the first lap but the mercury was dropping and the first few droplets of water began to splatter on my visor. Barry got past me then Marco and Randy, relegating me to fourth. Midway through the race we were caught in a deluge. It became messy trying to stay upright and fend off other riders who had elected to use intermediates or full wets. It was only a matter of time before riders started swapping positions. I knew Randy wouldn't be happy and soon he was back with me, riding on tippy-toes. I felt a surge of confidence and could see I was even catching Barry.

Then I tried too hard coming out of a slow corner and the back end whipped around sideways in a flash and then got grip again and flicked back. It happened so fast I broke the screen with my arms as I was doing pirouettes around the steering head. I came crashing back down on the seat, crushing my testicles on the back edge of the tank as I landed. Although my eyes were watering, I was still upright and in the race. I continued slipping and sliding my way around the track in the torrential rain until a sensible official decided to call a halt to proceedings with only three laps to go. I finished third with 10 points, and in the money again. More importantly, Kenny, Barry and I were now separated by just a few points.

My winnings were paid again in Italian lire, all in small denominations. I felt a bit like Santa Claus with a bagful of money over my shoulder. We had to hide the loot from Customs, as it was illegal to take cash out of the country without declaring it. Once clear of the border, out came a few bottles of Italian red which we appreciated on our way back to the UK.

SNETTERTON, 19 JULY 1981

Snetterton saw me on a high after winning all three races and breaking the outright lap record, and setting new lap records in both the TTF1 and 500 cc classes. To win the Race of Aces was a bonus but being the first person to do a 'ton up' lap sealed a memorable weekend. It didn't come much better than that, with five wins in a row on the 500 and four straight wins on the F1. I was enjoying this and what's more it seemed to be getting easier.

I even took the opportunity to have a scoot around on a G50 Matchless. They were very good bikes in their day, stable in the steering and not unlike a 2-stroke to ride, as you had to stay within a power band. We drove back to London where I packed for the Suzuka 8 Hour again.

SUZUKA 8 HOUR, 26 JULY 1981

Wes Cooley and I turned up at Suzuka with high hopes of repeating our win of the year before. It wasn't to be and we had to retire with an engine problem late in the race. The qualifying was much harder this year and I knew exactly how Wayne Gardner was feeling on his Moriwaki bike. I had been in a similar situation in '79 when the Moriwaki was so dominant.

The pace this time was again more like a sprint, probably because last year Wes and I fought it out with Lawson and Hansford at a cracking pace. We were all short-circuit racers rather than endurance riders, making the contest more exciting for the fans.

Qualifying was fun and we posted a time two seconds faster than the factory Hondas, but the scrap over pole position was a real family affair, just as it had been the previous year. Mamoru Moriwaki sent Wayne Gardner out and he set a time, then I produced a faster lap and so it went. I threw on a set new of tyres and went faster still before Wayne did the same. It was so competitive and in one last-ditch effort I asked for a new tyre right at the end of the session, hoping to eclipse Wayne's time of 2:14.7.

I had my 'race face' on and did the warm-up lap for the rear tyre's sake, then fired off down the start straight on my flying lap. It felt good and the grip was there so I squeezed it a bit harder. According to Moriwaki, on his stopwatch timing he was projecting me to be in the 2:13 range. I was one full second ahead at the halfway mark. Coming out of the esses and under the Dunlop bridge all hell let loose and down I went with bike tumbling after me. I felt a big thud as the bike hit the Armco barrier and everything went quiet. I took stock of myself and got up, miraculously unscathed other than a graze on my forearm. The bike looked a steaming broken mess as it was roughly picked up and quickly cleared out of the way by the circuit marshals.

I picked up the tail-light unit and carried it back to the pit lane. A huge crowd had gathered to check out 'Mr Hachi Tai' as I was being called — 'Mr Eight Hour'. It had been tight for pole position, with the commentator apparently screaming out over the PA system as Wayne and I diced for the best time. It was Wayne's pole this time.

I was standing at the pit-gate entrance waiting to be let in when Pops pushed his way through. 'Crosby-san, are you OK?' He was looking extremely concerned.

I went to move forward, then staggered backwards as if I was about to fall unconscious. Then I stumbled and fell forward, grasping for a handhold and went down on one knee as if in pain. The spectators were gasping in horror as I struggled to stand again, obviously in acute pain. The crowd parted as a medical team arrived to administer primary first aid to me.

Enough was enough; I had had my fun. I jumped up and stood

perfectly still, flicked some dust off my chest and walked off as if nothing had happened. Then I stopped, turned around and did a perfect Japanese bow. In my best Japanese I said, 'Excuse me sorry, don't worry I am not hurt.' Then I waved as I walked off at a fair clip with Pops next to me.

'Are you sure you are OK?' he asked again.

'Don't worry about me Pops, I'm not hurt.' Then I casually flicked the tail-light into his hand and told him this was the only bit that wasn't damaged. 'I am sorry, I tried too hard.' He looked genuinely happy now. He knew I must have pushed myself and the bike to the limit.

Unfortunately, after 141 laps and several unplanned stops we had to pull out of the race. Honda had a bigger presence this year and though they still couldn't get it right during qualifying they took the outright win with Americans Mike Baldwin and Dave Aldana. It was a good showing but highlighted the fact that qualifying had become just as important as winning the race. Pops was in a difficult position trying to please two groups, those who believed in going the fastest and those who wanted to be there for the longest.

Of course no visit to Suzuka was complete without a visit to Mama's Bar, where the host tolerated the kind of behaviour by foreigners that other Japanese bar owners might have found offensive. All in good fun, though, and I was still quietly protecting her cash register.

SILVERSTONE, 2 AUGUST 1981

I was shattered by the time I rocked up to Silverstone, having just flown in from Tokyo. Once back on the XR35 and the XR69 at Silverstone, I felt at home. Putting them both on pole gave me a boost all right, but bigger things were planned for me as I lined up for the British Grand Prix. A few laps into the race I had to suddenly switch to damage control mode as I picked myself up from the edge of the track.

'Croz, how do you feel about ruining Barry's Sheene's chances of becoming Britain's world champion this year?' a journalist asked me on the spot. I saw red and was livid at the audacity of this guy. I was shocked as well as dumbstruck that this low-life journo had the stupidity to even ask such a question. Responding out of desperation, I looked him straight in the eye and felt my top lip curl.

'Pal, if he wants to pull the brake on and crash when he did that's his problem, he could have avoided it. I was the one looking back, I was the one sliding along on my arse. I saw him grab a handful of brake and down he went. Don't blame me for that.' I continued walking back to the pit area. 'Fucking journalists!'

My mind was still racing as I made my way back to the security and safety of the paddock. 'Yes, I had crashed and yes I had caused Marco to crash along with me but to whoever is listening out there, it was not intentional — I am embarrassed and sorry but don't blame me for Barry's braking mistake.'

No one was listening once that idiot journalist had gone back to the press centre with his breaking story: 'Croz ends England's last hopes of having a British world champion'.

I was planning a response along the lines of 'OK, you Fleet Street wankers, when I woke up this morning, yes, I thought lap four would be a good time when I am right out front and leading. Of course I had to wait until Barry got into the right position just in behind me before I could grab a handful of throttle on my GP bike and spin up the back wheel in the corner and crash. Oh yes! It took planning and I pulled it off — what a crock of shit!'

Back at the paddock area I talked the incident through with Martyn, Radar and Mick. We went through all the possibilities, from lack of initial tyre temperature to perhaps a pitted steering head race bearing as a result of being at the TT. Without a technically plausible answer, I had to put it down to a lack of adhesion caused either by my opening the throttle a little prematurely or too aggressively. In any case the whole incident, seen by millions of television viewers, started a chain of events that would test my popularity in the UK.

Sheene used the incident to best effect in the tabloids and I had to defend my position as well. My fan-base had grown tremendously since I had arrived two years before. Rising from obscurity to an international motorcycle racing identity was quite an achievement for anyone and I didn't want to lose my credibility. Barry was good at stirring things up for his own benefit. If he was seeing mileage in creating a public rift with me, then so be it. I am not usually the one to back off. I was also aware that it made good press. Loyal Barry Sheene fans saw me as an evil person but the anti-Sheene crowd got in behind me. The tabloids ran stories back and forth, quoting and misquoting in some cases, and milking it for all it was worth.

Although Randy was running in third place, I had lost interest in watching the rest of the 500. It wasn't until Jack Middelburg and Kenny Roberts began dicing that I decided to watch the last few laps. Jack overtook Kenny on the penultimate lap and held him off to cross the line by only a split second in a truly great race.

Silverstone had started out really promising for me, with the two pole positions, but alas had ended up as a disastrous weekend. Following the crash in the 500 race on Sunday I still had an opportunity to make amends and lined up on the grid for the TTF1 race. The F1 bike was a delight to ride on this fast, open circuit and my pole time was not much slower than my 500 qualifying time.

For the TTF1 race I lined up on the grid in pole position and took a long look at the other riders to my left. I was on the best bike for sure, and their body language seemed to suggest they agreed. The look on each rider's face told me they knew I had three testicles and they had only two. It was a powerful thought that boosted my confidence.

Towards the end of the F1 race I had been engaged in a battle with 'Rocket Ron' Haslam on his Honda, changing places and generally enjoying the race. The XR69 was a brilliant bike and during the season we had developed it into a reliable and powerful beast. It was going great guns and was pulling strongly until I mis-shifted and it gave a brief rev over 9500 rpm. Immediately, I knew it had clipped a valve by the small but noticeable loss of power. A couple of laps later it suddenly rattled and slowed. I was quick enough with the clutch to save any further damage but it had haemorrhaged internally and would need surgery back at Beddington Lane.

Despite my two pole positions, it was not a good weekend. To have two DNFs at Silverstone was uncharacteristic for me, and the team for that matter. I'd have to look towards my next GP for some respite from the pressure of public opinion, good or bad.

21

CROZ — THE WORLD AND BRITISH CHAMPION, 1981

IMATRA, FINLAND, 9 AUGUST 1981

Finally, a street course that should suit me, I thought, as I drove around the tree-lined circuit. At almost 5 km it's a lot longer than the tracks back home but at least it has a railway crossing to remind me of Wanganui's cemetery circuit.

We had never been this far north and curiosity got the better of me about Finland's neighbour across the border. Russia was just up the road, so Brenda and I got in the car and drove to where we could look across no-man's land into Soviet Russia. It was bleak and featureless, making us think just how lucky we New Zealanders are. I could visualize life behind the Iron Curtain with its hardships and social problems but the weather would make anyone miserable. No wonder they all loved vodka. We stayed a few minutes and left the border guards to freeze in their huts.

Imatra is surrounded by trees and we were told that beautiful blonde women in this town outnumbered the men by three to one. It sounded like an ideal set-up and I could understand why some riders came all this way without their girlfriends or wives. Many of the Finnish women I saw had beautiful wispy blonde hair with steel-blue eyes and the perfect 34B bust. Brenda was keeping an eye on me and some of the guys couldn't believe that I had brought 'coals to Newcastle'. 'Yeah tell that to Brenda,' I challenged them.

In the paddock late one afternoon I needed to visit the toilet. To my horror I found it had a unisex shower with no curtains and two beautiful Scandinavian princesses were showering in full view of everyone. People were coming and going, seemingly oblivious to the fact that these two young women were in there in all their naked glory. It took me at least 20 minutes to wash the dirt from my hands.

I was here to race, but I would have to work extra hard to concentrate on the job at hand. Once qualifying was under way I had more than enough things to occupy my mind. From the outset the XR35 began suffering from an intermittent misfire and was shutting down on a cylinder or two when I rode over a bump on the track.

Randy was having the same problem and our times were both well down. We qualified sixth and ninth and I could see a repeat of Spa looming with me riding around like a dork at the back of the field. A couple of times we thought we had it nailed, only to have it reappear. It was so frustrating and it always happened where speed mattered most, halfway down the straight. That sudden loss of power meant I was head-butting the screen continually as the engine cut in and out. The bike was obviously starving for fuel and running on two cylinders as it hit the bumps along the straights. Unfortunately, we ran out of time to fix it.

With Randy and me struggling, Marco had a relatively easy run out front and despite an early challenge from Barry, his power valve broke a bracket and it remained stuck closed, ending his run. Kenny, however, had the same problem towards the end of the race but limped home with his power valve stuck fully open. My race was a boring one with a temperamental engine and a front brake that was still playing up. It was hot work riding, so you will understand why I was eager to take a shower.

Finishing fifth in Finland pulled me up the points ladder to be fourth in the championship chase, but only five points ahead of Barry.

ANDERSTORP, SWEDEN, 16 AUGUST 1981

The following week a group of riders representing all the GP classes met in Kenny's motorhome, I guessed because it was the biggest and he had the largest beer fridge. But this was a serious meeting to discuss what was happening at this Swedish Grand Prix. The off-hand treatment we were getting from circuit organizers was appalling and something had to be done. The poor old 250 cc class had had their race day changed to the Saturday to make room for a stupid street bike race on the Sunday. Already with precious little practice time allocated, they were now being required to qualify on Friday in the two scheduled 30-minute sessions, then have another two sessions on Saturday morning before being expected to race later in the afternoon. These riders would not have the time available to make adjustments to their machines and make the grid. We all asked what the hell these organizers were playing at. As if we didn't have enough problems on our plates with minimal practice times, we also had issues with the lack of straw bales available to provide a safe level of protection.

It was all turning messy again and I found myself getting sidetracked, thinking about how to improve the situation for all riders concerned, not just the 500 cc class. I knew there was a process we had to go through to get change but without all the riders working together, we would struggle to get any requests listened to, let alone acted upon. When the rumours began spreading about the threat of a riders' strike, the organizers were finally forced to address our concerns.

The difficulty was that as a group of riders we had no one voice to speak for us. While most competitors would strike for the benefit of the cause, there would invariably be those who just could not afford to miss a race or the opportunity of picking up the leftovers in the event of a boycott. We needed a spokesman who had international experience with Grand Prix operations, as well as having the trust and respect of his peers and a working knowledge of those key people responsible within the FIM and circuit organizers.

It wasn't hard to find someone, as Ian (Mac) Mackay volunteered to act as our voice that year. He would be charged with putting into place a procedure to find a fully funded representative going into 1982. Although it was a temporary assignment, we could not have picked a more suitable candidate. He was experienced at all levels of the paddock, being foremost an ex-GP mechanic and now a representative of Bel-Ray Oil Company. He knew the circuits and the people in the FIM and most of all he could represent all riders, no matter which class they competed in.

Seeing that the problem was not going to go away, the organizers made some changes by giving the 500 cc riders an extra hour of practice. The 250 cc race would still be held on Saturday but later in the day, and the local production race was moved to the end of Sunday's race programme. Extra straw bales were brought in and the groundswell slowly dissipated, albeit temporarily.

Randy's only hope of winning the world championship was if Marco failed to score a point; Randy would need to run third, giving him 10 points, just enough to win. It would be a big ask for Randy, especially given the weather forecast for the race was not going to be kind to him. His dislike of the rain meant it was again going to be a lottery. Even Boet and Jack again figured highly as possible upsets in Randy's last-chance bid.

All sorts of combinations of tyres were fitted for the start, each rider probably uneasy about his choice, knowing it could absolutely piss down or dry up completely. It started wet and the normal bunch of guys raced to the front — Randy, Korky and me with Barry, Marco and Kenny a bit further back. But it was those web-footed Dutchmen

Boet and Jack who soon joined us as the drizzle continued. The first casualty was Kenny, who after electing to change a tyre, then decided it was a futile task and retired. The rain arrived and backwards went Randy. Marco then crept up the leaderboard, being careful not to throw away his chances.

It was a slow and slippery race that ended with Barry taking the win from the two Dutchmen. I chased Korky home for fifth and in doing so ended the season in fifth place overall in the world championship. Randy found the rain just too much and finished a disappointing 13th, handing the 1981 world championship to Marco Lucchinelli.

ULSTER GRAND PRIX, 22 AUGUST 1981

The 500 Grand Prix season might have finally been over but I was still on the go with unfinished business back in the UK. Part two of the TTF1 world championship had arrived with the Ulster Grand Prix. Ireland just loves its road racing and this was a major event for them, along with the Northwest 200, but that circuit scared the hell out of me, mainly because of comments I'd heard about how ultra-quick and dangerous the course was.

I remembered that Aussie Warren Willing had crashed there a year or two back, effectively ending his racing career. Then in 1979 it had claimed the lives of three riders including local hero Tom Herron, and in 1980 with Mervyn Robinson's death I felt I should give it a miss. I had not even done a lap to find out for myself, but fortunately, clashes over the past three years prevented me from finding out anyway, so I kept my misgivings private.

However, going into the Ulster Grand Prix at Dundrod this year made us think long and hard about how we were to tackle the situation we now found ourselves in for the second consecutive year. It was all about tactics, and in a strange way it was a role-reversal from the year before.

If I was to win the race it would be my title again, even if I ran second to Ron Haslam (giving us each 27 points), and if I finished less than 1 minute 37 seconds behind him, I would still take it on aggregate time. I had that time advantage up my sleeve but when I looked out the window on race morning it suddenly became a vital factor. It was cold and miserable with a light drizzle, but the weather didn't stop the crowds appearing in their droves.

Honda's strategy of hiring Joey Dunlop, arguably the world's best true road racer, to run guard in the race and attempt to relegate me one place from Ron Haslam, was no different from what had happened the year before. Joey Dunlop on even an average day for him was simply superb around here. To back up both Ron and Joey, Honda had also employed Donny Robinson, another brilliant up-and-coming racer. After the fiasco at the TT, which had everyone up in arms with differing views and opinions, I could hardly believe it was still an issue. Some thought it was still up for negotiation and were hoping the FIM would step in and reverse the Isle of Man results in favour of Ron. This was not going to happen but I was still being affected by the comments of some fans.

I could just imagine myself saying, although I probably wouldn't have had the courage to do so, 'Are you for or against me?' and the moment I heard a sympathetic sound in support of Honda I could cut in and say 'OK, fuck off then! Next!'

It seemed like an eternity before the race was finally called. On this cold Belfast morning with no place to keep warm I just had to wait it out patiently; all the while my bollocks were being frozen off. My hands had already begun to change to that translucent colour indicating a lack of blood in the extremities. It was only a 10-lap race but at over 12 km a lap that's 40-odd minutes to be out there in the freezing conditions. I knew all my fingers would gradually become numb and I wanted to get it over and done with.

The race began in the damp with intermediate tyres selected for the conditions. Ron was off like a shot, knowing he had to get clear of me by 97 seconds. His crew kept him informed with signboards, as did mine. On the first lap Donny Robinson pulled up on his Honda with an electrical problem and Joey for some reason never really got going. This time I had no fogging problems and I followed Ron around, slipping and sliding but still keeping him in sight until the finish. Mick Grant followed me home with Noddy Newbold leading Joey in a lonely fifth.

It wasn't the 'fire and brimstone' race that everyone had expected but I had done enough to retain the 1981 TTF1 world championship. I found out later that Joey had witnessed a horrific car accident near the circuit, and he had crashed in the pre-race practice session which left him unable to perform to his usual high standards.

The presentation took place amidst the light rain and cold and I received an impressive engraved solid silver box. I figured the two solid gold Isle of Man coins from my TT double win would find a home nicely inside it.

With the world title now secure, but still with my feet and hands frozen, I asked Rex whether he would mind if I gave the Classic race a miss. He was relaxed and agreed that the job had been done. He said he would send a telex to Japan, informing them of the result as soon as possible.

DONINGTON, 30 AUGUST 1981

When Donington comes around I always think of aircraft. Planes had always fascinated me, so much that I thought at one stage it was interfering with my racing. I was introduced by John Cooper to his friend called Stewart. He was a dentist and a very interesting bloke with a cool job outside of his dentistry business. He acted as a personal pilot for the CEO of British Midlands Airways. They were based at Castle Donington only metres from the racetrack and he invited me to take a flight with him in the CEO's personal plane. It wasn't just any old plane but a SF.250 Marchetti ex-military trainer. It was a beautifully handling aircraft, fully aerobatic with side by side seating.

I had about 40 minutes of hooning around the Derby Moors doing loops and rolls and stall turns. It was fun and on the way back we got clearance to do a 'buzz and break' manoeuvre where we set ourselves up at about 4000 feet a few miles out from the airport and dived to maximum speed, then came down the runway only inches off the surface at over 300 kph.

He then pulled up in a climb and as the speed dropped off he lowered the landing gear and came around to land. It was impressive and the more I spoke to aviation people like Stewart the more passionate I became about flying. As with racing, it's not about taking risks, it's about managing them.

It was the sixth race in a row that I won and, with it, another silver tray care of the Shellsport series. I used the 500 in the two other international races. This event had attracted quite a few Grand Prix riders now that the world championships were over. Franco Uncini and Jack Middelburg had made appearances and even Marco had arrived, although he went tits-up in the first race and was unable to make the second. I followed Randy home in the first race and Barry won the second from Randy and again I followed him home for a third.

OULTON PARK, 31 AUGUST 1981

Oulton was not my favourite circuit but it was the third to last meeting of the year, with just Mallory and Brands to follow.

The F1 practice was scheduled to be first out and I had done only four laps when unexpectedly the steering gave way and folded under me, send me sliding up the road spread-eagled. By the time I picked myself up the flag marshals had the bike upright. It didn't look too serious. I had already figured that I needed to change the front fork setting so it wouldn't bottom out under brakes again. This part of the track had huge undulations and bumps leading into the slow corner. I had run out of front fork travel with it being loaded up, and the tyre had literally skidded out from underneath me.

Back at the paddock, Junior replaced some damaged components and did whatever needed to be done to get me back out again. I rode a little more easily into that corner during the race but still picked up 15 points to add to my tally.

The 500 race again proved to be a struggle keeping ahead of Korky on his KR500. It had shown good progress over the season, with Dozy working hard doing incremental changes. Being shortened in the wheelbase from 1980, it was certainly better but if he ever got ahead of me I had to make sure I had plenty of track to pass, as it was still quite a long bike.

My friend Keith Callow was there on hand with yet another silver tray. I now had seven of the buggers. With my lifestyle there was no place to put them. I'd joked with Keith about keeping one or two and the others could be used as drip-trays, perhaps.

With two wins in the weekend I was looking forward to finally having two weeks off. The gravel rash on my elbow would have time to heal. However, the next day we heard news that Dave Potter had died from injuries sustained in an accident during the MCN Superbike race. Dave had apparently slipped off his TZ750 and slid into an unprotected part of the Armco barrier at Cascades Corner. He did not regain consciousness and died in hospital, leaving a wife and two children. Dave was a great competitor and a friendly guy. Again I was reminded that this is a sport where anything can happen at any time and no one is safe from the roll of the dice.

RACE OF THE YEAR, MALLORY PARK, 20 SEPTEMBER 1981

At least we were in for a dry weekend's racing at Mallory Park. The whole team was present for the Marlboro-sponsored Race of the Year. I couldn't believe my rotten luck when my normal lightning-fast start failed me in the support Shellsport race. The engine bogged down, leaving me amongst the back markers, bashing fairings and rubbing shoulders with everyone as they all looked to share the same piece of the track. On every corner around Mallory as I worked my way through the pack there was a chance of being tipped off. If it happened it would not necessarily be my mistake; down the back of the field any old racing line seemed to do. I needed eyes in the back of my head as I rushed into bend after bend, not knowing which direction the bike ahead, beside or behind would take.

As I moved through the pack, the racing lines became more recognizable and I was able to plan my overtaking moves. Closer to the front everyone was running a lot harder with time ticking away and as I closed in rapidly on Randy it just ran out. My dismally bad start combined with this short course and only 10 laps meant I had effectively ruined my chances of doing a clean sweep of the series. I had been on target to win every round but seven wins and a second out of eight starts was still a bloody good effort.

'How can I take a positive out of this?' I asked myself. 'Well, you can't, sonny boy, you just got beat so move on!' At least Keith Callow from Shell got to present another silver tray and thankfully this time it wasn't to me.

I was quite happy to see our Moriwaki team performing well. Roger and Wayne had been plugging away at Scarborough a fortnight earlier and came away with their victories but their future with Moriwaki was uncertain.

The Race of the Year is the big one and there was talk this was going to be the last one to be held at Mallory Park. This race had a history of producing great finishes, one of the most notable being when John Cooper beat Agostini here in front of an enormous home crowd.

'Croz, how are you gonna run the race?' Mick Smith asked. It was a simple question requiring a complex answer.

'Good question Mick — it might help if I get a good start, don't you think?' I replied, taking the piss.

'Don't be such a wanker, it's a long race and you should think about how you're going to approach it.' He was right, I was joking and he probably thought a strategy hadn't crossed my mind. In fact I'd decided that this race was not going to be won by just getting out in front and hoping like hell someone waves a chequered flag at you at the finish.

The facts were that it's a 40-lap race with an average lap of say 50 seconds, so it's not long by Grand Prix standards. That's about 34 minutes around a right-hand course but it's not too hard on tyres providing the correct ones are chosen. On this short track it was going to be close and busy racing. I knew in my heart that in almost every rider's mind, it'd be game on with no holds barred as soon as the flag dropped. I'd played lip service to race plans before but once out there it's hard to hold back, particularly if you're desperately trying to hang on to the leaders. However, I needed to create a race strategy that might work around here. I formulated my simple plan by deciding that I didn't have to lead, but I had to be within striking distance at all times, and then be prepared to give it all I had in the last few laps.

I made it away safely with the front runners at the start of this main event and settled into a comfortable third ahead of Kork but behind Barry and Randy, who were already exchanging places. Barry was clever and often ran with 500 cc coloured plates on his 750 just to confuse the spectators into thinking he was on a smaller bike. I think we all knew why, though, and used to chuckle about it.

Barry and Randy continued swapping the lead, then Korky joined in and led from lap 21 through to 29. It became a game of cat and mouse but I kept back and with three laps to go made a move and surprisingly held on to win. I was positively blown away by the win but what made me more pleased was the realization that I had just run my first planned and controlled race. So the disappointment of only managing second place in the 500 Shellsport series due to a bad start paled into insignificance by winning this race.

I felt I had finally got to grips with the XR35. My performances had been improving during the latter part of the year and my confidence had been steadily growing. It was satisfying knowing I had just become the new British 500 cc champion and British TTF1 champion, so this was the icing on the cake to win the last ever Race of the Year.

Back at Beddington Lane I called Rolf Munding at R.A.T. Motorcycles. Things weren't too good financially with Moriwaki UK, mainly because the supply line from Japan was irregular and sales inadequate. Mamoru also informed us that he was not going to contest the British TTF1 or Superbike series in '82 which left Roger Marshall and Wayne without rides, so we decided to wind up the company and I sold my shares to the other directors who were better placed to deal with tax losses. Wayne had been talking about a deal with Honda so he would be OK and I wasn't sure what Roger was going to do for next year.

BRANDS HATCH, 25 OCTOBER 1981

Back at Brands again was like racing in your own backyard, with familiar faces and a great atmosphere. The same old officials got on and did the same job they had been doing for years, unaffected by the comings and goings of the multitude of riders who pass through the scrutineering bay annually. Some make it, some don't and there are others who leave an indelible impression.

This was the track I first raced on back in 1979 and now back here for my last race in 1981, nothing had changed in those three years. There's a sense of comfort in that, I suppose, and I guess perhaps that's why the UK had not been producing the international riders lately because they preferred the comforts of home. One look at all the Anzacs around the place, including me, is reason enough surely to make them think twice about their attitude to racing if they want to progress.

With two races to go and with both championships already sewn up, I was probably less hungry than I should have been. It showed in the TTF1 race when Suzuki made a clean sweep and only two Hondas finished in the top ten. Noddy Newbold had got the bit between his teeth, probably trying to impress Suzuki by riding hard and fast. I followed, with Mick Grant a close third.

The Shellsport 500 was another easy victory relatively speaking, and a little bit of excitement was added with the inclusion of Frenchmen Marc Fontan and Dominique Pernet on their Yamahas.

The curtains had come down on the season and it wasn't a bad effort for us. Over the last 34 weeks I had raced at 27 meetings. It was time for me to take a break. The XJS had to be shipped back to New Zealand. Suzuki had given me their freight agent and the XJS was last seen disappearing on to the back of a truck. I had thought of collecting all of our items up and throwing them into the car but the UK dock workers were not known for their honesty.

22

FUCK! WHERE DID THAT COME FROM? 1981

FREE-FALL

It registered but I had to hear those dreaded words again. I listened as Maurice Knight repeated, 'I'm truly sorry, Croz, but Suzuki Japan will not be able to supply you a 500 cc GP bike for next year.'

'Why, what's the problem?' I asked, expecting some plausible explanation I could easily rationalize and accept. Where did that come from?

'Japan simply does not have bikes for you,' Maurice went on. 'Look, Croz, we want you for the '82 season but to concentrate on TTF1 races here in the UK. Suzuki have guaranteed us 4-strokes for the championship so don't worry about the Grand Prix. I've tried my hardest to get you the GP bikes but Japan just won't do it.'

I sat there in Maurice's office listening quietly as my heart slid towards my stomach. What I was hearing was not what I'd expected. I had no doubt Maurice had tried to get 500's for me but failing to get Suzuki's consent suggested to me there was something missing, and I could not put my finger on it. He continued by explaining that Randy had already been signed by Suzuki. A second team rider had not yet been signed to back him up but he and I both knew it was not going to be me.

I knew that Doyle and Randy had had negotiations earlier. I knew Suzuki seemed to have a fixation on Randy and I had expected he would sign for next year. For some reason, however, I had neglected to think about my own situation, probably because I felt secure, given my results this year. I was so sure I'd be given the same programme next year. I was in a state of shock.

'Maurice,' I said, 'I had my heart set on doing another year with Suzuki, and here you are now offering only the F1 machines to me. I can't do it. I'm sorry, but I want to continue with the GPs.'

As the discussion continued, I was going into shut-down mode as the rug was being pulled out from under me. I was in free-fall. I simply could not make sense of Suzuki's rationale. Finally, I thanked Maurice for the last two years with Suzuki, we shook hands and I walked out a very despondent person.

'Where the hell did I go wrong?' I asked myself. I found my jaw was aching as I clenched my teeth; my knuckles had already turned white as the blood was being squashed from my fingers. 'Why?' I would ask that question over and over as I struggled to come to terms with having been dropped from the Suzuki Grand Prix team.

Back in the race shop I spoke first with Rex and I sensed he already knew the outcome of my meeting. He seemed a little taken aback and his big bushy white eyebrows rose as if he were genuinely surprised. Maurice must have talked with Rex earlier just to get all the ducks in a row before delivering the bad news to me. Perhaps they thought I would just roll over and accept their decision and take the F1 deal. Rex tried placating me by saying the UK race programme would be great next year and to think again about taking the F1 deal. He never seemed to get flustered but today he showed some real compassion by letting me know it was a case of us and them. The GP team was getting a new look and he suspected a change in command. He didn't know if he would be part of this new team either.

Rex reflected on the great relationship Suzuki GB had with Yoshimura and how well we had done this year. He genuinely felt for my situation but was powerless to do anything. We stood for a few moments just looking each other in the eye. I suppose he was contemplating my situation but unbeknown to him I had spied the chocolate biscuit in his open top drawer. I made a dive for it, picking it up cleanly in one swoop before he realized. The crumbs flew in all directions.

'Hey, you bastard,' he squealed.

'Gotcha,' I yelled, and walked off in search of Radar and Mick.

They were in the workshop cleaning down a chassis. I confronted them with the news and at first they appeared surprised but later developed their own views on what had transpired. Radar and Mick had been privy to the many discussions that took place before and after each race. They had valuable insight into the workings of the team. This decision impacted on both of them because without me their positions were also on the line.

We stood back scratching our heads and considered who would be the likely candidates responsible for pulling all the strings next year in the Suzuki team. The boys had heard that the structure of the team might change but nothing had been announced. The rumours had started a few weeks back. I couldn't change anything now but it would have been nice to know the real reasons why I had no GP ride next year.

I began feeling quite naive about the way things were panning out. I just had no clue or answers to my predicament. I could see no way forward with Suzuki and needed to be in another team quick-smart before all the good seats were allocated for next year.

My mind was playing out the various scenarios with the little available information I had. Politics is surely all about money and power, how the money goes round to make the team work and who holds the purse-strings. Who gets what and where are the trade-offs.

Someone has to be the driver of all this. I surmised that it might be Gary Taylor because he had become increasingly visible around the team as a PR man and he kept fairly close to Randy throughout the year. He had been helping Randy get over his fear of racing in wet conditions. He must have loved those mind games and that's why I'm sure he relished working with the likes of IMG and other personal managers, pitting his brain against theirs. He's very bright and a clever thinker, constantly looking out for that elusive major sponsorship. 'What's he up to?' I wondered.

Gary had been courting HB, the German subsidiary of British American Tobacco, and it was looking as though he might have pulled off a deal. The rumours were flying towards the end of the season as word was leaking out about HB entering the Grand Prix scene as a sponsor. I figured that Gary would have to have been the main contact to get them on board with the new team. I was not sure where I stood with him, though. Socially he was fine but you could never tell what he was thinking, which made me nervous at times. Was it him who did not want me in the camp, perhaps? Would having a New Zealander in the team reduce the likelihood of attracting sponsorship of any kind? That I could certainly understand.

Then there was Dennis Rohan lurking in the wings. He was an accountant with the Heron Group that owned Suzuki GB. Over the past year he and his wife had been seen increasingly with the team and I got the feeling that he too was making a play to be involved more directly. Still it didn't answer the question of why I was being let go. Maybe I'd used the wrong underarm. This was getting me nowhere, thinking about all the 'what ifs' and 'if onlys'; my head was spinning and I needed time to think.

'You bloody idiot, Crosby.' I was giving myself a good old talking to. 'It's almost the end of the bloody season and you have not made one move to check out what other teams have on offer. Christ, you could have Honda or Yamaha offering you more money and better bikes than you would get with Suzuki next year, but at the very least you would find out what you are worth, you dickhead! … No that's bullshit, anyway our Suzukis would be better.'

Jolted back to reality, I realized what I had said. 'Our Suzukis' were not going to be mine any more. I was wet arse and no fish, as they say. 'OK then, boys, where do I go from here?' I asked Radar and Mick. I could tell they were extremely disappointed, but it was Radar who volunteered a little gem of wisdom and I seized upon it.

'Croz, we are obviously not welcome here any more so we had better concentrate on finding ourselves a ride for next year.'

'You little beauty,' I thought; he had broken my mental block. This is not about me any more, it's about us, we're all in it together … a problem shared is a problem halved. Radar had probably been at Suzuki too long by now and he was up for a new adventure with me, wherever it took us.

WHERE TO NOW? NOVEMBER 1981

There are always more bums available than seats when it comes to allocating factory Grand Prix equipment for the upcoming racing season. I took a look at the other major manufacturers for any clue as to where I should start my search for a ride. With Suzuki GB out of the picture, perhaps the Gallina team could be a possibility but as it turned out, Roberto Gallina had already signed Franco Uncini and Loris Reggiani so Suzuki was now ruled out completely, unless I picked up a production RG. As a last resort I could probably do that but time was running out.

In desperation I decided to fly to Switzerland to see the Kawasaki endurance racing team based in Zurich. They were contesting the FIM Coupe d'Endurance championship which I thought might be OK. I didn't have my heart in it really and felt flat about the prospects of spending hours and hours riding around getting dizzy on dodgy circuits in all kinds of weather. It was, however, a few hundred quid spent wisely because I put endurance racing right out of my mind then and there.

With only Honda, Yamaha and Kawasaki having factory 500's, I thought I might first try Kawasaki. I was conscious Korky Ballington had pretty much taken up all of their resources. Whatever money Kawasaki had left for its GP programme was probably being directed to Neville Doyle and Gregg Hansford. They had been talking of running a KR500 in the championship. I decided to make the dreaded phone call to Kawasaki UK, just to check out the situation. It had to be a cold call to let them know I was on the market, though I held out little hope of success.

'Good morning, Kawasaki UK,' the pleasant-sounding girl answered; I had the right number at least.

'Yeah hi! It's Graeme Crosby here, can you put me through to the race workshop?'

'Sure, just one moment, putting you through,' she replied.

'Workshop!' someone answered.

'Hi it's Graeme Crosby, can I speak with the race team manager please.'

'What did you say your name was?'

'Crosby, Graeme Crosby' I replied.

'How do spell that?'

'Crosby, C- R- O- S- B- Y.'

'Someone called Crosby is on the phone, Graeme Crosby,' I heard him yell out.

'Who, what's his name, who's calling?'

'A bloke called Graeme Crosby!' he repeated.

'Never heard of him, what's he want?' Gulp, I thought, hmmm!

'Can I tell him what it's about, Graeme?'

'Nah, I'll catch up with him later,' I lied and hung up.

With Kawasaki now out of the picture I could concentrate on Yamaha. I knew they were totally behind the Kenny Roberts racing effort for '82 and he had the new OW60 already in testing. Barry Sheene was going to get a similar OW60 to race, as well as Frenchman Marc Fontan. I was not sure where I could fit in. There had been rumours of Agostini forming a team with Yamaha but nothing concrete had surfaced yet. Barry had apparently been asked to join with Ago and although not confirmed it seemed a likely scenario. If it was a two-man team, Barry and I would last only five minutes together before the claws came out.

There were choices to make if I wanted to race next year but identifying which company, if any, had the best deal going was difficult. I felt I had left my run too late to begin talking about getting my arse on any factory bike.

Out of the blue I received a message that Pops Yoshimura wanted me to call him. I did and he pleaded with me to reconsider taking the Suzuki GB F1 offer and he would try to get some assistance via Suzuki Japan for a GP bike. Although the conversation was brief, I think it was one of those times when Pops wished he could speak better English. I got the message that he wanted me to meet with him in Tokyo at the FIM congress and with him would be Mr Yokouchi, Suzuki's race team manager from Hamamatsu. I knew him well enough and respected his position and agreed to the meeting, not knowing what the hell to expect. I thought I had already been stonewalled by Suzuki.

To make things even more complicated I also got a message that Gerald Davidson from Honda wanted to talk to me while I was in Japan at the FIM congress. Things were heating up. I was stressed and didn't have anyone to turn to and show me a way out of this predicament.

I flew to Tokyo and booked into a hotel next to where the FIM congress was being held. I felt like a fish out of water, not knowing what to do and how to handle any negotiations. The hotel was humming with men in business suits wearing those European gold-rimmed spectacles, the kind you see in the inflight magazines advertising Pierre Cardin products. This was a classy bunch of people running our sport. However, we are only one section of the sport and it showed when I was summoned to receive my award. There was a broad representation of champions present to receive their medals and it was all over rather quickly.

'1981 TT Formula One World Champion, Graeme Crosby.' The French lady's voice sounded beautiful. I felt very proud for a few seconds. But after it was repeated in a dozen languages I was ready to grab my medal and go to the bar.

I met first with Gerald Davidson in a private room where he explained that he had been asked by American Honda to gauge my interest in competing in the AMA Superbike championship. This was a curve ball, as I had not given the American market any thought. I struggled getting to grips with what he was saying. He told me Freddie Spencer was contracted to do the 500 cc World Championship in 1982, leaving a gap in America. I would have to think seriously about that and mentioned I had a meeting with Suzuki in another room. I would get back to him.

I found Pops and Mr Yokouchi sitting in the waiting room and we got straight down to business. Pops wanted me to ride his bikes in the F1 programme and Yokouchi had already planned a response to my questions about a GP bike. They could not give me a bike directly because of an existing contract but would work on supplying a bike to me quietly through Riemersma Racing in the Netherlands. Alternatively, I could be supplied production bikes with special kits to make them as fast as the factory equipment supplied to Team HB and Gallina. It sounded too complicated and I was running out of time if they expected me to form my own team.

I wanted to believe they could deliver but I had grave doubts. I had been in the UK living off the smell of an oily rag for a year before being picked up by Suzuki for two years, when all I had to do was basically roll up to the grid and race. It seemed simple, but now I was faced with the potential problems of sourcing not only correct equipment, but finding money to run my own team. Mechanics needed to be paid and the set-up, travel and transport costs would be horrendous. Pops was prepared to fund some of it but we never discussed any figures. I knew it was too much of a gamble to try to put together a team myself. I needed a clean deal that would give me an amount of money I felt comfortable with and a race schedule. This Suzuki deal would not work for me; it would be too complicated to put together.

I went back to Gerald Davidson, explaining that I had a deal with Suzuki if I wanted it. Again he went through the programme and inevitably got on to the fees. I must have been bent in the head, crazy or stressed to the max but somehow I shook hands on a deal. The actual contract was to be sent to me within a few weeks for signing when I arrived back in New Zealand. I walked out of the room as the new Honda America rider for the AMA Superbike championship. The fee I had negotiated was for a brand new Piper aircraft. What the hell was I thinking?

Back in the UK the media was having a field day. Stories emerged of me being sacked by Suzuki, along with rumours that Randy's contract had indirectly pushed me out of a Grand Prix ride for next year. I doubted that Randy would have named me specifically in the contract, though. Good or bad press depends on the views you take of the situation but it was a newsworthy story and it had legs enough to make the papers for a number of weeks.

I flew back to the UK to clean out our motorhome and put it into storage. Brenda caught a flight home to start looking for a house to buy with our ill-gotten gains amassed over the last two years. I had been sending money home in lump sums and we had built up a nest egg. I loved it when I sent money home because the exchange rate was about $3 to £1 and it had been a pretty profitable year. But I was worrying about what next year would bring.

When it was time to go I made a quick lap around Suzuki GB's Beddington Lane facility and thanked everyone for their support and help both on and off the track. I asked Maurice Knight's secretary to distribute a short message via a memo to all of the staff. Then there was one last visit to Rex's top drawer to nick his remaining biscuits and then we were gone.

Radar and I visited Honda America's workshop in LA on our way home. I had arranged a meeting with the race team manager to look over what they had and gauge how I would fit in to living in America. He showed us around the workshop, which was roomy and light with plenty of equipment. The bikes had not arrived from Japan yet so we chewed the fat for a while, then we took up an offer to go to a party with one of the girls in the office. Her Redondo Beach house was pumping with perfect Californian girls with blonde hair, bronzed skin and whitened teeth. They were all partying hard and I was offered some dope to smoke. I couldn't see myself living this life; actually, I tell a lie — I could do it but I could also see myself getting into a lot of trouble.

Radar carried on to Sydney and I flew direct from LAX to Auckland, agreeing to keep in contact as things developed. He had bought a piece of land on the beach at Mackay but we all took the piss out of him because we reckoned he bought it at low tide.

I had been home only a few days when the phone rang and a stranger asked if I would kindly call Agostini in Italy. He said Agostini and Marlboro were forming a team and I was on the short list to be given one of their factory Yamahas.

'You beauty,' I thought. I knew something was happening with Yamaha and Agostini but I understood Sheene had his oar in there already. There was one other phone call I needed to make.

'Radar, hi it's Croz, mate can you deal with the Italians, cause I have to call Agostini and I think he wants me to ride for his new Marlboro Team.'

'I thought Bazza was in there,' Radar said immediately.

'Yeah me too, but anyway what I want to know is if you are going to come with me for next year if it's with Yamaha. I want to know how much you need as a contract and I'll do the same deal with 20 per cent of the prize money. And US$48,000 is what I have to get for you, right?' I asked.

'Yep,' Radar replied.

'Just one thing, Croz, don't you have a contract with Honda?'

'Bugger,' I said, knowing I had to call Gerald Davidson advising him I would not be going through with the US Honda deal. I was in a quandary as to what I should do. My first priority was to lock in the Yamaha deal if offered to me, then deal with the other issues.

We talked about the pros and cons of dealing with the Italians. Living in Italy had a nice sexy feel to it. Agreeing that although we both had had little to do with them, there was still plenty of anecdotal evidence to make us wary of any dealings with them. We were aware of their reputation for being slippery bastards and casual about meeting deadlines, but we were nevertheless excited about the prospects. I put the call through to Italy.

'Pronto,' a woman's voice answered.

'Hello, can I speak to Mr Agostini please?'

'Un momento, pervivore.' Yes, thank god he's there. Great, I thought.

'Pronto!' It was Agostini.

'Hi, it's Graeme Crosby calling from New Zealand. I have been asked to call you.'

'Ah! Crosby, hello, how are you? Thank you for calling me.'

I listened as he explained to me that he was getting his team together with Marlboro sponsorship to run a pair of factory Yamaha OW60's next year. I was on Yamaha's list of approved riders along with Barry Sheene. Graziano Rossi would be the other rider but only getting production Yamahas. I wanted to say 'Do bears pooh in the woods?' but said yes, I was available. I didn't mention Honda.

'Crosby, I have to check with Yamaha first because you are on the list but I have to confirm it. There are only two other riders, Barry and maybe Ferrari but I am not sure exactly what Barry is doing. I will call you back soon after I talk with Yamaha, OK?' It was starting to happen but I still didn't have a firm commitment from Agostini.

He phoned back a day later and said everything was OK with Yamaha, so we talked contract money and the fact that I wanted Radar to come with me. It was an easy negotiation; I asked for US$100,000 and $48,000 for Radar. With the terms agreed, Ago sent a copy of the contract. Then I went looking for Gerald Davidson's phone number. It was not a pleasant task but deep down I still harboured grudges about the TT and Honda's sportsmanship. I simply said that I wanted to go Grand Prix racing, this deal had come up and I was taking it. Understandably, he was really pissed off, more so as he had already informed Honda it was a done deal, made on a handshake.

It was a gentleman's handshake and I had reneged on it. I felt bad and disappointed with myself. On the flipside, negotiating to get an aircraft in lieu of a fee sounded a bit weird, proving I must have been off my trolley to make such a silly decision. What an idiot!

Brenda had found a suitable house and we set about making it liveable. We bought a huge four-poster waterbed that required an abseiling certificate to get in and out of. The house had white shagpile carpet throughout and a sunken lounge, its own bar and an open fire. Quite trendy really but I cursed the carpet when I was carrying in a photocopier with the power cord dragging behind. The door closed behind me, catching the plug and snatching the photocopier out of my hands, spilling black carbon powder all over the nice white shagpile. Although insurance paid for the repairs, it always looked like it had been patched up.

A regular visitor to our house was Pete Defty, who showed up on one of his scheduled flights to New Zealand just after we had moved in. He was now flying for United Airlines and often arrived at Auckland Airport early in the morning from LAX. The calls from the airport were always the same.

'Hey Croz, gidday! Pete here, I've just flown in (cough!). Can I borrow your car for the day?'

He always brought a bottle of Wild Turkey bourbon, which was my favourite, plus a cut of export meat. We left him all day to sleep off his jet lag, then he would get into the kitchen and prepare a nice dinner for us.

Pete was constantly clearing his throat as if he still had a cigarette butt stuck in there. He had taken an interest in the Professional Riders Association (PRA) movement by virtue of his friendship with Jim Doyle and Kenny Roberts. He normally coughed and spluttered his way through a half-hour discussion, bringing me up to date with developments.

I drove my car out to Ardmore Airport for some flying lessons. Pete was due to fly the 747-200 to Melbourne and back. Brenda had called to ask where Pete had left the keys to her car. I sat in one of the club's aircraft and dialled up clearance delivery, the departure frequency for Auckland International.

I heard the controller say 'United 811 cleared take-off, airborne contact approach on 124.3.'

A spluttering guttural response came back: 'Cleared take-off, 124.3 United 811.' It was Pete on the radio. I gave him a few minutes and called him.

'United 811, Echo Yankee Foxtrot.'

'811 (cough), go ahead,' he responded.

'Defty, Brenda wants to know what you've done with her car keys.'

Silence for a moment. 'Goddammit Croz, they're in my pocket sorry, (cough) see you tonight.'

I could hear the sound of the undercarriage retracting in the background. 'Cheers mate.'

23

PICKING UP THE PIECES, 1982

THE NEW TEAM, JANUARY 1982

Going into another season with the promise of new bikes and a revitalized mental attitude, I knew I had to be really fit; that was the plan anyway. Over the break between seasons in New Zealand I began a regime of physical training, mainly gym work and running. While I hated it, I knew it was necessary.

My best racing weight was always 77 kg, the weight at which I felt comfortable. Some of the other riders looked like greyhounds — all prick and ribs — but I liked some meat on my bones and, try as I might, my training programme seemed destined to be short-lived. It was probably my inability to say no to a beer or a bottle of wine when people showed up, as they did constantly.

Agostini rang through unexpectedly one day to say that Yamaha had set aside a few days for testing. I felt I was fighting fit and ready for work when I boarded a flight from Auckland to Tokyo. On arrival at Yamaha Japan's Iwata factory I was looking forward to throwing a leg over my new mount for the '82 season. I had a sense that the Yamaha factory would somehow be different and we would get more testing done in the few days allocated to us than we did at Suzuki. There I felt we were treated as the poor cousins, having to fit in and around the normal testing programmes scheduled for new products coming online.

Shortly after arriving we were taken to the race shop. My eyes scanned the area looking for my new bike. Our testing included doing a few familiarization laps on the YZR750, the bike earmarked for me to ride at Daytona. I had two to choose from: one was factory-prepared and the other was Kenny's old bike from last year, which had suffered a series of failures for one reason or another. Our testing programme meant I could give the factory-prepped YZR750 a shakedown for the race in early March.

When I saw it, I thought 'Oh shit!' It was a 1977 model, crouching in the corner covered in dust and cobwebs, like it had never been anywhere for years. I felt a little despondent, like I was taking a step backwards. Hell, I thought, I've done enough races around the world in the last few years, passing and being passed by these old dinosaurs, so I knew it was going to be a real test. Physically, it would be a hard bike to throw around for 200 miles; and mentally, I could picture myself lining up on the grid knowing everyone else had their new tackle to try out and there I was, poor old Croz who had drawn the short straw to race a camel at Daytona.

I turned my mind to tomorrow's testing session and began imagining having the whole track all to ourselves, perhaps breaking routinely for a drink of cold green tea and a chew on some rancid old tuna fish wrapped in rice rolls. I wished I could get in a solid 50 or 60 laps. Playing devil's advocate, though, I could see myself hanging around waiting for the track to clear after the flag marshals had pissed off to lunch just when we are ready to start.

That thought was short-lived because at the pre-test meeting we were informed of some scooter testing programme that had been given priority and we had to wait until 11.35 a.m. for the first of two short sessions. I was expecting another non-productive session and wondered if this happened only to me. The sessions would be long enough to get almost dialled in but short enough to raise a number of important questions. So it wasn't going to be any different from Suzuki — it would be the same old shit, just a different bucket this time. I would have to ride balls-out, running as many laps as I could in the limited time available, mainly to get to grips with my new bike, but of course also to impress our Japanese hosts. They had made the decision to allow me to race their OW60 in the 500 cc world championship and I wasn't going to let them down.

Like all competitive riders, I just wanted to go out and break the track record within a few laps of arriving. I was also painfully aware it would be a hard call to do because the test riders were very fast and knew the circuit like the backs of their hands. Although difficult, it was not impossible.

When we arrived at the circuit I asked one of the Japanese, 'Which way does the track go and what's the lap record?' As a tongue-in-cheek question that one got lost in translation and he walked away scratching his head with a strange look on his face. I think he understood, though.

Barry Sheene arrived with his Kiwi mechanic Ken Fletcher, who insisted on still taking the piss out of me about racing a 50 cc Suzuki back in New Zealand in the early 1970s. Luckily, he had conveniently forgotten our collision at Pukekohe. Another advantage of the early-season testing session was that it gave me a chance to meet those Japanese technicians who would be so important to our team for parts support.

Historically, Kenny Roberts and Kel Carruthers had earned the respect of the Yamaha factory with a long string of wins. This meant they had a reasonably free hand to develop and fine-tune their own bikes in close conjunction with the factory. I was really nervous when it came to climbing aboard the OW60.

It felt strange that a few months ago I was thinking my arse was safe with Suzuki for '82, and yet only a few months later, here I was about to join one of their arch-rivals, Yamaha. I was curious about what they had in store for us. It had better be an improvement on the Suzuki XR35's. I needed to prove a point and show Suzuki that they had made the wrong decision by letting me go. The OW60 was produced as an interim measure while a V-four version was being secretly developed behind the scenes. The OW60 did have some special features that Kenny had asked to be incorporated and I guess the boys at the factory figured if it was good enough for Kenny then we should also benefit by having those same modifications.

From that first lap at Yamaha's test course I knew I was in trouble — big trouble. The bike handled like a roller skate in a gravel pit and steered like a shopping trolley. It gave me no feeling of confidence, particularly as I turned into a corner when the front wheel felt as if it had not even arrived with me. The contact patch trailed somewhere under the middle of the bike. In consultation with Ken Fletcher, Radar and I established that the steering head angle was completely different from what I had experienced.

The triple clamps were machined with different top and bottom offsets to produce a divergence angle. The aim was to create a constant trail length under braking. Aside from the technical part, it was hideous to ride. While there was probably merit in the design, this bike was destined to go straight into the rubbish bin as far as I was concerned. On the positive side, it was quick enough and had similar characteristics to the Suzuki XR35. Before leaving Suzuki I had accurately measured the XR35 as it finished its last race. I wrote down all the data in my diary by recording the measurements of the chassis. I could transfer them to this Yamaha relatively easily, as the engines were of similar design. At least it would be a better starting point than what I was faced with now.

I felt snookered because the factory informed us they were unable to produce a new chassis in time for the first GP in Argentina. If it were just one chassis then maybe, but with my two bikes, Barry's two and Fontan's bikes that made six new chassis to be made, and that did not account for Kenny's bikes; but we couldn't talk for Kenny anyway. Yamaha informed us that for the South American GP we would have to do with what we had as an interim. Time had run out.

Leaning back on my chair in the hotel bar high above Iwata, I took time out to do a check on the state of the nations. I had a great team on paper, with leadership coming from Giacomo Agostini, a very respectable new team sponsor in Marlboro, and two brilliant mechanics in Dave 'Radar' Cullen and Trevor Tilbury, whom I had picked up from the Roberts camp. Both were reliable, trustworthy and highly experienced. The previous two years with Radar had proved without a doubt that he had outstanding capability. Trevor Tilbury would be joining us from Kenny's team and over the last couple of years I had got to know him reasonably well. I was looking forward to him bringing his wealth of knowledge to our stable.

OUR NEW HOME IN ITALY

Our new team's base in Bergamo was another story. Agostini's younger brother Felice would be acting as a kind of caretaker for the team when Ago was not there. His friend Boska, a tall gangly lad with a love of music, was given the job of doing the donkey work for the team and would drive the hospitality unit. When Radar and Trevor turned up they were laughing at the fact they only had with them a supermarket shopping trolley and a tool-kit that Trevor had stolen from under the seat of a new Yamaha road bike in Amsterdam. We reckoned we had a fair way to go to get where we wanted to be, and only had a short time to do it.

With no workshop or bikes and no sign of the race transporter, Radar and Trevor knew almost immediately it was going to be tough. Felice may have been there to keep an eye on things and offer assistance where possible, but he had no authority and would continually refer purchase requests back to Ago for approval. Ago held the purse strings tightly as our team began to take shape. I had figured that all the finance had not come through yet from Marlboro. It was proving a struggle for us and we would have to be patient and do our best with what we had.

My view of the situation was that Ago might have underestimated the workload to get all the pre-season preparation completed in time. He had informed Radar on a number of occasions about the progress of the race transporter that was being built to take the bikes and equipment necessary for the team to operate. It was becoming a joke and we started to think that the transporter might never eventuate.

From my perspective Ago was a busy man, looking after his property portfolio. His team, however, was also under construction and we struggled with no timelines to get things done by. Every item purchased by the team needed be run by Ago, which we all understood, but the delays in contacting him and the uncertainty were already having a negative effect on the team. We all seemed a bit lost for direction. When a workshop was finally found for us it was situated under a vehicle access ramp in a Ford dealership in Bergamo, just off the motorway. One of Ago's friends we guessed must have come to the party with some spare space for us to use as a temporary base.

Although progress was slow, the workshop was coming together in dribs and drabs. Sponsorship deals were happening but they seemed to focus on swapping equipment we needed for stickers on the bikes. More tools and equipment gradually began appearing. We figured this was the Italian way — there's always tomorrow.

Brenda and I arrived in Milan and made our way to Bergamo to check out our new base. Ago had arranged some accommodation for us across the road at a hotel. We soon realized it was being operated as a brothel. We were asked to go straight to our room and not linger in the foyer or lounge area during business hours. It was a brothel all right and a nice clean one at that. It was very stylish with lots of ceramics, glass and chrome in the bathrooms and huge big beds with fluffy duvets.

We checked out the girls a couple of times discreetly from the elevator and thought they were all nice looking, doing what girls do in places like this. Apparently, one of the local politicians' wives worked here and the owner was absolutely paranoid about anyone finding out.

In stark contrast, close to the Autostrada exit at Bergamo, the working girls were huddled around a 44-gallon drum. They were dressed in micro skirts up around their bums exposing their wares. We had to contend with them almost every night when we returned home late to the workshop. Our headlights once illuminated a Fiat 500 Bambina parked in the driveway blocking our entrance. One look at a pair of knee-length leather boots out each window was enough to figure out what was going on. The girls would be busy servicing their clients inside Italy's most famous little car. A bang on the door or roof was all it took to get some action and the girls feverishly started wiping the fogged-up windows on the inside before driving away as the poor old client was left desperately struggling to pull up his pants.

That sort of thing was always fun to watch but a walk up and down the driveway during daylight revealed the extent to which the area was being used. The ground was littered with used condoms and it was possible to have your shoes re-soled with rubber by the time you reached the road. We nicknamed our driveway 'Michelin Alley'.

Brenda and I flew to London to pick up our motorhome, which looked in a sad state and was showing the signs of being left out over a harsh English winter.

The infamous transporter, which we had begun to think was fictitious, finally appeared. It was a flash-looking new Iveco cab chassis unit with a box body. However, when the tailgate was dropped it revealed only one single steel table in the middle of the floor. Radar nearly died on the spot when he realized how much extra work would be needed to fit it out.

The hospitality truck was another matter, though. This smaller rig had been fitted out with the latest coffee machines and had a cooking facility designed for making pasta. It was swish looking and I soon began to understand the Italian way. It was more important to have the looks and the hospitality ready for the first race than, perhaps, the bikes. It was more about show than functionality. It looked stunning, though, with the fancy Marlboro paint scheme and we reckoned we were on pole position in the hospitality unit race.

Things started to happen once the first of two new OW60's finally arrived from Japan along with a few miserly spares. The boys got straight into making it ready for a test that we had planned for Misano. Graziano had his first reverse-cylinder YZ500 around the same time and the truck was loaded with the bare essentials and we set off. The first few laps of testing at Misano confirmed the need to have the steering head angle changed and without too much discussion the bike was stripped down immediately and Trevor had the chassis loaded into the team's Alfa Romeo bound for Amsterdam. He had all the geometry settings to make the changes and was able to cut the steering head off and have it re-welded, this time at the correct angle.

A few days later we were back at Misano doing laps on what felt like a completely different machine. It was one I could work with and I quickly got down to some really fast times. It felt fast and light and steered similar to the XR35. For the first time in a few months I felt we were ready, albeit with only one bike and half a race team.

Our team had grown with Graziano Rossi and me as riders, Radar, Trevor, Roland and Romero on the tools and Boska as the transport driver. The final piece of the team was Felice, who was acting as a conduit back to his brother Giacomo Agostini, who seemed to seldom grace us with his presence.

DAYTONA, 7 MARCH 1982

I turned up at Daytona for my first appearance for the new Agostini Yamaha team with a choice of two five-year-old bikes to play with, Yamaha's factory bike and Kenny's old bike. I was familiar with Daytona and knew if I could hang it together for the duration of the race I stood a good chance. I couldn't compete head to head with the new 500 Grand Prix bikes, so I had to go into the race with a tortoise-and-hare strategy. It was a tough call for me and I was under no illusion that it would be an easy ride.

Radar and I had cracked up at the fact we had one bike that had been race-prepared twice for Kenny but didn't get to travel more than a lap last time out. Jokingly, I said it only needed some air in the tyres and fresh fuel. I knew the other bike was ready to go as I had done a few laps on it in Japan.

Racing is strange at times, especially when we get curve balls thrown at us. I went out in practice and by the second lap the old girl cried enough and ground to a halt along the back straight. It seized solid for no reason and I remember saying to myself, 'One down, one to go.'

The other bike was in pit lane so out I went. It was perhaps faster than the Japanese bike but handled abysmally. It had atrocious suspension that was acting like a pogo stick and it wobbled when I least expected it. 'Bloody old nails these things; I think they're trying to kill me,' I told Radar. He had the solution: we simply exchanged the engines and worked with one bike from then on.

Honda had chosen Daytona to launch their new model V4 FWS1000 that was reported to have cost $1 million each, and they had two of them. They had spent a lot of time testing during the previous week and they were fast with Spencer and Baldwin on them. Kenny decided to run his new OW60 Grand Prix bike and Randy Mamola was having his first outing on his new Suzuki, all decked out in HB colours. Eddie Lawson had the new KR500 all dialled in apparently and it was expected to be a blindly fast race. And there was poor old Croz on his five-year-old dinosaur, in effect there just to make up the field. The pressure was off me as all eyes were focused on the new bunch of GP bikes.

The flag dropped and we sped off into turn one. The circuit had a layer of fine windblown sand covering the first turn and with our cold tyres it was very slippery. I followed the leading bunch into the first corner. It's a left-hand turn that is only used once while executing the start and when rejoining the track after a pit stop. The sand flew up to form a cloud as the first wave of 30-odd riders jostled for position. I took the wide line in and got a good clear run around the outside and as I began opening the throttle I saw Randy coming at me at a 30-degree angle. He was obviously running wide as a result of turning in too early. I was under power going in the same direction as everyone else and we collided. He ran his front wheel into my left side, leaving black tyre marks on my cowling. I don't think he meant to; perhaps he was just trying a little too hard early on. He went down and I felt a bump as my rear tyre either ran over him or his bike. I had a quick look over my shoulder and saw the carnage behind me. Someone was not going to be a happy chap crashing only a couple of hundred metres from the start.

From the beginning it was plain that I would be alone on the track as I skated around trying to work some heat into the tyres. Once I got going and slipped into a groove I watched the position up front change constantly. First it was Roberts who dropped out with a seized engine, leaving Spencer and Baldwin to battle it out until they pitted for tyres. That left Lawson in front but a broken transmission soon put paid to his chances. My old and ancient YZ750 just kept churning away lap after lap and it soon become apparent I might be somewhere near the front by the time this race drew to a close.

With Kenny out, our team suddenly took on an unexpected importance and we had the factory boys and Kenny's crew offering all sorts of help. My refuelling stop came and went without a hitch, but the big Hondas were harder on tyres, forcing them to make an extra stop. That left me with a nice run to the finish line and the chequered flag.

As I entered the winner's enclosure I was confronted by Randy's manager Jim Doyle complaining bitterly that I had deliberately knocked Randy off. I was looking at a man I thought had gone from adolescence to senility without bothering to pass through maturity. As if I had planned to deliberately take out Randy in the first corner of the first race after I thought he had screwed me at the end of last season! The thought had never entered my mind; I fought back the urge to say something, and I ignored his accusation.

One very observant British journalist roughly worked out the cost of Suzuki's effort at Daytona as being $10,000 per metre. I thought our effort at less than $10,000 all up was a steal, and we picked up $12,000 in the process, so it was not a bad start to the season. There's a wise saying, 'To finish first, first you have to finish', and once again Uncle Sam turned up for his 20 per cent cut of my winnings. Still, the race was a great result for us, now that it was in the record books.

On Tuesday I dropped in to say thanks to the organizers for putting on a great race. While no one was looking I managed to grab a very nice mounted photographic montage of me in the winner's circle. I nicked it off a wall in the Daytona administration offices; it must have been up there for only a matter of hours. I wondered if they would ever miss it.

Pan Am Pete Defty had been at Daytona with his size 12 alligator boots and his constant companions, that cough and his silly cowboy hat. We had spent a couple of good nights out enjoying the nightlife. Just before I was due to go, I threw him the big Daytona winner's trophy plus the mounted picture and asked him drop it off in Auckland next time he was flying down that way.

ARGENTINA GRAND PRIX, 28 MARCH 1982

My new OW60 had been crated up and sent airfreight to Buenos Aires and it was delivered to the track. Radar was in fits of laughter when he saw the crate with our new Yamaha in it. The bike was jammed in with wooden packers pushed in and around it and looked hideous. Whoever made up the crate must have been either drunk, on drugs or trained at making wooden wine barrels because that's what it looked like. This was going to be one hell of a year.

Honda had spent some valuable testing time before we had arrived so they were up to speed; however, the lap times being quoted were irrelevant, as we soon found out. The track was changed several times using straw bales so no direct comparisons could be made until the first official practice session. The circuit was just under 4 km, that is if you took the correct turn. It had extensions with short cuts and long versions all built into the design. I needed a map the first time I went out.

We were quietly confident that the changes to the chassis we had made over the last few weeks would be enough for us to start the championship chase in good form. I also felt our new team was slowly getting the rough edges knocked off it. Radar, Trevor and I worked at getting the bike sorted as fast as we could with the correct jetting. The fuel was not exactly the quality you get from your local petrol pump and working with the atmospherics the carburettor jetting had to be spot on.

The training and qualifying sessions ended with less than one second covering the first eight riders. This was going to be some season if we had this level of competition throughout.

I organized with John, the tyre fitter from Dunlop, to go out for a meal. I had in mind a true Argentine steak restaurant and as they were staying in the same hotel the numbers soon grew to a dozen. The restaurant I found had an almost complete beast cooking over fiery coals in the front window. John had picked the mixed grill and when it came out he jokingly muttered something about coming back early next week to pick him up, by which time he would have eaten about half of it. The plate was as big as the table and had various kinds of dodgy-looking offal on it. We left John there with a few other hardened meat-eaters, happily chewing away on what looked like the remains of a bull's testicle.

On race day I arrived at the track to find our team in a flurry. Felice had apparently poured all of the race fuel into Ago's hire car. He knew Ago had always used freshly mixed fuel and I guess he thought we would be mixing up a fresh lot for the race. But we didn't have any more fuel or oil to mix up for the pre-race warm-up or for the race.

Radar and Trevor were really pissed off, as they had to make do with a blend of some other dubious fuel. We had no time for testing what effect it would have on the jetting and were basically snookered. We had to take a chance and run with the blended mix.

From sixth on the grid I got a blinder of a start and led for the first lap, being extra careful not to take a wrong turn. Freddie slipped by on his Honda then Barry got the better of me as well but it was to last only a few laps. My engine felt strong but as I changed up into third all hell broke loose; the engine vibrated violently, as if someone had thrown a handful of ball bearings into the crankcase. 'Fuck,' I thought, pulling in the clutch and coasting to a stop.

I was picking it to be a crankshaft or even a broken rod. Having a failure is one thing but being stuck on the infield with a broken bike and no way of getting back to the pit area is cruel, even more so as I had to watch valuable championship points disappear. With the 32 laps completed I was able to get back to the pit area with the bike. I found the boys and explained to them what had happened. Radar and Trevor looked at each other, both fully aware of why it had happened. At least Ago wouldn't run out of fuel going back to his hotel tonight.

'What a long way for no bloody points!' I said to Radar as he rolled his eyes and shook his head in disbelief. Trevor was more vocal and between his expletives he explained that a failed main bearing caused the problem, perhaps to avoid me breaking someone's head with a tyre lever. Either way, no one ever knew we had lost control of our fuel supply. He was genuinely disappointed that we failed to show the Yamaha factory our full potential. This would have to wait.

As racers we are fairly well informed about mechanical things but on matters of a political nature at times we came up short. I had no idea about the scrap Maggie Thatcher was having with the Argentine government. The word had got around that the Argentine military had invaded South Georgia and the Falklands War was about to start.

The results of the race and its importance were left way behind when we realized we could be caught up in the war. Our Alitalia Boeing 747 was due out in a few days' time. We packed the bike into its wooden barrel and made sure it got to the airport. The effects of war were not yet evident at the airport but the route our flight took was rather strange. I was expecting a steady climb to perhaps 30,000 feet en route to Italy but we stayed only a few hundred feet above the ground, with the leading-edge slats activated for a short flight to what looked like a deserted airstrip. We landed and some shady looking people pushed a ladder up to the front door, someone boarded and we took off again, this time climbing to our planned altitude.

Who the hell did we just pick up? That was the question, and it's one I've never learned the answer to.

24

MUDDLING THROUGH ALONE, 1982

IMOLA, ITALY, 4 APRIL 1982

Another international that Ago had organized as part of my contract was Imola. Since the installation of chicanes, the Autodromo Internazionale Enzo e Dino Ferrari circuit was not my favourite racetrack but as an event the typically flamboyant style of the Italians would ensure it was at least fun. It wasn't a Grand Prix, so no valuable points were at stake and the depth of competition was naturally a lot less, although I still had a few hard-chargers to deal with. Current world champion Marco Lucchinelli on his new three-cylinder Honda would be the main drawcard and threat. Team Gallina had entered Franco Uncini and Loris Reggiani on those super-quick Suzukis and a host of other top-notch riders had signed up to ride. Graziano Rossi would surely put up a fight on his local track but the reverse-cylinder YZ500 I thought was a spent force.

While 200 miles around here sounded like an endurance race, it would actually be split into two legs of 32 laps each. The fuel-burn on our OW60 virtually guaranteed that a pit stop was needed, and while it would be the same for others, Radar and Trevor worked out a strategy. In the first leg we started with less than a full tank and planned to stop early to refuel, hoping we had made enough of a break not to lose sight of the leaders when we rejoined the race. From the start it was hectic, with Marco, Franco and me circulating in a tight pack. No one could really get away until Franco had a machine failure, leaving Marco and me to battle it out.

Radar showed me the 'PIT IN' sign early in the race and prepared for the fuel stop. It would be a straightforward stop with the engine still running. Our aircraft-style quick-release nozzle should allow 20 litres of fuel to be transferred in a matter of seconds.

Leading into the last corner prior to the pit entrance, I shoved my leg out the side indicating I was stopping and dived into the pit lane. Marco had positioned himself to my outside just a few metres behind me and suddenly found himself being carried into the pit entrance whether he liked it or not. He had obviously not seen my signal and was forced to carry out an unscheduled fuel stop. His mechanics were surprised by his unannounced arrival in search of fuel. He lost valuable seconds in the scramble for a top-up and I benefited hugely and went on to win by a comfortable margin.

The second leg turned out to be largely a repeat of the first but we had changed our fuel stop time to midway through the race. This time Marco would be a lot more attentive but his crew bungled his fuel stop and again I pulled out an unassailable lead.

I climbed off the OW60 feeling rather lucky to have got away with the two wins. It could have been a lot harder if Franco had not pulled out and Marco not cocked up his stop. Boy, did I cop it on the rostrum, though, when we were presented with our prize trophies. Marco was gutted with the overall result, accusing me of poor sportsmanship in the first leg and blaming his crew for the bad stop. He had hold of the microphone and was yelling at me at the top of his voice. I couldn't understand what he was saying but I was just getting to grips with the fact he was stirring the spectators into a frenzy. I was about to try to speak in my defence when I felt a tug from behind. My crew had gathered around and led me off the presentation platform, protecting me from an increasingly violent crowd. I threw my beautiful winner's trophy into the motorhome and changed out of my racing suit into my old jeans and a T-shirt. With sunglasses on, Brenda and I went down to the local village square to get some beer and watch the happenings from the safety of a park bench, incognito.

Later that night I went back and as everything had died down I was able to pick up my winnings. Thankfully, this time there was a good-sized crowd and I didn't have to wait for someone to get more cash out of the bank like we had to back in 1979.

Someone pointed out that I had achieved a similar string of victories to Agostini's, in winning the Daytona 200, Imola 200 and the TT. I would have liked them to have extended that to include the Suzuka 8 Hour. But I had yet to win a bloody Grand Prix.

HENGELO, THE NETHERLANDS, 12 APRIL 1982

If there is one country in the world that has ownership of the most enthusiastic road racing event, then it is the Netherlands. The annual Dutch GP is one thing but the other international races attract huge crowds too, and Hengelo is no exception. This was another race that Agostini negotiated in my contract but it didn't worry me. I had raced street circuits before so it couldn't be that bad, but I had to think twice when I realized I was going into the lion's den with Jack Middelburg and Boet van Dulmen.

The racetrack had straw bales everywhere protecting the riders from trees that lined the track. It reminded me of Wanganui but it was a lot faster and more open. The well-drilled team of volunteers had stacked hay bales around anything that looked remotely dangerous. Although it wasn't a particularly hard track to learn, with only four tight corners, it had those flat-out left and right flip-flop curves that if you get wrong can end up really messy.

This was Jack and Boet's turf; they were hard-chargers who ate gravel for breakfast. They were as tough as old iron but lightning-fast on open country roads like Hengelo. My saving grace was to use the power of my bike to try to get away from these gladiators. However, I was worried about whether this would be enough to overcome their hard riding. I knew Boet would be difficult but Jack had me more worried. God forbid if they got charged up by the enthusiastic crowd — I would have a race on my hands.

I loved this type of racing and those who compete on these street circuits are a breed in their own right.

Although I got in a few practice laps, enough to get my gearing sorted and a plug chop done to adjust the jetting, I was still also nervous about the track.

The weather was cold from the outset, then the wind got up and made riding precarious in the strong crosswinds. Coming out of the slower corners, if you pulled a wheelie the crosswind would push your bike towards the trees on the edge of the track. Just as the wind abated, the sky opened up and it felt like the whole of the North Sea dropped on us, complete with huge hailstones. The start was postponed and then within minutes the skies cleared and the sun came out, sending everyone in search of sunblock.

After a good start I was soon locked in a three-way battle with Boet and Jack. It was a 12-lap race of only about 44 km. Jack slipped off on a slow corner, leaving me to scarper around with Boet and another hard-charger, Jon Ekerold, who was sniffing at our tails. I had the horsepower and was glad of it.

I slurped back the victory bottle of Champagne and headed back to the motorhome. I was on my fourth Heineken when all hell broke loose outside. A bus that had been converted into a workshop and living area complete with an attached awning was billowing smoke from a fire inside. It was already a lost cause but we were worried about the gas cylinders that had the potential to spread the inferno, where vehicles were packed in like sardines.

I cranked our Chevrolet engine into life and made a beeline for the farm gate. It was a quagmire with mud from the downpour earlier in the day. While most of the paddock had got out, we were left slipping and skidding with no traction.

I used speed and the four Heinekens as Dutch courage to race through the bog up onto the narrow road and turn all at the same time. I ploughed up the bank and swung the wheel to get the front wheels pointing in the general direction. The back came up and around and I corrected by counter-steering. I finally got it under control after narrowly missing a house and although our cupboards had emptied themselves on the floor, we were out of danger. We had the after-race party to attend in the Hengelo village and I parked to get out to inspect any damage and found a pile of branches poking out of the rear bumper. They belonged to the house; until then, I hadn't realize just how close I had got to taking out the whole house, bricks and all.

I picked up my prize money at the function and partied until the late hours. It was great grass-roots fun; the Dutch know how to do it better than most. Boet was the life of the party but the locals drank a toast to my victory and proclaimed me as an honorary Dutchman.

AUSTRIAN GP, SALZBURG, 2 MAY 1982

I felt comfortable with Salzburg as a track, but was apprehensive about the weather forecast, as I hated the cold. Yamaha Japan had hired the track for a private training session earlier in the week. Kenny brought out the OW61 for a track test and all eyes were on this new bike. Technically, it was very advanced and quite different from the OW60. The twin crank V-four with disc valves should be capable of producing the horsepower required and in conjunction with Peter Ingley of Dunlop they had produced a big fat rear tyre to make the power usable. We would have to wait and see if it would before jumping to conclusions, but at least there was some R&D happening. I just hoped Yamaha weren't yet ready to abandon the OW60's as we still needed technical development on them.

We had already questioned why the FIM had not moved the date to get better weather. The first practice session got under way. As always I focused on getting a time recorded to at least guarantee a position on the start line. When the sleet came down, the freezing rain stung my hands at speed. In the warm I had no problems with the wet conditions but when the temperature was close to zero it became intolerable. The risk of injury was high anyway but going out in atrocious conditions that restricted your vision greatly increased the risk of getting hurt. I always gave my visor a liberal coating of anti-fog on the inside to prevent misting up. Sometimes it worked well and at other times it was ineffective and I had to resort to breathing out of the corner of my mouth.

I had been noticing for some time that when I raced in the cold my circulation was restricted. A wave of white slowly worked its way from the outer extremities of my little finger across my hand until all my fingers were opaque and bloodless. I would also lose the sense of touch and although I knew I had a pair of hands at the end of my arms I just couldn't feel them. In this state, every application of front brake and twist of the throttle happened as if by second nature. Fortunately, I still had feeling in my thumbs, so I was able to hold on properly to the handlebars.

I counted myself lucky, though, because I knew a few riders who suffered from carpal tunnel syndrome, which has a greater impact on a rider's ability to compete. You can be the most talented racer in the world but if your hand starts tingling and goes numb and you can't hold on any more, it's curtains for you. Australian Jeff Sayle was a prime example, as he suffered CTS and, with its onset, it was only a matter of time before he'd be forced to retire. Thank god I only had to worry about cold weather and my irritating nipples, which I remembered to cover in sticky plasters before going out.

The atmospheric readings of temperature, humidity and pressure all affect carburation settings. The wet and dry bulb thermometer danced up and down all day, sending mechanics back and forth to the jet box.

Heaps of crashes were happening and the injury toll began to rise. Englishman Keith Huewen, who had effectively replaced me at Suzuki GB, ended up going home early. It was not a good start to Keith's time with Suzuki as he had already experienced a number of crashes and the season had only just started. I knew how he felt, having once been in the same predicament. Both Randy and Freddie had taken a tumble in private practice and Randy again slipped off in qualifying, along with Lucchinelli and Jack Middelburg; even Korky Ballington threw his Kawasaki away. The paddock was full of the walking wounded.

In the 500 cc race I found myself on pole position, having got a reasonable lap time tucked in before the weather crapped out. Barry got the jump on us all at the start and a gaggle of riders followed him, all chopping and changing places with every lap. From a spectator's point of view it must have been marvellous to see so many top riders battling it out. A blanket could have covered us all. Marco and Franco were flying and somehow managed to get a break. Between them they had been chipping away at the lap record, with Marco finally recording the quickest time. It would have helped if he had completed his last lap but he cocked up a corner and took a detour into the hay bales.

Mechanical failures and a couple of crashes in the last lap helped Franco Uncini win his first Grand Prix, on a bloody Suzuki as well. Randy was almost lapped, so perhaps Suzuki GB did me a favour after all. I retired to the bar with my first eight points of the season safely tucked away.

FRENCH GRAND PRIX, NOGARO, 9 MAY 1982

I sensed we were in for a difficult time at the French Grand Prix before we had even left Austria. With not much space in the paddock it begged the question why we were going in the first place, given the

FIM were acting like ostriches; something was bound to happen. The year before at Silverstone, the PRA in its infant state had put the FIM on notice that the riders and teams would no longer tolerate Grand Prix events being held on unsafe and inferior tracks. Nogaro had been allocated a GP on the published tentative list of dates and although we were informed the circuit would be resurfaced, we expected it to be dropped from the approved list.

Nogaro had by all accounts been used for F1 testing and was extremely bumpy, so it was going to be interesting to see how things would pan out. Most of the factory riders held the view that the French had three good tracks to choose from — Circuit Paul Ricard, Circuit De Nevers Magny-Cours and Circuit Bugatti at Le Mans. So why Nogaro?

I had my own theory on why it had been allocated a Grand Prix. Such an event attracts a huge number of spectators and the competitors are expected to arrive and perform for a small amount of prize money. It was a miserable amount that rarely exceeded the FIM mandate as a minimum. Operating costs to run a Grand Prix are high but in one respect lower than other major motorcycling events as they are not paying the performers. The net result means a Grand Prix is a cash cow. The income can then fund future improvements but these happen long after we have packed up and left. So the following year it goes to another circuit, one that might be needing some capital to upgrade facilities and they get the nod. I'm sure a lot of politicking is done behind closed doors but by the time the GPs are cycled through each of the four circuits the track has deteriorated and it's time to start over.

The Marlboro, Yamaha, HB Suzuki and Kawasaki teams were all camped together in one area of the paddock. I parked next to Kenny's motorhome and we did our usual arrival routine. Once set-up had been completed and our mobile single-bedroom apartment on wheels was bedded down, I went wandering around talking to others. It wasn't long before we realized that the paddock was becoming tight for space and when the Honda transporter arrived there was little room left for anyone else. But they kept coming and soon the paddock had filled to over-capacity. The circus had arrived in town; it was bigger, brighter and had more transporters, team vehicles, motorhomes and caravans than ever. A few teams even blocked the fire exits. Something was about to give.

There were a lot of factors to consider prior to making any decisions. While we in the 500 cc class could afford to boycott the event, we wanted it to be a unanimous call. This wasn't going to happen because everyone had differing opinions and could justify them individually. Some needed the money to continue to the next GP, so would ride anyway. Some were not doing all GPs this year and many had turned up just in the hope of qualifying. The lack of unanimity played into the organizers' hands.

The top factory 500 cc guys and a few other high-profile 350 cc and 250 cc teams got together to discuss how to deal with the problems. The overcrowded paddock was a non-negotiable item. The condition of the paddock itself was also unacceptable — too few power points and the ones in use had 10 or more leads connected, risking a fire. The bumpy circuit was also a major issue, worse for the 500 cc riders perhaps than for the smaller classes. We drew up a letter outlining our concerns and most factory riders signed it, with support from the manufacturers. In it we explained the reasons why we would not be riding this weekend. We wanted to give the organizers a chance to inform spectators that we would be leaving on Thursday so they knew not to expect a full contingent of GP riders here.

The letter met with some sympathy to our cause within the FIM representatives and with contempt from the organizers, as expected. They still maintained the circuit was not as bad as we had claimed. After some discussion we decided to postpone our departure by a day, pending a meeting scheduled for the Friday morning.

A free practice was available on Thursday and Radar had the OW60 out and ready for me to do a few laps. I had to run in a cylinder and get the gearing about right before the first official practice started. The bumpy parts of the circuit were mainly in places that were not good for your health, particularly under brakes into the slower corners. It had a washboard effect that had your eyes spinning like the wheels of a poker machine while holding on to a jackhammer. Bad as it was, I felt I could have dealt with it and had a strange liking for the circuit in the few laps I rode. Ironically, the conditions suited me because of my road racing experience.

I had never been to Nogaro before so I had no idea what to expect. Now I was faced with the dilemma of protesting the condition of a track when I had cut my teeth on circuits twice or three times as bad as this. I was a road racer at heart and raced the Isle of Man TT and Ireland, so I would be seen by many true road-racing fans as a hypocrite. 'Croz has gone soft,' I could hear them say, mainly with an Irish or English accent.

Before long it was clear that everyone was unhappy about how things were panning out and to add insult to injury a National Yamaha Cup race was also being planned for the weekend, in breach of the FIM regulations. Apparently, they had applied for and got permission to run the extra race.

Friday produced no change of heart from the organizers and in full agreement with our sponsors Marlboro and Yamaha we prepared to leave, along with several top 500 cc factory teams. There was just one problem: we were stuck in the paddock unable to move. Kenny and I cut down a wire holding the huge netting fence and I drove my motorhome out over it. This made way for the next truck and another motorhome to follow until all those who were boycotting had left the circuit.

Those remaining at the track suddenly found themselves faced with the question, do I stay or do I go? Every remaining rider had a free choice. Some riders supported our stand and some opposed it. I could have gone either way as well, but my choice to go was made out of a desire to improve the general paddock conditions and to show the FIM that we would not be fucked around any more.

Leaving early meant a leisurely drive down to Madrid for the Spanish Grand Prix at Jarama, not my favourite place but it was going to be warm and dry. I looked at the map and thought it would be great to drive over to the sea at San Sebastian via Bilbao and take in some sights on the way.

It was pitch dark and I was getting tired of driving and looking for a spot to stop for the night. I wanted a place that was just right. I felt like a dog doing circles in its basket in preparation for settling for the night. Finally, I gave up and found a park close to the beach. Half an hour later I was awoken by a noise outside. Our Marlboro team's 'coffee and pasta' truck had arrived with Boska and Felice aboard.

I peered out the window and noticed we had parked in a rubbish tip. The two vehicles were amongst smelly household garbage, rusty old bicycle wheels and worn-out mattresses. We had a look around after breakfast and then went into town. It was market day and fresh fruits and vegetables were in abundance. Old women in black shawls scurried around bartering for the family provisions and vibrantly dressed young girls displayed themselves to the young men. Whole families had come to town. Dads gathered around tables drinking coffee or sipping plum brandy, talking and laughing. It was a great feeling to see so many people having fun.

I walked past a butcher and got a hell of a surprise. It was like a zoo in there with live animals in cages and others on the end of ropes. The old butcher had a cigar hanging out of his mouth and, brandishing a large knife, he was systematically slicing up what looked like half of a horse. I watched as people bought chickens that were dispatched and plucked in front of my eyes. I could see no sign of refrigeration but I reasoned that if it was alive 20 seconds ago no one would complain about its not being fresh.

SPANISH GRAND PRIX, JARAMA, 23 MAY 1982

Jarama, on the outskirts of Madrid, is a hell-hole and bloody hot. I never liked the place and equally the circuit didn't care for me either. My thoughts went back to the first time I was there in 1980. I was struggling not only with the bike but also with my head. I was a lost soul trying to fix a front-wheel chatter that today I could have done in my sleep. The previous year the Spaniards threw their toys out of the cot, insisting that the Spanish GP would not include a 500 cc race, probably because the Spanish motorcycle market is based on small bikes. It went ahead without us, although for me it made no difference as I had Brands Hatch on that weekend.

This weekend at Jarama, however, was a sad affair as news spread quickly that John 'Noddy' Newbold had been killed at the Northwest. He was riding for the Suzuki GB team and using one of my old bikes. I took a gulp when I heard, because John was a personal friend and I had enjoyed his company over the past couple of years. Sadly, the death rate continued seemingly unabated. Who the hell was going to be next?

I figured it was more good luck than good management that had allowed me to get through the last two years without getting seriously injured or killed. I had stepped into a Suzuki team that did not have a particularly good track record in the safety department. John Williams, Tom Herron, Pat Hennen, all top riders and now John Newbold. And Ikujiro Takai had also lost his life in a testing accident on the V-four Yamaha. Ike went back to the Marlboro days in New Zealand in the late 1970s and of course at Macau. It was all getting a bit too close to home.

I couldn't get to grips with the circuit and struggled again with settings but managed to qualify quicker than Randy. Team Suzuki had been here testing privately for some time and I expected more from them. It was one of those poignant moments when I could have walked up to Jim Doyle casually and said a small thank you in his ear. Although I was still battling with our OW60, the Suzukis were experiencing major development pains. It might pay off for them later; time would tell.

The race began in typical dry Madrid heat. Roberts was on fire with the V-four. He was scorching around the track hanging on for dear life as every corner promised an opportunity to buck him off. It was fast down the straight but he rode the wheels off it around the corners where it was not behaving as it should. Sheene rose to the occasion with another gutsy ride and Randy unfortunately retired after a couple of laps. He had been complaining of a sticky throttle and to be fair his Suzuki had biffed him off already in practice so he would have been riding cautiously. I slipped and slithered around the track back in fifth spot and had a lonely, uneventful ride. I was pleasantly surprised at picking up an extra place when Jack Middelburg had a rear wheel failure. Fourth place in the championship so far with 16 points was OK but Kenny had already streaked out to a lead of 24 points. Things were looking ominous.

As we were about to leave, I found out many riders were taking the ferry from Barcelona to Genoa. Roberto Gallina had organized the trip by doing a group booking, then offered the deal to the paddock. I was in boots and all — bugger driving all the way to Misano for the next Grand Prix, it was too far and much less fun than taking the overnight ferry. It was only a short drive then from Genoa, so we would be at Misano all revved up and ready to go, in a refreshed state.

25

UNABLE TO CONVERT, 1982

GRAN PREMIO DELLE NAZIONI, MISANO, 30 MAY 1982

We had a few days to settle in at Misano and I began feeling more confident on the direction we were going as a team. The FIM had issued us notices of intention to fine us for our Nogaro antics but as yet no one had paid nor was likely to pay. We might have won a moral victory at last.

My Italian was improving with help from Boska and the weather was being kind to us. The gentle humming of the generators at night and the smell of barbecues were part of a sociable scene that I found very relaxing.

Because we had tested here earlier in the year, our race set-up was effectively dialled in from the first session. However, we were greeted on the first lap by some huge slippery patches of freshly laid tarmac. The repairs were made to bumps on a few corners but they were on the racing line which made them unavoidable. As practice continued it got marginally better and on race day we all had pretty much forgotten those hairy laps of a few days ago. Practice and qualifying went well on the Friday and Saturday but Graziano Rossi should have stayed home. He threw his reverse-cylinder 500 up the road and broke his collarbone — his second crash in two weeks.

In the warm-up lap I set off from the pit area to find that the power valve was faulty. I had only half the normal power, so I was sweating when it came time to form up on the grid. Radar had a spare battery and exchanged it immediately — good old Radar, always prepared like a Boy Scout and he wasn't easily flustered. I was in third spot on the grid behind Franco and Freddie Spencer. I was ready but my bike failed to fire up on cue, leaving me on the grid while 30 riders raced by into the first corner. It finally fired into life and away I went, desperately chasing the back markers.

On lap four I noticed a small vibration in the front end that puzzled me. Was it a thrown wheel weight or a tyre failing? It was noticeable enough to make me do something silly. The back straight at Misano was split into two sections with a very fast left-hand bend connecting the two. As I leaned into the left-hander I poked my head down the side of the bike and tried looking at the bottom edge of the tyre. I couldn't see anything, not even a hint of chattering. It was a quick look but long enough for me to run wide off the track and I found myself on the dirt at over 200 kph. Luckily, I was able to steer it back on the track and carry on as if nothing had happened. I would have to explain the lost 3 seconds over a few beers later.

It was going to be a long 40 laps around this 3.5 km circuit. I kept my head down and easily dealt with the rest of the back markers as I carved my way through the field. But as I got closer to the front, it became a more difficult job to pass as the speeds were getting closer to mine and opportunities to pass became fewer.

Up front Franco Uncini had got a flyer and was comfortably leading Freddie, with Kenny doing his bucking bronco imitation again aboard the V-four Yamaha. I caught and passed Barry, who later complained he was having trouble with a poorly handling bike, which I hadn't noticed as I had the bit between my teeth. I got Kenny late in the race but fell short of catching Freddie and eventual race winner Franco Uncini. I even lapped Randy who must have been having a shocker for that to happen but it was a satisfying feeling for me. He retired on the next lap with brake problems.

This had been a good race for me in many respects, I had enjoyed the whole 52 minutes of balls-out racing and other than my little excursion off the track it was incident-free. I must have been at a heightened state of concentration because it seemed to be over very quickly. That's always a good sign, but even so I was still in fourth place in the title chase.

DONINGTON ITV AND JOHN PLAYER CUP, 19 JUNE 1982

Ago had agreed with Donington Park to bring his whole team over from Italy. It was part of my contract to do three internationals on the basis of us splitting the start money, which was about £3000. It was only a week before the Dutch GP at Assen and I needed to show the English crowd that Suzuki's decision to drop me last year was wrong. I loved the East Midlands circuit because it held so many fond memories from the previous three years. I was on familiar territory now and enjoyed seeing the English crowd again.

I won the ITV cup race on Saturday and was credited with the fastest lap time. On Sunday in the 500 cc John Player International I had a win in the first leg but failed to finish the second race, while still managing fastest laps in both races. I began focusing on my chances of winning a Grand Prix. If I could ride like I did here in the last two days, then I felt a Grand Prix was not out of the question.

It was a big field with most top riders there including Kenny, Barry, Randy, Jack Middelburg and the Gallina team. However, of all those there I was surprised to see the progress Korky Ballington's bike had made. It was fast and extremely good under brakes, and Korky was riding really well. Dozy must have been working late. I asked him one time how it felt being a mechanic for his own brother.

'Croz,' he said. 'I try to make Korky's bike go very fast in a straight line so he can go slowly and more safely around the corners.' I cracked up at that but Dozy was full of little gems of wisdom and was hilarious to talk to, especially when he'd had a few too many.

I loved catching up with John Cooper and Tom Wheatcroft, both larger-than-life characters. John rode with a famous pudding-style helmet with huge eyes painted on the front. Nicknamed 'Moon Eyes', he was a real hard-charger in his day, one time beating Giacomo Agostini in the Race of the Year at Mallory in 1971. It was his finest moment and he could recall every lap of that race.

Tom was the circuit owner and he had an infectiously loud laugh that could be heard a mile away. He was extremely passionate about the sport and had extended an invitation to me to join him in his special hospitality suite located on a corner at the end of the back straight. I was unlucky enough one time to be high-sided off the bike at that corner. I returned to earth on the grass amongst a pile of broken fibreglass pieces, mud and grass clippings. As it happened right outside his suite, I stood up and took refuge behind the fence in front of him.

Tom bellowed out, 'Bloody good of you to make it Croz but you could have come in the main entrance. Would you be wanting a Heineken, me lad?'

DUTCH GRAND PRIX, ASSEN, 26 JUNE 1982

We were halfway through the season when the Dutch GP suddenly appeared on our radar screen. Circuit van Drenthe was a great track with a good surface but as usual at Assen the forecast was not good.

Fortunately, practice went well and with a dry track I was able to get on the pace quickly. I spent a lot of time cocking around with gear ratios and trying an overdrive-type set-up. It turned out to be a waste of time and effort for no appreciable speed gain. Five close ratios for the corners and then a long sixth gear to get the top speed right. I had problems matching corner speed and rpm with the power delivery and thought that by changing gear-sets it might help.

Hindsight is a wonderful thing; I even briefly contemplated reverting to my old style of racing from Australia, braking later and just hoping like hell to get around the corner. I ended up totally confusing myself. We had one bike with a standard set-up so I concentrated on that one and zoomed around the 7.5 km circuit to stick it fourth on the grid behind Uncini, Kenny and Barry, but three seconds ahead of Randy. It would have to do.

When the 250 cc race was on we all walked over to the back of the pit area to cheer on Jeff Sayle (who was riding a 250 cc Armstrong) and Graeme McGregor (on a 250 cc Waddon). These guys made riding a 500 look like a doddle. The skies opened up during the 250 cc race but Jeff rode hard and fast, only losing second position to Jean-Louis Tournadre on the last lap. We were proud of how well he did. As soon as the race was over the sun came out and it looked like it would be a dry race for the 500 cc event.

With slick tyres selected for the race we pushed the bikes onto the grid and got away for the warm-up lap, keeping a close eye on the billowing cumulus clouds forming, the type that hide those wretched thunderstorms.

I was usually quick off the start but today it didn't fire cleanly, leaving me in the midfield dashing to the first corner. It was absolutely critical to get a good start because in parts this track was quite narrow. I was trying to get a rhythm and flow going but was struggling back in eighth position.

The first big drop of water hit me on the visor and then another followed. The thunderstorm arrived and with it torrential rain. On my seventh lap I was gingerly exiting the left-hander behind the pit area; it felt as if I was riding using only fingertips and toenails. Off to my right a rider was skating to a stop with mud flying everywhere and I recognized the red, black and yellow suit of Kenny Roberts. A huge sheet of water lay directly ahead and I went right through it. Although I was not carrying too much power, all the grip, both front and rear, was lost and the bike spun around at about 140 kph. Both tyres had aquaplaned and I was on my way to join Kenny in the creek some 70 metres away. I slid along the wet grass until finally dropping into the ditch next to Kenny.

'Goddammit, sonofabitch,' I could see Kenny mouthing from under his visor. We were both out of the race, retired wet but unhurt.

It was not long before we realized that the race had been stopped and could be restarted, so a mad panic set in to get the bikes back to the pit area. Luckily, it was a short distance and our two bikes were dragged on to the back of the truck and taken back to the Parc Ferme. Radar and Roland were waiting to carry out repairs. Radar told me that the race had been stopped on lap eight and as I was upright at the time, I could restart if we could get the bike repaired.

I left Radar and the boys working feverishly inside, cannibalizing the spare bike for its useful parts. To make sure it would all hold together we taped the broken cowling back on and crossed our fingers. The back of our truck and the workshop resembled a second-hand parts dealer when we finally wheeled out our repaired bike. We had virtually no new spare parts to play with, so the bike was brought back out of the pit area to take its place on the grid still looking in a sad state of repair. Radar whispered that it would do the distance, adding that it might not feel the same after the crash.

On the start line and ready to go, one of Freddie's mechanics noticed a broken steering damper bolt. Unfortunately for Freddie, it was apparently a left-hand threaded bolt that was hard to replace in time and his bike was pulled from the grid. Kenny had got his V-four back on the grid as well.

The restart was a mess again but I trundled off just behind

the leaders, circulating without being able to get fired up. About mid-distance I got a surge of energy and concentrated again to begin the task of moving up to the leaders. Unfortunately for the thousands of fans who had come to see 'Jumping Jack' Middelburg win his home GP, he had a shocker and crashed his works Suzuki early in the opening laps, leaving Sheene out front with a clear track ahead. Uncini was holding second place with Roberts and Mamola dicing it out for third. Kenny finally made a pass that would stick and began pulling away and I was dragged along in pursuit of him.

Somehow I passed Randy on his superfast Suzuki but it was such a technical track and so quick in places that I had to plan my every move. I caught and passed Kenny in the closing laps as his tyre began balking at the punishment he was giving it. I was happy to be on a dry track. Sheene had an 'oops' towards the end but managed to stay upright, though he damaged his cowling and had to ease off the pace. It was enough for Uncini to take the lead and the win, also allowing me and Kenny through.

I came back elated after the finish, thinking I'd taken second place, but the euphoria lasted only minutes before an official called Barry and Kenny to join Franco on the rostrum. I was puzzled until Radar explained the rules about a two-heat race.

In this case the regulations clearly stated that if the race was stopped with less than 75 per cent of the time completed, and then restarted, the points were to be defined by the aggregate results of both legs.

It was disappointing and confusing for me. Feeling a little dejected, I found the paddock bar and settled in for the night, focusing on how good Jeff Sayle and Graeme McGregor's performances had been in the 250 cc race. I waited until the queue at the race office was short enough and picked up my winnings. Radar would get his normal share that night for a job well done.

SPA-FRANCORCHAMPS, BELGIUM, 4 JULY 1982

The treatment of riders and teams was getting out of control. The paddocks were becoming overcrowded and the risk of a catastrophe grew as more and more people were squeezed in. Fire would be the killer because we simply could not move once we had set up our camp.

I was disgusted that the circuit organizers were still allowing children to sell toilet paper by the sheet to those in desperate need. I had become one of them but I didn't have any money on me so the problem was elevated to super-critical. I fixed it by telling the kid to take a hike and then threw his collection tin out the window, scattering Belgian francs in the grass. As I'd done the year before, I bought a supply of toilet rolls and stacked a few in each cubicle. I even made representation to the circuit owners through the organizers about this degrading situation, but to no avail.

While Brenda headed off to Spa for shopping I prepared myself for a spot of fishing. I knew it was illegal but it was a hell of a lot of fun to sneak out with a few mates into the forest under cover of darkness. A stick with a line and a hook with some bread was all we needed to catch a bag of trout. Philippe Coulon had shown me a pond the previous year and I wouldn't have been surprised to find him lurking in the bushes again. We got a few but not the big bag I'd hoped for. The little buggers were a lot more difficult to catch than I had remembered.

I arrived back to find Brenda and her friend Bronwyn home from their shopping expedition with a little more than I had bargained for. Lying on the motorhome table was a pregnancy testing kit showing a 'Positive Indication'. Everyone was beaming and all excited with the news and I quickly worked out that next year we two were going to be three. I was going to be a dad.

The naming issue became an ongoing topic of conversation over the next few months. Everyone had suggestions but we all knew people with the same name and it affects your decision-making process. When you think of a name all you can see is either a fat, ugly, smelly, nasty, dopey, short, tall or just stupid person with the same name. It would have to wait until closer to the time.

Now we were facing another major problem in that the FIM explicitly prohibited the sale of paddock passes to the general public. But this weekend everywhere I looked I could see spectators walking in and around our working areas. Equipment and personal effects became targets for thieves. Anyone could fork out some money and get a pass.

We had a mixed bag at qualifying but as always any indication of pending bad weather meant the first priority was to get the bike on the starting line for the race. It's no good wobbling around running in a new gearbox or a new cylinder in dry conditions knowing it will piss down later and you won't have a chance of posting a good time. It had to be locked in as soon as possible. Afterwards you can experiment and cock around because you have already guaranteed yourself a start.

This was an opportunity to try a new compound Michelin rear tyre again and as I had been happy with my existing one I could still not convince myself of the need to change. It did not produce any faster lap times and was marginally slower getting up to working temperature. Michelin said it would last longer but I needed to be away with the leaders every time or risk having to play catch-up as I'd had to do on several occasions this year.

Some say the name 'Spa' is derived from the Latin word 'spargere' meaning to scatter, sprinkle or moisten. If that's true they got that one right, as it rained and sprinkled and we all got moistened. Trying to set up a bike and qualify it in inclement conditions is quite stressful. Saturday was a waste of time and eventually the practice sessions were cancelled. Sunday morning we had our final goes at qualifying, then the frantic job of getting every bike race-ready for the afternoon.

It was my birthday on race day so I had planned a little celebration at the local hotel with some close friends. It's funny what goes through your mind but I was thinking that I should be extra careful not to make a mistake today because I would miss out on my party. Then the moment of realization hit me: if I was more worried about missing my party than performing at peak in a Grand Prix event, perhaps I didn't have my heart in this racing game any more.

Our OW60s were working OK but there was still no news about the supply of new go-faster bits. Radar and Roland had their work cut out squeezing every bit of power from the engine. I put the old girl third on the grid behind Jack Middelburg, Freddie, Barry and Kenny. From the start I was third on lap one, then led on lap two but only for a short time before Kenny came steaming past me. I tried to hang on but his bike was clearly a lot faster and gradually he pulled away. Now I had Spencer on my tail and he snuck by on lap four. The next few laps I spent fending off Sheene and Uncini but they got past too. Mid-race I saw Kenny coming back into view, desperately hanging on to a bucking, sliding, wobbling beast. Better him than me, I thought as I passed him.

The engine was strong on my OW60, but when you are riding so hard and concentrating so much any small change in vibration or noise or a very slight power reduction is noticeable. I felt the vibration and noise change immediately and I backed off but the engine gave a bigger vibration and I pulled the clutch in and coasted to a stop. Only 14 bloody laps out of 20; I was pissed off. I would not have won but I could have been third or fourth. I reminded myself of a Jim Halliday saying: 'If your aunt had balls she'd be your uncle.' I'd get over it but it was disappointing to get so far and end up nowhere.

That night I had my party at a hotel up from La Sourse hairpin. We wanted to have lobsters that were in the restaurant display tank with their pincers safely tied up with big rubber bands. Before anyone knew it, the bands had been cut and ferocious lobsters were being carried about the place with pincers gnashing and flailing away in mid-air trying to catch some poor unsuspecting person's index finger.

Brenda woke up first next morning and noticed something strange about where we had parked. By the noise of the traffic whistling past us I soon discovered that I'd stopped on a main road. I had blocked one whole lane of a two-lane street which was now clogged with trucks, cars and buses. I opened the windows, stretched, scratched my bollocks, got into the driver's seat and moved the motorhome to a safer spot.

26

SKIN, BLOOD AND SCABS, 1982

YUGOSLAVIA, 18 JULY 1982

It was looking as though Radar would have to miss the Yugoslavian Grand Prix at Rijeka because he was an Australian passport holder. Yugoslavia's communist government was going through an institutional reorganization and Aussies and South Africans were not being given visas. This posed an interesting problem for the various sporting codes holding international events in the country. If you came from a blacklisted country you could not compete.

Initially, I joked about his doubtful heritage, being descended from convict stock; given the same situation I would probably also ban him. But the thought of not having either Radar or Trevor there to make it all happen was no laughing matter.

It was imperative that Radar come to Yugoslavia because he was a key member of our team. Trevor was South African but he also held a Dutch passport, so he could get a visa. Radar had been travelling on his Australian passport and until now had had no problems getting visas. This Grand Prix at Rijeka threw a curly one at him. As soon as we found out we had a problem, Agostini got on the blower to work out a solution. I don't know who was responsible, but Radar ended up with an Italian passport and drove over the border from Italy via the northern city of Trieste.

I nicknamed Radar 'Luigi Paspalum' for the duration of the weekend. It was brilliant weather for a Grand Prix with hot, cloudless days — perfect for sunbathing, wearing shorts and drinking local wines. It felt like a real Mediterranean holiday atmosphere.

New cylinders for the bike arrived from Japan and Trevor and Radar went about making sure they were perfect, taking off any casting dags that could create trouble if a piece broke off and went through the engine. It was great getting new stuff from the factory; getting a bike is one thing but keeping it going and developing it over the season required constant input from Japan. To know that the factory remembered we were out on the battlefield, fighting for the brand, made for good vibes. Just getting anything that might give us an advantage we were glad to accept. I think the Japanese underestimated the psychological lift it gave a rider when he was presented with new parts for his bike. We were still perplexed as to why there had been so few new parts made available for the OW60's. A set of new carburettors or cylinders might be nice, but we also wanted to feel that our contributions were valued and that we were being shown some respect.

We kind of knew that the OW60 had been produced as an interim model while the V-four was being developed. If that was the case and knowing how the Japanese think, we were probably lucky to get anything at all. The OW60 was built and supplied to do a job but was not designed to be a world-beater. The V-four engine was the direction for the future but without a solid testing programme Yamaha had got behind. Once a decision has been made to make another version the foot comes off the throttle on development of the previous model. It was as if we were between seasons.

Kenny was still struggling with the V-four's development. It seemed to me they were chasing their tails. Barry had been pestering Yamaha desperately, trying to get a hold of the bike before the British

GP so he could spend some time testing and making changes that would progress its development and give him a chance of winning Silverstone in two weeks' time.

In qualifying, our OW60's worked nicely around the track and even carburetted well. It was the gearing that required attention and we tried a few different ratio changes. I had finally accepted Ago's method of getting the final overall top gear sorted. We made changes so that the bike was almost gasping for breath in the last 100 metres of the longest straight. Although it sounded a little harsh, I was able to cope with it and it gave me a better drive out of the final corner onto the straight.

The circuit was smooth as a carpet to ride on, so I was able to get good feedback through the shock units both front and rear but it was difficult to tell how much grip existed. The corners were slightly banked so G-loading made the units work hard. I liked the track and managed to get my bike fourth on the grid. Sheene was trying hard to shore up support for him to get the V-four. He put a great effort in to get pole position about 0.7 seconds ahead of me in fourth place. He was welcome to it; I didn't like the idea of him getting his hands on it if it meant he would be beating me, but I sensed it would be a distraction, knowing what it was like to ride.

The race itself was a Franco Uncini benefit as he stormed away on his Suzuki, seemingly oblivious that we were all scratching around trying hard to follow him. He looked so smooth, effortless and under control. A large part of the race was taken up fighting it out with Spencer and Sheene. I got a break on Sheene and managed to maintain an advantage for some time before my concentration lapsed and I thought I might be overhauled. I got myself together again and hung on for second place.

I was presented with an exquisite crystal vase, along with Champagne of course, but the biggest surprise was counting out my winnings in the motorhome while driving back towards Trieste. I began counting out the funny paper money and just when it should have been about to run out there was more to count. The silly buggers had given me the winner's purse instead of the second placegetter's money. Oh dear; it took me all of one millisecond to decide what to do.

SILVERSTONE, 1 AUGUST 1982

The British round at Silverstone was mid-season. I had been based at Bergamo about 50 km from Milan for the first half of the year. My loyal fan base that I'd had with Suzuki last year had surprisingly not forgotten me. I was really keen to put on a good performance for them. I still felt I had a point to prove, that Suzuki were wrong to let me go, so I needed a good showing to jog their memories. A good finish here would give me a great sense of satisfaction.

Arriving at Silverstone, I was treated like a long-lost kid by the fans and it made me feel special to be mixing and mingling amongst these genuinely friendly faces. I marvelled at those familiar old stalwarts who turned out religiously race after race. Rain, hail or shine, these fans were tough customers and I enjoyed having a laugh and a beer with them. This year was to be different, though, as I was soon to find out.

Last year's 500 cc fiasco saw me crashing out spectacularly, taking Sheene with me. Silverstone has always been challenging for me because the circuit is fast and has a smooth surface with no slow sections. Third, fourth and fifth seemed to be the only gears I used here.

We were scheduled to have an unofficial practice session on the Monday and Barry had finally persuaded Yamaha to give him Kenny's spare OW61 V-four. After a few laps, Barry had sent it off to get the steering head angle changed. Technically, it was almost there but lacked something basic. Kel Carruthers and the Japanese technicians had been working hard to fix it. I thought the design was somehow flawed from the outset but the talk seemed to be focused around its intake tracks and carburettors and the inherent difficulty of controlling the airspeed. Later in the year I would get an opportunity to tyre-test and prove myself right about my initial thoughts.

However, this year's practice sessions for the 1982 British round of the 500 cc world championship were marred by horrific crashes. Barry Sheene collided with the remnants of Patrick Igoa's 250 cc that lay on the racing line. He had been thrown off it in the closing stages of a late private testing session on the Wednesday after tangling with a slower rider. The bike slid across and stopped in the middle of the track. Barry arrived at the top of the hill, hotly pursued by Jack Middelburg on his Suzuki. He couldn't have seen the bike in the middle of the track and slammed into it at high speed.

Barry suffered massive injuries to his legs and completely destroyed the V-four. The front end was literally ripped out of it. I heard the noise from where I was watching and ran over and saw the carnage. At first it was Jack Middelburg I spotted lying on the track with severe cuts to his back. He had hit the debris and was brought down in the mess. I went to his aid but there was little I could do without first aid training — clear a windpipe or stop some bleeding perhaps but Jack was conscious and the medics were arriving. There appeared to be bodies and broken bikes and bits everywhere. Patrick Igoa was lucky to suffer only a broken collarbone.

Barry was taken to hospital where surgeon Nigel Cobb literally created two new sections of shinbones out of the minute fragments found when he opened up the wounded legs. By attaching screws and plates to the broken bones, Mr Cobb was able to save both legs from amputation.

My testing session so far had provided few surprises, although I had turned down the chance of testing the OW61 because I thought it was a distraction rather than an opportunity. Radar and Trevor possibly thought I was an idiot for not grabbing the offer. But having watched Roberts wrestle with the beast for race after race, it was not a pleasant thought. My OW60 square four 500 may have been old technology but at least it was familiar, comfortable and easy to ride. I really did feel for Barry and to this day I can still hear that explosive wallop on impact that rang out across the infield at Silverstone.

Official practice commenced amidst accusations of poor track safety and of allowing 125 cc bikes out with the faster 500's. Everyone began ducking and diving for cover with threats of lawsuits over culpability. Those who could have been held responsible suddenly became Teflon-coated. A high-profile crash, like the one that unfortunately effectively ended Barry's racing career at that level, was bound to stir controversy. His horrific accident detracted from what was shaping up to be a great British GP event.

Lurking somewhere out on the periphery was a new subject that was being discussed at all levels within the paddock. The journalists wanted to know about the formation of the PRA, which by all accounts was finally getting traction. This new association would mean the riders and team owners would have one voice with which to negotiate circuit safety, conditions and other matters. It seemed as though the first nail had been driven into the coffin of the establishment. Although the PRA was to morph eventually into the International Riders and Teams Association (IRTA), those involved were still carrying on very much as if it was business as usual as the groundswell increased.

We, and I include myself by virtue of association and the fact that I was a factory rider, attended the various meetings staged at what seemed increasing regularity to keep everyone informed of developments. The real drivers behind the PRA were in my opinion Barry Coleman, Kenny Roberts and Mike Trimby. This small core of determined individuals all had one thing in mind and that was to be listened to as a body of riders, teams and sponsors hoping to improve conditions for those involved in the GP scene, which to date was the domain of an antiquated regime called the FIM. I did not really understand how it all worked. I just wanted to race bikes; fuck the politics.

Practice as usual was confined to four 30-minute sessions, two on Friday, and two on Saturday with the race on Sunday. Having had the benefit of a few laps in the days preceding the official sessions, I was quickly on the pace and managed to set a time of 1:31.57. While a full second slower than last year, I was happy, given track and weather conditions. The bike handled great as always but that did not stop us forever chasing small suspension setting changes and experimenting with gear ratios. Carburettor jetting proved as fickle as ever; if we got it spot-on then things generally fell into place and times improved.

Towards the end of Friday afternoon's practice session I was coming off a good lap down the front straight and had a quick look at the lapboard, confirming the last lap time was somewhere in the ballpark. I braked into Copse Corner and accelerated out towards Maggots Curve. As I rolled the bike upright, making sure I was using every bit of track available to get me positioned perfectly for the run up to the next corner, I picked third gear and let the rpm build briefly then slipped into fourth. At this speed and with the extreme bank angle I just couldn't get my foot off the foot-peg to change gear so it had to be a 'short' change. Assuming I got it right with the rev counter touching 8900 rpm as I rolled up right towards the entry to Beckett's Corner, this was going to be another quick lap.

All that changed halfway through the corner when the stiff 25-knot crosswind that was blowing left to right lifted the front end momentarily, relieving my front tyre of the necessary grip and I found myself losing control of the bike. Things go very slowly after realizing you have just blown it and are skidding and sliding down the road on your arse. There is a natural tendency to hold on to the bike but despite the overwhelming feelings of pending pain I remained quite calm and pushed the bike free from me. Coming off at 180 kph, believe it or not, has its inherent benefits because the higher the speed you come off at, the less is the angle or vertical component on impact. Not like those slower-speed high-sides that cause fractures — I hate that.

I lost the front end and was now travelling spread-eagled on my face, using my hands as brakes and to help me manoeuvre so I could roll over on to my back and move to a legs-to-the-front in some form of defensive posture. I could feel the tarmac creating friction heat on my hands and every area that was in contact with the ground became rather hot, like being seared with a red-hot poker.

My speed across the tarmac decreased to a point where I felt it was slow enough to stand up, but wisely I hesitated. I knew only too well that judging speed while on the bike is one thing but when drawing to a halt after sliding off at 180 kph, the tendency is to stand up before you reach walking speed. In the past I got it all wrong and thought it was OK to stand up, then realized I was still doing 30 kph. That would invariably end up with the inevitable 'face-plant' — literally, not a good look. While highly embarrassing for any rider, it is always seen as amusing by the crowd. With this in mind I stayed prone until I stopped, which was in amongst fine loose metal chips on the edge of the track. The bike was some 30 metres away lying on its side and showing all the signs of a rough landing after it had done several somersaults over the catch fence. The back end of the bike looked nasty and it had lots of scuffing and friction burns and bits of broken cowling sticking out. I would have liked to call it superficial but it looked unrepairable from where I was lying.

I stood up to find myself being stalked by several flag marshals. A quick check revealed I had taken the majority of the slide directly on the palms of my hands and both bum cheeks. My beautiful Marlboro Agostini Kushitani leathers were scuffed and scraped but largely intact, other than holes worn through either side of my bum.

The stinging pain began as I extracted my short little fanny scratchers from the torn remains of my gloves. There was no blood present, only raw skin with visible white dots and patches indicating that the friction burns were deep into both palms of my hands.

The bike was picked up unceremoniously and dragged to a safe area by flag marshals. It would be transported back to the paddock area for collection after the close of this practice session. All attention was then directed at me for medical help. The circuit's RT radios were busy issuing instructions and reporting back to race control. An ambulance was directed via the infield to the scene of the accident and shortly thereafter the yellow caution flags were withdrawn, allowing the balance of the field to get on with practising and searching for their own 'hot lap'.

I was ushered into the back of the ambulance where a zambuck checked for signs of shock, fractures or potential head injuries. I managed to keep my head up and was conscious throughout the ordeal but I was still wired high with adrenalin. On arrival at the St John's emergency centre I was greeted by the course doctor who took a quick look and established that I was not going require anything more than a couple of aspirins, a Telfa pad or two and a bit of sticky plaster. He left the room after issuing instructions to the attending nurse to thoroughly cleanse my open gashes before releasing me to face the mercy of the press and to explain my crash.

The nurse was a big buxom woman with enormous breasts that threatened to smother me as she scraped away with what can only be described as a sterile wire brush. My palms had been impregnated with hundreds of tiny stone chips from the Second World War runway tarmac. These were a potential source of infection and the nurse was blunt about what needed to be done. 'Better to deal with it and get it all out now lad, than have an infection set in.' No indication of how painful it was going to be — she just began scraping away as if she was enjoying herself. With my head buried between her bosoms I was not enjoying the procedure, but painful as it was there would be no tears from the 'Croz'.

Before I was released she handed me a bunch of tissues to remove damp patches from my red eyelids. 'Bitch,' I thought.

Returning to the paddock area, I went straight to my pit. The bike had already been delivered back and looked a sorry sight. After a cursory inspection I sat down with Radar, Trevor and Ago to go over what had happened. Like any racer I was concerned not so much about getting the bike back together and into race trim again; I was more concerned about whether I could ride on Sunday.

I was faced with the prospect of not even being able to wear gloves, let alone hold on to a GP bike at 290 kph for 30-odd laps. I needed help. I knew the first line of assistance was the St John's Ambulance service which had provided initial medical help, but I would be needing ongoing treatment to get me back on the track sooner than later. I walked around the paddock in a search of Dr Claudio Costa, an incredible Italian who had a passion for the Grand Prix scene. In true Italian style he'd formed and headed up a team of private Italian doctors to provide medical services to riders. Although primarily designed with crash victims in mind, his Clinica Mobil (mobile hospital) was capable of all sorts of surgical procedures. However, I suspected that riders and mechanics with the odd case of the 'clap' or more likely alcoholic poisoning would have seen the clinic also swing into action.

Claudio took one look and began treating my hands with a special surgical cream that need to be changed every few hours. He explained that in order to get my hands working, the healing should start from the inside out, not from the outside in. I knew it was going to take time and he began changing the bandages regularly. Incredible as it seemed, I could almost see this new opaque skin growing in front of my eyes.

However, my back end was another issue, because the focus had been on my damaged hands. I had completely neglected my sore bum. It soon became a daily ritual in the mornings that when I woke up I would slip out of bed, dragging sheets that had 'healed' themselves to my bum overnight. It was very painful peeling the sheets and scabs off my wounds.

I made an attempt at riding in Saturday's qualifying session and I tried various glove combinations to alleviate the pain. Radar even shortened the handlebars so I could ride with the ends nestled into the wells of my hands. I did a couple of laps, then came in and made an adjustment. But the end of the session could not have come quick enough. I was dejected and it looked like I would miss the British Grand Prix.

Later that day Murray Walker swung by. Murray never fails to amaze me with his enthusiasm and passion for motorcycles, having been brought up with them as a kid. He asked me to talk him through a lap of Silverstone aboard my OW60. I could appreciate where he was coming from because to sit high up in the commentary box watching and calling the race as it is unfolding is no easy task. With the possibility of a lull in proceedings if the race is boring or lacking action, it is important to have lots of technical info at hand to use. Mind you, having accurate technical details is also extremely important. Now, I am not entirely stupid and I would think Murray might have already talked with Kenny, Randy, or Freddie about their 'tech lap tour'.

So, not wanting to reveal any of my secrets, I picked up a speed chart that showed various internal gear ratios, primary and final ratios, engine rpm and speed in kph. Our bikes had a cassette-type side-loading transmission that allowed for individual ratio changes that did not affect the overall speeds. Murray and I sat down on a tool-box and I explained that my chosen internal gearbox ratios were made up of 'E — 1st', 'D — 2nd', 'C — 3rd', 'D — 4th', 'E — 5th', 'E — 6th'. I had selected a fictitious set-up with an internal ratio that could only be described as the first notes to the melody 'Mary Had a Little Lamb'. I set about working out speeds that corresponded to any given corner at Silverstone. Murray clung to my every word as I took him around the course, pointing out and marking on the circuit diagram my braking points and all associated speeds, gear-change points and rpms.

I was delighted to hear him use my information most informatively during his commentary of the race later. No one was the wiser.

On race day I plucked my bed sheets carefully away from my bum scabs and then dressed. I was really apprehensive about how I would perform. I ate a little toast but it was difficult to swallow, which was usual for race day.

When I told Radar we were going to do this race, his eyebrows lifted and an expression appeared on his face as if to say 'Oh fuck!' Radar had assumed I would not be making the grid on Sunday and had gone about doing some routine service work in preparation for the next GP in Sweden. In next to no time Radar had enlisted the assistance of the factory Yamaha mechanics who had been working on Barry's V-four. It was a mad panic — the bike now required a serious amount of preparation for the race. The flurry of activity continued right up until it was pushed out to the grid.

Man, what a race it turned out to be. I got a blinder of a start, then settled quickly into working my way 'backwards through the field'. I could not stand the pain and my concentration suffered badly as a consequence. I felt so hopeless seeing my lap times so slow and having privateers passing me didn't do much for my confidence. It wasn't until Randy, who had got an unusually bad start, came past me mid-race that something clicked and the pain vanished and suddenly I was in the zone. I had quite a bit of catching up to do but I began making ground steadily. I had forgotten about the pain, probably because the adrenalin had kicked in, providing all the anaesthetic needed, and I was able to concentrate again.

The last several laps were probably the quickest I have ever done in a GP, in terms of overall time. I guess this was another case when you are at your best and focused and riding in the zone. I managed to cross the line after fending off a few desperate challenges from Katayama on his Honda three-cylinder NSR500 and Loris Reggiani aboard the Team Gallina Suzuki to finish third behind Franco Uncini and Freddie Spencer. The trophy for third place proved it was worth the effort — a handsome bronze statuette of the world wrapped in tobacco leaves and emblazoned with the Marlboro logo.

During the race I was credited with the fastest lap which made my chest swell, considering the circumstances. However, my aching palms, now bleeding through the bandaging, were to become less important as Radar, Trevor and the boys slurped back from a large bottle of Champagne.

I didn't have the heart to thank Randy for giving me a wake-up call halfway through the race. That would have to wait for a more appropriate occasion.

27

OK, BEEN THERE, DONE THAT — WHAT'S NEXT? 1982

SWEDISH GRAND PRIX, ANDERSTORP, 7 AUGUST 1982

We caught the overnight ferry from Harwich to Gothenburg and had a great time catching up with other teams heading the same way. It was an eclectic bunch of rogues — a smorgasbord of nationalities, most in their 20s, having fun, seeing the world and with a positive outlook on life. With bars and a disco aboard, we made the most of our time at sea.

As soon as we arrived at Anderstorp Raceway I knew it was going to be a hard task again riding for 30 bloody laps with the way my hands were. They had been responding quite well to the treatment but were still far from being healed. I was in no condition to give it 100 per cent on the racetrack, at least not without feeling the pain intensely. The beautiful new translucent skin had been growing steadily from the base of the wounds. I knew it was good to see it growing but Claudio Costa had kept insisting on removing any new scabs that were forming on the outside of the wound. He had supplied me some gunky cream resembling axle grease that I was supposed to apply twice a day.

I did this as instructed but thought I should just find a beach somewhere and go for a swim. I would get plenty of salt water into the wound and then let it dry out and heal naturally from the outside. Dr Costa gave me a playful flick on the head when I told him of my plan. He re-emphasized the reason why his method of treatment would be more effective long term. 'Think of meat pie with juice in the middle and a crust on top,' he said in his broken English. 'Every time you have a crust form the squishy bit inside stays wet so it heals slowly. So we keep wiping the wet stuff off so the base can grow. Plus you risk infection — that's why I want it to heal from the inside out, not from outside in.' I had no option but to follow his recommendations.

Once we were parked and settled in, the real work began, carrying out repair work from our Silverstone crash. I thought this was going to be no problem but I'd forgotten we had made one bike out of two at Silverstone for the race. Now I needed both bikes again to take advantage of the lack of training time. I remembered the fiasco last year when we almost had a strike over lack of practice time.

Radar had been working from another angle with my injuries in mind. He had been busy on a small project making a leg brace so I could take the weight off my hands under brakes. I was not looking forward to riding here, for a number of reasons. Aside from my hands there was also the track. I was not confident with the course or its layout. It just didn't work for me. It was essentially an airport that could double as a racetrack. The main runway was used as the straight and then we dived off at right-angles onto a taxiway that was flat with no camber and the corner was squared off. A typical taxiway layout but the infield corners were almost a constant radius turn with a high degree of banking. A very tight bumpy left-hander led on to the short front straight where the pits were located. This was a racetrack that lacked soul. The circuit was cut from a forest and was not well maintained. It could have benefited from a cash injection.

I had been here before and I was expecting it anyway, but the spectacular display by a delta-wing Saab fighter jet made a visit to this track tolerable. The jet came out of the north, fast and very low, then pulled up into a loop for a couple of aileron rolls and then disappeared into the distance, chased seconds later by the roar of its own turbo jet engine. I identified it as a Saab Viggen by its trademark canard front wing.

I struggled to get through qualifying and was three seconds slower than Freddie's Honda. Come the race day I had discarded all attempts to make life bearable and elected to tough it out, hoping adrenalin would kick in again like it had at Silverstone. Whether it was the effect of the forest I'm not sure but our carburation was causing problems. I could not get it to accelerate cleanly out of the corners and I was frustrated knowing I was losing valuable time every lap.

Seventh on the grid was a disappointing result but poor old Freddie's bike had developed a cough on the warm-up lap. He had lapped about 1.5 seconds quicker than anyone else in qualifying. With a minute to go before the start, his mechanics were still searching in vain for the cause. Freddie retired it to the pit lane soon after the start.

Randy had begun seeing the fruits of his development and I was able to watch from my comfortable fifth spot. This event was one of the most difficult mentally for me. I was conscious of the pain in my hands and also aware that I didn't want to be there. My drive and aggression had evaporated and I just wished it was all over. I asked myself where the fun and excitement had gone. I was not concentrating and my mind darted from one thought to another. Sooner or later I was going to hurt myself.

When the flag finally came down I was surprised to find myself elevated into third place. I told myself I'd take 10 points any day if they came like that — unexpected and almost undeserved. I had been wallowing around in fourth and fifth place and when Uncini stopped after his rear sprocket fell off it gave me a glimmer of hope.

I'd got stuck behind Marc Fontan who was riding really well and it was a tough call getting by him. Eventually, I managed to get past and set off after Randy, but by that time I'd run out of laps.

I couldn't find the little spark that burned in me. The bike was slower perhaps than the Suzukis and Hondas but with no improvements due from the factory I had to resign myself to the knowledge that this was about as good as it was going to get this year.

Then I decided there would be no next year for me. I had a life after racing to look forward to, and this was now occupying my thoughts. The various directions the riders and teams were taking in their plans for next year started becoming apparent. Neither Agostini nor Yamaha had discussed their plans for next year, at least not with me. I could have put the hard questions to them, but I was tired and mentally exhausted. I just wanted to go home and focus on pursuing a flying career.

I had heard rumours of younger guys like Didier de Radiguès being approached as potential riders but I had purposely ignored them. My team was headed by Agostini who, to me, was clearly a part-time manager. He seemed to be acting in a caretaking role for Marlboro. While I felt he didn't have his heart in it, I could see other ominous signs developing. Behind the scenes I could see a situation that would see Yamaha offload more of the financial burden to sponsors like Marlboro and Gauloises. Talk to any of the top mechanics and they know what's going on. Any plans for the Marlboro team did not appear to include me; that I was sure of. The politics of the Grand Prix paddock were being played out right under my nose from the onset of the opening round with rumours, claims and counterclaims. That was the nature of the business and with big money at stake, there were bound to be casualties.

It seemed to me a case of the tail wagging the dog. Kenny was able to have a degree of influence on the Yamaha Motor Company about how the team's management and structure should be organized for the following year. I imagined he had a group of talented guys with various skills looking after him. Undeniably, Yamaha held Kenny in high regard, and Kenny to his credit had vision. He did not need me competing against him or for that matter Sheene, because we both wanted to win the world championship just as much as he did. There was not enough room for two egos in one team.

Through the fog I could see a future being created for Kenny that would ensure his longevity in this field long after he had pulled off his racing suit for the last time. I felt a little lonely and disappointed that I might be paying the ultimate price for being a Kiwi. A foreigner, a johnny-come-lately, a lightweight without any commercial clout.

I had to rely on Brenda, Radar and friends to provide support and encouragement to keep me going. I loved racing but this was one aspect of international competition where I was naive and inexperienced. I recalled the time in Sydney when I arranged to meet with IMG, the sports management company. The guy I met with could not see past Bob Charles and golf. So being rejected by the Aussie branch of IMG in such an off-hand manner was insulting. I needed to have a professional manager but by now I realized it was too late.

On the rostrum we were given our trophies, which would have been the smallest I'd seen. I'd got better rewards when I got six out of ten for a spelling exam back in 1968. And then bugger me dead, just to rub salt into the wounds we were presented with some sparkling grape juice. Then it dawned on me why I didn't like coming here.

With Kenny back in the US recovering with a broken finger from his Silverstone crash, Franco Uncini became the 1982 FIM 500 cc world champion. He thoroughly deserved it and with Team Gallina making it two in a row following Marco's 1981 effort, the party was going to be big. Well, it would have been, except the Swedish alcohol laws made it almost impossible to get a little drunk and celebrate. I had more chance of drowning in the beer than getting drunk. That took the fizz out of the after-race party.

At least I was still alive and kicking. Jock Taylor wasn't so lucky; he was killed at the Finnish Grand Prix at Imatra on his sidecar. He slammed into a telegraph pole and even before they could free him he was hit by another out-of-control sidecar. The conditions were atrocious but at least the FIM had made some headway by not including the 500's in that Grand Prix. It was too late to help Jock, though.

MUGELLO, 5 SEPTEMBER 1982

The Yamaha factory team contacted Agostini and asked for me to be available for their scheduled tyre-testing session with Dunlop on the V-four the week prior to the Grand Prix at Mugello. My role was to do the riding on 'that' bike again. I had been talking with Kel about what had been happening development-wise and he muttered something about the length of the inlet tracks being too long, therefore the airspeed was slow, making tuning difficult at slow rpm. All the things that I didn't want to hear if it meant it was hard to ride.

The Mugello circuit is set in a small valley in the rolling hills of Northern Tuscany between Firenze and Bologna. I drove down in the Alfa Romeo and arriving at the track I was struck by its apparent unfinished state. Cement-filled block walls with reinforcing rods poking out the top was a sign that work had ground to a halt at some stage. The circuit was about six years old and looked like its owners had run out of money to complete it. I couldn't help but think our Grand Prix road show was here purely for the benefit of the track owners. A Grand Prix would bring the much-needed funds to at least partially finish another section of this potentially brilliant circuit.

We ran into the owner who was a real live wire. Enthusiastic about the prospects of a great GP the next weekend, he was skilled at selling the advantages of his circuit to anyone with a sympathetic ear. Despite its unfinished appearance, the track looked exciting and technically challenging. There were lots of adverse camber corners, banked corners and descending downhill curves as it twisted through the valley. Differing radius corners and a decidedly long front straight added to the excitement. Thankfully, there was plenty of run-off in most places. It was hard to imagine that back in 1976 there were 70 crashes in practice, including two fatalities. That was the last time a GP had been held here. It was a sobering fact but I shrugged it off.

Initially, I would ride the bike then provide feedback to both Kel and the Yamaha representatives about the bike's performance and any changes I thought might be needed. Dunlop wanted information on a range of tyres they were developing and as far as I was concerned I didn't need to have information on what was being tested because it might have interfered with my assessment. Dunlop had clearly been talking with Yamaha and both companies were working towards producing competition tyres for the future racing models. The development at that time included testing of a very wide and triangulated rear tyre.

Kel and Nobby Clark prepped the bike and did the normal safety checks before I was pushed out to the track. My testing method was to do a warm-up lap to bring the tyres up to the optimum temperature. By this time brakes, engine and transmission all had enough temperature in them for a faster lap. I would have known if anything else needed attention by then. I would do about four to five laps, each at a progressively quicker pace. In my mind I was establishing the overall gearing ratio. I wanted the engine to be at maximum power just short of the braking area. My reasoning was that if I needed to get a draught from another rider, the engine should be able to handle a few hundred more rpm without failure. If I was to over-gear it would be slower to accelerate and my top speed would be slower.

This was a trick that Agostini had taught me at Misano. We checked the speed charts and worked the top speed out to be very close to 300 kph at the end of the straight.

Once the overall gearing was set, I worked back through the gearbox, checking each ratio against corner speeds and rpm. I would pick a mark on the track, usually at the exit point of a corner, and check my rpm at that point. Bearing in mind that one gear might be used in four corners, a compromise might exist. These rpm readings would be recorded as an overlay of the track and I could then get a mental picture of my ratios and make the internal ratio changes necessary to get what I wanted.

With Kenny's bike I found I had one additional factor to consider. It was the ever-changing rolling circumference of the rear tyre as it went from maximum angle of bank to upright. When cranked right over and running on the edge of the tyre, the effective rolling circumference is a lot less than if measured in the centre of the tyre. The big Dunlop tyre accentuated this fact because of the huge triangulation.

Coming out of a turn the big V-four had plenty of torque and power but getting it to the ground via the chassis suspension and tyres was another matter. It was a strange phenomenon to be cranked over with 7200 rpm showing on the tachometer and accelerating while bringing the bike upright as it drove out of the corner still with 7200 rpm showing. It made the bike seem flat but it was actually accelerating, trading bank angle for rpm.

I did about 30 laps, coming in every four or five laps for data collection and new tyres, which kept the tyre-fitters busy. We took a break for lunch and wandered off down to a little cafe beside the track for pasta, and the boys had some local Chianti. As always, I ate little when I was riding, but had just enough to keep the hunger pangs away.

We returned to the pit area where a few changes were made to the carburettors and new tyres fitted for my next session. I went out and did a lap. I went down the long straight on my second lap and shot around the course in identical fashion to just about every other lap.

I ripped into the wide left and right chicane leading up to the final corner before the long straight.

My first reaction to the two consecutive loud clanging thuds was that I had broken something in the front end or gearbox, the way the front suddenly dipped. I was just changing into third gear and flicking it from left to right when the bangs and thumps happened. The front end dipped and the tyre slid at the same time as another thud happened. My immediate reaction was to close the throttle and apply brakes and get it stopped but I was still doing around 130 kph. I grabbed at the front brake lever to find it went straight to the handlebar. I had no front brake and only the rear to stop me as I careered towards the last corner. I made a split-second decision. I was not able to slow it up enough to stop; instead I locked the rear brake to throw the bike sideways so I could drag it down, preventing a high-side. I got it close to the ground then somehow I slid away, giving it a kick for good measure to push it away from me.

As the dust settled I was shocked at how quickly it all happened. I dragged myself upright and took a look at myself. I was intact but my hands looked like they had been used as brake pads again. Blood poured from the left palm of my hand where the scab from Silverstone had been healing slowly. 'Fuck, not again!' My first thoughts were of embarrassment — I had just trashed the V-four. The factory, Kel and Nobby would not be pleased. I couldn't really care less about the bike; it was only a piece of equipment made from parts. I had learned long ago that you had to take care of a bike of course, but it has to be ridden with an almost reckless abandon to get the most out of it. It was best to have no emotional ties with the machine; to start worrying about how much the equipment costs will only detract from your effort.

I peeled off my glove and walked slowly over to the bike, noticing how quiet everything was. I pulled at my chin strap and slipped my helmet off my head, having a casual glance for signs of damage. None.

I was alert all the way through this crash and had kept my head up while I slid towards the grass verge.

As I reached the bike my eyes caught a glimpse of what had caused the crash. The front right-hand brake calliper was hanging loose by its brake hose. The bolts had come loose and dropped out just prior to the chicane and, on exiting, the calliper dislodged itself and fell down, tangling itself in the spinning magnesium front wheel. The bangs and thuds I felt were where it got caught in a spoke and then got spat out again.

I picked up the bike and started to push it back in the direction of the pit area. A group of guys arrived and took it from me and within minutes I was sitting in the Yamaha truck amidst a deathly silence. We all knew what had happened and it was inexcusable at this level of racing to have bolts left undone. Especially calliper bolts, for the very reason I was sitting here licking my wounds. I rationalized and then commented, 'Hey guys, it could have been worse if it had been at the next corner.' It then sank in what I had just said. One millimetre more of thread and the calliper would then have come off a few seconds later, perhaps at the end of the straight. I would have been doing about 300 kph. Nothing needed to be said by anyone. I had just come within seconds of meeting my maker.

On race weekend, Mike Trimby was lurking around waving papers and demands to the FIM for increased prize money and conditions. The costs of running the teams had increased dramatically. While the FIM had maintained its position on prize money, I felt for the first time that we were being listened to, albeit through one voice that had our backing. Mike was doing a great job and for no money other than small contributions we made to enable him to meet his expenses.

Our Marlboro team arrived and set up camp, all excited by the fact it was a home GP for most of those in the team. I was feeling a little cocky perhaps as I prepared for this race, knowing that both

Barry Sheene and Kenny Roberts were recuperating. Barry would be out for the season, but Kenny was still waiting for an operation on his knee and it gave me a chance to put extra points on him. Even Franco had an injured foot and would struggle. My main rivals would be the Hondas of Spencer, who was nursing a sore hand, Lucchinelli and Katayama plus a handful of Suzukis that seemed to be getting quicker as the season progressed.

I was given the opportunity to run the V-four but didn't have the confidence in its handling so I elected to use the OW60. It performed as expected, being down a bit on power and a fourth-fastest time was about all I could hope for. Michelin still wanted me to run their new compound tyre and although Freddie was using it I found more stability and reliability in the standard production tyre. They made another attempt at persuading me and I did another test. I was thinking that its slightly different compound might provide more endurance before going off. I was still unconvinced that it made a difference in my lap times but perhaps if anything it might hold its edge a little longer. I thought about it then decided to try my luck with it in the race.

In the last practice session Marc Fontan crashed his Yamaha and was a non-starter. His name was added to an ever-increasing list of injured riders.

On race day the organizers were asked to shorten the 500 race due to the extreme heat. Citing safety concerns and with temperatures in the high 30s, it seemed a reasonable ask. 'Not possible' was the response and the 25-lap race started, depleted of stars. Spencer tore off into the distance, followed by the other Hondas until Lucchinelli ran out of steam and Katayama crashed, leaving Mamola in second while I followed a distant third.

This race was more a procession, during which my bike became more difficult to ride, probably as a result of overheating in both the front and rear suspension. The tyres also began sliding and skidding, making the bike feel floaty and squishy. I blamed the temperature.

I was getting used to the rostrum now and I looked forward to the cups and trophies. I had to hand it to the Italians — they appreciate the importance of quality silverware. I gave my magnum of Champagne to Radar, to stop me from spraying it around and wasting it. Our team would deal with it as soon as I got back from talking with the press. With 10 points here I moved into second place in the standings with one race to go.

HOCKENHEIMRING, 26 SEPTEMBER 1982

It was my final race and there was still no word from Ago about his plans for next year. I was resolved to get the race over and done with and get the hell out of Dodge, as they say. Even if he gave me the courtesy of five minutes to talk about next year it wouldn't have made any difference. I had had enough; I was on my way home.

This Grand Prix might have marked the end of the racing season for 1982 but the silly season had been under way for some time. For a number of reasons, I had not actively sought a further year with Ago. I'd heard he had been talking to a number of riders including Didier de Radiguès and Jean-Louis Tournadre. It would have been nice if he'd let me know if I was going to be part of his plans. It was yet another example of his lack of communication. Rather than dancing to someone else's tune, I now had other aspirations to occupy my mind.

While most of my reasons for heading home permanently were loosely based around the fact I was not enjoying my racing any more, it was more that I had no confidence in the team. Putting aside his unquestionable riding ability, which is well documented, Ago had played the role of an absent team owner. With no disrespect I can say that I firmly believe Agostini was not mentally prepared for his role as team manager or owner in 1982. It required dedication and management skills plus effective communication. Perhaps it was the timing that was wrong for him in this first year because he seemed more focused on his construction business. I could see little changing in the way the team would be operated in the following year or two, except that they would have to find a rider to replace me.

West Germany was one of the countries that had introduced a tobacco advertising ban, so at Hockenheim our team had to cover all the Marlboro logos on the bikes, the truck and on our team clothing. It was the same for the HB and the Gauloises teams. It was hard to understand why the cigarette companies spent so much money on sponsoring teams internationally when they could not put signage on the bikes.

I heard that Graziano Rossi had crashed in a national event at Imola the week before; it sounded really bad. He came down on the big sweeping left-hander after the start-finish straight. It's a hellishly quick curve and he could not have chosen a worse place. Graziano apparently had to be resuscitated by the medical team from Clinica Mobil. At least he was in good hands with Dr Costa.

When Boska finally arrived in the team truck we were keen to find out what was in it as we had our suspicions. Sure enough, Radar discovered that all of his preparation for this final Grand Prix had been wasted. The machine Graziano had crashed at Imola was our OW60. The boys had prepared it in advance of Hockenheim. It was a bloody mess; all of the careful planning to ensure reliability had gone out the door. We were short of engine parts for the square four anyway and now we were faced with the prospect of running the bike with time-expired crankshafts and pistons. This was the final straw and another example of mismanagement. Although Ago had the final say in everything, I was somewhat surprised he hadn't discussed this with Radar or me.

Radar had been experimenting with bigger carburettors and different exhaust pipes to get more top-end power. We knew we would have to sacrifice some mid-range power but were confident of picking up top-end speed where we needed it. Hockenheim was fast and our old OW60 had been left behind in the power stakes as the season wore on.

Kenny turned up after his knee operation but it was clear he did not intend to ride. Yamaha asked me to try the V-four in the first practice session. It had been modified again and according to the factory it promised great things. I was less confident, however, but I agreed to try it. The engine was a revised version of the one without power valves and a new rear suspension set-up had been fitted that was similar to the OW60 square four's.

I decided after practice that I was wasting my time trying to ride this bucking monster that had come close to throwing me off on every corner. I guess the timing was wrong, trying to fix a problem with a bike that had so many other inherent design problems. I could see no future with this particular bike.

I wanted safety and reliability with my old OW60, which by now had been prepared for the second time. Although it was a good bike it was showing its age and was slow compared with the works Suzukis. Any further development had pretty much stopped, other than some cylinder modifications and new exhaust pipes. The Hondas and Suzukis seemed to have finally found their legs and we were being left behind.

Going into the last race of the season I was in second place in the world championship. The pressure had been building as the season drew to a close. I could easily lose second place to Freddie, who was only four points adrift. Kenny and Barry were both a further four points behind, and luckily for me they were both sidelined with injury. My fight would be to hold on to my points lead over Freddie in this final race.

Spencer, Uncini, Lucchinelli, Middelburg and Mamola all put in serious times to qualify ahead of me. Although I was still over a second quicker than my previous year's pole position time, the top five were nearly three seconds quicker than that. It demonstrated to me that our OW60 was now obsolete.

From the time the flag dropped I was fighting a losing battle, down on top-end speed. The Hondas scorched past with noticeable extra power. I tried to hang on but lap by lap the leaders kept pulling away until eventually I lost contact. I was conscious that only four points separated Freddie and me. If he won and got his 15 points I had to at least finish second, which looked unlikely. I tried even harder but with only a slight improvement in my lap times; my only chance now was if there was an accident or mechanical failure.

I had come back into the amphitheatre on lap 15, scuttling around the first of five infield corners, Onkokurve. Then I whistled around the tighter left-hander Sachskurve in the infield. Looking up to get a distance on the rider in front, I attacked Elfkurve and finally the Opelkurve, the corner leading to the start-finish line.

My right knee scraped the tarmac as I leaned into the corner. There is a slight crest in the middle of the track where the bike lightens a little before dropping off the ridge again. The suspension takes over, absorbing the combined weight of rider and machine. With the bike at maximum angle of lean, the front wheel suddenly lost grip and tucked away and down I went.

I could feel the scuffing and ripping of leather as I sped across the track heading for the grass verge. I slid freely to the edge of the track then I felt like I was lifted and slammed back on to the grass again. I stopped and immediately found I could not take a breath. I was winded but everything else seemed intact. 'I can deal with gravel rash and scrapes,' I thought, 'but not broken bones, please!' In what felt like 10 minutes but was probably more like 30 seconds I got my breath back. I lay there for a few seconds, then slowly dragged myself to my feet. The bike lay on its side with the cowling and screen broken and a layer of dirt all over it.

I looked around and saw about 15,000 people either standing or clambering into a position to see me as I walked awkwardly towards the bike, nursing my embarrassment. I turned to the crowd and gave a cavalier's exaggerated low bow and salute. Those who weren't already on their feet now joined the rest of the crowd by responding with a standing ovation, cheering with relief that I was evidently not much the worse for wear. I retired to a safe area, acutely aware that there was not a single flag marshal in sight. I watched two more laps while I was quietly bidding goodbye to my world championship second place.

'I'm such a bloody idiot, so close but I couldn't finish the job. What a wanker I am,' I told myself.

Suddenly the crowd erupted again and I spun around to see the cloud of dust, bikes and bodies on the Sachskurve. I couldn't believe my luck — the trio of Mamola, Spencer and Uncini all duelling for first place had tangled and two riders went down. Only Mamola continued. At that moment I realized I had just placed second in the 1982 500 cc world championship. I picked up the OW60 and gave it a pat on the tank which was now sporting a dent and scratches on the right side.

'More battle wounds for my faithful old warrior. You have been a great bike and we shared some good times together.' Now it was over. I pushed the bike back across the track and into the pit area, where I shook hands with Radar and Rolando. My mood was seesawing from elation to disappointment at finishing the season this way.

'Crosby please, please come this way.' I looked around to find a circuit doctor reaching out to guide me to the medical room. 'How do you feel Mr Crosby, any pain? We want to check you over — is this your helmet?'

I followed the doctor who was looking at my helmet which had a graze across the back of it. His assistant looked into my eyes and using a small torch asked me to follow the light.

'I'm all right, a few scratches but perfectly fine,' I protested.

Seeming not to hear, he replied 'You will get into the ambulance for a check of your head at the local hospital please.'

'Yes sir!' I muttered, reluctantly deciding it wouldn't do me any harm to be checked out. They must have been concerned I was concussed so I let them do their job. Brenda had arrived by this time and I assured her I was fine as I stepped into the ambulance and took a seat right next to Freddie. He had been knocked out and was on his way to be checked too.

'They won't find anything when they X-ray my head,' I told Freddie. He laughed, still looking a little wired after his crash.

A quick check at the medical centre revealed no damage. I was free to return to the paddock and pack up for the last time. I felt a huge sense of relief when I finally drove out through the gates and onto the autobahn heading towards Mannheim.

I was wondering if this was really it, or was it just a passing phase I would get over in a month's time? Would I then regret my decision? No — I knew I'd been there and done that, and my only regret was that I hadn't actually won a Grand Prix. I wanted a fresh and interesting new challenge, perhaps one of a more intellectual nature, less reliant on physical skills and more stimulating to my brain. I would not rest on my racing laurels but head off to new adventures with a smile on my face and thanks in my heart to those who had helped me along the road so far.

POSTSCRIPT

2010

My decision to call it quits was not taken lightly, but the truth was that the fire had almost burned out inside me. Those lapses in concentration and my inability to be energized to a sufficient level during the last few races made me think I was about to enter a grey area that was fraught with danger. Maybe not today or tomorrow, but as long as my arse pointed to the ground, if I wasn't fully committed and passionate about what I was doing, I would eventually get hurt. So when I finally made the decision, I knew it was the right one for me, and I was also aware that there would soon be three people to consider in my family.

The sport had changed and with it came a greater level of professionalism that was inevitable. Although I was enjoying all the trappings of a Grand Prix rider, I needed to work on my personal development to safeguard my future. I had to upskill myself in preparation for civvy street.

The strong American influence on the GP scene had also become evident with the likes of Lawson, Rainey, Spencer and Roberts, who were heralding a new era. I felt there would be fewer opportunities for me, and besides the fun had gone out of it.

I had known several great riders who had continued past their 'use-by' date; they had gradually faded away and it was sad to see. They kept on riding when they were no longer competitive and had ended up just making up the field. I did not want that, and I was still young enough, with a long list of other things I wanted to do.

Back home in New Zealand, it took time to extract myself from the Grand Prix scene. I slowly drifted away and lost contact, preferring to put my brain power to good use elsewhere, for example in gaining my Commercial Pilot licence.

Building flying hours took time, so I bought into a retail

motorcycle dealership in Auckland and got involved in a few other small businesses, including an aerial advertising company. I used to tow advertising banners around the sky but always kept my résumé filed with several airlines in the hope that one day I would get a call seeking my services. It was déjà vu, the same as motorcycle racing, with just too many arses for the small number of seats available.

I tried my hand at car racing with some success but soon figured there was no money in that. In fact it was a big soak-hole for money, with little or no return. By this time I had a wife and three children so I concentrated on my businesses.

In 1996 I sold my motorcycle dealership in Auckland and took up a flying position with Northern Air based at Auckland Airport as a line pilot carrying freight and doing charter work. It wasn't paying much, so after a year I accepted a job selling Mercedes-Benz passenger cars and became their top salesperson in New Zealand in 2000.

In 2002, I paid the penalty for a life in the fast lane, rather harshly I thought, by having cardiac surgery to fix a blocked 'main jet'. As so often is the case, following major medical intervention, I reassessed my life, splitting with Brenda after 24 years of marriage. Over time we had become flatmates and we both needed to start again. We had three great kids, Renee, Michael and Ashlee, who are all doing well for themselves.

I remarried in 2004 to a wonderful lady who has encouraged me to put pen to paper and record my life on two wheels. Helen has been able to rekindle my interest in my chosen sport and now I have a shed full of old bikes awaiting restoration. We are living the good life on a small property north of Auckland, complete with a pair of poodles, 12 chooks and a large potager garden I designed in the shape of a tiki. Our garden is full of fresh vegetables and with the constant stream of visitors we plan to grow old disgracefully.

RESULTS

Date	Circuit	Class	Machine	Position
1974				
Apr	Hamilton	Open Production	Kawasaki H2	1st
May	Baypark	Open Production	Kawasaki H2	1st
Aug	Manfeild	Amco National	Kawasaki H2	1st
		Open Production	Kawasaki H2	1st
		Open Production	Kawasaki H2	1st
Sep	Pukekohe	Open Production	Kawasaki H2	1st
Oct	Napier	Open Production	Kawasaki H2	1st
Nov	Manfeild	NZ Castrol 6 Hour	Kawasaki H2	3rd
Dec	Gracefield	Marlboro Series – Production	Kawasaki H2	1st
	Wanganui	Marlboro Series – Production	Kawasaki H2	1st
1975				
Aug	Pukekohe	Open Production	Kawasaki Z1 900	1st
Sep	Pukekohe	Open Production	Kawasaki Z1 900	1st
Oct	Amaroo	Australian Castrol 6 Hour	Kawasaki Z1 900	12th
Nov	Manfeild	NZ Castrol 6 Hour	Kawasaki Z1 900	1st
1976				
Mar	Amaroo	Unlimited Feature	Ross Hannan Superbike	12th
Jun	Amaroo	A Grade Feature Race 1	Ross Hannan Superbike	5th
		A Grade Feature Race 2	Ross Hannan Superbike	7th
Aug	Oran	Unlimited A Grade	Ross Hannan Superbike	9th
		Unlimited Improved Touring	Ross Hannan Superbike	1st
Oct	Amaroo	Australian Castrol 6 Hour	Ducati 900SS	DNF
Nov	Oran	Unlimited A Grade	Ross Hannan Superbike	2nd
		Unlimited Improved Touring	Ross Hannan Superbike	1st
Nov	Manfeild	NZ Castrol 6 Hour	Kawasaki Z1 900	1st
1977				
Apr	Bathurst	Unlimited Production	Kawasaki Z1B 900	2nd
		Superbike	Ross Hannan Superbike	1st
Apr	Oran	125 cc NSW Titles	Yamaha TZ350	7th
May	Adelaide	Unlimited Production	Kawasaki Z1B 900	1st
	Adelaide	Improved Production	Ross Hannan Superbike	1st
	Adelaide	Australian Unlimited Title	Ross Hannan Superbike	6th

CROZ

Date	Circuit	Class	Machine	Position
Jun	Amaroo	125 cc	Dowd Honda 125	3rd
		Unlimited Production	Kawasaki Z1B 900	1st
		Unlimited Improved Touring	Ross Hannan Superbike	1st
		Unlimited Feature	Ross Hannan Superbike	1st
Jul	Amaroo	Unlimited Improved Touring	Ross Hannan Superbike	1st
		Unlimited A	Ross Hannan Superbike	1st
		Unlimited Production	Kawasaki Z1B 900	1st
		Unlimited Feature	Ross Hannan Superbike	3rd
Oct	Amaroo	Australian Castrol 6 Hour	Kawasaki Z1B 900	6th
Nov	Manfeild	NZ Castrol 6 Hour	Kawasaki Z1000	1st

1978

Date	Circuit	Class	Machine	Position
Mar	Amaroo	Unlimited NSW Titles	Ross Hannan Superbike	3rd
		Unlimited Feature	Ross Hannan Superbike	4th
		Unlimited Production	Kawasaki Z1B 900	1st
Mar	Adelaide	Advertiser 3 Hour	Kawasaki Z1B 900	6th
Mar	Bathurst	Australian GP Senior	Yamaha TZ350	6th
		Australian Unlimited GP	Ross Hannan Superbike	6th
		Bathurst Unlimited	Ross Hannan Superbike	9th
		Unlimited Production	Kawasaki Z1B 900	1st
		Superbike	Ross Hannan Superbike	1st
Apr	Adelaide	Australian Junior Title (SA)	Yamaha TZ350	3rd
Apr	Oran	Junior Championship	Yamaha TZ350	1st
		Unlimited Feature	Ross Hannan Superbike	4th
Jun	Amaroo	Unlimited Production	Kawasaki Z1B 900	1st
		Superbike	Ross Hannan Superbike	1st
		Unlimited Challenge	Ross Hannan Superbike	1st
Oct	Amaroo	Australian Castrol 6 Hour	Honda CBX	DNF
Nov	Oran	Unlimited A	Ross Hannan Superbike	7th
		Swann Series Leg 1	Ross Hannan Superbike	6th
		Unlimited Improved Touring	Ross Hannan Superbike	1st
		Swann Series Leg 2	Ross Hannan Superbike	9th
Nov	Manfeild	NZ Castrol 6 Hour	Kawasaki Z1R	1st

1979

Date	Circuit	Class	Machine	Position
Mar	Amaroo	Interstate Match Race	Kawasaki KR750	2nd
		Unlimited Improved Touring	Ross Hannan Superbike	1st

RESULTS

Date	Circuit	Class	Machine	Position
		Interstate Match Race	Kawasaki KR750	4th
		NSW Unlimited Championship	Kawasaki KR750	1st
Apr	Bathurst	Unlimited International	Kawasaki KR750	1st
		Australian Grand Prix	Kawasaki KR750	2nd
May	Brands	British TTF1 Championship	Moriwaki Z1000	2nd
Jun	TT	World and British TTF1	Moriwaki Z1000	4th
Jun	Mallory	British TTF1 Championship	Moriwaki Z1000	DNF
Jul	Donington	British TTF1 Championship	Moriwaki Z1000	2nd
Jul	Snetterton	British TTF1 Championship	Moriwaki Z1000	2nd
Jul	Suzuka	FIM Coupe d'Endurance	Moriwaki Z1000	2nd
Aug	Oran	NSW State Title	Kawasaki KR750	1st
Aug	Silverstone	British TTF1 Championship	Moriwaki Z1000	2nd
Aug	Ulster GP	World and British TTF1	Moriwaki Z1000	3rd
Aug	Oulton	British TTF1 Championship	Moriwaki Z1000	6th
Sep	Scarborough	British TTF1 Championship	Moriwaki Z1000	3rd
Sep	Cadwell	British TTF1 Championship	Moriwaki Z1000	3rd
Sep	AGV Donington	International	Kawasaki KR750	4th
Sep	AGV Imola	International	Kawasaki KR750	DNF
Oct	Amaroo	Castrol 6 Hour	Kawasaki Z1R	DNF
Oct	Brands	British TTF1 Championship	Moriwaki Z1000	3rd
Nov	Macau	International	Kawasaki KR750	2nd
		British TTF1 Championship		**2nd**
		TTF1 World Championship		**3rd**
1980				
Mar	Daytona	International	Suzuki GS1000	1st
Apr	Brands	Trans-Atlantic International	Suzuki XR23 653 cc	2nd
		British Shellsport 500 cc	Suzuki XR34 500 cc	2nd
Apr	Mallory	International	Suzuki XR34 500 cc	5th
		British Shellsport 500 cc	Suzuki XR34 500 cc	1st
Apr	Oulton	International	Suzuki XR34 500 cc	DNF
Apr	Salzburg	World 500 cc Grand Prix	Suzuki XR34 500 cc	Cancelled
Apr	Olivers Mount	British TTF1 Championship	Suzuki GS1000R XR69	DNS
May	Misano	World 500 cc Grand Prix	Suzuki XR34 500 cc	DNF
May	Jarama	World 500 cc Grand Prix	Suzuki XR34 500 cc	12th
May	Paul Ricard	World 500 cc Grand Prix	Suzuki XR34 500 cc	5th

Date	Circuit	Class	Machine	Position
May	IOM	Senior TT (500 cc)	Suzuki XR34 500 cc	1st
		TTF1 and World Championship	Suzuki GS1000R XR69	2nd
		Classic TT	Suzuki GS1000R XR69	DNF
Jun	Mallory	British TTF1 Championship	Suzuki GS1000R XR69	DNF
Jun	Assen	World 500 cc Grand Prix	Suzuki XR34 500 cc	8th
Jul	Zolder	World 500 cc Grand Prix	Suzuki XR34 500 cc	4th
Jul	Snetterton	British TTF1 Championship	Suzuki GS1000R XR69	1st
		British Shellsport 500 cc	Suzuki XR34 500 cc	1st
Jul	Finland	World 500 cc Grand Prix	Suzuki XR34 500 cc	DNS
Jul	Suzuka	FIM Coupe d'Endurance 8 Hour	Suzuki GS1000R XR69	1st
Aug	Silverstone	World 500 cc Grand Prix	Suzuki XR34 500 cc	13th
		British TTF1 Championship	Suzuki GS1000R XR69	1st
Aug	Ulster	TTF1 World Championship	Suzuki GS1000R XR69	1st
Aug	Nürburgring	World 500 cc Grand Prix	Suzuki XR34 500 cc	2nd
Aug	Oulton	British Shellsport 500 cc	Suzuki XR34 500 cc	DNF
Aug	Donington	British TTF1 Championship	Suzuki GS1000R XR69	1st
Sep	Cadwell	British TTF1 Championship	Suzuki GS1000R XR69	1st
Sep	Mallory	British Shellsport 500 cc	Suzuki XR34 500 cc	3rd
Oct	Brands	British Shellsport 500 cc	Suzuki XR34 500 cc	2nd
		British TTF1 Championship	Suzuki GS1000R XR69	1st
Dec	Australia	Swann Series	Suzuki GS1000R XR69	1st
	Adelaide	Boss Trophy	Suzuki GS1000R XR69	1st
		World 500 cc Championship		**8th**
		World TTF1 Championship		**1st**
		British 500 cc Championship		**2nd**
		British TTF1 Championship		**2nd**
1981				
Apr	Cadwell	British TTF1 Championship	Suzuki XR69 998 cc	1st
Apr	Donington	British TTF1 Championship	Suzuki XR69 998 cc	1st
		World of Sport Challenge	Suzuki XR35 500 cc	2nd
		John Player Gold Cup	Suzuki XR35 500 cc	2nd
Apr	Brands	British 500 cc Championship	Suzuki XR35 500 cc	1st
Apr	Mallory	British 500 cc Championship	Suzuki XR35 500 cc	1st
Apr	Oulton	British 500 cc Championship	Suzuki XR35 500 cc	1st
Apr	Austria	World 500 cc Championship Grand Prix	Suzuki XR35 500 cc	2nd

RESULTS

Date	Circuit	Class	Machine	Position
May	Germany	World 500 cc Championship Grand Prix	Suzuki XR35 500 cc	13th
May	Italy	World 500 cc Championship Grand Prix	Suzuki XR35 500 cc	2nd
May	France	World 500 cc Championship Grand Prix	Suzuki XR35 500 cc	3rd
May	Brands	British 500 cc Championship	Suzuki XR35 500 cc	1st
May	Yugoslavia	World 500 cc Championship Grand Prix	Suzuki XR35 500 cc	4th
Jun	IOM	TTF1 World Championship	Suzuki XR69 998 cc	1st
		Classic TT	Suzuki XR69 998 cc	1st
Jun	Donington	World of Sport Challenge	Suzuki XR35 500 cc	3rd
Jun	The Netherlands	World 500 cc Championship Grand Prix	Suzuki XR35 500 cc	DNF
Jul	Belgium	World 500 cc Championship Grand Prix	Suzuki XR35 500 cc	7th
Jul	San Marino	World 500 cc Championship Grand Prix	Suzuki XR35 500 cc	3rd
Jul	Snetterton	British TTF1 Championship	Suzuki XR69 998 cc	1st
		Race of Aces	Suzuki XR35 500 cc	1st
		British 500 cc Championship	Suzuki XR35 500 cc	1st
Jul	Suzuka	FIM World Endurance Round	Suzuki XR69 998 cc	DNF
Aug	Britain	World 500 cc Championship Grand Prix	Suzuki XR35 500 cc	DNF
		British TTF1 Championship	Suzuki XR69 998 cc	1st
Aug	Finland	World 500 cc Championship Grand Prix	Suzuki XR35 500 cc	5th
Aug	Sweden	World 500 cc Championship Grand Prix	Suzuki XR35 500 cc	5th
Aug	Ulster GP	World and British TTF1 Championship	Suzuki XR69 998 cc	2nd
Aug	Donington	International Winter World Cup	Suzuki XR35 500 cc	2nd
		International Winter World Cup	Suzuki XR35 500 cc	3rd
		International World of Sport	Suzuki XR35 500 cc	3rd
		British 500 cc Championship	Suzuki XR35 500 cc	1st
Aug	Oulton	British 500 cc Championship	Suzuki XR35 500 cc	1st
		British TTF1 Championship	Suzuki XR69 998 cc	1st
Sep	Mallory	Race of the Year	Suzuki XR35 500 cc	1st
		British 500 cc Championship	Suzuki XR35 500 cc	2nd
		British TTF1 Championship	Suzuki XR69 998 cc	1st
Oct	Brands	British TTF1 Championship	Suzuki XR69 998 cc	2nd
		British 500 cc Championship	Suzuki XR35 500 cc	1st
		500 cc World Championship	**Suzuki XR35 500 cc**	**5th**
		World TTF1 Championship	**Suzuki XR69 998 cc**	**1st**
		British TTF1 Championship	**Suzuki XR69 998 cc**	**1st**
		British 500 cc Championship	**Suzuki XR35 500 cc**	**1st**

CROZ

Date	Circuit	Class	Machine	Position
1982				
Mar	Daytona, USA	International 200 Mile	Yamaha YZR750	1st
Mar	Argentina	World 500 cc Grand Prix	Yamaha OW60	DNF
Apr	Imola, Italy	International Leg 1	Yamaha OW60	1st
Apr	Imola, Italy	International Leg 2	Yamaha OW60	1st
Apr	Hengelo	International	Yamaha OW60	1st
May	Austria	World 500 cc Grand Prix	Yamaha OW60	4th
May	France	World 500 cc Grand Prix	Yamaha OW60	Boycotted
May	Spain	World 500 cc Grand Prix	Yamaha OW60	4th
May	San Marino	World 500 cc Grand Prix	Yamaha OW60	3rd
Jun	Donington	International – ITV Cup	Yamaha OW60	1st
Jun	Donington	International – John Player	Yamaha OW60	1st
Jun	The Netherlands	World 500 cc Grand Prix	Yamaha OW60	4th
Jul	Belgium	World 500 cc Grand Prix	Yamaha OW60	DNF
Jul	Yugoslavia	World 500 cc Grand Prix	Yamaha OW60	2nd
Aug	Britain	World 500 cc Grand Prix	Yamaha OW60	3rd
Aug	Sweden	World 500 cc Grand Prix	Yamaha OW60	3rd
Sep	Italy	World 500 cc Grand Prix	Yamaha OW60	3rd
Sep	Germany	World 500 cc Grand Prix	Yamaha OW60	DNF
		500 cc World Championship	**Yamaha OW60**	**2nd**